WAR WITHOUT BLOODSHED

The Art of Politics

ELEANOR CLIFT
AND TOM BRAZAITIS

A LISA DREW BOOK

SCRIBNER

SCRIBNER
1230 Avenue of the Americas
New York, NY 10020

SCRIBNER and design are trademarks of Simon & Schuster Inc.

DESIGNED BY ERICH HOBBING

Set in Caledonia

Manufactured in the United States of America

1   3   5   7   9   10   8   6   4   2

Library of Congress Cataloging-in-Publication Data
Clift, Eleanor.
War without bloodshed : the art of politics/Eleanor Clift and Tom Brazaitis.
p. cm.
"A Lisa Drew book."
Includes bibliographical references and index.
1. Politics, practical—United States. 2. United States—Politics and government. 3. Political
consultants—United States. 4. Lobbyists—United States. 5. United States. Congress—
Leadership. 6. United States. Congress—Officials and employees. I. Brazaitis, Tom. II. Title.
JK1726.C55   1996
324'.0973—dc20   96-7790
CIP

ISBN 0-684-80084-5

To our children:
EDDIE, WOODY, and ROBERT CLIFT;
MARK and SARAH JEAN BRAZAITIS

ACKNOWLEDGMENTS

This is our first book, individually or together, and we could not have done it without help from a lot of people. The concept for the book came from our first editor, Carlo De Vito, who had to give up the project before it really got started. Lisa Drew took it from there, not only editing skillfully, but giving us the unwavering encouragement that made us believe we could do this. Our agent, Bob Barnett, smoothed the way.

The final product reflects the constructive criticism and gentle advice of the following people who acted as editors at-large: Evan Thomas, *Newsweek*'s Washington bureau chief; Steven Schier, professor of political science at Carleton College; Steve Waldman, who helped find the forest in our trees, and Fred W. Wright, whose early combing of the manuscript was valuable.

Bebe Bahnsen, a friend and fellow political junkie, steered us through the final stages of the project with her exacting eye for story and chronology, and by issuing "non-junkie alerts" that made the manuscript more reader friendly.

We had reporting help from Edward Roeder, the money and politics analyst who founded Sunshine Press and is largely responsible for the "Money Matters" appendix; Lisa Shepard, a freelance journalist and native Californian, who charted Maxine Waters's political rise in that state, and Mary Jacoby, a staff reporter with *Roll Call,* the newspaper of Capitol Hill, who contributed insights on both Maxine Waters and Sheila Burke.

Fredric Alan Maxwell, a writer himself, provided layers of research on each of our characters, and maintained a level of enthusiasm for the project that more than matched our own. "Book manager" perhaps best describes Gail Thorin's many contributions in bringing this book to fruition—from acting as our liaison between all the players involved in book production to sharp-eyed copyediting and diligent research. Her experience, foresight, and precision saved us from ourselves many times over. In the face of deadline pressure, her equanimity was marvelous.

Newsweek's Guy Cooper opened up the magazine's photographic resources, and Tom Tarnowsky assembled a portfolio for us to choose from. William Rafferty, who heads the *Newsweek* library in Washington, responded to our many and varied queries with dispatch and good humor, as did his able assistants, Kevin Lamb and Shirlee Hoffman. Lorna Wisham, in the Washington bureau of the *Plain Dealer*, proved invaluable on numerous occasions. Our tape transcribers, starting with Tom Asimos, a student at nearby American University, and extending to Irene Haley, an e-mail correspondent in South Dakota, faithfully rendered many hours of interviews.

We are especially grateful for the time that each of our subjects gave us, and for the confidence they showed in us as journalists by agreeing to participate in this project. Our thanks, too, to key aides who helped with things as mundane as scheduling, but more importantly deepened our understanding of the men and women they work for. Special thanks to Lawrence O'Donnell (Daniel Patrick Moynihan), Tony Blankley (Newt Gingrich), Patrick Lacefield, and Bill Zavarello (Maxine Waters).

Finally, we are indebted to our bosses at *Newsweek* and *The Plain Dealer* for giving us the leeway to expand our journalistic horizons.

CONTENTS

WAR
WITHOUT
BLOODSHED

INTRODUCTION

Rough Justice

T his book is an examination of government through the eyes of eight individuals who are generally regarded as among the best at what they do. They include elected officials and nonelected political operatives, Democrats and Republicans, men and women, who have in common that they all operate at the highest levels of the political game today. We began this project in September 1993 when President Clinton's dream of extending health coverage to every American through sweeping government reform was very much alive, and there seemed to be a renewed spirit of hope about what Washington could do to improve the lives of ordinary people.

Our book, we thought, might even be a celebration of politics and the much-maligned political professionals. But health care reform died an ignominious death, and it was soon apparent that Clinton's election in 1992 had done nothing to change the cynicism of the citizenry toward politicians, except to make it worse. Midway through our research and reporting, in November 1994, the Republicans recaptured the Senate and, for the first time in four decades, gained a majority in the House. The ill-fated health care reform effort and the stunning ascendancy of the GOP provide the two main themes for the book, and link our eight characters.

What we have is neither a celebration nor a condemnation of politics today, but simply an effort to show what it is like. Each of our subjects agreed to cooperate, and much of the reporting and dialogue comes directly from them. Where others were involved, we of course cross-checked the information. We interviewed dozens of people in the Clinton administration, on Capitol Hill, and in the political consultant community for their perspective, and their views are part of the narrative. We gave each of our principal characters a chance to read the manuscript before it went to press. There was some spirited debate over interpretation, most of which was resolved amicably.

The idea for this book comes from George Will's *Men At Work,* which is about professional baseball. Will picked four positions—manager, pitcher, batter, fielder—and focused on four men who filled these positions in an exemplary way. The result was an insider's look at the game of baseball that even a fastidious fan would find revealing. We set out to do a similar book on the game of politics in Washington. In choosing our positions, and the people who filled them, we knew we could not cover every base, any more than Will could. We settled on six jobs—pollster, lobbyist, committee chairman, opposition leader, member of Congress, and chief of staff—through which we hoped to show how the game is played. In choosing our players, we looked for people who had achieved prominence and would likely be around for some time, who would grant us the access we needed, and who could step back periodically to explain and reflect upon what they were doing.

The title, *War Without Bloodshed,* comes from Chairman Mao Zedong, founder of the People's Republic of China, who said, "Politics is war without bloodshed while war is politics with bloodshed." Newt Gingrich often uses the phrase to describe what he does, although his critics and even some of his admirers ask plaintively, "What do you mean, without bloodshed?" Gingrich warmed to the idea of this project more than anybody else at the outset. When we first approached him in late 1993, he was the House minority whip, a job that he used mainly as a forum to denounce Democrats, liberals, and the "corrupt welfare state" he said they had created. He was famous inside the Beltway for bringing down Democratic House Speaker Jim Wright, but he had little name recognition around the country. Over dinner on February 16, 1994, at the 1789 Restaurant, located in a Revolution-era house in Georgetown, Gingrich clicked off what we had to do to fulfill our mandate: "You need a sense of what we do, how we do it, and then why we do it. You need four or five cycles of that per person. Each of these people has an art. They have a set of things they've done that are skills—and it's one of the great dangers of term limits—because you learn by apprenticeship and practice. It's not a science. It's a taste—it's a feel."

Seven months later, on September 27, 1994, Gingrich stood on the steps of the U.S. Capitol, surrounded by Republican incumbents and challengers preparing for the upcoming election, championing a Contract With America that presented term limits as one of the objectives of a Republican-controlled House. He campaigned for 129 challengers that year, and when seventy-three of them won, they made him Speaker of the House. He had been a congressman for sixteen years. If term limits had been in effect, there would be no Speaker Gingrich.

By the time we began to write the chapter on Gingrich, we had watched him through three life cycles. The chapter about Gingrich was originally titled "The Opposition Leader." He had barely graduated from being a fringe ideologue when we first turned on the tape recorder and heard him spin out his vision of a Republican majority. When the Republicans took over the House, he became the Speaker, and so did the title of our chapter. Gingrich received easily as much publicity as a new president, much of it glowingly positive about his energy and ideas. And, indeed, he saw himself as the modern-day equivalent of FDR ushering in and shaping a new political era. Less than a year later, his image tarnished by ethical questions and a string of intemperate statements, Gingrich's hold on the speakership seemed tenuous. Was he a supernova who would burn out from his own intensity?

The book opens with a chapter on polling, which is the foundation of modern-day campaigns and issues. Stanley Greenberg was the obvious choice when we embarked on this project. He had just helped elect a Democratic president, a feat in itself, and he was an authority on the middle-class discontent that drove the 1992 election. When that angst turned to anger in the months leading up to the November 1994 election, Greenberg seemed to have lost his touch. His goal, as the presidential pollster, was to build a new governing majority. The collapse of health care reform, the centerpiece of Greenberg's strategy to woo back the middle class, set the stage for the Democrats' debacle. There are a number of memos to the President and First Lady cited in this chapter. Greenberg did not provide us with these memos, citing his loyalty to the President. We obtained them elsewhere.

Even before it became clear that Greenberg was falling out of favor at the White House, we were drawn to the hot new pollster on the block, Frank Luntz. Barely over thirty years old and a combustible mixture of unbridled ambition and desperate insecurity, Luntz was an expert on disaffected voters, the portion of the electorate who would make history in 1994. "I want to be the next Greenberg," Luntz declared. He set out to be at the side of the next prominent political figure, in this case Newt Gingrich. Pollsters are like the archaeologist in *Raiders of the Lost Ark*, sifting through public attitudes and perceptions to unlock the secrets of the next election. We started talking with Luntz early in 1993 and charted his rise until he was heralded as the boy genius of the 1994 campaign. By the time we completed our chapter, he was fending off negative attacks in the press from some of his fellow GOP pollsters.

The characters in this book revealed themselves at some risk, and that is especially true of the lobbyists who operate beneath the radar, and whose tactics, when exposed, are often not pretty. Michael Bromberg, who opened the Washington headquarters of the Federation of American Health Systems in 1969, represented hundreds of profit-making hospitals in the health care fight of 1993–94. Known in Washington policy-making circles as "Mr. Health Care," Bromberg was accustomed to being on the inside, and thought he could help the Clintons shape a health care compromise. He even had a personal interest: Having had bypass surgery, he had a preexisting condition that made it difficult to get insurance. His battles with Hillary Rodham Clinton made him realize that the White House viewed him as the enemy, yet without the support of special interest groups like the one he represented, health care reform was doomed. Once he failed to influence what was in the Clinton plan, Bromberg actively worked to kill it. At the time of our writing, Bromberg, a former Democrat, was supporting Bob Dole's presidential campaign.

Paul Equale started out as a McGovern Democrat, and like so many young idealists who come to Washington, he grew more conservative, or, as he would say, realistic, over the years. Some of his friends got jobs in the Clinton White House, and he prided himself on his close ties to the new administration. But he, too, was at odds with Mrs. Clinton, who singled out his organization, the Independent Insurance Agents of America, as a potentially dangerous opponent of health care reform. Equale is a foot-on-the-bar-rail kind of lobbyist who spends a lot of time with members of Congress. He sensed the coming Republican revolution, and "reoriented" a substantial portion of his association's campaign donations away from Democrats and into the coffers of Republican candidates.

After the 1994 election, lobbyists waved goodbye to the Democrats who had lost their seats and quickly adjusted to the new powers on the Hill. Equale did his part by rounding up Democratic support for restrictive libel law legislation that was part of the GOP's Contract With America. He talked confidently about being able to get an invitation, if he wanted one, for his family to watch fireworks on the Fourth of July from Speaker Gingrich's balcony overlooking the Mall. Equale is disarmingly frank about the way lobbyists and their money are embedded in our system of representative democracy. "You know some people think I'm smooth, but people who are smooth have a tendency to be the most self-revealing once you get them going," he said.

Daniel Patrick Moynihan, our committee chairman, brings a sweep of history and an obstinacy about ideas that make him maddeningly original. He is no one's ally for long, not even his own. He is just as likely to debunk a social program one day as he is to defend it the next. The Clintons counted on Moynihan, a fellow Democrat, to shepherd their health care plan through the powerful Senate Finance Committee. Instead, he is blamed by many for the bill's failure. If the Clintons had studied Moynihan more carefully before coming to Washington, they would not have been surprised by the treatment their legislation received in his committee. Moynihan was not meant to be a legislator. He is a senator in the Greek sense, a wise man engaged in educating through rhetoric. He is also a proud man, easily offended. He cannot be ordered around, as the Clintons learned to their dismay.

Of his dispute with the White House, Moynihan would say that presidents by definition have no experience being president and few have much previous contact with Washington. By contrast, Congress rewards experience through seniority. Moynihan had been sixteen years on the Finance Committee when he became chairman, and had served under four previous chairmen, two of each party. He would argue that he, more than the President, had a sense of what could and could not be done.

Moynihan is best viewed as an original thinker in a world where other people reflect polls instead of their own beliefs. Some Democrats, including the Clintons, will never forgive him for his dismissive handling of the Clinton health care plan. But Moynihan lost his chairmanship in the Republican landslide of 1994, and happily returned to his role of social critic. By the time we closed this chapter, Moynihan had reclaimed his Democratic roots and was back in good graces with the liberals, defending the sixty-year-old federal entitlement to welfare with the energy and intellectual verve of the last civilized man holding off the barbarians at the gate.

Maxine Waters came to Washington wanting to legislate. It is what she did quite successfully as a member of the California Assembly, where she rose to become the majority whip, the first woman to hold that powerful position. Under the tutelage of Speaker Willie Brown, she learned how to make deals, extract favors, and seek revenge against her political enemies. She gained a reputation as a skillful backroom negotiator. When she arrived in Washington in 1991, she discovered that as a freshman member of Congress she was not welcome in the leadership circles where the wheeling and dealing was done. Rigid rules of seniority and tradition kept her out, so she resorted to a tactic familiar to backbenchers, the same one Newt Gingrich used to great effect during his rise to power. She became in Capitol Hill parlance a bomb-thrower.

It is a way to get noticed and a way to exercise power, especially if you are a woman and a minority in a political world that is overwhelmingly male and white. After the 1994 election, the Republican-led revolution to return power to the states threatened many of the federal benefits that go to the district that Waters represents, which includes South Central Los Angeles, the scene of riots in 1992. She came to Washington to make deals that would help her constituents, but most of the time she has had to settle for making a point. Waters brings the perspective of a lawmaker representing people who are mostly voiceless in a political system driven by moneyed special interests. Her job is made more difficult in a Congress increasingly oriented to suburban voters and less concerned with inner-city problems.

Our final chapter focuses on the job of chief of staff to show how real power in Washington frequently is wielded anonymously. When we selected Sheila Burke, chief of staff to Sen. Bob Dole, few people outside the congressional community had ever heard her name, much less had any inkling of what she did. A nurse who was once a registered Democrat, she is an unlikely sidekick for the dyspeptic Dole, politically and stylistically. Yet he trusts her completely, and for a man who trusts few people, this is an extraordinary leap of faith. Burke's placid exterior belies her skills. She is a crafty inside player, who has mastered the legislative game in a way few others have. Conservatives suspect that she uses this mastery to advance moderate policy goals, and they are right. Burke offered to resign after the 1994 election, fearing that she would become a target of the Right, but Dole resisted. Instead, he expanded her power.

Our characters deal with important issues, yet their actions sometimes come across as petty. We do not wish to deepen the cynicism about public officials, and urge fair-minded readers to understand that the behavior of Washington politicians is not unique. Anyone following the players in a city council, a state legislature, or, for that matter, a corporate boardroom, would find the same clash of egos and agendas.

We have attempted to understand how good people do some good things and a lot of things that are mediocre, and some things that are indefensible. Perfectionism is not compatible with achievement in a democracy. In the end, when the reader has digested all six chapters, and the appendix on the role of money in Washington politics, we would hope that he or she emerges with a sense that there is a rough justice to the political arts. Imperfect as it is, politics reflects the reality of the human condition: high ideals compromised by what is achievable.

CHAPTER ONE

THE POLLSTERS

Throwing the Bones

I n the last days before the 1994 election, Stanley Greenberg had
trouble sleeping He would awaken in the middle of the night, and
then lie in bed for what seemed like hours frozen with anxiety at the
prospect of widespread Democratic losses. After helping elect Bill Clinton president, and receiving all the adulation the media typically heaps
on winners, he now faced the possibility just two short years later that
the Democratic Party he had worked so hard to renew would be repudiated by the voters. He was also deeply pained by the thought that he had
failed his President, and that the political ideas that had carried Clinton
to the presidency would be discredited.

A pollster whose role is limited to taking the public's pulse would not
react so viscerally. Greenberg saw himself in a larger context as the cre-
ator of a new Democratic majority. He cared about advancing Democratic ideas. He used polls to figure out ways to bring back the Democratic
constituencies that had drifted away to vote for Ronald Reagan in 1980.
Bill Clinton's victory in 1992 seemed to validate Greenberg's notion that
a different kind of Democrat, one who did not come from the party's liberal elite, could foster a new bond with working-class Reagan Democrats. Now the Democratic Party was collapsing and threatening to take
Stanley Greenberg and his theories with it.

For months, he had been sending conflicting signals about the outcome of the election. In the spring and early summer, he had written
memos warning that the Democrats would likely lose the Senate and
House. The memos were so despairing that top White House officials
decided that Greenberg should be kept away from the President. They
reasoned that Clinton had to play the primary role in uplifting the party's

spirits, and meeting with Greenberg would only grind in the bad news and break his spirit. He had had some meetings with the President canceled and top aides had instructed him to tone down his predictions.

Then, as the election approached, Greenberg's pessimism seemed to dissipate. He lulled himself into thinking that if the White House made the right moves and the Democrats got some breaks, disaster could be averted. His advice was for the embattled White House to give up on a health care bill that was now doomed to fail and blame the special interests for "killing health care." He urged that Clinton wage an all-out campaign for welfare reform and a crime bill that called for putting 100,000 more police on the streets. Greenberg got permission from the White House to sound out Democratic leaders in the House on the prospects of quickly passing a welfare reform bill. The reaction to the pollster's desperate pleadings was mostly bemusement.

Greenberg's election strategy called for Democratic congressional leaders to adjourn early to shift the focus away from Congress. The more voters watched the gridlocked Congress, the angrier they got at Democrats, who were in charge. For the first time in decades, polls showed a majority of people would vote for almost any Republican for Congress over a Democrat.

Greenberg kept hoping that the gloom would break. Each morning, an assistant would hand him a list of the latest polling information faxed in from around the country, and he would search for evidence that Democratic candidates were rebounding. After Congress finally adjourned, the President's approval ratings went up and public polls showed Democrats regaining some of their strength. But in the last ten days before the election, when the President returned from a trip abroad and began campaigning for congressional candidates across the country, the Democrats' poll ratings worsened again. Greenberg, with backing from other advisers, had urged the President to make the final campaign swing, a strategy that backfired.

When the Democrats' momentum stalled, he stopped looking at the polling data because it was too depressing. He tried to convince himself that the bad numbers would not hold up, and that the Democrats would close the gap in the final days. He gave briefings and made press statements that projected an outcome more favorable to the Democrats than the raw numbers themselves suggested.

A pollster's role goes beyond gathering the numbers to putting a public face on them. On the one hand, Greenberg had to be honest about the realities of the Democrats' predicament; on the other hand, he felt he simply could not say in large meetings or on television that the Democrats were on the verge of losing. He could imagine the headline that would result: "President's Pollster Says Democrats to Be Repudiated Next Tuesday."

Because he restricted the worst news to a tight inner circle, there were some at the White House and at the Democratic National Committee who came away from his briefings thinking that Greenberg had lost touch with reality. At a session in the Roosevelt Room of the White House the day before the election, he prepared presidential aides and Democratic Party officials with talking points so they could react to the press. He sketched out three scenarios: horrid, or "tidal wave," losses of forty-plus congressional seats; moderate, or "wave," losses of thirty seats; smile, or "relief," with losses in the twenties.

There was a good chance the results would defy expectations, he said, speaking in an emotionless monotone. Greenberg sounded so detached that he could have been delivering a lecture on the legislative races of some European parliament. Oddly, Greenberg's dry, academic tone made him more convincing. What started as a doomsday briefing turned into a relatively upbeat session on how White House aides could spin a loss of twenty-five or thirty seats to make it look like a victory.

That night Greenberg predicted on *Nightline* that the Democrats would retain control of the House and Senate. He had convinced himself that the best possible scenario was achievable: an even split in the Senate, with each party holding fifty seats, and a loss of some thirty Democratic seats in the House, not enough to lose majority status. Besides, he rationalized, as the President's pollster, he had to be something of a cheerleader in his public pronouncements.

On election day, a final strategy session was held in chief of staff Leon Panetta's West Wing office. Afternoon exit polls fed to the White House by the television networks signaled huge Democratic losses around the country. Greenberg had little to say, and the others did not seek his counsel. With catastrophe imminent, the glib White House aides who had elevated spin to an art form could not come up with a positive gloss. The meeting dissolved early.

Of the advisers who came to the White House with Clinton, Greenberg was the house philosopher. Other aides got caught up in the crisis du jour; Greenberg stepped back and pondered its impact on the fragile Democratic coalition. To the extent there was any coherent view of government in Clinton's ragged leadership, it was Greenberg's. A former Yale professor who specialized in civil rights and African studies, Greenberg believed that the way to reach out to disaffected middle-American voters was through new government programs that serve everybody, not just the poor and minorities. Greenberg's theory was shaken when Bill and Hillary Rodham Clinton's health care plan foundered among confused and frightened middle-class Americans.

A neon sign that says "Meltdown" hangs over the doorway of Greenberg's office on Capitol Hill. That was the word he used in a late-night phone call to the governor's mansion in Little Rock to describe Clinton's plunge in the polls during the final days before the 1992 New Hampshire primary. Now he was facing meltdown again. He had reached the pinnacle of polling only to have it all taken away. This had happened to him before when, as a young professor building a promising academic career, Yale University inexplicably denied him tenure.

There would be no tenure in politics either, he discovered. In roughly seventy-two hours, he had gone from sage to scapegoat. At countless Washington seminars examining the election results, pundits blamed Greenberg's advice for making Democrats believe they could propose government solutions to the country's problems. What five things should Bill Clinton do to reinvigorate his presidency? "The first thing he should do is tell Stan Greenberg he never wants to see him again," said *Newsweek*'s Howard Fineman at a panel at the National Press Building.

Many analysts faulted Greenberg's theory that the disaffected middle class could be won over by the promise of a health care entitlement. The obsession with making health care a guaranteed right for all Americans had cast Clinton as a big-government liberal and obscured his accomplishments, including a robust economy. Blame was plentiful, and Greenberg got his share.

In the gloom after the election, Clinton cast around for a new pollster. He was convinced that poor marketing of his policies was the problem, and that better advice was the solution. "If you had told me when we started that I would accomplish all these things and be this far down in the crapper, I would have told you you were crazy," he railed in a private meeting with one of Greenberg's potential replacements.

For a time, it looked as though Greenberg might be fired. But that was far too decisive a step for this most indecisive of presidents. After much agonizing, Clinton stubbornly stuck with Greenberg and the other consultants who had been with him in 1992. "Those are the people who got me here," he told those pressing him to make a change. But the President had lost confidence in Greenberg, and the pollster would play a much diminished role from then on.

Stan Greenberg grew up in Washington, D.C., where his attitudes about race and politics were shaped by direct experience. He lived in a small

brownstone in the city with his parents and grandparents, who were
Orthodox Jews from Russia. They were the only white family in an all-
black neighborhood. All his childhood friends were black, but the school
he went to was all-white. Segregation was the law of the land.

When Stan was in the third grade, the family moved to Riggs Park, a
Jewish working-class neighborhood. Up until the time of his bar mitz-
vah, Stan went to synagogue every day after school. "Everybody I knew
was Jewish unless they were black, and the blacks were the people who
were not kosher," he says.

Stan's world was divided into Jews and non-Jews; skin color was not
an issue. Neither was politics. His parents were Democrats, but so was
everybody else. In 1954, the Supreme Court's ruling in *Brown v. Board
of Education* desegregated the schools. Two years later, Stan's sixth-
grade class was bused to a black school. "Busing meant you were simply
transferred," he recalls with a laugh. "You went on public transportation.
I took three buses to get there. We were this white class in the middle of
this black school." Stan was small for his age. He remembers being
taunted and chased by the bigger kids. The black friends that he had
made in his old neighborhood were his defenders.

The civil rights movement was well underway when Stan reached
high school. By then, his family had migrated to Silver Spring, a Maryland suburb just outside the District of Columbia, where he took part in
demonstrations against various restaurants that were not integrated. His
father, who worked at an instrument engineering plant, was always nervous that he would show up for lunch somewhere and find Stan out front
picketing. The elder Greenberg did not like to make waves. The
McCarthy era, with its communist witchhunts, had so frightened him
that he broke off relations with several family members who leaned left
out of fear that their affiliations might endanger his security clearance.
Stan only discovered this in high school when his father forbade him to
join a Jewish youth group because it was too left-wing.

For working-class families with immigrant roots, nothing can surpass
the importance of a college education. One of Stan's friends in Montgomery Blair High School's class of 1963 shocked her classmates by pursuing a different dream. "At graduation, everybody thought she was
failing because she wasn't going to college," Greenberg recalls. The
young woman was Goldie Hawn.

The summer of 1963, after graduating from high school, Greenberg
worked nights at the NAACP helping to organize the March on Washington. His commitment to civil rights led him into politics, and when he
entered college that fall at Miami University in Ohio, he immediately

joined the Young Democrats. The following summer, as a nineteen-year-old intern at the Democratic National Committee, he was assigned to write a position paper in support of the Vietnam War. The arguments he made were not convincing, and a year later, he traveled to Washington to picket the White House against the war. It was 1965, and anti-war fever was intense. But in the evenings, Greenberg sometimes socialized inside the White House. He was dating a friend of President Johnson's daughter Luci. After Clinton was elected, Greenberg recalled, "I told the President that I used to make out in the solarium. . . . That's probably overstating it. But we used to party in there."

Vietnam derailed Lyndon Johnson's presidency, but not his Great Society programs. Liberalism was still ascendant in 1967 when Greenberg enrolled as a graduate student in political science at Harvard. He developed along with other students a forecasting model for how well Robert F. Kennedy would do in the 1968 presidential primaries. All the work was done on keypunch cards and stored on metal shelves. When Kennedy was assassinated just after claiming victory in the California primary, the students were so heartsick that the project came to a standstill. Sometime later, when they returned to retrieve the boxes of data for course credit, they were horrified to learn that older material was routinely destroyed to make room for newer work. Greenberg reconstructed the project without the data. Interpreting the Kennedy phenomenon was far more fascinating to him than the absolute numbers.

Greenberg had come to resent the elitism of Democratic liberal politics. He saw the battle between Robert Kennedy and Eugene McCarthy in 1968 as a cultural struggle within the party. "Clean Gene" McCarthy attracted people who were more suburban, and college-educated. Kennedy's strength was in the working-class and ethnic communities. The cultural split was even true in graduate school at Harvard, where support for the two candidates divided along class lines. "I was never comfortable with McCarthy," Greenberg says. "I very strongly supported Robert Kennedy."

Greenberg was drawn to Kennedy's vision of the Democratic Party as a place where working-class whites and blacks found common ground. His career has been a Sisyphean struggle to promote progressive policies in a way that does not offend more people than those policies are designed to assist. From the rise to national prominence of Alabama Gov. George Wallace in the 1960s to the divisive debate over affirmative action in 1995, the issue of race would return again and again to bedevil Greenberg and the Democrats.

While still a student, Greenberg oversaw a government-funded study on the attitudes of the poor toward the War on Poverty. It became his doctoral thesis and then a book, *Politics and Poverty*. What he discovered to his surprise was that poor blacks were less alienated from the American dream than blacks who were better educated and better off. He concluded that housing segregation, by making it difficult for middle-income blacks to leave poor neighborhoods and materially improve their lives, accounted for their increased alienation and made it more likely that they would embrace radical forms of politics. He sent a copy of his findings to the White House, where urban affairs adviser Daniel Patrick Moynihan had said he wanted ideas from the university community.

Greenberg had made the connection between his civil rights advocacy and his academic work, another step in his march to prominence in electoral politics. It was a journey that he undertook at some personal cost. When he submitted the dissertation in September 1971, he included this plaintive note: "I am hard pressed to explain my wife's tolerance of this work, given the responsibility for home and children which fell largely to her. Now that we are all liberated, myself from this research, my wife from 'home-making,' and our children from the effects, we can proceed, confident that we would never do it again." The note notwithstanding, Greenberg continued to publish scholarly articles and books about the politics of race, and his marriage eventually ended in divorce.

His next marriage proved more felicitous when it came to accommodating political passions. Greenberg has been married since 1978 to Rosa DeLauro, a member of Congress from Connecticut. They met during a Democratic mayoral race in New Haven, for which DeLauro was the campaign treasurer and Greenberg, by then on the faculty at Yale, was an adviser. They got to know each other over pizza with anchovies and began dating a year later. Early on, DeLauro set some guidelines. Upon learning that Greenberg and another male adviser were meeting each evening without her, she stopped providing them information on the campaign's finances. When they complained to the candidate, DeLauro proposed solving the problem by having the three of them get together on a regular basis. Greenberg got the message. DeLauro, elected to Congress in 1990, is now a member of the Democratic leadership in Congress. Known for her unstinting liberalism, she is one of the party's most vocal critics of the new Republican majority.

Greenberg expected to spend his professional life in academia, but in 1979, Yale turned down his request for tenure. There is some speculation that support for Greenberg's areas of specialty, comparative studies, race relations, and South Africa, had cooled in the eyes of university administrators. At any rate, his rejection was so unexpected that some graduate students developed the verb, "to be Greenberged." It meant being on the fast track and then suddenly running into a brick wall, a phenomenon Greenberg would later encounter in politics.

That same year, he lost a lucrative consulting job with the Rockefeller Foundation. He had traveled to South Africa and angered some bureaucrats in the all-white Afrikaner government with his outspokenness about race. They demanded his ouster, and the foundation complied to prevent possible retaliation against others affiliated with the foundation who were applying for visas to visit South Africa.

A combination of luck and nepotism drew him to polling. DeLauro was running Chris Dodd's 1980 campaign for the Senate, and had tapped Greenberg for an advisory committee of academics. Dodd's pollster was Patrick Caddell, a brilliant but mercurial analyst who was also President Carter's pollster.

Caddell was too busy trying to shore up Carter's collapsing presidency to devote much time to Dodd. A critical meeting had to be rescheduled several times. When the session finally took place in Boston, Caddell delivered a meandering presentation that impressed no one. "Dodd was crazed," recalls Greenberg. "It was obvious Caddell hadn't read the data." Dodd decided on the spot to replace him with the dependable academic who was married to his campaign manager. They proved to be a winning duo.

With a Senate candidate as a client, Greenberg founded The Analysis Group in the basement of the sprawling, 1906 vintage house that he shared with DeLauro in New Haven. After Dodd's victory, DeLauro began commuting to Washington, where she was Dodd's chief of staff, the most powerful position in a congressional office. With the Dodd race over, Greenberg went back to Yale, where he had resigned himself to a nontenured position teaching African studies. He polled on the side, mostly for local races.

In 1982 he got his next big break, thanks to a young man who had been the candidate's driver in the Dodd campaign. Traditionally the candidate's driver is a junior staff member, but the job offers extraordinary opportunity for seeing a campaign up close and having access to confidential strategy discussions. Jimmy Carter's press secretary, Jody Powell, began as Carter's driver on his first Georgia gubernatorial campaign. Two years after hearing Greenberg deliver poll results to a Connecticut candidate in the back of a van, Dodd's driver, Doug Sosnik, was managing a congressional race in Michigan. He hired Greenberg to do the polling, his first race outside Connecticut. The candidate, Bob Carr, won election to Congress in 1982 and again in 1984.

A footnote on the serendipitous workings of the political network: Sosnik, the young man who unwittingly launched Greenberg's career, a decade later joined the White House staff as Clinton's political director. By then, Greenberg had been ousted from the inner circle and rarely saw the President. Sosnik became one of his primary contacts in the White House.

The connections Greenberg had made through the Carr race led to an invitation in 1985 from the Michigan Democratic Party to come to Macomb County and find out why so many white, middle-class suburbanites had turned away from the party. In 1960, Macomb had been the most Democratic suburb in the nation, a thriving bedroom community just outside Detroit where many of the city's autoworkers had migrated with their families to achieve the American dream. Lyndon Johnson won Macomb in 1964 with seventy-four percent of the vote. Twenty years later, Macomb's working-class families overwhelmingly supported Ronald Reagan with sixty-six percent. The phenomenon of Reagan Democrats was born and the importance of Macomb County reached far beyond Michigan. The *Los Angeles Times* called it Ground Zero for the 1992 campaign.

Greenberg's study of Macomb concluded that many of its white, blue-collar voters felt abandoned by a Democratic Party that they perceived as caught up in the civil rights movement and catering to the interests of minorities. That analysis has since been widely accepted, but it was revolutionary at the time. The Macomb County study concluded that the racial issue had to be addressed if Democrats were going to reclaim their base. Greenberg warned the party that it had to find ways of reaching ethnic, white, middle-class voters as part of its overall strategy. Part of his critique was that the Democratic Party did not identify with, and did not really respect, working-class culture. Democrats had to recognize that the uproar over busing, for example, was not just racism; people felt, justifiably, that their values and their neighborhoods were being threatened.

Greenberg was asked to present the study findings at a meeting of state party chairs in Chicago. His report was enthusiastically received, and Greenberg was invited to brief Democratic Party officials in Washington. Paul Kirk, then chairman of the Democratic National Committee, reacted negatively to the racially volatile findings. At the least, Greenberg's conclusions were sure to infuriate Jesse Jackson, the black civil rights leader and candidate for the Democratic presidential nomination in 1984, who was expected to be a player again in 1988.

"I found the conclusion inflammatory," recalls Kirk, "that what Democrats have to do is pay less attention to minorities." Kirk moved to squelch further discussion. "He just flipped out," says Frank Greer, a

Democratic consultant who worked with Greenberg. "The conclusions are so painfully obvious that it's amazing today that anyone could think they could be concealed."

In 1992, Macomb County appeared on Clinton's campaign schedule so often that he once asked Greenberg how many electoral votes it had.

Clinton's rise from governor of Arkansas to President of the United States was linked closely to the Democratic Leadership Council (DLC), an organization of moderate elected Democrats formed after Ronald Reagan's second landslide victory in 1984. Adherents to the DLC philosophy referred to themselves as New Democrats. Civil rights leader Jesse Jackson ridiculed the group of mostly white southerners as "Democrats for the Leisure Class." Clinton headed the organization in 1991 and used it as a stepping-stone for his presidential candidacy the next year.

In his keynote speech at the DLC's May 1991 convention in Cleveland, titled "What We Believe," Clinton said, "Governments don't raise children; people do. It is time they were asked to assume their responsibilities and forced to do it if they refuse." The statement shattered liberal orthodoxy and foreshadowed the themes of smaller government and personal responsibility that Clinton would employ in his presidential campaign beginning five months later.

Ironically, Greenberg came to the New Democrat agenda with an expansive sense of government, rather than a plan to reduce the role of government. His goal was to unify the party with programs that would serve blacks and whites, poor and middle class together. To overcome racial division, he advocated something closer to Swedish universalism than New Democrat moderation. He wanted the umbrella of government to reach the middle class, rather than be reserved for the truly needy. He wanted a greater role for government, particularly in the guarantee of health services, in an era when the public had no confidence in the government's ability to do anything. Greenberg operated on the theory that the disaffection of white suburbanites was a reaction to the Democratic Party's perceived preoccupation with the race issue. But it was about more than race; it was about the role of government.

Greenberg had a tendency from the start to let his ideology influence his advice. He had an agenda. During the 1980s, he urged Democratic candidates to speak out in opposition to President Reagan's policies toward Central America even though most analysts considered the issue a loser at the ballot box. "He tried to convince me to use El Salvador in races in central Michigan because he believed so strongly that U.S. policy was wrong," says Jill Buckley, then a Democratic consultant. Buckley ignored the advice.

Greenberg managed to thread the needle through the Reagan Revolution by helping elect Democrat Carr to Congress in Michigan. By the end of the decade, as candidates began gearing up for the 1992 presidential election, Greenberg's ideas were receiving closer scrutiny, and he came to Clinton's notice.

Clinton wanted to be president, but first he had to get reelected as governor of Arkansas. It was June of 1990, and the polls did not look good. Clinton was at forty-four percent and dropping. He put out an SOS to Frank Greer, a fellow southerner. "I'm in deep trouble," Clinton told him. "I'm getting ready to lose this reelection race. You've always wanted me to run for president. If I don't win this race, I'll never be able to run for dogcatcher, much less president."

Greer flew to Little Rock and met with Clinton and Dick Morris, who was then Clinton's pollster. Greer, looking ahead to 1992, knew that Morris, a Republican, would not cross party lines for a presidential run, at least not then. Also, Morris was not doing focus groups, which were being used increasingly in political races. A focus group allows the give-and-take of real conversation, and allows a pollster to plumb the public's psyche for nuances in a way that conventional question-and-answer polling does not. Greer proposed bringing in Greenberg, who had used focus groups in Macomb County.

Clinton had read an article that Greenberg wrote in 1991 for the liberal opinion journal *American Prospect,* in which Greenberg took seriously the frustrations of a middle class that felt squeezed between the rich who benefited from tax breaks and the poor who received welfare benefits. Clinton later told Greenberg that he read the article three times. Clinton wanted to hear what Greenberg would advise, and Morris approved. "If he had been hostile to the idea, it wouldn't have happened," says Greenberg.

What makes a truly gifted pollster is the ability to catch the little puffs of wind and see where they are going. Predicting the exact decimal point in an election is less important than divining themes that can sway voters. The real action is in asking the right questions and correctly interpreting the answers, and that is where Greenberg excelled.

Greer and Greenberg set up a focus group in a motel in Darnell, Arkansas, a couple of hours from Little Rock. Typically, focus groups are held in special facilities with two-way mirrors. Nothing like that existed in Darnell, so they put chairs in one end of the motel conference room. Greer, Greenberg, and Gloria Cabe, Clinton's campaign manager, watched the focus group on a television monitor from the other end of the room behind folding accordion doors.

They returned to Little Rock quite late, but Clinton was anxious to know what they had learned. "I'm a morning person, and in any case, I don't like to do immediate reaction," Greenberg recalls. "I like to read the transcript, but he wanted to have a conversation that night, so we went back to the mansion to do it. He was fine, alert and ready to go. I was exhausted. My lips wouldn't move."

Clinton agreed to put off the analysis until morning. Greenberg got back to his room at 1:00 A.M., then spent two more hours reading and interpreting the written responses from focus group members. He had a hard time falling asleep, then slept through the alarm at 6:30 for the scheduled 7:00 A.M. meeting. Greer called at 7:45, saying Clinton was waiting. Greenberg threw on some clothes and got to the mansion by 8:00 A.M., an hour late. Bleary-eyed and not quite sure he was making sense, Greenberg somehow got through the presentation.

The focus group results confirmed what Clinton had suspected. Arkansas voters thought that he had been in office too long, having served four consecutive two-year terms, and that all he had done was raise taxes. "All they think about is ten years and taxes," he said glumly. Greenberg developed a theme that turned Clinton's longevity in office into an asset. "Don't turn the clock back," which emphasized Clinton's accomplishments, especially in education, where much of the new tax revenue had been directed. Clinton handily won reelection in November 1990, and Greenberg became Clinton's new guru, displacing Dick Morris.

Planning for Clinton's presidential race got underway immediately. Greenberg, still a Washington outsider himself, was in charge of message development. Domestic policy was Clinton's strong suit. He knew a lot, and he had a record that he could tout. But Clinton lacked experience in foreign policy, especially in contrast to George Bush.

In September 1991, Greenberg arranged a series of issues briefings for Clinton in a private conference room at the Washington Court Hotel on Capitol Hill. The lengthiest session covered foreign policy. Several top House and Senate Democratic staffers attended, including an aide to then Armed Services Committee Chairman Les Aspin, and Lawrence Korb, an assistant secretary of defense during the Reagan administration who was at the Brookings Institution, a progressive think tank.

Clinton got right to the point. "How can I get out of this national security box?" he wanted to know. He did not have to explain what he meant. George Bush was on a stratospheric high in the polls, fresh from his triumph in the Gulf War. He was a World War II hero. He had served as U.S. ambassador to the United Nations. Clinton was the governor of a small southern state. He had avoided the draft and had no experience in foreign affairs.

The participants in the meeting thought they were there to talk foreign policy. But Clinton, with Greenberg at his side, was only interested in probing for ways to undercut Bush that would somehow boost his own credibility. "Where is Bush vulnerable?" Clinton asked, searching for specifics that he could use. "What issues can we pick to get some military backing? What weapons can we support?" Clinton subsequently called for completing existing orders for the B-2, which Defense Secretary Richard Cheney had said was nice to have but too expensive. According to one of the participants, when the Bush administration's policy of turning back fleeing Haitian refugees came up, Greenberg made the point that if Clinton let in the Haitians, "That puts us on the moral high ground." The observation was an obvious one, but that it had come from a pollster made the foreign policy professionals uneasy. When the discussion turned to Israel, Greenberg recused himself because he is Jewish and left the room because he did not want anyone to think he would bring his biases to the discussion.

When it came to packaging Clinton's strong domestic policy experience, Greenberg's background as an academic gave him added cachet. Finally the party had a thinker. He understood the cultural alienation of the middle class, and how ordinary, hardworking Americans were falling behind economically. They were not racists; they wanted their share of the American dream. Clinton would offer a "New Covenant" of rights and responsibilities that would reward work and exalt family values in language that sometimes jarred the party's liberals. This Democrat would not cater to the poor and minorities, but to the middle class—a far more costly proposition as it turned out. Clinton was never able to reconcile the dueling themes of universal government largesse with his New Democrat message of smaller government and personal responsibility.

Greenberg and Greer screened films of Franklin Roosevelt's speeches to prepare Clinton's presidential announcement speech. FDR had called for "a new deal for the forgotten man." It was an easy transition to "forgotten middle class," the phrase that Clinton used when he declared his candidacy on October 3, 1991, in Little Rock.

Clinton's efforts to win the presidency by forging a New Democrat majority were threatened by revelations about his past womanizing and his avoidance of the draft. Developing a strategy to overcome these negative stories was difficult. There was so much that Greenberg and the other campaign consultants did not know about Clinton, and Clinton was not forthcoming, even in the midst of a campaign crisis. James Carville, the hyperkinetic Cajun strategist, once said that Clinton was the political equivalent of a blind date.

A few intimates were designated to raise sensitive questions with the candidate; Greenberg was not one of them. In the midst of the controversy over the draft, Greenberg fired off a strategy memo that began, "I'm not a part of these [discussions], nor do I want to be." Getting the full story out of Clinton was extraordinarily difficult. "It didn't need another player, and it didn't need polling judgment," Greenberg says, parsing his words.

Other aides envied Greenberg's ability to coldly analyze the steamier side of Clinton's life. After tapes of phone conversations between Clinton and Gennifer Flowers that included sexual references became public, Greenberg drolly inquired in the midst of a conference call with Clinton and other campaign officials whether he should poll on oral sex. An aide who was on the line remembers how Greenberg raised it in the context of "a mishmash of things, including scheduling decisions and arranging a doctor's appointment for Clinton's voice." The suggestion hung in the air for a millisecond until Carville uttered one word: "Damn." Then everyone realized Greenberg was joking.

Greenberg did draw up questions that probed public attitudes about Clinton's infidelity. For example, "If you found out a candidate had an affair while married, would that tend to lessen your support?" There was always a core of people who would not vote for such a candidate under any circumstance. But the majority of voters were willing to forgive marital infidelity if it was in the past, and if the candidate was worthy in other ways.

Hillary Clinton, the most influential member of the campaign team, approached the talk about her husband's private life as a political problem. Doing so gave her emotional distance. In May 1991, Hillary sat down with Greenberg and Greer and said, "There are all these rumors about Bill's philandering. We've got to figure out how to deal with it." She wanted a strategy to preempt what she knew would be a problem. Out of that session came the idea for Clinton to do a mini-confessional with a small group of reporters before he officially announced his candidacy. They chose the Sperling Breakfast, a Washington institution of well-connected print reporters who meet with newsmakers over eggs and cereal.

Clinton's strategy of admitting past problems, pledging fidelity, and invoking a "zone of privacy" worked for a while, until a woman named Gennifer Flowers stepped forward to publicly accuse him of adultery. Clinton got through the scandal, but everyone was waiting for the next high heel to drop. Behind the scenes, Clinton's evasion continued to trouble his political intimates. They felt like lawyers defending a reluctant client. How could they prepare his case? "You've got to give us everything," Greenberg implored, knowing that his pleas would go unheeded.

Lack of candor was not the only problem Greenberg had with Clinton. The candidate's tendency to include a wide range of people in campaign decisions also bothered him. So many people had to be consulted that decision-making often came to a standstill. Greenberg found comfort in his careful questionnaires, one thing he could do without getting mired in the Clintonland group culture.

At the start of the campaign, Clinton insisted on personally signing off on the questions for every poll. When he was late in getting back his comments, Greenberg went into the field without his okay. They had a dustup over that, and Greenberg agreed he would not do it again. But when Clinton missed the very next deadline, Greenberg ignored the protocol and proceeded on his own. By then, Clinton was so busy he forgot about it.

The issue came to a head again in the late spring of 1992, a particularly sensitive time. Clinton had the Democratic nomination virtually in hand, but the doubts about his character and values had taken root and raised real questions about his electability. The campaign had just completed highly secretive research on the Clintons' image, dubbed the Manhattan Project, and Greenberg was readying the campaign's first real national survey based on the project's data.

The survey had gone through many drafts and many people, but Susan Thomases, a prickly New York lawyer friend of Hillary's, was still not satisfied. Thomases was extraordinarily protective of the Clintons, especially Hillary. Whenever Greenberg did a "favorability battery" that asked for thermometer readings, cool to hot, about a variety of public figures, the results on Hillary were blacked out for all but the President and Hillary herself. Greenberg concluded this was just more of the same protectiveness. After much heated discussion, and without Thomases's approval, he went ahead with plans to do the poll.

As the poll was about to hit the field, Greenberg went to Arkansas for a campaign meeting. He had just arrived at the Little Rock airport when his pager signaled that Clinton aide George Stephanopoulos was trying to reach him. Using his cellular phone, Greenberg called Stephanopoulos, and was told by Clinton's young aide to pull the survey; Thomases had gone to the Clintons with her objections. Greenberg responded in an instant. "I quit," he said.

That night, he refused to attend a meeting with Clinton and the others at the governor's mansion. But other aides who had had their own encounters with Thomases urged him to stay and confront Clinton. The next day, a Sunday, he met with the candidate. Clinton characteristically tried to smooth over their differences. Thomases was only trying to protect him, he said. "Look, you've got more leeway on this than any pollster who's ever worked with me," Clinton told him. "With Dick Morris, I always saw the questionnaires."

From that point on, Greenberg had total control of polling. But he never had the intimate relationship with Clinton that Morris had had, and would have again after the 1994 election. Morris's cause was Clinton; Greenberg's cause was the advancement of his theories about building a new Democratic majority by bringing blacks and middle-class whites together.

Greenberg wanted a slogan for the campaign that would embody this vision for the party. He was part of a team that suggested the phrase "It's time to do right for those who have been done wrong." The other advisers hated it and mocked it mercilessly. They pointed out that it was bad grammar and played into the stereotype of the ignorant southerner. Greenberg liked it because he thought it spoke to the "forgotten middle class." He backed down a week later when the slogan was panned by focus groups. Clinton eventually settled—with Greenberg's backing—on the theme "Putting People First."

Clinton's election was a giddy time for Greenberg and the others. They had done what the pundits said could not be done—elected a Democrat. But the joy of winning soon gave way to the reality of governing.

Clinton squandered much of the goodwill surrounding his election in the messy transition. He spent too many hours balancing gender and ethnicity in his Cabinet and not enough time setting his governing priorities.

It was clear that Greenberg and the other consultants would have to maneuver adroitly if they were to continue to have access and influence to the President-elect. Clinton had delegated power to them during the final months of the campaign only after he was forced to as a matter of self-preservation. Now that the campaign was over, he wanted to regain control. Stephanopoulos stayed as a spokesperson, but the political operation was gone.

Greenberg turned to an unusual person for advice. Their meeting was secret, so only the letters DW appeared on Greenberg's office calendar that November morning when he and Dick Wirthlin had breakfast together at La Colline on Capitol Hill. Wirthlin had been President Reagan's pollster. He met regularly with Reagan, maintained a research operation at the White House, polled with the frequency of a permanent campaign, and kept his corporate clients. Greenberg wanted to know how Wirthlin managed such an arrangement for eight years in the midst of the inevitable White House infighting. "Access is the name of the game," Wirthlin said. He advised Greenberg to push for private time with the President each week.

On November 23, Greenberg sent a memo to the President urging that he adopt a "modified Wirthlin model" for polling. Under the arrangement, Greenberg would be assured time alone with Clinton each week for fifteen minutes, and a research operation, to be controlled by Greenberg, would be established at the Democratic National Committee.

Greenberg proposed a polling program that would surpass even Wirthlin's: a nationwide survey each month to assess Clinton's job performance; issue surveys every month; statewide surveys, at least two a month; six focus groups a month "to allow a continuing conversation with the American people"; and dial groups, a new technology for instant reaction to major presidential speeches. Eventually this was somewhat scaled back to four focus groups a month and fewer state polls until the midterm elections.

In what he called "a first draft of political tasks and goals," Greenberg reported the findings of a survey conducted the day after the election, and what it meant for the Clinton agenda. Fifty-one percent wanted the new president to address the economy and create jobs. "Just nineteen percent say attack the budget deficits . . . and just four percent say health care." Clinton did just the opposite in his first two years. Deficit reduction was Clinton's central theme in 1993, overwhelming the "investments" in education and job training he had promised in his campaign. Driven by pressure from Wall Street and the bond market, he produced a budget worthy of an Eisenhower Republican—and got no credit for it from Republicans or Democrats. Clinton's second year, 1994, was swallowed up by health care reform.

The sense of hubris in the Clinton camp blinded them to the early warnings of the problems that eventually would overwhelm the Clinton presidency. Samuel Popkin, a California political scientist and polling consultant who worked with Greenberg, remembers getting a call from a member of the inner circle in Little Rock after the election asking him to be one of ten people to write memos on what Clinton should do after the first hundred days. When Popkin asked what the hundred-day plan was, he was told that Clinton would do health care and the budget—a naively ambitious agenda.

Despite data from his own polls showing that health care was politically risky, Greenberg advocated a major overhaul. He believed that anything less than comprehensive reform would not impress cynical voters. The problem was that the same people who worried about health care were even more nervous about the government fixing it. He sent a post-election memo to Little Rock that did not attempt to reconcile the contradiction.

"Voters are deeply worried about health care and give the Democrats and Bill Clinton a strong advantage on addressing the problem (sixty-nine to twenty-one percent). Moving effectively is essential if Clinton is to have any hope of reducing the deficit and funding new initiatives. But this issue bodes big potential problems and should only be addressed with great care. When Clinton moves, he must move boldly, but there is no current mandate on health care. The issue barely comes up as a priority for the new administration or as a reason to have supported Bill Clinton—ranked in behind the economy, jobs, and deficit reduction."

Greenberg accurately forecast the Republicans' attack, and he knew how fragile a mandate the Democrats had. "When Clinton moves on health care, we should expect the Republicans to take their stand against a government too big and too ready to spend and tax. There is only a bare philosophic majority for an expansive government role (fifty-two percent), and Republicans can play effectively on the deep public ambivalence about overriding the judgments of private actors. . . . This is a battle that Clinton must join and win, but the administration and the public are not ready for it."

Greenberg emphasized repeatedly that people wanted health care reform, but there was no consensus on how to do it, and people were nervous about the government getting involved. Nevertheless, taking on health care reform against all odds would allow Clinton to address what Greenberg called the "political/trust dimension." Greenberg's numbers showed that Clinton had an image of being too political and too willing to give in on issues of principle. Pursuing an issue of this magnitude in the face of political opposition would restore trust. What Greenberg did not calculate was the devastating impact of the fight if Clinton were not successful.

Clinton had run a campaign on job creation, welfare reform, and a middle-class tax cut, with health care reform a late entry. Greenberg's polling showed that this agenda was popular with the American people. After the election, those were the issues people expected the new administration to address. During the transition, it was decided that health care reform should take precedence over welfare reform on the theory that young, single mothers remained on welfare to secure health coverage for their children that they could not get in the workplace. To give Hillary Clinton the substantive role she desired in his presidency, Clinton named her to lead the health care reform effort, a historic appointment for a first lady, but one that carried considerable risk.

Greenberg could not gauge the fallout from the appointment. The protectiveness around Mrs. Clinton prevented rational discussion about her role in the White House. Clinton had named her health care czar on January 25, 1993, without a full understanding of the public's likely reaction and the possible consequences, particularly if she failed. Greenberg was allowed to do only the most rudimentary polling on the First Lady, which rankled other aides. "If she's going to carry the flag on health care, we should be asking a lot of questions about her," an adviser said at the time of Mrs. Clinton's historic appointment, adding, "People are terrified to talk about anything that has to do with Hillary. And that hasn't changed since the campaign."

With Hillary in charge, Greenberg was not involved in the design of the plan. "There was incredible paranoia about *not* using polls to design the plan," says Samuel Popkin. The fact that the Clinton plan was, or could be, painted as big-government liberalism dashed Greenberg's hopes that bold health care reform would win over voters attracted to independent businessman Ross Perot. Greenberg and the political advisers were briefed on the details of the plan only after it was ninety-five percent complete.

Having been elected with only forty-three percent of the vote, Clinton's major task as the leader of a new governing coalition was to solidify his support among New Democrats, even if it meant loosening his ties to traditional Democratic constituencies. Greenberg wrote, "Clinton can forge a New Democratic Party if he takes on broad battles to uplift America and its people. Obviously, Democrats need to honor their historic commitments to labor and minority communities that have been discriminated against. We should live and breathe our commitment to equality. But this election was not about finishing old revolutions; it was about starting new ones." The passage presaged Greenberg's support for the North American Free Trade Agreement, bitterly opposed by organized labor, and for a scaling back of affirmative action programs based on racial preferences.

As the inauguration drew near, Greenberg was finalizing his polling contract with the DNC, but could not get through to the man whose political future the polling was designed to protect. He dispatched several unsolicited memos to Little Rock in an effort to penetrate the curtain around the First Couple.

On January 17, 1993, three days before Clinton was sworn in as President, Greenberg wrote urgently to the President-elect and Hillary: "We have lost our focus. . . . We are losing control of our agenda, just as we are about to assume the position to set it." Clinton's popularity was at seventy-one percent, the highest in recent history for any president taking office. Yet he had allowed his agenda to be defined by stories of indecision and disarray. "It matters when a Jay Leno begins making jokes about 'broken promises,'" Greenberg warned the Clintons.

Greenberg wanted Clinton to convey a larger sense of purpose and coherent goals. Quoting Carville, whose plain talk could move Clinton when no one else could, Greenberg concluded, "James said it pointedly, 'Tell us the message, tell us the mission, and we'll figure out how to sell it. We'll tell you where you are going to run into trouble, but we'll sell your ideas. But we have to know your core purpose and goals.'"

Clinton was making his way in a triumphal caravan from Monticello to Washington the day before the inaugural, when Greenberg wrote this sometimes cranky memo. "You would think from watching the news that cutting the budget deficit in half was our only goal. . . . The public has not changed its priorities. They are focused on growth, job creation and rising incomes. Over two-thirds still think we are in a depression or recession." Clinton's emphasis on deficit reduction would steady the financial markets and lower interest rates. But the benefits to middle-income voters were not as tangible as traditional Democratic spending programs. Indeed, the notion that a Democrat would cut the deficit was so counterintuitive that Clinton never received political credit.

"Our fate is in the hands of middle-class voters," Greenberg wrote Clinton, urging him not to become too identified with liberal social policy. "The prospect of realignment, and of winning in 1994 and 1996, depends on our ability to show the middle class that we are New Democrats, committed to growth and spending discipline, and who understand their values. . . . We are opposed to moving on abortion, gays in the military and other subjects in the first days and weeks." Less than a month later, Clinton's advocacy for gays in the military would undermine his attempt to appear as a centrist Democrat, and brand him as a social liberal.

Greenberg urged that the President-elect push "an unrelenting reformist agenda" as a way to win over Perot voters. "Stick with your twenty-five percent cutback of staff budgets in Congress and the White House," Greenberg advised. "Sell off limousines; insist on a line-item veto; announce management reforms, and propose lobby and campaign reforms. In the survey data, real reform means spending reform, [eliminating] perks, and political reform, in that order."

In an almost desperate tone, Greenberg wrote that the transition between the election and the inauguration had failed to produce "a common understanding of priorities" for the new administration. "Obviously, we start with the economy. Health care is a close second. But where does political reform fit in?" Greenberg said Clinton's repeated promise to "end welfare as we know it" was the equivalent of George Bush's "read my lips" promise on taxes, yet Clinton paid scant attention to the issue after the election.

Clinton's inability to set clear priorities encouraged warring factions to flourish behind the scenes. Greenberg felt political reform was essential to reach Perot voters. But Democratic congressional leaders had already persuaded Clinton to back off reform in exchange for their cooperation in passing key legislation. Many analysts of the Clinton presidency would view the deal as a pact with the devil. The 1992 Democratic Congress would be swept out two years later by Republicans preaching the reform message that Clinton set aside.

Greenberg finished drafting the memo at 6:40 A.M. on inauguration day, adding a personal note to the President: "The 'Reunion' on the Mall and at the Lincoln Memorial . . . was an extraordinary event that left me dumbstruck. I have had difficulty writing the last few paragraphs. The country will never experience anything like it again—a cultural revival, not just a generational change. We've lost track of how tired and mean the country has become. . . ."

But Greenberg did not let his emotions override his concern about Clinton's emphasis on achieving racial and gender balance in his Cabinet. "I want to express a dissent in hopes of influencing where you take us in the next few days," Greenberg wrote. "The power of the reunion theme, we found in our research, lay in the concept, 'working together to lift up America, to get her moving.' Diversity is a powerful and ennobling concept, but only if it is genuinely broad and inclusive and only if it lifts us up as a nation for some purpose."

Clinton had concentrated on naming women, African-Americans, and Hispanics to his Cabinet. Elevating these groups to prominence hurt efforts to woo white ethnics, the weakest part of the Democratic coalition. Greenberg noted that Catholics—Italian, Irish, and Eastern European— were not part of the Cabinet and that the larger meaning of diversity had been lost in the effort to include representatives of certain groups.

All the warnings were there. But Clinton was being pulled in so many directions that long-range planning was about getting through the week. On January 26, 1993, less than a week after Clinton took office, Greenberg wrote a confidential memo on the public's attitude toward new taxes. He titled the memo, "The Political Moment." He sent it to the President, Vice President Al Gore, and the economic team.

"There is a new willingness to entertain new taxes, though our support and leeway on this issue is very narrow," he said. Greenberg found that voters overwhelmingly supported taxing the wealthiest taxpayers but strongly opposed an energy tax and a rumored fifty-cent gasoline tax. "Voters are watching Bill Clinton to see if he raises taxes on the middle class," Greenberg said. "They are already aware that the middle-class tax cut is moving off the table, though few voters ever expected it to happen. But they are nervous that the opposite will happen which, for many, will prove a betrayal."

Greenberg would later privately advocate dropping a modest gas tax that was part of the President's budget. Members of Clinton's economic team were aghast that a pollster even entered into such policy discussions. Greenberg defended his involvement on the grounds that any Democratic president getting ready to raise taxes in an anti-tax climate deserves to know the subtleties of the public's thinking. He said he proposed dropping the gas tax because the amount of money it would raise was not worth the political heat Clinton would take.

Although Greenberg had a reputation as a strong liberal, his early memos show that he tried to get the administration to move away from liberal positions that ultimately proved disastrous. He opposed the President moving ahead so quickly on abortion and gays in the military. He pressed for welfare reform. He criticized the preoccupation with diversity, and would eventually support scaling back affirmative action programs.

Greenberg was still trying to figure his way into the chaotic White House. His standing weekly meeting with the President would often be shifted around or canceled entirely depending on what crisis was brewing. Whatever he told the President when he did see him was closely held. Copies of Greenberg's memos were numbered to help trace any leaks that might occur.

A February 2, 1993, memo was addressed to "Mrs. Hillary Clinton" and offered suggestions on health care "positioning." It was the first of many pieces of advice from Greenberg that emboldened Mrs. Clinton to push for major health care reform. The very naming of Mrs. Clinton to head the health care task force, and the media emphasis on the issue, had made health care Bill Clinton's Persian Gulf. Greenberg reported that "growing majorities" believed the health system was in need of an overhaul.

Although reforming the health care system had been low on the public's wish list immediately after the election, Greenberg saw the new interest in the subject as an opportunity for Clinton. "We should describe our recommendations as 'major reform,' reflecting the sense of urgency and providing the President with the space to make bold proposals. Health care is the area where voters expect Bill Clinton to make the biggest change and accomplish the most," Greenberg wrote. He urged Mrs. Clinton to recruit "important authority figures" like former Surgeon General C. Everett Koop to reassure the public. He cautioned the First Lady about making unnecessary enemies. "Our attacks on fraud and excessive profits should not be so sharp that they preclude the co-optation of some major figures from insurance and the health field." It was not advice that the combative First Lady was able to follow.

Clinton had been in office two weeks and two days when Greenberg hit him with a memo that was pointedly titled "Post-Inaugural: New Kind-of-Democrat?" Clinton's job performance ratings were dropping, and his negatives rising. Liberals loved him, up from seventy-seven to eighty-one percent, but support was falling everywhere else across the ideological spectrum. Greenberg subtitled his biting analysis with headings that told the story: "The Gay Fallout," "Not Very Solid South," "The Perot Voter: Missing Our Target Audience." "We have let slip away a lot of what we forged over the course of the campaign—in particular, the sense that we are not a predictable Democrat. . . . Being 'too liberal' is now the strongest negative predictor of feelings about Clinton."

If it was so obvious what Clinton was doing wrong, why couldn't he change course? The question plagued the President months later as his poll numbers continued to drop. He wanted to know how to reverse the downward spiral. "It was very hard to give the poll numbers when we were sinking," Greenberg acknowledges. "The President really at that point did not want to see poll numbers on how fast we were sinking; he wanted to know what the strategy was for getting out of it, and that wasn't my role. I mean, it is a collective role that I have with other people, but that's not what these presentations are for. I don't lay out my strategy. That's a process that we go through with the political advisers and with George [Stephanopoulos] and others. This is not the political advisory meeting."

Clinton's frustration with Greenberg bubbled over at the May 1, 1993, White House Correspondents' Association dinner, a black-tie event where the President is expected to deliver self-deprecating remarks. With hundreds of reporters in attendance, Clinton read a mock telegram from Greenberg that said, "I don't have a clue what you should do. Follow your instincts. But send the check anyway."

A Greenberg questionnaire just before Memorial Day asked people what they had read, seen, or heard about Bill Clinton in the news lately.

Thirty-three percent said, "Haircut," referring to news stories of the high-priced haircut Clinton got on Air Force One while reportedly holding up air traffic at the Los Angeles International Airport. That was more than four times the eight percent who cited health care, the next highest response. Side issues that cast Clinton as a self-indulgent yuppie were defining his presidency, while public interest in health care reform foundered.

Clinton's health care plan would not be unveiled until September, but there was growing skepticism that he could do what he had promised. The doubts were more evident in focus groups than in the raw numbers. Greenberg used a focus group facility in Paramus, New Jersey, a community just across the river from New York City and a hotbed of what today might be called Rush Limbaugh Democrats—working-class men and women who say their party left them. It is Macomb County East. Greenberg sat behind the two-way mirror, studying body language and listening intently. He knocked on his side of the glass to remind participants they were being observed, which is a courtesy. But he did not reveal himself, or his client, the President.

The moderator read an outline of Clinton's proposed health plan, which included a Health Security Card for every American, guaranteed coverage even for the unemployed, and out-of-pocket expenses limited to $200 a year. "It sounds too good," was one comment. Another was, "Pie in the sky."

Questions about Clinton's resolve dominated the discussion. "Everything he has promised can't come to be," said Cheryl K., an older woman. "He covers too many issues at once."

The moderator asked, "What bad thoughts or doubts come into your head when you hear the name, Bill Clinton?"

"Waffles, can't make a decision, doesn't back up staff, and doesn't have priorities in order," said Nancy K., a homemaker with a small child. Lisa B., a hairdresser who was seven and one-half months pregnant, wondered, "Did you really cheat on your wife?"

It was focus groups like this one that helped Greenberg shape Clinton's health care strategy. Some of the changes were cosmetic. For example, the phrase "managed competition" was discarded early on because the public reacted negatively. After research showed that middle-income voters equated universal coverage with taking away some of their benefits to cover the poor, Greenberg advised using the phrase "guaranteed insurance for all."

Clinton began to realize that the promises of cooperation he had gotten from the Democratic leaders in Little Rock before the election meant nothing in the rough-and-tumble of everyday politics. Every Democrat in Congress had won with a higher percentage of votes than Clinton. Many were envious fellow baby-boomers, who were reluctant to give Clinton the loyalty and respect he needed. Democratic elders second-guessed him privately and, in the case of Senator Moynihan, publicly. In June, top advisers gathered in the White House solarium for a strategy session. Greenberg advanced a new theory that the ability to master Congress is the equivalent test of strength for a post–Cold War president as handling the Soviets was in an earlier era.

There was a lot of chest-thumping among the consultants about how Clinton had to get tough with the Democrats. One adviser suggested "cutting off" Democratic lobbyists whose clients opposed the President's budget. Listening to the proposal, a White House aide thought to himself, "What do we do about Tommy Boggs?"—Boggs and other lobbyists being major financial contributors to the Democratic Party whom Clinton could ill afford to punish. The idea died there.

Clinton badly needed a political victory. Pressing for ratification of the North American Free Trade Agreement initially looked like a loser. Labor unions opposed NAFTA, and Ross Perot was threatening to mobilize his base of independent voters against the treaty. But Greenberg was convinced, based on his polling, that Democrats could vote for NAFTA and not be punished in the next election. "No one will remember this vote a year from now," he said. Rosa DeLauro, who had to cast a vote on this issue, was not persuaded by her husband's arguments. When Greenberg presented his data on Capitol Hill, disbelieving Democrats jeered: "Why should we believe you if you can't convince your wife!"

In the summer of 1993, Greenberg escaped the White House infighting about Clinton's troubles and went halfway around the world to do pro bono work for another presidential campaign. Decades of apartheid had ended in South Africa and the first election in which blacks could vote was scheduled for late April 1994. Greenberg and media consultant Frank Greer offered their services, without charge, to the African National Congress (ANC), the party of Nelson Mandela, who had been released from prison after twenty-seven years. For Greenberg, this was a dream realized, validation of his outspoken stand against apartheid, which as a young man had cost him a job in South Africa.

The first South Africa polls in the summer of 1993 took about three months to complete: a month and a half in the field and a month and a half to analyze the data. Once enough interviewers were trained, Greenberg polled nationally every week. He thought focus groups would be impossible, but they proved easier to arrange than in the States. "Here [in the United States] the way you do it is you call people up, you interview them to find out if they meet the criteria, then you try to persuade them to come to a focus group. You offer them a financial incentive. You invite fifteen people, you call them back three times, you hope you get ten." In South Africa, because there are so few phones, Greenberg would go to a busy place, like a bus station, interview people, offer them a modest cash payment, and pile them into a van on the spot. One-stop shopping eliminated the problem of no-shows.

Despite the conventional wisdom that Mandela would win easily, polls had him just barely over fifty percent. Greenberg discovered in the focus groups that the ANC was seen as out of touch and maybe even arrogant, with the leaders having been in exile and engaged in three-years-long negotiations with the white South African government. "This is a liberation movement. For people to view them as distant, that was a real problem," Greenberg said. He and others knew that in order to get the ANC to campaign in a more populist way, Mandela, the ANC's candidate for president, would have to hear the complaints firsthand—not just in a report, but actually in the words of ordinary people.

Greenberg personally read Mandela comments from focus group participants to impress upon him the depth of their concern. These words and feelings persuaded Mandela and the ANC to hold "People's Forums," which were modeled after Clinton's town hall meetings. This was a drastic change for a revolutionary movement, whose idea of a rally featured Mandela and ten other speakers of comparable rank speaking interminably.

Persuading the ANC to elevate Mandela and exploit his greatness took some doing. "Even when you convinced Mandela, you had to make the case to the Western Cape Regional Committee," says Greenberg. Mandela adapted remarkably well to Western-style campaigning, but he joked about returning to tribal rituals, telling Greenberg, "If we don't like your numbers, we can always have the witch doctor throw bones."

The campaign they fashioned in periodic visits to South Africa, like the Clinton campaign in 1992, focused on the economy. The theme was "Better Life for All," which local campaign operatives translated to "Vote ANC: Jobs, Jobs, Jobs." Watching a focus group in Cape Town, Greenberg felt he was back in the Clinton campaign when a voter demanded to know how the ANC would pay for all its promises. "It's just like Clinton," the man exclaimed. "The numbers don't add up." It was about the same time that the Congressional Budget Office had attacked the financing of Clinton's health care plan, pointing out that the plan did not generate enough revenue to cover everybody in the country and still cut the deficit substantially, as Clinton had promised.

It took all the finesse they could muster for Greenberg and Greer to prepare Mandela to debate his white opponent. They wanted Mandela to be conciliatory toward F. W. de Klerk, who had taken courageous steps toward democratizing South Africa. But it upset Mandela when de Klerk took credit, as he often did, for ending apartheid. Mandela felt it trivialized the sacrifices of his ANC colleagues, many of whom had been jailed or killed in the struggle for liberation. "We urged him not to take the bait," says Greenberg.

Mandela was tougher on de Klerk in the debate than his Western advisers would have liked, until the very end, when he extended his hand in a gesture of conciliation and said, "We have to do this together." The photograph of that moment made front pages around the world and defined the debate. It looked choreographed, but Greenberg insists it was not. "Everybody believes it was the American handlers who produced this, but it had nothing to do with us," Greenberg says. "What Mandela said afterward is, 'I got to my closing arguments and I figured I had been so hard on him that I had better reach out.'"

Working to achieve Mandela's historic victory brought together the two parts of Greenberg's life, his academic study of South Africa and his parallel career in polling. "I never thought I would experience anything as exhilarating, as intense as Clinton's election," he said. Pictures of Mandela's election replaced the framed *Newsweek* account of the Manhattan Project, the image remake that helped elect Clinton, on Greenberg's office wall.

On May 4, 1994, the day that Greenberg returned to Washington from Johannesburg, *The Washington Post* had a front-page story on a sexual harassment lawsuit filed against the President by a former Arkansas government worker, Paula Jones. Greenberg called Greer from the airport, sounding discouraged. The summer and fall of 1994 would be Clinton's worst period as president. His health care proposal was collapsing, and the country had lost confidence in him as commander in chief.

Voters were disgusted by the image of young marines snappily saluting a bag of golf clubs carried off the presidential helicopter by a White House aide scouting a golf course in Maryland. Clinton promptly fired the aide, an Arkansas pal, but the incident cut as deeply into his credibility as the airport runway haircut a year earlier. The Clinton presidency was being defined by a landing at a golf course and a fraternity house governing style symbolized by late-night pizza deliveries.

Greenberg would nervously try to jolly Clinton out of his gloom by attributing the slide in popularity to the June 8 jinx. Three years in a row, Clinton got his lowest polls on that date, beginning in 1992, after the California primary, when media attention shifted to Ross Perot; in his first year as president, after the loss of his economic "stimulus" package; and now, in 1994, his authority eroded by questions about Whitewater, a land deal he and Mrs. Clinton had entered into years before in Arkansas, and Paula Jones's charges. He had rebounded then; he would do so again, Greenberg assured him.

At a strategy session at the Democratic National Committee offices, a rival Democratic pollster challenged Greenberg on his approach to health care reform: "At no time did the cry for universal coverage drive the public, yet that was what Stan presented to the White House. I remember sitting across the table from Stan and saying that our polls showed that portability and cost are far more important to this debate than universality." Greenberg said that in the dial groups he conducted during the President's health care speech, Clinton's comments on universal coverage and his holding up of the "Health Security Card" got the strongest response.

Dial groups instantly measure reaction with electronic dials that selected voters turn to show approval or disapproval. Greenberg says he hates dial groups, that he only does them defensively because everyone else does them. But in at least this one case, he cited them as a basis for concluding that selling the public on health care by promising lowered costs would not work.

Greenberg's research showed that people think government spends money recklessly, and they have no faith in government's ability to lower the cost of health care or anything else. But people did regard government as capable of imposing mandates to make sure everyone was covered by health insurance. Greenberg knew that containing runaway costs was the policy priority, and the plan developed by Mrs. Clinton had two provisions for restraining costs, neither of which was very popular. The first was a broader use of managed care, a concept the public recoiled from; the second was price controls, an approach so abhorrent to the medical community that administration officials were barred from talking about it in public.

In the early spring of 1994, Greenberg told the President and his aides that if they lost health care, they would face a "disaster" in the fall elections. "And I'm not saying thirty to thirty-five seats," Greenberg added. "I think we could lose a lot of seats."

What Greenberg was looking at were "thermometer scores" for each party. In nonpresidential election years, the Democrats usually held an advantage of ten or twelve points. The lowest Greenberg could remember in thirty years was seven. In May and June of 1994, the Democrats actually trailed the Republicans by five or six points, which was an extraordinary turnaround. Greenberg spent less time at the White House and more on Capitol Hill, giving extensive presentations alerting Democrats to the scale of the problem.

However, Democrats felt that Greenberg, as much as anybody else, was to blame for creating the party's difficulties. They had no idea what he was counseling in the White House inner sanctum. They associated him with a health care plan that had labeled them as the party of big government. In the search for scapegoats, Greenberg was convenient. His emphasis on domestic policy was also implicated in the administration's failure to appreciate the importance of foreign policy as a symbol of leadership. Outside advisers said Clinton should get off MTV, quit talking about his underwear, and hold some state dinners.

Clinton had fallen into the trap that Greenberg first warned of in his Macomb County study, when focus groups revealed that traditional Democrats were no longer voting Democratic because they thought the party "only cared about blacks and minorities." Greenberg thought white ethnic voters did not like government because it excluded them; even worse, he discovered they did not like government, period.

Clinton presented health care reform as an entitlement in what many of his critics in Congress and the media said was an era of post-entitlement politics. A year and a half spent pushing health care reform and convincing the country there was a crisis made it impossible for Clinton to then get credit for an improving economy. He was tarred as a big-spending, big-government liberal.

Throughout the summer of 1994, there was growing disenchantment with Greenberg and his advice. The White House brought in other voices, including Geoff Garin, a respected Democratic pollster, and Bob Shrum, a talented wordsmith and media consultant who had worked for Senator Bob Kerrey against Clinton in the primaries. The DNC invited in several Democratic pollsters for what it hoped would be a series of brainstorming sessions with Greenberg, the only one on the payroll. Many of these consultants were polling for Democratic members of Congress and their own polls told them disaster was looming.

"I was amazed how willing they were to share information for the greater good," said a party official. "Basically, Greenberg wouldn't tell them anything. He wouldn't trade. He would just be mum." After two meetings, the other pollsters concluded it was a waste of time. For all of Greenberg's mild-mannered exterior, he jealously guarded his position as the sole funnel of information to the President. When Clinton was told by a number of outsiders how they were frozen out, he expressed great surprise. "I didn't know people were shut out," he said.

As the President's pollster, Greenberg felt constrained about sharing his findings, although he knew as well as any of the other pollsters that disaster was indeed looming. In his defense, he says that it is not unusual for a White House pollster to operate in secrecy, citing similar Lone Ranger behavior by pollsters for Bush, Reagan, and Carter. The difference this time, however, was that Democrats had not held the White House for a dozen years and a generation of pollsters felt they had a shared stake in Clinton's succeeding.

With the Democrats' plight growing more desperate, and his own stock falling, Greenberg began convening small groups of Democratic consultants in the White House Roosevelt Room. Using research he had done in eight congressional districts, he told them that Democratic incumbents could run successfully on the votes they had cast. He cited the "three strikes and you're out" measure on crime, cutting the federal bureaucracy by 250,000 positions, the Brady Bill, and the assault weapons ban; he even threw in welfare reform, though Clinton had done little to advance the issue. "If your candidates are for welfare reform, they should take ownership and tell people they fought for it," he urged.

Greenberg bolstered his presentation with a computer model that showed the correlation between presidential popularity and the number of seats lost in a midterm election. His message was, "If Clinton does better, so will you." Some of the consultants left the session grumbling. It was the first time they had been inside the White House since Clinton had taken office, and they resented being summoned to be team players only when all else was failing.

The sentiment in the country in the early summer of 1994 had not yet crystallized into anger against the Democrats. That would happen later with the collapse of health care. Greenberg sent his eleven-page "Strategic Guide to the 1994 Election" to Democratic state chairs around the country, and it soon showed up on the front page of *The New York Times*. Democrats could win if they ran on welfare reform, cutting the bureaucracy, and the "three strikes and you're out" crime measure, the memo said, a strategy that bore little resemblance to the issues that so far had defined the Clinton presidency.

The section of the memo dealing with welfare reform tap-danced around reality. "The biggest single accomplishment not on the list is welfare reform. That legislation has not yet passed the Congress, but when in the survey we suggest that it did, the issue quickly rises to the top of the list of accomplishments. Democratic candidates should give high consideration to emphasizing their battle to achieve welfare reform that limits payments to two years."

When Greenberg presented his findings to a group of moderate Democrats in Congress, recalls former Rep. Dave McCurdy, "We almost hooted him out of the room." McCurdy and other moderates had begged the White House to reform welfare so they would have something tangible to run on in November. They blamed Greenberg for allowing a health care plan that was unachievable to dominate the public discussion. And now Greenberg was giving them the same advice he had ignored only months before. They had no way of knowing that Greenberg, too, had been pushing the White House to take up welfare reform. Again, citing the peculiar prerogatives of a presidential pollster, Greenberg said he was in no position to tell the moderate Democrats what he was advocating privately at the White House.

Two remodeled Capitol Hill row houses serve as headquarters for Greenberg's business. The house in front serves as the reception area and the one behind it is the "nerve center," the computer equivalent of the campaign war room. So many posters cover the walls that, when the IRS audited Greenberg after the 1992 election, an agent thought he was a poster maker.

As election day 1994 approached, the buildings were frequently busy around the clock. A subculture of young people—the breed of computer nerds and political junkies that are essential in campaigns—worked at gathering and crunching data.

Postcards to Clinton written by voters in focus groups are tacked onto bulletin boards. "Bill Clinton keep trying!" says one. "Conservatives eventually die and progress is made!" says another. There are Ronald Reagan reminders everywhere, from the Van Heusen shirt ad he did as a young man to a poster depicting "The world according to Ronald Reagan." The poster shows Democrats and "welfare bums" vying against Republicans "and other real Americans." Reagan's style of leadership is a model for Greenberg and his minions even though they are at odds with his ideology.

When Greenberg needs to get away from office distractions, he heads for nearby Union Station, a restored train terminal that houses several movie theaters and a variety of shops, restaurants, and fast-food outlets. He usually sits alone at a tiny table in the communal eating area sipping gourmet black coffee from the Bucks County Coffee Company, and tapping away on his laptop computer. It is noisy and congested, but he treats it as a sanctuary. Somehow it is exhilarating, all that noise that has nothing to do with him. He just shuts it out. "It's where I do my best writing," he says.

On this August day, however, Greenberg is anything but relaxed. He keeps checking his watch because he has an appointment with Sen. Joseph Lieberman, one of his clients and a holdout on health care among the Senate Democrats. Greenberg has reluctantly agreed to lobby Lieberman. "I've never done it before. I don't think it's my place," he says. But the White House is desperate, in part because Greenberg has told them that the success or failure of health care reform will be the prism through which the voters evaluate Clinton and the Democrats in November. Legislative accomplishment, Greenberg believes, is the only way that Clinton can convince voters he is "for real" and overcome their unease about his character. "We need a health care bill," Greenberg says quietly.

When Greenberg called Lieberman's office on Capitol Hill, the senator was suddenly unavailable. "I think he was avoiding me," Greenberg said. Questioned months later, Lieberman said, "I had already crossed the bridge. He was one of an onslaught of calls. You know when you're being targeted big. Why put up with it?"

Republicans in Congress were emboldened by the Democratic defections from Clinton's health care plan and by data that showed they could be rewarded by the voters for stopping "a bad bill." Clinton's credibility was at such a low point that Democrats lost a procedural vote on a crime bill August 11, 1994, "which should have been a no-brainer," says Greenberg. Republicans successfully portrayed money for youth recreation programs like midnight basketball in inner cities as "pork." Rosa DeLauro, campaigning for her third congressional term, was derided as "Porky Greenberg . . . because she sleeps at the White House and goes after pork."

"Some people would call that an anti-Semitic slur," Greenberg said angrily, "and that is how I am taking it."

On September 26, 1994, Greenberg was waiting to address the National Restaurant Association when he got the news, quite by accident, that health care reform was officially dead. The speaker before him, Republican Sen. Bob Packwood, announced that Majority Leader George Mitchell had pulled the bill, ending any chance of a compromise.

The hall erupted into wild cheering, followed by more cheering when a questioner suggested cutting Social Security benefits for workers, reasoning that younger people did not expect benefits to be there for them anyway. The Restaurant Association was a formidable opponent of universal coverage, which would have forced its members to provide health care benefits. Greenberg could not have been in a weaker position before such a hostile audience. He tried to make light of his plight. "I am used to having a spirited speaker and spirited audience, and sometimes a dispirited audience—I am not sure what to do with a dispirited speaker."

The tension over the failed effort on health care heightened the personal animus that many Democrats in Congress felt toward the Clintons. When Donald Sweitzer, the DNC's political director, was quoted in *The Washington Times* saying Democrats should distance themselves from the President, he was suddenly removed from the list of people authorized to receive Greenberg's strategy memos. In any event, the memos were sanitized before they were distributed, with sensitive polling data deleted for fear it would be leaked to the press.

Members of Congress thought the Clintons lived in a dreamworld. Clinton convinced himself that even without health care he had a record that Democrats could be proud of. The White House toted up his accomplishments, from the family leave bill to tougher crime measures and deficit reduction.

"Why aren't we taking our case to the people?" Hillary Clinton demanded of the political advisers. The President had to be talked out of doing advertisements for the Democratic National Committee. He wanted to go on camera himself and tell his story, while Democrats running for office preferred that he stay hidden. They did not want to be linked to Clinton, whose approval rating was below fifty percent. If the 1994 election became a referendum on an unpopular president, Democrats would surely lose. At one private strategy session, the First Couple proposed that they lead the fight. Hearing this, a DNC official thought, "Doesn't Greenberg brief these two?"

The day after Mitchell pulled the health care bill, Republican incumbents and challengers from across the country gathered on the steps of the Capitol to announce their Contract With America. Greenberg was delighted. He was convinced that it projected the wrong image to a country fed up with Washington. He welcomed the Contract with its Reaganesque promises to cut taxes, boost defense spending, and balance the budget. "We should make the Contract our friend," he said. "People don't want to go back to the Reagan years."

California Rep. Vic Fazio, a member of the Democratic leadership, instinctively reacted against any negative reference to Reagan, and Greenberg responded with some force that most people separate their fondness for Reagan as a person from their negative attitude about the 1980s. Greenberg said his opinion was based on polling data, but Fazio thought it was wishful thinking.

The GOP Contract nationalized the elections and made it easier for

Republicans to run a unified assault on Democratic rule. Greenberg made a great deal out of his findings that Newt Gingrich was "the most unpopular figure in American politics." That may have been true, but Greenberg's surveys also found that less than a third of the voters knew who Gingrich was. "A lot of people felt misled by Stan," says a Democratic Party official.

Greenberg struggled to understand a phenomenon that he had never seen before. The election was just a few weeks away, and a majority of the undecided voters were Democrats. Typically, when Democratic incumbents are running, the undecideds are overwhelmingly Republican. "And you have to assume you are going to lose them all," Greenberg explained at the time. "So, if you are not over fifty percent, you are not going to make it. That is a standard assumption. What is peculiar this year is that there are more Democrats than Republicans who are undecided. We don't know where they are going." To get a better fix on these voters, Greenberg did focus groups in late October where he had undecided Democrats in two Texas districts and in Cleveland actually step inside a voting booth and, with their hand on the lever, talk about what was holding them back. What did he find? "Deep trouble," he said. "They were just in revolt."

The media use polls to define reality. The numbers and the momentum were with the Republicans, and the media were repeating that every day. Part of Greenberg's job, he says, is "to contest reality" with the press by offering an interpretation of the numbers that might be more kind to his clients, the Democrats. But when Greenberg predicted on television on election eve that the Democrats would retain control of both houses of Congress, he was no longer helping to shape media perceptions. He had lost touch with reality.

Greenberg spent election night in New Haven celebrating his wife's victory and trying to absorb the magnitude of the Democratic losses. DeLauro won a third term with sixty-three percent of the vote, but the Democrats had lost the Senate and the House with the biggest turnover in forty-eight years.

On the Thursday morning after the election, Greenberg was scheduled to appear with Frank Greer on C-SPAN. "I know you're going to think I'm crazy, and this is just rationalizing," he told Greer moments before they went on camera, "but this is a better outcome than if we had lost the Senate and kept the House. We wouldn't have been able to govern, and they would have thrown us out in 1996."

"Stan, within a day, had a rationale why this was good for the country and how it would benefit Bill," Greer chuckled.

There was a growing determination among the White House staff, led by chief of staff Leon Panetta, to break the monopoly of ideas that Greenberg had enjoyed. Greenberg further aggravated the situation by conducting a post-election survey in Macomb County for the Democratic Leadership Council (DLC), the group of moderate Democrats that Clinton had headed before his election as president. The survey, which Greenberg and DLC officials presented at a televised news conference at the National Press Club, showed how Clinton's failed quest for health care had reinforced his image as a big-government liberal.

Clinton watched the news conference on C-SPAN and "went ballistic," says an adviser. Mimicking the President's hoarse intensity, the aide quoted Clinton, saying, " 'Stan Greenberg stood up there and talked about how health care was a disaster. He told me what could be in and what could be out. He told me not to talk about cost containment, and then he stands up in a press conference and blames me.' "

In Clinton's view, Greenberg, not Hillary Clinton, was the architect of health care. The President, for his own peace of mind and the future of his marriage, could not bring himself to fault his wife. In a version of the devil-made-her-do-it rationale, Greenberg was the devil. He had advocated a bold plan, and encouraged Mrs. Clinton's disdain for incrementalism. He had been the health care hawk, pushing for an expansive government role, telling the Clintons that universal coverage was a popular idea, and steering them away from talk of controlling costs.

Republican pollster William McInturff also watched the DLC press conference and could not believe what he was seeing: Greenberg undercutting the President in a public forum on behalf of a minority wing of the party. "I said to my wife, 'Can you imagine Dick Wirthlin working for the Ripon Society [an organization of moderate Republicans] in 1982 and saying that the trouble with Ronald Reagan is that he wanted to cut government too fast and go after Social Security?' "

Greenberg shrugged off the criticism and told friends that the White House—"and not just anybody," he stressed, implying the President or at the very least a top aide—had approved his doing the project. But he did feel caught between two masters. The night before his televised presentation, he stayed up very late reworking his remarks because the DLC officials who had commissioned the study felt Greenberg was offering too much of an "apologia" for the President.

In the fourteen months before the November 1994 election, Greenberg's firm collected $2.7 million from the DNC, a sum that drew fire from many quarters and, eventually, from the President himself. Clinton was "ripshit," said an aide, after watching a CBS report in January 1995 that flashed dollar figures on the screen for what Greenberg and the other political consultants had received from the DNC.

By the midpoint of Clinton's presidency, no White House had been in touch so much for so little apparent result. *Harper's Index* noted that the ratio of money spent by Clinton for polling in 1993, compared to what George Bush spent in the comparable year of his presidency, was twenty-eight to one. The obsessive attention paid to polling underscored the public's view of Clinton as "too political."

Clinton spent several weeks alternately fuming about Greenberg and defending him when others were on the attack. At the urging of Panetta, Clinton met with two or three Democratic pollsters and consultants. One of them remarked that Democrats in Congress felt "misled and mishandled" by the White House because they were led to believe that votes on the budget and health care would not be tough and unpopular. Clinton flared. "Who the hell told them that? A pollster?" The consultant told the President there was a feeling among members of Congress that Greenberg "kept the data hidden away." He would selectively release the responses to one or two questions, the consultant said. For example, he would cite a strong majority for universal coverage or note that most people supported an increased tax on the rich, without showing the downside. Democrats on the Hill felt he acted more as a cheerleader for the administration's position than a dispassionate pollster.

Part of Clinton's pique had to do with the way Greenberg capitalized on being the President's pollster. Given the insatiable appetite of the press, there is no way that Greenberg could have concealed Clinton's reliance on polling. But when Greenberg countered a *Los Angeles Times* report that he would have a diminished role with the assertion that he was polling on the President's upcoming State of the Union address, Clinton was furious. "I am sick and tired of reading that I have to have a poll or a focus group before I go to the bathroom."

Clinton said this and more to Greenberg in a midnight phone call that went on for an hour. Greenberg let the President vent, but he resisted one of Clinton's favorite rationalizations—that he was the victim of poor marketing and communications. Greenberg believed that the failed health care effort so overshadowed everything else Clinton had done that it was foolish to expect the public to judge him on other grounds. "It is a lot to ask of voters to say, 'Forget about the last nine months.'"

Greenberg sought in that phone call with the President to put what had happened on health care into a larger historic context. It could be a good campaign issue in 1996, he said. Remember, it took thirteen years to get Medicare through Congress. President Kennedy fought for it, campaigned on it, and did a national tour that included a Madison Square Garden rally that was telecast on all three networks. He still could not get it passed. It was only after Kennedy's assassination that Lyndon Johnson convinced a majority Democratic Congress to enact Medicare.

Greenberg was uncertain about his future with Clinton after that phone call. But the President would later tell him to forget it, that he was just blowing off steam. It was characteristic of Clinton to want to smooth things over.

Clinton floated the idea of a team approach to polling. That struck everybody as unworkable, but it made Clinton feel better temporarily. He did not have to fire anybody. Greenberg signed a new contract with the DNC when Senator Chris Dodd became party chairman in January 1995. The contract was valued at $329,000 for the first six months of the year, a fraction of the $4.5 million he had earned over the first thirty months of the Clinton administration. As the President's pollster, Greenberg had divested himself of his corporate clients in order to avoid a conflict of interest. Now conflicts be damned, he needed the money. "I put out the shingle," he said. "It's true." He had to furlough several analysts.

Greenberg had lost his exclusive franchise on presidential polling. He shared those duties with other pollsters. He rarely saw the President, and then only when others were around. Their relationship had changed, irrevocably. "Clinton gets really pissed off when he thinks how much money we burned in 1994, and nothing will ever change that," said a White House aide.

The vacuum left by Greenberg was soon filled by a familiar presence. Even before the election, Clinton had begun telephoning Dick Morris, his old pal and pollster, secretly seeking his counsel. Morris had engineered Clinton's comeback as governor in 1982 after Arkansas voters had turned him out of office at the end of his first term. Morris had no discernible ideology, other than what worked politically. He was a slick easterner from the Upper West Side of Manhattan who had drifted rightward with the rest of the country. He worked mostly for Republicans, but not exclusively. His wandering allegiance made him suspect in both parties, but he was good. He had what the political tacticians called "edge"; he could break through and catch the attention of a cynical electorate.

Morris was a master of the black arts of politics. Among his political heroes was the late Lee Atwater, who managed George Bush's 1988 election as president, a campaign remembered most for its unabashed use of negative TV ads. The revival of Morris, a nonideological, nonintellectual gut fighter, threatened everything Greenberg stood for.

Just days before the 1994 election, Morris had warned Clinton in a phone call that he was going to "lose it all," meaning the House and the Senate. When Clinton turned to him after the election, Morris begged off at first. He was mostly working for Republicans now. "Well then, what Democratic pollsters would you recommend to me?" Clinton probed. "I don't think much of any of them," Morris replied. "And if you don't mind my saying so, your pollster is among the worst."

Morris kept his relationship with Clinton under wraps for a period of time. He stayed at the Ritz-Carlton Hotel on Massachusetts Avenue under an assumed name, and when a Republican Party official asked him point-blank in January 1995 whether he was working for the President, Morris chose his words carefully. "I have never been with Bill Clinton in the Oval Office." It turned out that they were meeting in the residence.

Unlike Greenberg, who is dedicated to advancing progressive Democratic ideas, Morris cares only about winning. After Clinton won the Democratic nomination in 1992, Morris sought to capitalize on his knowledge of Clinton among Republicans. "I know how he thinks; I worked for him," he boasted. Alex Castellanos, a media adviser working for George Bush, remembers Morris assuring him that Clinton was "a fatally flawed candidate with a time bomb strapped to his back—and I have the detonator." Morris implied that for the right price, or the right client, he would sell out his old friend.

Greenberg undermined what chance he had to win back Clinton's favor by speaking out on the sensitive issue of affirmative action. Senate Majority Leader Bob Dole, positioning himself for the Republican presidential nomination, had called for legislation to end affirmative action. Hoping to find some middle ground between the status quo and all-out abolition, Clinton ordered up an internal review of race-based programs in the federal government. Everyone in the White House was under orders not to comment on any possible change in policy until the review was complete. But Greenberg had just published a new book, *Middle Class Dreams: The Politics and Power of the New American Majority*, in which he bluntly discusses the role that race played in the Democratic Party's decline.

Before the 1960s, civil rights did not belong to either party. Indeed, Martin Luther King, Sr. initially endorsed Richard Nixon over John Kennedy for president in 1960. He switched only after JFK himself called Coretta King to express sympathy over the jailing of her husband, civil rights leader Martin Luther King, Jr., in Atlanta after he had requested service in a whites-only restaurant. The embrace of civil rights as a cause, which began under a reluctant Kennedy, had by 1965 defined the Democratic Party.

Greenberg believed that white working-class men, disaffected by what they saw as the Democrats' preoccupation with race, could be won back by a government that paid attention to them. That is what led Greenberg to favor universal programs, like health care, that would benefit the middle class.

The flip side of Greenberg's argument, usually left unspoken, is that government could no longer promote programs exclusively for minorities. Appearing at a breakfast with reporters, principally to promote his new book, Greenberg was asked about affirmative action. He said that the Democratic Party's coalition "cannot be based on social justice claims for one segment" of the public. The remark was entirely consistent with his long-held beliefs. A *Washington Post* headline the next morning declared, "Clinton Aide Urges Shift on Affirmative Action."

Greenberg's remarks caused chaos for Clinton, who had promised liberal activists he would do nothing precipitous. Rev. Jesse Jackson was livid. A meeting was hurriedly arranged at the White House for Clinton to assure Jackson of his commitment to affirmative action. Jackson's decision to challenge Clinton in 1996 could hinge on how the President handled this issue.

Angry Cabinet officials called the White House to find out what was going on. The topic had been debated internally for weeks. If Clinton moved too far to the right, he risked losing his base of liberals and minorities. "It's a little late for a white man strategy," Commerce Secretary Ron Brown told the President. An exasperated White House official groused, "The last thing we need is a pollster out there talking about affirmative action. He got his knuckles rapped."

Clinton's State of the Union address on January 24, 1995, his first major speech before the new Republican-controlled Congress, had been in the works for weeks. But Clinton was not happy with the draft he was given and added whole chunks to the text. Leon Panetta and George Stephanopoulos were dispatched to gently tell him the additions did not work and to get license to edit the speech so it flowed.

The result was a speech that flowed with so many currents that it set a record for the occasion at one hour and twenty-one minutes. Greenberg and about twenty-five of the President's aides crowded into Room 173 of the Old Executive Office Building next to the White House to watch the speech on television, and simultaneously to see the reaction of a group of voters in Dayton, Ohio. As Clinton spoke, each member of the dial group in Dayton indicated pleasure or displeasure with what the President said by turning a circular dial right or left on a portable, handheld device. In Washington, aides watched a white line on a separate TV that moved up when the group liked what Clinton had to say and down when it did not.

New technology, involving a remote transmission over a telephone through a computer to a television set, made it possible for the first time to visually monitor the reaction of a dial group sentence by sentence as the speech progressed. Off the House floor, in the Democratic cloak room, White House political aide Rahm Emanuel got the information the old-fashioned way. He sat with a phone cradled to his ear taking down the numbers from Dayton.

Emanuel annotated the text, jotting down the numbers as Clinton spoke. When the speech stretched over an hour, a nervous aide asked, "Are they still paying attention?" Emanuel pointed to the numbers, still in the sixties, and gave a thumbs-up. He was perhaps too sanguine. The meter's neutral setting is fifty. "It's at fifty when you're clearing your throat," an aide explained.

The dial group was intentionally weighted toward Perot voters and Republicans skeptical about Clinton. Surveys at the time showed only nineteen percent of Perot voters and Republicans approved of the way Clinton was handling the presidency. The line rocketed upward when Clinton called on members of Congress to stop taking gifts from lobbyists and took a plunge when Clinton appealed for a multibillion-dollar rescue plan for Mexico. Most of the speech tracked between sixty and seventy, peaking in the high seventies at Clinton's attack on lobbyists, and dropping to forty-eight when he spoke about aid to Mexico.

By its lukewarm response to bailing out Mexico, the dial group told Clinton the public was wary, even hostile. Still, Mexico's faltering economy needed an immediate infusion of capital. Clinton did not have the political clout to persuade Congress to act in the face of such negative public opinion, so he went ahead on his own authority to extend to Mexico $20 billion in short-term loans and longer-term guarantees. House Speaker Newt Gingrich said the President had acted courageously.

Nowhere is a president more sensitive about being led by polls than in foreign policy. Yet every president since Franklin Roosevelt has used polling data to help determine the role of the United States in the world. Greenberg liked to say he did not poll on foreign policy, and that was literally true. But he would toss in an occasional question about whatever was in the news. And during Clinton's first months in office, as the war in Bosnia raged on the front pages of American newspapers, Greenberg instructed his focus group moderators to ask participants how much attention they were paying to the situation in Bosnia and what they thought the United States should be doing.

Whether he polled on foreign policy or not, Greenberg knew he would be accused of doing so. To arm himself against critics, he went back and looked at how polling was used by former presidents. Roosevelt polled to pick the bomb targets in Europe, and to see how Americans would react if churches were bombed. Wirthlin polled for Reagan on the arms control negotiations, and how belligerent the President should be versus how forthcoming. Nixon polled extensively on renewing relations with communist China, and the impact of his visit there on various constituencies. Greenberg concluded that he had done far less polling on foreign policy issues than was done in previous administrations.

"When I did the research, I said I am badly serving the President," Greenberg concluded. "I'm not doing anything in this area compared to what has been done in the past. . . . I am actually doing less than I probably think I should do because I expect people to exaggerate my role . . . to make the case that he [Clinton] doesn't stand for anything."

People think politicians do not move without consulting the latest poll, and, in many cases, they are right. Today's pollster is similar to a playwright writing dialogue. Having such refined information increases the danger that politicians will pander to voters and never take a courageous stand in the face of negative public opinion. But any politician trying to navigate serious policy changes through a cynical public has to be mindful of the land mines that await and devise strategy around them.

When Doug Bailey entered the polling business in the mid-1960s, candidates did not like to admit they had hired a pollster. He left the business in 1987 disgusted over the way polling had progressed from information-gathering to agenda-setting. "The poll's God," Bailey said in an interview for this book. "Any number of candidates would come to us, and they wouldn't have a position on issues like abortion and gun control. They wanted to know, 'What should I say?' If you don't know what your views are on the most controversial issues out there, what business have you got running in the first place? That's a dramatic difference from the time when I started, maybe partly because the polling wasn't so accurate that you really could rely on it."

The father of modern polling is George Gallup, Sr., who used scientific sampling to predict FDR's landslide win over Alf Landon in 1936 when the most famous poll of that time, the *Literary Digest* mail ballot of ten million people, predicted his defeat. The *Digest* sample was drawn from automobile license lists and telephone directories, an upscale group during the Depression that was biased against "that socialist Roosevelt."

Presidents Truman and Eisenhower did not rely much on polls, though Eisenhower was briefed on public attitudes toward Korea and Sen. Joe McCarthy's anti-communist crusade. Truman had doubts about the accuracy of polls, and in 1948 was delighted to be proved right. The picture of Truman holding up the *Chicago Tribune* front page declaring Thomas Dewey president is the classic reminder of the fallibility of polls. "I wonder how far Moses would have gone if he'd taken a poll in Egypt," Truman wrote in a memo to himself. "What would Jesus Christ have preached if he'd taken a poll in Israel? . . . It isn't polls or public opinion of the moment that counts. It's right and wrong."

In the 1948 election, Elmo Roper, the pioneer pollster, announced in September that he would not do any more polling. Even as the election approached, he saw no reason to change his mind, for no "political miracles" had taken place. In fact, early polls that showed Truman lagging prompted the whistle-stop tour that carried him to victory. Roper said it was the first case that he knew of where the polls affected what they were allegedly measuring. "What the polls did was make the Republicans complacent," he told *The New York Times*. "The unions dragged their supporters to the polls while the fat cats played golf."

Nixon wrote in his memoir that campaigns should poll less and pay less attention to polls, but as president he and his aides used polls aggressively, often conducting them undercover. Chief of staff H. R. Haldeman set up a polling operation in the White House that was so secret Nixon's own pollster, Robert Teeter, was not told of its existence.

Kennedy was the first to invite his pollster, Louis Harris, to be part of the inner circle. Harris briefed Kennedy on the campaign trail, often while the candidate was taking a bath. Yet after Kennedy was elected, Harris kept his distance, at least technically. None of his polls was directly commissioned by the White House.

He did go to work for *The Washington Post*, whose publisher, Philip Graham, was a friend of the President's. The "Harris Survey" appeared regularly in the *Post*. After Kennedy read the bulldog edition, which comes out late the night before the paper's publication date, he would call Harris at midnight to discuss the findings, especially if his ratings had slipped. "He would say, 'What are you trying to do, destroy me?'" Harris recounted. "And then he would go on and on for a few minutes, and then say goodbye, and then about noon [the next day] without fail, he would call me up, never apologize at all for his outburst, and we would talk about current issues and problems he faced."

The technology of polling has advanced as rapidly in this century as computers since Univac. As a Harvard undergraduate, Patrick Caddell

visited the Kennedy Library to study Harris surveys of religious preju-
dice. He was amazed to find there were no cross-tabulations, where
opinion responses are examined according to a second variable, such as
gender, age, income, or education. The questioning and the analysis was
primitive by today's standards. Harris essentially asked voters whether
they would or would not vote for a Roman Catholic. The results determined where Kennedy would campaign and shaped his "Catholic strategy." During the summer of 1972, Caddell's foot soldiers conducted
fifteen-thousand face-to-face interviews for Democratic nominee
George McGovern, a practice now rendered obsolete by random-digit
dialing and computer-generated calling.

Caddell was the first presidential pollster to expand the role into setting themes, sometimes with disastrous results. His findings about
"malaise" in the country in 1979 sent President Carter into a tailspin that
ended in the forced resignations of the entire Cabinet. Caddell fled
Washington in 1980 for a new career as a Hollywood consultant and
scriptwriter. He made a cameo appearance on the national stage advising Jerry Brown in 1992. When Brown faltered, Caddell tried to finagle
himself onto the Perot bandwagon. A memo he sent to Perot offering to
help the insurgent candidate was dated February 17, 1992, the day
before the New Hampshire primary, when Caddell was still publicly
promoting Brown. Caddell viewed political candidates as vehicles to
advance his ideas about campaigning and governing.

Richard Wirthlin, a courtly Ph.D. and practicing Mormon, worked for
the most ideological president and was himself the least ideological.
Trained as an economist and with a doctorate from the University of California at Berkeley, Wirthlin had once chided a colleague who worked
for Reagan for "selling out to that Hollywood right-winger."

How Wirthlin ended up in Reagan's employ is a story worthy of James
Bond. Wirthlin had agreed to do a statewide issues poll for a group of Californians represented by a man who identified himself as Tom Green.
When Wirthlin flew to Los Angeles to present the results, Green met him
at the airport and said his real name was Tom Reid, and he was a political
adviser to Governor Reagan. Reid drove Wirthlin to Reagan's home in
Pacific Palisades where, for ninety minutes, the Berkeley-trained professor and the governor, who was the scourge of Berkeley, chatted across
a cozy table in the library. At the conclusion of their talk, they shook hands
to signal the start of a long professional relationship.

"After that, there probably wasn't a thirty-day period from December
of 1968 until fairly recently that I didn't have one contact or another with
him every month," recalled Wirthlin a quarter-century later. "I briefed

him in the library of his home, in the kitchen; on two occasions, I briefed him in the bathroom because he wanted some privacy. I briefed him in airplanes, hotels, the back of limousines. It's been quite a ride."

Wirthlin's "Black Book" guided Reagan to victory in 1980. Wirthlin was on his way to New Hampshire for the February primary when Reagan reached him in his hotel room at Boston's Logan Airport to say he was firing his campaign manager, John Sears, and replacing him with an old friend, William Casey. Reagan asked Wirthlin to take over as campaign strategist. The strategy document that Wirthlin put together was really a long philosophical essay, supported by polling data. It laid out Wirthlin's thesis that American democracy is not only a system of governing but a "romantic preference for a given value structure." Wirthlin believed that the candidate who understood values and knew how to tap into them would be the winner.

"Whatever the realities about our elected leaders—negative or positive—they are almost irrelevant in predicting public acceptance or rejection," Wirthlin wrote. "Not what is, but what appears to be, determines the image of public figures." With Wirthlin's help, Reagan, divorced once, estranged from his children, and an infrequent churchgoer, would become a symbol of strong family and religious values.

Of the recent presidents, George Bush is thought to have paid the least attention to polls. But pollster Robert Teeter ran his campaign in 1992. The self-effacing Teeter, a midwesterner who never moved to Washington, stayed out of the spotlight. Bush had another pollster, Fred Steeper, do tracking polls on American public opinion during the Persian Gulf War. The work was done in secret, and Bush was briefed daily on reactions to the bombing, on whether to pursue Saddam Hussein, and on attitudes about when and how to end the war. Aides say that Bush often acted in the face of negative public opinion, which then responded positively to his leadership. But the decision to conclude the ground war phase after a hundred hours remains controversial in part because of the suspicion that it was poll-driven. Bush also found his most potent campaign issue in 1988 when a focus group uncovered the intense emotion associated with a Massachusetts convict named Willie Horton, whose weekend parole and death spree Bush used to portray Governor Michael Dukakis as soft on crime.

When the numbers are good, a pollster is the resident guru; when they are bad, he is more like an abused spouse. After front-runner Bob Dole lost the New Hampshire primary in 1988, he referred to his pollster, Richard Wirthlin, as "Dr. Worthless."

Looking back on the episode, Wirthlin is philosophical. "Bob Dole needed someone to blame, and I just happened to be there." He recalls that Dole was ahead the Friday before the Tuesday primary. By Sunday morning, Dole's lead had slipped, and on Sunday night, Dole refused in a debate to take a no-tax pledge. The next morning, seventeen percent of the voters were undecided.

Wirthlin recalled that fateful day: "Dole came out of a meeting and for some reason he became very angry with . . . it wasn't even a heckler, it was a twenty-one-year-old, clean-cut, well-groomed student who held up a sign. I think the sign simply said, 'Vote for George Bush.' He was very innocuous, and he wasn't yelling or screaming. He was just standing at the rope.

"For some reason, he set off Dole. Dole went over to him and growled in his face, 'Why don't you crawl back in your cave?' and with the boom microphones, that was the story for that day. Dole asked me on the bus, 'Where do we stand?'

"I said, 'Well the vote is fifty percent plus or minus four percent that you'll win, so that means forty-six to fifty-four percent.' The only thing he heard was the fifty-four, and so that set him up psychologically."

Wirthlin's postmortem on New Hampshire showed that Dole's refusal to take the no-tax pledge and the sense that he was "mean-spirited" had turned the seventeen percent undecided vote almost entirely against him. Wirthlin dropped off the analysis at Dole's apartment at the Watergate in Washington and called Dole later, but Dole did not take his call. "The only thing he did was read this study, which in isolation could be viewed as, 'You lost the election.' I think that's the reason he's never forgiven me."

Frank Luntz spent election day 1994 shopping in Atlanta. Two years before, the disheveled young pollster could not have imagined being escorted through a shopping mall by Marianne and Kit Gingrich. But the wife and mother of Newt Gingrich knew that a Republican takeover of the Congress was imminent and that Newt would be the new Speaker. They appreciated the role Luntz had played in getting Newt there, but Marianne Gingrich in particular was determined to spruce him up before the big celebration. In her mind, Frank Luntz looked more like a scruffy Democrat than a neat, button-down Republican.

Luntz dresses so that he would never be mistaken for an establishment country club Republican. For him, dressing down is a political statement like it used to be for the Democratic left. Whatever Luntz's reasons for sartorial slovenliness, the Gingrich women were looking out for Newt's interests. When national reporters came to Luntz that night to get his spin on the Republicans' great victory, Luntz would look acceptable. Marianne would see to that. When he was outfitted to her satisfaction, the flattered but uncomfortable Luntz accompanied the women back to Gingrich headquarters at the Waverly Hotel in Marietta. He and they would be at Newt's side when history was made.

"I want to be the next Stan Greenberg," Luntz had said some months earlier. Luntz admired Greenberg's technique, which included a greater reliance on so-called qualitative data, or focus groups, than quantitative data, which is polling by numbers. But more to the point, Luntz yearned for the recognition that comes with being the embodiment of a new idea. Luntz's work in developing the GOP's Contract With America would make him the voice of the angry white males who turned out in decisive numbers to vote Republican, much the way Greenberg was once the authority on the forgotten middle class.

What Greenberg and Luntz have in common is that they use polling to advance an ideological agenda, a way of viewing government and its role. Like Greenberg, Luntz has a mission: to put the alienated segments of the electorate center stage, whether they be Reagan Democrats or Perot Republicans. That approach distinguishes them from most pollsters of the past and marks a new trend in polling. It increases their influence but also, sometimes, undermines their credibility. They use polling to prove a point, instead of to make a point.

Luntz, however, will not press an ideological point if he does not think he can communicate it well. He specializes in crafting language to get across conservative ideas, and if he cannot find the right words he would rather shelve an idea than present it poorly. For example, Luntz warned House Republicans that talking about abolishing the Department of Education might make them look "anti-education" unless they said it in just the right way. Luntz's polling illustrated his point: Telling Americans that you want to abolish the Department of Education and return control of education to parents, teachers, and local communities will earn the support of only a third of the electorate. However, by reversing the order and telling Americans that parents, teachers, and local communities should have control of education, and this can be done by abolishing the Department of Education, Republicans could bring a clear majority to their side. The words are the same, but the new order stresses results, not process.

In his early thirties, Luntz was a generation behind Greenberg, who had come of age in the 1960s, when the aspirations of minorities and women shaped the decade's idealism. Luntz matured during the Reagan years, when blacks and women were marginalized as special interests, and the stirrings of the Reagan Revolution made Republicanism popular on college campuses. Luntz himself is a curious mixture of shy nerd and brash self-promoter. "He reminds me of me at that age," says Newt Gingrich.

From the time he was very young, Luntz displayed a prodigious memory and a fascination with numbers. He likes to recall how he was once so drunk at seventeen that he could not walk, but he could still recite the names of the presidents backwards and forwards in under a minute.

Luntz grew up in a comfortable Connecticut suburb, the only son of a dentist and a mother who, while indulging his interests in history and politics, was otherwise strict. At the University of Pennsylvania, he was one of the first students with a personal computer, but he had the tiniest record collection. Today, his CD, tape, and album collection approaches a thousand, including a large collection of Beatles bootlegs. Luntz's late father may have precipitated his son's rebellious dress code by always wearing a tie, even around the house. His parents were independents, and did not register as Republicans until Frank became state chairman of the teenage Republicans and asked them to.

A Thouron fellowship, a less prestigious (though financially more remunerative) version of a Rhodes, allowed him to study at Oxford. Reagan was in the White House and Luntz, a devout and very public Reaganite, had trouble finding dates among the liberal student body. He finally resorted to conducting a survey on sexual attitudes. "It allowed me to go out and ask women what their opinions were on various things," he admitted. Among the questions were how many sex partners students had, and whether they used contraceptives. He discovered that Oxford students were remarkably conservative even in 1985 before the impact of AIDS on sexual behavior. "It was a good way to meet people," Luntz says.

When Newt Gingrich came to Oxford in 1985 to debate the merits of American intervention in Nicaragua, Luntz was among the minority of students who sided with the militant congressman from Georgia. Luntz wrote a story about the event for the school magazine, and took the photograph of Gingrich that accompanied the article.

Luntz was starstruck. Washington was to be his Hollywood. He got a job as a research analyst with Richard Wirthlin, who was then polling for President Reagan. Luntz turned his doctoral thesis into a book, *Candidates, Consultants and Campaigns*. In the questionnaire that formed the basis for the book, Luntz asked pollsters: "Overall, which is more important in recent congressional and senate campaigns: issues or the candidate's image and personality?" Their unanimous response was image.

Luntz adopted Wirthlin's view that the only reality in politics is what people perceive. Change the perception, and you change the politics.

Wirthlin wrote the introduction to Luntz's book and Luntz, in turn, is respectful, even worshipful, of Wirthlin as a careful professional who never lost his moorings regardless of who was paying the bills. Luntz's brashness caused conflicts with other analysts at the firm and sometimes offended the courtly Wirthlin, who was not unhappy to see Luntz leave after two years to form his own company. Later, however, Wirthlin missed Luntz's innovativeness and tried unsuccessfully to lure him back. By then, Luntz liked being on his own, but rivalries with colleagues would remain a constant in his career.

It was not always easy for Frank I. Luntz and Associates. Some of his clients, such as the National Rifle Association and the Beer Institute, were poor public relations vehicles. For the most part, they hired people to keep themselves out of the news. He initially had few political clients. Still, Luntz's name began to show up regularly, often attached to "The Quote of the Day" in *Hotline*, a computerized compendium of political news.

Luntz understood political commentary, and he could put together a good sound bite. He once called a friend of his at *Hotline* to nominate what he had said for the next day's edition, a story that made the rounds and contributed to his reputation as a self-promoter. Soon, Frank Luntz was in every political reporter's Rolodex. He was a good quote; he called back quickly, and as an adjunct professor at the University of Pennsylvania, his alma mater, he had academic standing as well.

Luntz took the first of the big risks that mark his rise to the top when he polled for Pat Buchanan, the conservative commentator who challenged President Bush in the 1992 primaries. Buchanan's candidacy was not looked upon with favor in Republican circles. On the day of the New Hampshire primary, Luntz shared with reporters his projection that Buchanan would get thirty-six percent of the vote against an incumbent president. Few believed Buchanan would do that well, but when he finished with thirty-seven percent, reporters clamored to talk to Luntz.

Luntz knew that in the upcoming southern primaries, Buchanan would be campaigning on social issues, and when he was pressed on which ones, he named affirmative action, prayer in schools, immigration, and foreign trade. "That sounds like David Duke," a reporter said.

"I'm not an idiot, and I thought to myself, 'It does sound like David Duke.' And so the professor in me said, 'Good point there,' but the pollster in me said, 'Oh shit, what am I going to say now?' So I come up with the response, 'No, it's not.'"

That was like throwing red meat to the lions. Two, three, then four reporters pressed Luntz to explain why Buchanan was any different from

David Duke, a segregationist who had run as a Republican for the Senate in Louisiana. Two cameras were trained on him. "I could have been destroyed that night," Luntz recalls with a shudder. "All I was doing was the Monty Python school of arguing, which is just taking the contrary point of view. I'm dying. I'm thinking, 'Oh my God, I'm killing my guy.'"

A reporter from *U.S. News & World Report* came to Luntz's rescue. "I'm on deadline. I need to talk to you," the reporter pleaded, promising his colleagues, who were glaring at him and protesting, that he would return their prey in thirty seconds. The reporter, Don Baer, who later became President Clinton's chief speechwriter and then his communications director, did not really need anything from Luntz. He could see what was happening and thought Luntz did not deserve it, at least not yet. "I will be forever grateful," says Luntz. "I was a kid. It was my first time."

What Baer got out of that incident was an inside track to Luntz. Before Baer went to the White House, Luntz made it a practice "to give him heads up before anybody—that's how Washington does work, and I owed him." For someone professing to reflect the sentiment of the outsider, Luntz diligently worked to be accepted as an insider.

To journalists covering the 1992 election, Luntz's data and interpretation were key to understanding the protest vote. The voters who were dissatisfied with the two major parties held the balance of power and would be the key to victory in November. Many had voted for Buchanan in the primaries and many more seemed attracted to Perot's populist message. In May 1992, after the Buchanan campaign faded, Luntz headed to Dallas, Texas, and joined the Perot campaign.

The billionaire industrialist denied he had hired a pollster. In fact, he had hired two, Luntz and Democrat Paul Maslin. It was the Noah's Ark of campaigns, with both parties represented throughout the high command.

Perot called Luntz a "director of research," and was antagonistic to his surveys. Luntz put up a sign where he and Maslin sat that said, "Stealth Pollsters." They would joke about how they did not really exist, and fantasize about running up imaginary expenses. Luntz had no contact with Perot. He funneled his memos and surveys through third parties, usually Ed Rollins, a Republican consultant, or Tom Luce, one of Perot's business partners. He was never certain Perot even read them. They disappeared into a black hole.

"It's hard to poll for a maniac," says a Luntz colleague. "You show him numbers, and he says, 'Who cares?' And you say, 'Why am I doing these polls then?' and he says, 'I don't know.'"

Perot never trusted the campaign professionals, and would soon fire them. On the July day that Rollins and the others were told to leave, Luntz stopped by the office of one of Perot's top advisers to ask if he would arrange for him to be photographed with Perot. The adviser saw no harm in providing the young man with a memento, and readily agreed. The resulting photo suggests an intimacy that was never there. Other than attending an occasional staff meeting where Perot was present, Luntz had no personal contact with Perot.

After leaving Dallas, Luntz billed the Perot campaign for several thousand dollars, which Perot declined to pay. Never having employed pollsters and media consultants before, the billionaire industrialist had no idea of the costs involved, and assumed they were excessive. "He didn't do anything," Perot protested. After extended negotiations, Luntz reduced his charges in exchange for a ticket to a presidential debate. "It was all so ordinary, so lowbrow," sniffs a Perot associate.

When Perot dropped out of the presidential race, Luntz offered to share his polling data with the Bush campaign. He was treated like a traitor, rebuffed and rejected. He then got feelers from the Clinton camp, which interpreted his stints with Buchanan and Perot as a Generation Xer's search for a new kind of politics.

"I was told to call Greenberg," says Luntz. "When I left Perot, Democrats wanted to get me over. They thought this was the chance. Use Perot as the bridge. Republicans were beating the hell out of me. Democrats thought, 'We'll treat him nice, welcome him in, and we'll get him on to our side.'" Luntz says he thought about it "for a millisecond." Others say he agonized, as he does about most things. In the end, Luntz renewed his vows with the GOP, although he was not fully trusted by party loyalists.

Luntz's relationship with Perot, brief and unsatisfying as it was, made him a hot commodity in Washington. It was as though he had made contact with some alien being, and had just returned from the mother ship.

Journalists and political consultants alike yearned to understand what was going on "out there." He appeared on *Nightline* to talk about Perot and what he had learned from focus groups about the mind-set of Perot's followers. Invited to dinner at the Washington home of Democratic political consultant Bob Shrum, Luntz brought along a book with biographies of Perot's potential vice presidential candidates. The list included journalist Cokie Roberts and Reagan's attorney general, William French Smith, who was dead.

"You know why I brought that book?" he says. "If worse came to worse, I could always use it as my contribution to the conversation."

Luntz need not have worried. His rumpled exterior and his obvious insecurity make everyone rush to be his protector, and that night was no different. Among the guests were *Washington Post* editorial page editor Meg Greenfield and Democratic Sen. Barbara Mikulski. After the 1992 election, Luntz was the first Republican to appear on Greenfield's opinion page with his analysis, the result of the connection he made that night. In November 1994, she cleared space for his "Lessons Learned" column the Friday after the election. "And I hope that I will be the one who does that every year until she's no longer editorial page editor," says Luntz. Also, Mikulski promised to speak to Luntz's class at the University of Pennsylvania. Not bad for one night's networking.

His dinner companions might have been shocked to learn that Luntz was advising the bane of the liberal elite, the National Rifle Association, on how to improve its image. Luntz had grown up with guns. His father collected guns and was a top pistol marksman in Connecticut for five years.

Luntz feels an allegiance to the NRA, but in the face of mounting violence from guns and the overwhelming popularity of gun control measures, he advised the organization to seek a compromise on the Brady Bill, a gun control measure then pending before Congress. The NRA leadership reacted the same way as the Bush campaign high command, turning away Luntz and treating his analysis as an act of disloyalty.

"This is an issue in Washington: Do you tell the truth when it hurts?" Luntz reflects. "There's a loyalty question, and there's an honesty question."

For a professed Republican, Luntz had a lot of explaining to do. He had polled for Buchanan against a Republican president, and for Perot, who many thought had cost Bush the election. Zelig-like, Luntz even maneuvered his way onto the stage at the Democratic National Convention, a close-up spectator as Bill Clinton made his nominating speech.

After President Bush was defeated for reelection, Luntz's data on the Perot vote was in vogue among Republicans. It was a matter of math. Bush lost by five million votes; six million Perot voters were up for grabs. A *Washington Post* headline on March 1, 1993, declared: "Perot's Ex-Pollster in the Limelight at GOP Retreat."

Republicans meeting in Plainsboro, New Jersey, in the wake of losing the White House were eager to hear Luntz's prescription. His meal card was filled: breakfast with Haley Barbour, the party chairman, and lunch with Newt Gingrich. They did not know it then, but Luntz's ten-point plan to win Perot voters would become the foundation for the Republican counterrevolution. Among the proposals: stick to economic or political reform and avoid divisive social issues; appeal to the forgotten middle class; speak in plain, nonpolitical English; avoid ideological labels; and undermine Clinton's honesty.

Republicans flocked to Luntz's seminars, but they weren't hiring him. So Luntz did something that was unheard of in the polling world: He offered a rebate to attract business. He promised to return $8,500 to Republican Rudolph Giuliani's mayoral campaign if his final poll did not come within 2.9 percentage points of Giuliani's share of the vote. The flip side was that Luntz would get a $20,000 bonus if his numbers were accurate. Luntz got the account. When Giuliani won the New York mayor's race in November 1993 with nearly the exact percentage Luntz had predicted, Luntz's rehabilitation in Republican Party politics was almost complete.

He was still blacklisted by the Republican Senatorial Campaign Committee under the chairmanship of Texas Sen. Phil Gramm. The executive director, Paul Curcio, did not think Luntz's disloyalty should be rewarded. Candidates who considered hiring Luntz were told that they risked losing funding from the committee. Luntz made a vow to himself: "Don't get mad and don't get even. Get ahead."

Luntz continued to strengthen his ties with Gingrich and the House Republicans. In the fall of 1993 Gingrich was under attack for teaching a college course on "Renewing American Civilization" that his critics charged was a political venture masquerading as education. Luntz volunteered to write an opinion piece defending Gingrich. He sent it to *The Washington Post*, where it was rejected by Meg Greenfield. "She turned it down because she said that comparing Newt to Aristotle was a bit of a stretch," says Luntz. The piece did run in *Roll Call*, a Capitol Hill newspaper, where it undoubtedly earned Luntz points with Gingrich, if no one else.

Luntz found the inspiration that solidified his entrée into Gingrich's inner circle in an unusual spot: President Clinton's speech introducing the details of his health care plan in the fall of 1993. Luntz marveled at Clinton's salesmanship and the way he had woven themes from the threads of Greenberg's research. "I knew the numbers were going to be great," he said. Dismayed by the reaction of Bob Dole and other senior Republicans who dismissed the President's call to arms on health care as "no crisis," Luntz went to see Gingrich to argue that the GOP had to counter Clinton more effectively.

No one understands the disaffected voter better than Luntz, and Gingrich was intrigued with what he had to say. He sent Luntz to see the key members of his inner circle. "They all have to vet me; they have to make sure I'm for real," recalls Luntz. The process took six weeks, and was not unlike fraternity rush. Luntz talked on the phone to Steve Hanser, the retired associate professor of history who has counseled Gingrich since they were fellow academics at West Georgia College. He had coffee with Jeff Eisenach, who heads the Progress & Freedom Foundation, the think tank that underwrote Gingrich's college course. And he met with Joe Gaylord, the veteran Republican operative who oversees all Gingrich's enterprises and maintains tight control over who sees Gingrich. Gaylord is congenitally hostile to outsiders, and was suspicious of Luntz. He wondered what this young man was up to, and if he could be trusted.

During this period, Luntz was as nervously anticipatory as a high school student waiting to hear from his first-choice college. "It's not yet happened, but it's about to unless I screw it up," he said. "Newt Gingrich is going to hire me as the consultant for the House Republican Conference to fight Bill Clinton over the next year, to sit there in rooms like this [the richly paneled dining room of the Willard Hotel where he was being interviewed] and come up with crazy, wacky ideas and words to fight him, which is such an awesome opportunity."

Gingrich offered the job to Luntz on Dececember 16, 1993. It was a controversial move given the fact that Luntz had only recently insulted some of the party's leading lights. While urging Republicans to be less formal and wooden in their public appearances, he had remarked that Indiana Sen. Richard Lugar, a droopy-faced former mayor, and Utah Sen. Orrin Hatch, thin and ministerial, looked like undertakers. "That solidified me as a loose cannon on deck," Luntz said. When the remark appeared in *The New York Times,* Hatch took it in good fun. Lugar has not talked to Luntz since.

Moreover, Jeane Kirkpatrick, former U.S. ambassador to the United Nations and doyenne of the GOP, had heard Luntz speak disparagingly about George Bush and complained that he was too young to be making fun of presidents. "Well, I was making jokes about presidents when I was ten," says Luntz, "and George Bush deserved every bit of it. I could not give him enough."

Still, Kirkpatrick's rebuke was in Luntz's mind when he made a similar presentation before Gingrich and other House Republicans. He bashed Bush but then quickly apologized. "You don't have to apologize, but we don't really need to do it," Gingrich said solemnly. "We all know how bad, terrible, rotten, dreadful, evil, and despicable George Bush was." By the third or fourth adjective, everyone was laughing. The tension had been broken.

Luntz finally had the status that he craved. He became a Washington insider because he had honed an anti-Washington message. The insight that he brought was as obvious as it was daring: To capture the Perot vote, shorthand for the swing voters who held the key to victory, the GOP had to offer something positive. "The Perot people would not have turned out if we did not give them a good reason to vote for someone," says Luntz. "Otherwise they would have said, 'I hate the Republicans. I hate the Democrats. I'm not going to vote.'"

In mid-January 1994, Luntz handed Gingrich a first draft of his memo "Looking for Waterloo." It included a proposal to freeze congressional pay. "No way I'm going to take that to the members," Gingrich told him. "I have enough things to convince them about. Why should you and Ed Rollins get rich consulting for us while we cut our pay!" (Rollins had earned $250,000 a year in the 1989–90 election cycle as an adviser for the Republican Congressional Campaign Committee.) The pay proposal stayed in the memo, but Gingrich did not highlight it, and neither did Luntz.

Luntz unveiled his Waterloo memo at the Republican retreat in Salisbury, Maryland, on January 26, 1994. Gingrich had read the memo and decided that he wanted Luntz to share it with the others, knowing that Luntz's audacious views would shake up the complacent Republican members. "The purpose of this document is to issue a House Republican wake-up call—to see, hear and utilize the new politics that will make you a majority in 1994," Luntz wrote.

Statistically, the opportunity for Republican control existed for the first time since the 1950s. To achieve it, Luntz set five objectives: capture the crime issue; articulate a reform agenda; capture the mantle of change; communicate and empathize with voters; and convince voters that "the real Bill Clinton" not only raised taxes and increased government spending, but that in doing so he broke his campaign promise to the middle class to do neither.

When Luntz made his presentation, Clinton had a fifty-five percent approval rating despite Whitewater and personal infidelity scandals. "Every time he delivers a speech, his favorability rating shoots up to the moon," Luntz said. Clinton, Luntz warned, is a far more clever and agile adversary than the last Democratic president, Jimmy Carter. "Clinton's empathy—the 'I feel your pain' emotion—is as powerful a public relations tool as Reagan's 'Morning in America' vision."

Luntz went on to outline a communication strategy that would eventually evolve into the House Republican election strategy, culminating in the GOP's Contract With America. Among his findings: Denying welfare to noncitizens is supported by sixty-nine percent of the public. Cutting off *legal* immigrants who were not citizens from benefits would become a key element of the House Republicans' welfare reform plan.

Luntz urged the Republicans not to think of themselves as the opposition, but as a government in waiting. The concluding chapter of the thirty-nine-page memo is titled "Carpe Diem."

The document would serve as the blueprint for the GOP takeover. But the part that attracted media attention was the section on communication strategy. "Americans think politicians in general, and Republicans in particular, are out of touch. . . . Too many of us are seen as suit-and-tie Republicans trying to represent a jeans-and-T-shirt electorate. We're watching *The MacNeil/Lehrer NewsHour* while they're watching *Roseanne*. We're listening to NPR while they've tuned in to Rush Limbaugh or Howard Stern. We're reading *The Wall Street Journal*. They're reading *USA Today* and *People* magazine. . . . In 1992, it was George Bush's apathy versus Bill Clinton's empathy—and empathy won. In 1994, if we want to be heard, we must start connecting."

When these quotes appeared in *USA Today*, Luntz got a call from Texas Rep. Dick Armey, who admonished him in the same earthy way that Lyndon Johnson might have two decades earlier: "Frank, we're trying to bring you inside the tent so you can piss out. Why are you still pissing in?" After the conversation, Luntz referred to himself as "the late Frank Luntz."

Luntz has a talent for biting the hand that feeds him. A poll he conducted on the attitudes of Ivy League students ranked the University of Pennsylvania last in "academic quality and overall reputation." The finding contributed to one department where he taught discontinuing its relationship with Luntz, whose political science students had done the survey.

Luntz has no social graces and is stupendously shy, yet he makes his living drawing other people out. And he does it with a defiance of dress and decorum that would guarantee oblivion if he were a lesser talent. It is his way of stating that he is not one of them—them being the Establishment. He says, "Establishment people don't walk into a presentation with a dozen congressmen in a wrinkled shirt, jeans, and this sweater that was keeping me warm. I didn't even realize it was dirty. . . . I don't care because the Establishment is too slow, and the Establishment in our party will sink us. I never came up through the Establishment, and I don't owe them anything."

His clothes are populist; his car is an Acura. Otherwise, he lives like a graduate student. He will take a three-stop flight over a direct connection to save money and get the extra frequent flyer miles. He is a parody of the New Republican who has left the party's patrician, country club past behind.

Luntz recognized early the reach of talk radio and how it could carry the Republican agenda. He urged Republicans to "stay in touch with our greatest cultural icon, Rush Limbaugh." And he began to fashion his own presentations before business groups and others after those of television talk show celebrities, using a roving microphone and encouraging audience participation. He carried a blue and white Nerf football imprinted with the words, "Talk to me." He tossed it to the audience, and whoever caught it had to speak out. "Republicans can learn a lot from Phil, Sally and Oprah," he wrote in his Waterloo memo.

In the spring of 1994, Luntz's loyalty to Gingrich and his ideology almost got him fired. He was quoted as saying that Newt Gingrich has a vision for the future while Bob Dole is trapped in the past. Dole himself never confronted Luntz, but Republican elders warned the pollster to keep his distance.

Dole's dark side often surfaced in polls and focus groups. Testing voter attitudes, Luntz asked, "Which candidate would you want to sue your ex-spouse in a divorce?" Dole led the field. One respondent volunteered, "That SOB would take her for every cent she has, and she deserves it." After Gingrich's rise to power and once the GOP presidential contest got underway, the party had taken on such a hard edge that Dole seemed an almost comforting presence next to Gingrich and Texas Sen. Phil Gramm.

Luntz's glibness brought him publicity, but a good quote does not build a career. In the end, he would be judged on the accuracy of his polls. Even those who decry his boisterous style acknowledge that he was the first pollster to publicly predict a Republican House and Senate majority, and that as early as May 1994, he had predicted the Republicans would gain thirty-five seats when others were saying fifteen or twenty.

Luntz wanted very much to work on a presidential campaign. That summer, he appeared on a panel at the National Press Club with former Education Secretary Lamar Alexander, a colorless but competent Republican who had not yet announced his candidacy but already was running for president. Stepping to the podium, Luntz turned to Alexander and said how pleased he was to be appearing with "one of the leading contenders for the *vice* presidential nomination."

The joke flopped. Alexander consulted some with Luntz over the next few months, but when he hired Mike Murphy as his campaign manager, one of Murphy's conditions was that Luntz not be part of the campaign. Murphy thought Luntz's hunger for publicity would lead, ultimately, to the young pollster's self-destruction.

After the Salisbury retreat, Gingrich instructed Luntz and others to translate the ideas in Luntz's memo into a "contract" that Republicans could run on that fall. Gingrich had wanted such a document for several years, and Frank Luntz had given him the basis for what would become known as the Contract With America.

The initial reaction of Louisiana Rep. Bob Livingston was that the encounter group atmosphere at Salisbury was a waste of time, but he later praised Luntz, saying, "He was, in fact, the brains behind the Contract in terms of confecting the message and providing the behind-the-scenes momentum to make it stick." Rep. Chris Shays of Connecticut said Luntz was the first person other than Gingrich to convince him that the Republicans could win a majority. "He made me a believer," Shays said.

The first task was to find the issues that would unify Republicans. Luntz helped prepare an eight-page questionnaire for all House Republicans running for reelection, and for GOP challengers around the country. He listed sixty-seven specific issues in twelve categories and asked candidates to rank each item according to how much they personally liked the idea, and then how much including it in the Contract would help them in their district.

The issues that emerged were oldies but goodies, measures that the Republican minority and the business community had advocated for years. Among the most popular were a balanced budget amendment, line-item veto power for the President, term limits for members of Congress, tougher measures to fight crime, and limitations on punitive damages in product liability laws.

Gingrich had ordered the Contract be limited to ten items, a mythical number in any competitive exercise. There was heavy lobbying among Republicans over which items would make the list. Luntz is quite ideological, and he loves Gingrich for being the same way. Yet he recommended that the Contract include only what was politically popular. Issues like school prayer that could divide Republicans were excluded. Representative Armey, a Gingrich ally, lobbied furiously for school prayer, and had an aide call Luntz to obtain polling that would back his stand. Luntz pointed out that Perot voters, whom Republicans needed to sway, are "less religious than liberals." School prayer stayed out of the Contract.

The final wording of the Contract flowed directly from focus groups. It was the first time that a political party would quite so blatantly give the public what it wanted. The concept of a contract had been tried in 1980 when Ronald Reagan met with Republican members of Congress on the Capitol steps. But Luntz and others brought a level of sophistication to the effort that was not available fourteen years earlier, when focus groups had limited political application and survey research was not nearly so probing.

Luntz tested every word of the Contract. Each element of the document was carefully phrased to attract the support of at least sixty percent of voters. The idea was to slowly start rebuilding trust by offering limited, focused promises that could be kept. Voters responded positively in focus groups to the slogan "A campaign promise is one thing—a signed contract is quite another." Decades of politicians' overpromising had left the country so cynical that government could no longer accomplish anything that required public support.

Luntz understood the intensity of the electorate's anger, and he helped shape it into public policy proposals. "Throw out the line, 'Why should we be giving people on welfare a raise?' and you want to see twelve people in a room scream," he said. "The camera shakes, people are so angry. That's when some three-hundred-pound guy with a mustache from Detroit yells, 'Fuck 'em!'" A radical overhaul of the nation's welfare programs became a cornerstone of the Contract's "Personal Responsibility Act."

The two major political parties had so little credibility that Luntz advised that the word "Republican" not appear in the Contract because party affiliation was seen by many voters as a negative. Luntz's research showed that even people who called themselves Republicans responded better to the Contract without the party label.

Anger was the operative emotion in the fall of 1994. Listening to hostile voters in focus groups took fortitude. It was more primal scream than rational discourse. Frank Luntz walked out of a focus group in Denver because he could not take it anymore. He had tried everything to open up a line of conversation, even putting people on the spot and shaming them about how little they knew about current events. Few could even name their representative in Congress, but that did not stop them from showering abuse on the nameless member. The mindless rage got to be too much for Luntz.

"I walked out because I couldn't even communicate with them. I'd say, 'Look, I know you're angry. Now tell me something good. Who do you respect? What do you want Congress to do? Tell me something good about democracy. You're all just grumbling and complaining.' I was going to put myself and all twelve of them through the window at that point. If I cannot relate to them, and I'm an angry person, and they're just so far beyond me, I did not know what to do to pull them back in. There was no common ground. They wouldn't give any of these people a chance, Republican, Democrat, liberal, conservative, whatever."

Representatives from the Republican National Committee, sitting behind the mirror and monitoring the session, did not know whether to be more alarmed by the voters' behavior or by Luntz stalking out of the room. A young Luntz staffer reassured them, "Let him vent; he'll go back in." One of the Republican elders, anxious that the evening not be a dud, told Luntz not to worry about the seeming lack of progress. "Just get back in and fight with them," he counseled.

Luntz reentered the room and introduced the Contract With America. The Denver dozen initially were skeptical, not believing they could trust any politician or party. But as they heard more, Luntz sensed he had pierced their wall of hostility. He flew home early the next morning feeling he had found the secret weapon that would win for the GOP.

Back in Washington, Luntz conducted numerous training sessions for Republican challengers. He told the largely male candidates to shed their suit jackets and talk like ordinary people. He briefed them on the Contract With America, telling them that the document would give them something to say in language that had been polled to please. And he advised them on other issues. In a memo dated August 9, 1994, Luntz urged Republicans in Congress to oppose the crime bill before them and offered language to caricature the prevention programs that were part of the legislation. "Ridicule is a powerful weapon," he wrote. "Dance lessons, arts & crafts, midnight basketball, and the 40,000 new social workers are all obvious targets. . . . For example, ask your audience to imagine calling 911 and, instead of getting the police, they get a sensitivity awareness counselor. 'That's not a mugger pointing a gun at you, madam. That's an individual who's crying out for help.'

"We need a SWAT team of cops, not social workers. . . . If you want to play it straight, just say, 'If they're under eighteen, they should be at home studying or in bed; if they're over eighteen, they should be at home or working the late shift.'"

All but eleven Republicans voted against the crime bill, ensuring its failure. Tony Blankley, Gingrich's spokesman, called it "one of the major plays of the season." Luntz was the impresario; Republican members of Congress were his chorus.

It was a stunning defeat for President Clinton. A compromise crime bill passed later, but the skirmish proved to be the death knell for health care reform. Time was running out on the session of Congress. With Clinton weakened and Democrats divided, Republicans were able to kill Clinton's health care bill, without ever having to vote on it.

Democrats did not have much to cheer about that fall. But they were certain the Republicans had made a big mistake when more than three-hundred incumbents and candidates for Congress gathered on the steps of the Capitol on September 27 for a ritual signing of the Contract With

America. With the country hating everything about Washington, why would Republicans pose with the Capitol dome in the background?

Actually, Gingrich's people had debated the location. Some wanted the Lincoln Memorial. It was pointed out that most people identify the Lincoln Memorial with civil rights events, and that a comparison with Martin Luther King, Jr.'s "I have a dream" speech would not help the Republican cause. Lafayette Park across from the White House was also considered, but a rally could easily get out of hand there because it is home to so many protesters. The Capitol won out in part because of growing Republican confidence that they could persuade the country they were ready to "take back" the Congress for the people.

Gingrich had gotten Republican Party chairman Haley Barbour to agree to finance a political advertisement of the Contract in *TV Guide*. Luntz tested several different versions of the ad. The production and space cost the RNC more than $250,000. Gingrich urged voters to cut out the Contract and put it up on their refrigerator door.

The Contract was attacked by Democrats and by many pundits as the worst kind of poll-driven pandering. Some found the Contract's implications disturbing. Mark Siegel, a Democratic consultant, said on a panel televised over C-SPAN that anyone who creates public policy from survey data is "Goebbels-like." Luntz was so offended that he did not talk to Siegel for six months. "A friend called me a Nazi on nationwide TV," is how Luntz interpreted the remark.

Democrats were not the only ones attacking the Contract. Two of Luntz's rival pollsters, John McLaughlin and Tony Fabrizio, were quoted in the conservative *Washington Times* mocking Luntz. "Frank Luntz has given bad advice that could cost us the majority," McLaughlin said. Fabrizio added, "When the Contract takes down a few of our candidates, which it will inevitably be blamed for, everybody is going to lay the blame at the feet of the person who created it: Frank Luntz."

To Luntz, the Contract was more than an electoral tool. He believed that it was a critical first step in demonstrating to a cynical and bitter electorate that elected officials could be trusted to keep their word. His polling after the election showed fewer than a third of voters had even heard of the Contract, but it served to rally Republicans throughout the election and into the first months of the new Congress.

Promoting the Contract became a personal crusade for Luntz. He traveled the country tirelessly conducting focus groups, watching the anger against government build and devising ways to exploit it for the Republicans. He said he felt like the late actor Peter Sellers, whose total immersion in each character he played made it hard for him to know who he was. "My problem in life is that I have none," Luntz said regretfully. "I spend my life sitting around tables listening to people bitch about government not working." Luntz experiences life primarily through the responses to his questionnaires and his interaction with focus groups. "I like to run naked with my feet through the data," he once told a colleague, a metaphor meant to reveal his almost primeval connection to his work.

Luntz became the *enfant terrible* of the pollster community. At thirty-two, he had shaken up the profession like no one since Patrick Caddell had helped engineer George McGovern's 1972 presidential nomination while he was still an undergraduate at Harvard. Luntz was the Right's answer to Caddell—brilliant, eccentric, filled with insecurities. Would he flame out, a victim of his own brilliance, the way Caddell had in the political world?

In late October, Luntz flew to Georgia to spend quality time, he hoped, with Gingrich, away from the hostile interference of Joe Gaylord. Luntz went out to the new house on a cul-de-sac in suburban Marietta that Gingrich and his wife, Marianne, were busy moving into.

"I fell asleep on his couch," Luntz recalled. "That let me know that I felt really comfortable with him, that I would let myself do that. I love talking to him. I love listening to him because he is such a great educator. He's the uncle that I never had. If he were my uncle I'd worship Thanksgiving and Christmas and all family gatherings.

"The opportunity to be involved with him is my life. It is what I've waited and learned and done all this stuff for. It's why I will go back to the office and work for another couple of hours. It just means so much because he wants to do for America what I like to do for America."

Luntz's intense feelings of admiration for Gingrich were not unusual for those who came under Gingrich's spell. Such hero worship typically does not last beyond the infatuation stage. The country, from Carrollton, Georgia, to Washington, D.C., is full of people who believed in Gingrich as a new political messiah and were later disappointed. Gingrich fell in and out of love with his admirers as well. In the race to see who would cool a relationship first, Gingrich always won. He had a well-earned reputation for discarding people once he had no use for them.

Luntz had no reason to think his close relationship with Gingrich was in any jeopardy. He believed, in fact, that there was a "perfect symmetry" between them. For that reason, he dared to broach the subject of a remark Gingrich had made recently to a group of lobbyists suggesting that Clinton Democrats be portrayed as "the enemy of normal Americans." The pejorative phrase, which was leaked to the press, prompted a cascade of negative comments. "Newt, that's dumb," Luntz said during their time together in Atlanta. Gingrich bristled. "I didn't get where I am by playing defense," he said, and left the room.

That Sunday, on CBS's *Face the Nation,* Gingrich was asked about the "normal Americans" comment. His apologetic explanation indicated he had paid attention to Luntz after all.

Back in Washington, a week before the election, Luntz went to a party at *Washington Post* publisher Katharine Graham's Georgetown home. The party was given to celebrate the publication of *Newsweek*'s book on the 1992 election, *Quest for the Presidency.* As Washington's glitterati gathered in conversational bouquets, Luntz stood off to the side in his running shoes reading sections of the book.

By election night in November 1994, Luntz thought he had worked his way back into Gingrich's favor. At the headquarters hotel in Marietta, Luntz headed for the "war room" where computers tabulated voting returns from around the country. Joe Gaylord, who was in charge, told Luntz he would have to leave and escorted him out. Gaylord, who had dutifully climbed the ladder of Republican politics, was not going to share this important night with an upstart. "I'm not his kind of Republican," Luntz said. "He's Establishment. The idea that I would go to work for Ross Perot against the Republican nominee was horrible to him."

Luntz was crushed. "Imagine, the night your hero is going to become Speaker of the House, and you've devoted your last year to this, fifteen hours a day. . . ."

Luntz took refuge with others who were watching the returns on television. After the Republican landslide was official, Luntz went to a room where the faithful had assembled for a private celebration with Gingrich. This time, no one moved to evict him. He presented Gingrich with two framed magazine covers side by side, one of Gingrich and the other of Joe Martin, the last Republican Speaker of the House. Luntz had searched antique stores for three months until he found the August 9, 1954, edition of *Time* magazine that featured the unmemorable Martin. The caption beneath the covers, which Luntz had had triple matted, read in big royal maroon Roman letters, "The Once and Future Speaker."

Back in Washington the next day, Luntz poured out his thoughts to the new Republican leadership in a fifty-four-page memo that he called "Year Thirty." He chose the title because of an analogy he had read. On day one, there is one lily in the pond; on day two, two lilies; and the lilies keep doubling every day. If on day thirty-one, the pond is completely choked with lilies, on what day was the pond half full? Most people would say on day fifteen, but the answer is day thirty. "I wanted to send the message that we really were one day away. We're only halfway there, but what happens in the next two years is just going to blow people away."

The battle lines had not been so clearly drawn between the two parties since Ronald Reagan's election fourteen years earlier. Yet the following weekend, where did Luntz go to unwind? Tony Coelho's Delaware beach getaway. A former member of the Democratic House leadership, Coelho was regarded as one of his party's sharpest minds. Never mind that it had been a nasty campaign and Coelho had shaped strategy for the Democrats. They had been in the trenches together.

After the election, Coelho was among the first to call with congratulations. When he threw in the beach house invitation, Luntz was initially unsure whether he should accept. He was in awe that Coelho, a grand master of the political arts, was treating him, a newcomer, as a valued equal.

The two adversaries took a long walk together on the beach. Coelho, the loser, was in better spirits than Luntz, the ostensible winner. Luntz worried about being cut out of Newt's inner circle. Coelho advised him to relax and broaden his contacts throughout the House and into the Senate GOP leadership. Gingrich would come back to him. Luntz poured out his anxiety over the way the other pollsters seemed to shun him and how he missed having those collegial relationships. "He helped me through it because I was really having trouble," said Luntz. "He told me I could either get out of the business now or, if I stayed in the business, I'd better develop a tougher skin or I'd die; he said don't worry about everything, every attack and all that." Over the Christmas holidays, Luntz and Coelho would face off on CNN's *Inside Politics*. Viewers could never have guessed from the testy exchange that they were anything other than mortal enemies.

Earlier in December, Luntz circulated the first draft of a memo that in his mind marked a career shift from pollster to policy strategist. He called the memo "Communications Strategy for the Upcoming Budget Battle," and over the next six weeks, he distributed it to nearly two hundred House and Senate Republicans.

No one had directly commissioned the memo or paid Luntz for the work. Indeed, he had few paying clients among the members of Congress. He was prospecting for a broader role in Republican politics.

He wanted to be the party's personal trainer in language arts. He believed that Republicans would succeed in selling their tough budget medicine to the country only if they selected the right buzzwords, phrases, and concepts. Luntz's memo, which he kept rewriting and redating, proposed a new user-friendly language of politics, as gleaned from focus groups. In the peculiar mix of immodesty and modesty that characterizes

Luntz's personality, he says, "Not much that I do is great. More than half is good. Some of it really is lousy, not too much. This is a great memo."

The memo tells Republicans how to sculpt language to make their programs more appealing. For example, to maintain support for a balanced budget, the GOP should avoid specifics and talk about "irresponsible debt, runaway spending, destructive welfare . . . fostering all the wrong values in our society."

The rhetoric in Luntz's memo was raw meat for the Gingrich-led House freshmen, dubbed "Shiites" for their unyielding radicalism. Luntz fed their paranoia about the liberal media with an attack on "the pseudo-moralists" at *The New York Times* for running two pages of pictures of homeless people sifting through dumpsters for food and on NBC's Tim Russert for "decrying the inhumanity of the Republican cuts even before knowing what they are. . . . We need to frame the debate in terms of a moral commitment to our children and their children. We must match our opponents story-for-story—the personal and national immorality of passing along increasing debt to our children and future generations versus their budget cutting horror stories. . . .

"Individual programs have friends. Bureaucracies and bureaucrats don't. . . . Every budget statement by every Republican official should include the words 'cutting the Washington bureaucracy.'"

After copies of the memo were leaked to the press, an angry Russert called Luntz to question why he had impugned his journalistic integrity. Luntz said he had been irked at the unflattering lighting and camera angles of a preelection *Meet the Press* interview with Gingrich and had cited Russert as an example of the hostile media. Luntz acknowledged over the phone to Russert that he had gone too far, and later sent a written apology.

Luntz found in focus groups that people accepted the elimination of the Department of Education, but did not want to reduce spending on education or give up student loans. "The communications lesson: be ready with assurances that any 'truly important' program will be maintained even while entire departments are being eliminated."

The public believes "overwhelmingly that the budget can be balanced by cutting out waste, fraud and abuse," Luntz wrote. "But that will change as the debate moves forward and as Americans come to realize that deficit reduction involves sacrifice. . . . It would be a serious communications mistake to implement a capital gains tax cut ('for the rich') now while only phasing in the 'middle-class tax cuts' over multiple years. Regardless of the economics, this will look like you're putting the 'wrong people' first."

Politicians who use the language of ordinary Americans, and who say what voters want to hear, are likely to be popular. That is the essence of Luntz's theory and one that he defends as essential if politicians are going to rebuild the public trust in government. "You can't lead if people aren't willing to follow, and you can't be willing to follow until some politician keeps his promise," he says.

Repetition is important, he told Republicans. "No single event will convince America you are real budget cutters. . . . Without continuous repetition, Americans won't hear you. . . . If we talk about pain, we lose. If our words invoke a better future, we win."

Luntz proposed several "responsive chord" questions guaranteed to elicit knowing smiles and nods of approval:

Who delivers charitable services more efficiently, the Salvation Army or the federal government?

Who builds higher quality and less expensive housing for the poor, Habitat for Humanity or HUD?

Do you think the same welfare programs work in the South Bronx and in South Dakota?

Politicians who could not come up with their own bromides were advised by Luntz to say, "It's time to put the government on a diet"—a phrase that "resonates extremely well."

On welfare reform, Luntz advised caution. "Words matter—and almost any word is better than 'orphanage.'" After an early foray into defending Boys Town-style orphanages, Gingrich quietly retired the word.

Luntz hoped his data would temper some of the more draconian aspects of the GOP welfare reform. "Americans recognize common sense when they see it," he wrote. "Let the social scientists compare regressions and try to figure out whether cutting off welfare will stop young girls from having babies.

"And let the moral philosophers debate whether unwed mothers should not be allowed to receive welfare benefits. Despite their dissatisfaction with current welfare, Americans aren't yet ready to make either of these changes. For now, talk about denying cash benefits to people who have more kids while on welfare—that strikes a chord with the public."

Luntz's memo warned Republicans not to whine about how hard it is to be in power. "The public has little patience or sympathy for the situation you are now in. They know the federal budget is a complex problem, but they don't care. They expect YOU to make the tough choices, regardless of the political consequences. They want a 'fair' solution, and they want it NOW."

He proposed an across-the-board reduction in spending, an idea that has superficial appeal even though most economic analysts oppose it. "After completing the line-item targeting process, put whatever remains on a three percent diet. (In a pleading voice, ask: 'Can't we save just three cents out of every dollar Washington spends?') After two hours of discussion, it is easier to sell a focus group on $100 billion in across-the-board cuts than eliminating a specific $2 billion program."

From his beginnings in the business, Luntz had worked at self-promotion to attract attention. Now that he had achieved stardom, he needed to adjust his behavior, tone down his visibility an f-stop or two. He continued to appear on television, but granted fewer print interviews. Reporters complained that he no longer returned their phone calls. "It's easy to be open when you're irrelevant," he said.

Luntz proved no more successful than his idol, Newt Gingrich, at restraining his natural impulses. Two quick examples make the point. In an appearance on *Fox Morning News* with Democratic Rep. Joseph Kennedy, Luntz acted as though it were a presidential debate, and he were Ross Perot. In a discussion about cutting the deficit, Luntz taunted Kennedy, who voted for the balanced budget amendment, "Bring it to zero, bring it to zero, bring it to zero." When Kennedy confused "deficit" with "debt," Luntz interjected, "That's why a majority of Americans are for term limits." He mocked Kennedy's defense of programs for the poor as "the same old crap . . . McCarthyism from the left."

It was not only on television that the "old" Luntz surfaced. He likes to shake up people. He calls it interaction. In a presentation to the National Association of Wholesaler-Distributors, he surveyed the sea of men in their white shirts and ties, and declared, "This is depressing." He then singled out various members of the audience and used them to make the case for the GOP's nouveau populism.

"Alex here, stand up and turn around so they can see your suspenders and tie. You see, the average American does not wear suspenders. I see Republicans campaign in a bowling alley and they'll be dressed like Alex—you know, thousand-dollar suits. . . . I don't think yours is quite that high. Polyester doesn't cost that much. [Laughter.] They'll be dressed in Armani suits and loafers that cost 250 bucks. And there's no way that anyone who talks to them will feel like they can relate."

Luntz believes the country is in an age of "post-partisan" politics and that Republicans do better if they don't look like, well, Republicans. As if to demonstrate his point, Luntz appeared on CNN wearing a maroon turtleneck sweater and sporting a pronounced stubble of strawberry beard.

The political message escaped some of Luntz's friends, who figured it was just Frank. "He's the worst schlep," despairs Jennifer Laszlo, a friend and sometimes date. Laszlo worried about Luntz after the election. He had vaulted to the top of his profession at a young age. It was what he wanted. Yet he was paying dearly. "He misses real life," says Laszlo. "He's like me, over thirty, not married, no kids, and wondering if he'll ever have that. He went home for New Year's, well not home—his family is in Connecticut—but home to the University of Pennsylvania to hang out with kids he went to college with. He is in an emotional crisis right now."

Laszlo ran for Congress in 1994 as a Democrat. She never got past the primary in her North Carolina district. "I got creamed," she says. Luntz promised to send her $1,000 for her campaign, but in the end did not. They met when Laszlo was at *Campaigns and Elections* magazine, and Luntz had a crush on her. "He was sending me flowers. This was years ago," says Laszlo. "I wouldn't talk to him."

Finally, the publisher intervened, insisting that Laszlo give the nice young man a chance. The three of them went to dinner. Laszlo has been a devoted Frank fan ever since. "We talk about maybe getting married someday," she says, but confesses, "We've never even kissed." (Luntz later said he had rectified this romantic contradiction.)

Luntz polls relentlessly on family values, yet he is terrified of marriage. "He sees marriage as an overwhelming commitment. No one has ever gotten divorced in his family, so he wants to be sure he does it just right," says Laszlo.

Among the things he worries about is having a politically correct spouse. "He has told me that he would not want the mother of his children to be a Democrat," says Laszlo. Luntz rejects a lot of what is superficial in the Washington culture, from dress code to dinner parties, but airtime is another matter. Laszlo describes a pivotal point in their relationship. "I had invited Frank to Yom Kippur dinner. He canceled to go on *Nightline*. I was so mad and disappointed. I told him, 'If work is more important than God, that tells me a lot.'"

Luntz so longs to be accepted that he agonizes over every slight, real or imagined. He has, for example, never been asked to appear on *Larry King Live*, one of the stepping-stones to superstardom. A friend has a thousand-dollar bet with him that he will eventually be invited. She said that she called the show and asked why he had never been on and was told, "He dresses like a pig. Our viewers won't understand that he's important. Nobody's heard of him, and he doesn't look important." She pointed out that Luntz wore a suit when he did John McLaughlin's *One on One*. "They could make that a stipulation," she added helpfully.

Luntz's determination to be included surfaced again when the Fund for a Republican Future organized a panel on "Empowerment" that did not include him. He called up and demanded that he be added. "It's my issue," he said. When it was explained that the flyers had gone out and that it was too late, Luntz was more upset than he had reason to be. Displays like that did not win him friends in the consultant community.

It is hard to find a Republican pollster or consultant who likes Luntz. Part of it is jealousy. He rocketed to the top and they did not. Some of the animosity goes back to the Bush campaign, where they were loyal and he was not. And his style can be infuriating; a sound bite and a soft-shoe routine, and he is the quote of the day.

Ruminating about his reputation among other pollsters, Luntz said he could still find comfort in the raw materials of his profession—the numbers. "There's a certain cruelty in this profession that does not exist anyplace else, and numbers are not cruel to you. I could do my polling and disappear and still do a good job for people. Numbers don't lie if you do it right. Numbers don't beat you up in the newspaper. Numbers don't yell and scream and all that. And I know that that had something to do with why I was attracted to polling when I was younger, and even now."

Popular or not, Luntz had reached the top. And he was on hand when the new Republican members were sworn in. He went to the floor of the House on January 4, 1995, the opening day of the 104th Congress, without a tie, a violation of House rules. No one seemed to notice, or care. Luntz had expanded his reach in the Republican-led Congress beyond Gingrich to the rank-and-file members.

Luntz had arranged to have two bottles of special "Speakers Choice" whiskey from the House of Commons in London flown to Washington at great expense. He presented one bottle to Gingrich on opening day. The other bottle, he stashed away for a presidential campaign, his next big goal.

On Presidents Day in February 1995, Luntz walked into the House Budget Committee hearing room expecting to do a presentation on the politics of cutting Medicare. Some fifty people had assembled in the historic chamber that day, but for a different purpose. "Happy birthday!" they cried as Luntz entered the door. Under one arm were a dozen copies of a memo he was prepared to distribute on the political perils of cutting Medicare.

He was stunned, and after several long seconds, managed only, "Hi, Mom. Hi, Dad." Besides his parents, who were there from Connecticut, the guests were mostly professional friends, including lobbyists, a couple of bookers for TV talk shows, and several journalists. A dozen Republican members of Congress stopped by.

After the guests sang "Happy Birthday," it was Luntz's turn. "I have nothing to say," he began haltingly, his discomfort so raw as to be painful. "I see some strawberries over there. I'm going to go eat." His father, who would die of a heart attack a year later, recorded every moment with his camcorder.

A PBS camera was there, following Bob Livingston, the new chairman of the Appropriations Committee. "Mom, see that camera. Don't talk to it," Luntz said, only half-joking. He doesn't want her giving away family secrets on national television.

Luntz's mother confides that he is sensitive and thin-skinned. "We tell him you can't be that way in politics," she says. A *Newsweek* item that week skewered Luntz for "cashing in" on his relationship with Gingrich because several of his clients, including Merrill Lynch, the Golden Rule Insurance Co., and a business lobby seeking to dismantle the Food and Drug Administration, have business before Congress.

"He prepared us for the *Newsweek* piece," says Mrs. Luntz. "It didn't bother us. What's wrong with being successful?" Luntz had a different view. His clients would love it; Gingrich would hate it. The author of the piece would thereafter be on Luntz's enemies list. Luntz says he pointed out to the reporter that the accounts that were listed had been his clients before the election and that his first post-election client was *Newsweek*, which had commissioned him to do a focus group.

The same day that Frank Luntz was feted in a historic public chamber, President Clinton was allocated a utilitarian basement room of the Capitol for a meeting with House Democrats. *The New York Times* noted that it had "gray walls and low ceilings and not much room for dignity."

The centerpiece of the Republican revolution was a daring plan to overhaul Medicare, the health system that serves the nation's elderly. In order to keep their promise to balance the budget, Republicans proposed cutting $270 billion over seven years from the popular program. Politicians traditionally shied away from tampering with Medicare, a topic whose very mention alarmed elderly voters. If the Republicans were to get Medicare's runaway costs under control, they would have to devise a new way of talking about the government program, one that would reassure seniors, disarm Democrats, and keep the various interest groups at bay. Luntz was fond of saying that whoever defined the issue would define the 1996 election, from the White House to the lowliest district seat. Senator Moynihan called the Republicans' wordplay "semantic infiltration."

Republicans searched for soothing language and thought they had

found it in the slogan "preserve, protect, and improve." But Luntz discovered in focus groups in Florida that the word "improve" to most
seniors meant free prescription drugs, free eyeglasses, and free hearing
aids. "You want to get in even deeper trouble than you're in?" he asked
Republican leaders. Luntz suggested substituting "strengthen," which had
tested favorably in focus groups. So Republicans began talking with one
voice about how they would "preserve, protect, and strengthen" Medicare.

Far more lethal was the word "cut." Asked, "If your member of Congress voted to *cut* Medicare spending, would that make you more likely,
somewhat less likely, or much less likely to vote for him or her?" seventy-
two percent of seniors said less likely. Only seventeen percent said more
likely. But if Luntz asked the same people how they would feel if their
lawmaker voted to increase spending but at a slower rate, he got a dramatically different response. More than half, fifty-three percent, would
be more likely to vote for that person; forty percent less likely. From then
on, Republicans challenged not only Democrats, but any reporter who
said or wrote that the GOP intended to "cut" Medicare.

In the kind of trick question that could have been lifted from the high
school Scholastic Aptitude Test, Luntz asked, "Which would you support: Increasing Medicare spending from $4,800 per person to $6,700 by
the year 2002, or increasing Medicare spending from $178 billion to
$260 billion between now and the year 2002, or increasing Medicare
spending by 6.4 percent every year between now and 2002?" Each says
the same thing in a different way. Not surprisingly, most people chose
the formulation they could relate to personally—an increase from
$4,800 to $6,700. From interviews with local newspapers to national
television talk shows, Republicans repeated the optimistic-sounding
numbers like a mantra.

Nevertheless, the poll ratings of the Republican Congress plummeted as it advanced its plan to overhaul Medicare. The finger-pointing
started, and there were stories suggesting that Luntz had overestimated
the public support for the GOP's radical reduction of government, and
that his polling had been flawed. Democrats portrayed the Republicans
as callous and uncaring. Fellow GOP pollster Bill McInturff explained,
"Frank is so obsessed with language, he didn't take into consideration
what happens when the other side uses their language."

Luntz had, in fact, tested the Democratic message on Medicare with
focus groups, pitting a hypothetical Mr. Green (the Democratic
approach) against Mr. Smith (the Republican approach). He discovered
that when people heard the GOP's full explanation, they could be won
over. He urged the GOP to stick with sound bites describing its propos-

als as "specific," "realistic," "plain English," and "not politics as usual." Even so, the Democrats had their own sound bites, and the threat to Medicare posed by the Republican budget cuts made a greater impact on a nervous public.

Republicans had made the tactical error of equating Medicare with balancing the budget, Luntz said. "They sounded more like accountants and bankers when they needed to talk like social workers," he said. In his memos, Luntz had advocated having more women members of Congress talking about Medicare, and fewer male committee chairmen fighting over which economic forecast to use by spouting acronyms like CBO and OMB. Nevertheless Luntz accepted his share of responsibility: "If the Republicans lose control of the House in 1996, then I did fail."

Pollsters can be smart or dumb, but ultimately they look smart or dumb based on their last win or loss, and on their relationship with whoever is the maximum leader. So there are inevitable ups and downs. Greenberg was the hot pollster in 1992 when Clinton won the presidency. Luntz was hot in 1994 and the beginning of 1995 when Gingrich took his turn at the top. The reputation of pollsters, not always fairly, is tied to the fortunes of the people they work for.

The other pollsters seemed to enjoy watching Luntz squirm. He was a full decade younger than most of them, and they were in awe of his resilience and productivity. "Gee, I hope he gets married and has babies, and has to go home once in a while," McInturff said. "The rest of us are trying to figure out how to have some kind of balanced life. . . . Like Bob Dole said about Phil Gramm, he's so relentless—like a bug, you squash him and you think he's finished, but he keeps coming back."

At thirty-three, Luntz had advanced, by dint of talent and determination, to the high-profile position of communications adviser to the Republican revolution. *Time* magazine named him one of the nation's fifty most promising young leaders. His success had been stunning. Yet Luntz suffered from those same dark nights of the soul that his onetime role model, Stanley Greenberg, had endured before the election that exposed his fallibility. Luntz recognized the tenuous nature of his success. "I don't think it's going to last," said Luntz. "I think there are too many people out after me."

CHAPTER TWO

THE LOBBYISTS

Mind Games

arry and Louise, the yuppie couple in a series of TV ads raising doubts about the Clinton health care reform plan, had been on the air for only a few weeks when lobbyist Michael Bromberg got an urgent phone call from the ad's sponsor. "We've got a bombshell here," said Charles (Chip) Kahn, an executive vice president with the Health Insurance Association of America (HIAA).

As the senior strategist for a coalition of groups opposing the Clinton health care reform plan, Bromberg grew worried as Kahn poured out the story in a nervous torrent of words. A young woman connected to the Democratic National Committee had contacted the actress in the ads. The actress, it turned out, was a Democrat. The DNC woman urged the actress to appear at a press conference with the President in the Rose Garden to endorse his plan.

The ads never mentioned the couple's names, but they had come to be known as Harry and Louise, after the actors' actual names. Bromberg knew if Louise Caire Clark were to endorse Clinton's bill, it would contradict her very convincing objections as the fictional Louise and undermine a multimillion-dollar advertising campaign. Bromberg could imagine the headline: "Actress Who Plays Louise Says Ad Deceives Public." But as Kahn went on with the story, Bromberg began to see a way out of this predicament. The Democratic operative who had approached Louise had tried to intimidate her by hinting that if she failed to cooperate, her career would suffer. She went so far as to tell Louise, "The Clintons have a lot of friends in Hollywood." If Louise felt defensive about what she had done, she also was angry. After all, she was only an actress earning a living who happened to be a Democrat.

Besides, in her mind, the Clinton plan did need some fixing, so she was not lying.

For Bromberg, this was a crisis that called for "mind games," the most subtle of the lobbying arts, and, after three decades in Washington, he could play with the best of them. Sure, it would be a hard blow if Louise publicly disowned the very ads that had started to have the desired effect on opinion-makers. But the coercion by the DNC operative had given Bromberg the ammunition he needed to make Clinton, not the health care industry, the big loser. No one would blame Louise for feeling she was being blackmailed, Bromberg thought. What was the best way to expose the Democrats' heavy-handedness? He considered holding a news conference to charge the Democrats with McCarthy-like tactics. But knowing that Louise really did support the Clinton plan, Bromberg did not want to take the chance. Threatening to expose the Democrats' intimidation tactics might work just as well, he reasoned.

Following the strategy devised by Bromberg and other lobbyists opposed to the Clinton plan, HIAA president Willis Gradison called White House aide David Gergen, going through the White House switchboard to reach him at home, a tactic meant to convey a sense of urgency. Gradison left a message on Gergen's answering machine saying it was "really important" that they talk. Gradison, a former Republican member of Congress from Cincinnati, made the call because his association was sponsoring the Harry and Louise ads. Gergen was the one called because he had worked in the White House for Republican presidents and was thought to be fairer on partisan issues than the young Democrats relishing their first taste of real power. At age fifty-one, Gergen was considered an elder statesmen in the Clinton White House. Gergen had not been returning Gradison's calls as punishment for the Harry and Louise ads. This time, however, intrigued by Gradison's insistent tone, Gergen phoned back immediately.

Gradison laid out the story of the Democratic operative bullying Louise, adding ominously, "This could harm you if it became public. We don't want to harm you, but we want you to call off the dogs." Gergen knew nothing of the DNC's attempt to get Louise's endorsement of the Clinton plan, but he said he would check it out. Within a few days, Bromberg learned that the attempt to get Louise's endorsement for the Clinton plan had been a rogue operation that the DNC promised would not be repeated.

Bromberg's strategy had defused the bomb. Harry and Louise would go on to become one of the most successful campaigns in the history of public policy advertising. Between September 1993 when President

Clinton introduced his health care plan and February 1994, the series of ads received much of the credit for the precipitous drop in public support for the Clinton plan.

When the Clintons moved into the White House in January 1993, Michael Bromberg was in his twenty-fourth year as the executive director of the Federation of American Health Systems. He had become known around Washington as "Mr. Health Care" because of his knowledge of the issue, his access to Democrats and Republicans, and the money that he controlled on behalf of the federation's 1,700 hospitals, management companies, and residential treatment centers, all profit-making institutions. Over the previous five election cycles, his political action committee (PAC) had contributed an average of more than $162,000 each election, mostly to incumbent members of Congress to encourage and reward them for their help on issues.

In the late 1970s, another Democratic president, Jimmy Carter, had attempted health care reform with a hospital cost-containment bill. Bromberg had been instrumental in the bill's defeat, but he believed some kind of health care reform was inevitable, so he set out to shape any reform along market lines and to business's liking. In August 1989, he founded the Healthcare Leadership Council with Pam Bailey, a former Reagan aide and health care lobbyist, and several other health care company CEOs, who represented insurers, pharmaceutical companies, and hospitals. A lobbyist for nonprofit teaching and research hospitals said a more apt name for the group would be the "Screw the Consumers Coalition."

Bromberg is accustomed to being on the inside of the debate. When President Bush developed a modest health care proposal, Bromberg met with him five times, prodding Bush to act, then helping to write the legislation. Bromberg recalled how Richard Darman, Bush's policy adviser, had alerted him partway through one presentation that the President's attention was flagging.

"You're losing him," Darman whispered.

Bromberg raised his hand and said, "Mr. President, there's a tremendous analogy here to the situation in Eastern Europe."

Foreign policy was Bush's favorite subject, and Bromberg's craftily planted buzzword got the President's attention. Darman stifled a laugh. Having found his opening, Bromberg talked about centralized government control of health care in the Eastern Bloc, easing Bush's entry into an area he knew little about.

"You can make fun of it, but what struck me was how sincere and honest he was," says Bromberg. "He turned to us at one point and said, 'Will someone explain to me the difference between an HMO and managed care?' He wasn't one of those phonies with index cards.

"On the other hand, you could tell he was very uncomfortable with the subject. Bob Teeter [Bush's pollster] and John Sununu [the chief of staff] were telling him over and over that health care reform was a terrible issue for Republicans: 'Stay away from it. It's no win. The Democrats will outbid you. You'll get into a price war that you can't win.' Those of us who thought that was stupid tried hard to get the President into it."

It is hard to imagine health care reform clearing the legislative hurdles in Washington without Bromberg's blessing. That was what House Ways and Means Committee Chairman Dan Rostenkowski tried to tell Hillary Clinton. "Spend some time with Bromberg," he told her the first time she came to see him in his office in the Capitol.

"She is sitting to my right, doing what newcomers do, polishing the apple with the chairman—they can't do it without me and that stuff," Rostenkowski recalled. "I said, 'Hillary, if you want to write a health care bill, you're going to have to sit down with your adversaries.'"

Mrs. Clinton, appointed by her husband to head the health care reform task force, listened as Rostenkowski explained how his thirty-six years as a legislator had taught him that lobbyists bring to the bargaining table valuable insights based on their research and experience. "Mike Bromberg is a person who by his nature has to be at the table," he told her. "He will have bottom lines, and he'll roll his eyes and throw his arms up in retreat, but Mike Bromberg wants to be at the table. May I suggest you talk to him?" Rostenkowski was a regular recipient of campaign contributions from Bromberg's PAC, but their professional relationship and friendship went deeper than dollars.

The Clintons' longtime friend and policy adviser Ira Magaziner accompanied Hillary on the first visit to Rosty's office. Intellectually uncompromising and personally aloof, Magaziner had already earned the moniker "The Iratollah" on Capitol Hill. Rostenkowski, a tough-talking, blue-collar ethnic pol from Chicago, had no understanding of or use for Magaziner.

"I told her she should get some people that got a little dirt under their fingernails working on this thing," he recalled. "All he was doing was irritating my members." With Magaziner sitting there, Rostenkowski told Mrs. Clinton she ought to fire him. She listened politely, but had no intention of firing Magaziner. As for the chairman's advice to pay attention to Bromberg, the First Lady wanted reform that would be painful for Bromberg's clients, the for-profit hospitals. He was the enemy and not to be trusted.

When Rostenkowski was at the peak of his powers, most supplicants could not act fast enough to carry out any suggestion he made. His support was vital to pass legislation and his advice had the infallible aura of a papal decree. Having offered his guidance, Rostenkowski phoned his pal Bromberg to tell him to expect a call from Hillary's people. The call never came. It was months before Hillary Clinton, pressured again by the Democratic chairman, agreed to invite Bromberg to meet with her at the White House.

"Hillary is a very intelligent girl and a very aggressive young lady," Rostenkowski allowed, intending to be diplomatic. "But she and Bill Clinton had no idea how to use the power of the President and the First Lady."

Despite the best efforts of Rostenkowski and other knowledgeable Washington veterans, Hillary Clinton urged her task force to come up with the best policy and not to worry about the politics. It was a noble approach, better suited to an academic exercise than real-world legislation. Even Ira Magaziner, generally thought to possess the political instincts of a blind pilot fish, had qualms. In a memo to Mrs. Clinton dated May 3, 1993, he predicted "an awful roller coaster ride on an untested course."

Magaziner tried to prepare the First Lady for the criticism ahead. "Much of it will be legitimate criticism from people who feel we are making mistakes, and in some cases they may be right," he wrote Mrs. Clinton. "The truth of the matter is that we cannot be sure about what will work best. I tell you this not to alarm you but to be honest about the minefield upon which we will travel these coming months."

Bromberg finally met with Mrs. Clinton at the White House in August 1993, an hour-and-a-half session he would later refer to as "my first shoot-out with Hillary." Mrs. Clinton had one objective: to persuade Bromberg to be present in the Rose Garden when the President announced his health care reform plan in September. He said no, explaining that he would lose his credibility. He had some problems with the draft plan that was circulating on Capitol Hill and had torn out a page that he found particularly troubling.

"Mrs. Clinton, we're both attorneys," he said, handing her the evidence. "If you represented anyone in the health care industry, could you look at this page and tell them that this bill isn't filled with price controls?" The First Lady turned to Magaziner, who insisted that Bromberg was misreading the bill and that there were no price controls.

Their dispute over price controls only hinted at the real gulf between Bromberg and the White House. Bromberg comes from what he calls the Lyndon Johnson school, where politicians and lobbyists beat up on each other in public and cut deals in private. He did not feel comfortable negotiating with the dewy-eyed idealists who had taken up residence in the White House.

Mrs. Clinton did not let up. She wanted Bromberg in the Rose Garden for the bill introduction. Bromberg held his ground. He said he would be happy to join the First Couple at the appropriate time, after the contentious points had been negotiated. His presence at the start would give the wrong signal to the health care industry—"that I didn't think this was serious enough to fight," he said.

Three days later, Bromberg returned to the White House, this time to meet with Thomas F. (Mack) McLarty III, then the President's chief of staff. Bromberg and McLarty knew each other because Bromberg's dog, a 210-pound English mastiff named Winston, had knocked McLarty off a curb one day in the northwest Washington neighborhood where they both lived when he expressed a neighborly interest in the animal. McLarty, an affable sort, did not take offense. He had once owned the same breed of dog. After the incident, he made it a point to always ask about Winston.

When Bromberg walked into McLarty's corner office in the West Wing of the White House, McLarty had a folder in front of him. He opened it and deadpanned, "I've got a two-page report of your meeting with Mrs. Clinton." Then McLarty burst into laughter. He had known Hillary Clinton long enough not to be surprised by the First Lady's negative review of Bromberg, who fit her definition of politics as usual.

President Clinton unveiled the broad outline of his health care plan before a joint session of Congress on September 22, 1993. His nationally televised sales pitch got favorable reviews. The ceremony that Hillary Clinton had wanted Bromberg to attend was held the next morning. All the interest groups that are traditional allies of the Democratic Party were there: labor, women, and senior citizens. The American Medical Association, historically a foe of health care reform, sent a representative. The gesture symbolized a huge change in attitude on the part of the doctors' lobby. Seated in the audience was a who's who of health industry lobbyists, except that Bromberg was not among them.

That fall, the Clintons' health care reform plan, or something very close to it, seemed like a sure bet to become law. Public opinion polls showed support was up following the President's speech. Newspaper editorials praised the plan. Clinton and his wife seemed poised to make history. In October 1993, Bromberg himself sounded like a closet supporter of health care reform. Over lunch at Sam & Harry's, a steak house that is a favorite hangout for lobbyists, he confided, "The White House doesn't know what an ally they have in me." He put the odds at ninety percent that Clinton would get some bill through Congress, probably a much smaller bill than his original proposal, but one the President would at least get credit for signing.

Bromberg had a personal stake in the Clintons' goal, which was to achieve guaranteed coverage for all Americans. The year before, at age fifty-four, he had undergone a triple heart bypass operation. As a result, he had what insurance companies call a "preexisting condition," which made him one of the hard-to-insure Americans the President had talked about in his speech.

While he understood the need for health care reform, Bromberg had to protect the interests of his client hospitals. There were aspects of the Clinton plan that they opposed, mostly having to do with more government regulation of health care spending, and he thought that he could quietly work with the White House to smooth over those differences. That was how he had done business with past presidents. But when the Clinton administration shut him out, he launched a broader attack on the reform plan.

Bromberg knew that he could stop the Clinton bill if he had to. That was half a victory. The other half was salvaging a health reform bill that would put market-based reforms in place. Without it, the next Congress was certain to call for drastic cutbacks in Medicare and Medicaid, the government health programs for the elderly and the poor. Bromberg's for-profit hospitals would bear the brunt of those reductions. "Democrats regulate us to death," Bromberg said. "Republicans starve us to death."

The ponderous Clinton plan was delivered to Capitol Hill in November. Critics immediately began undermining the lofty promises Clinton had made in his speech two months earlier by interpreting the bureaucratic language of the bill itself as threatening to the world's best (if most expensive) health care system. With such a big target for opponents to shoot at, it was not long before the tide of public opinion turned against the White House.

Bromberg and the other lobbyists targeted aspects of the plan that they opposed rather than endorsing the parts of the bill they supported. Bromberg's hospitals teamed with other opponents of the plan to eliminate three provisions: a "global budget" that would have put caps on spending; price controls on insurance premiums; and large mandatory alliances of consumers. All three were considered dead before Congress even opened discussion on the bill. Bromberg's hospitals actually would have benefited from the cornerstone of the Clinton plan: employer mandates that required businesses to pay for a substantial portion of health coverage for workers. Mandated insurance coverage would have relieved the hospitals of millions of dollars in emergency room costs for the uninsured. As his support was never cultivated by the White House,

Bromberg did not have to offend allies, such as the National Federation of Independent Business, who fiercely opposed mandates on employers.

By excluding lobbyists from participating in the development of the policy, Hillary Clinton forced them to find creative ways to penetrate her biosphere. Enlisting the help of a prominent figure as a "door opener" was one tactic. Magaziner felt flattered at first that former Senate Majority Leader Howard Baker wanted to see him, until Baker, a lawyer-lobbyist, turned up with an insurance executive in tow. Magaziner saw some CEOs four or five times accompanied each time by a different former member of Congress turned lobbyist. Michael Berman, a lobbyist and former top aide to Vice President Walter Mondale, pressed Magaziner to pay more attention to Bromberg, who had written Magaziner a dozen memos on various aspects of the plan. At the same time, Berman was advising the White House on political strategy. Bromberg could not have found a better-connected ally, but Berman's entreaties went nowhere.

The White House purists remained impervious. When Bromberg saw a newspaper photo of Health and Human Services Secretary Donna Shalala with her golden retriever, Bucky, he sent a photo of Winston to Shalala with a note: "If you want to discuss health care, have your dog call my dog." Bucky replied on Shalala's letterhead that he had a lot of friends who are doctors and already knew all about health care reform.

Bromberg understood that Mrs. Clinton did not want the medical industrial complex dictating health care policy and did not blame the Clintons for excluding lobbyists from the policy-development phase. What was missing, he felt, was a reality check. Ira Magaziner had a history of thinking too big and ensnaring others in his grandiose schemes. Bromberg said the White House should have paid attention to no more than half of Magaziner's advice, but no one knew which half.

Magaziner said Bromberg was frustrated because the Clinton White House did not play the game by his rules. "Bromberg came in with pieces of legislation all written for us," Magaziner said. "And we basically told him, 'We're not going to do it that way. We will meet with you and we will listen to you and we will get your reactions, and so on, but we're not gong to let you write the bill.'" Magaziner said he met with Bromberg as many as eighteen times. "He's a very smart guy and he knows a lot about health care," Magaziner said. "He had some ideas that were good ideas, but there were certain interests he was trying to defend which we felt were not in the public's interest."

Michael David Bromberg did not set out to be a lobbyist. He says his mother was embarrassed by the job description. Once, she confronted him: "You're a lawyer. You graduated from law school. Why do they call you a lobbyist?"

Bromberg is a fast-talking New Yorker with a compact build and a Type A personality. Although his major at Columbia University was English, he once envisioned being a musician, and sang with a group that included Art Garfunkel. After graduating from New York University's law school, Bromberg joined a law firm. When one of the firm's partners, Herbert Tenzer, ran for a congressional seat in 1964, Bromberg was his campaign manager. Tenzer invited Bromberg to go with him to Washington as his legislative aide. When Tenzer announced his retirement before the 1968 election, Bromberg considered running himself but concluded he would have more control over his life as a lobbyist. "It's better to be a chess player than [one of] the pieces," he told *The Washington Post.*

Bromberg's first lobbying client was American Express. It took him ten months to push through a bill making it a federal crime to steal a credit card. Some senior lobbyists warned him that that was too fast. The real money, they said, is in long-term, by-the-hour contracts. Bromberg has been suspicious ever since of "hired guns" who run up billable hours.

In 1969, Bromberg joined the Federation of American Health Systems as its Washington representative, and, two years later, became executive director. In a quarter-century of legislative battles, his political acumen failed him only once, when a catastrophic health insurance plan that he helped develop was repealed by Congress after senior citizens protested. The bill's fate was sealed after angry elderly people in Chicago demonstrated their opposition by banging on the car of Ways and Means Chairman Rostenkowski, a sponsor of the bill.

Bromberg's politics are pragmatic. He started by working for a liberal Democrat, Tenzer. As a lobbyist, he holds fund-raisers for politicians from the opposite side of the ideological spectrum, such as Dan Quayle, when he was a senator from Indiana, before being tapped as George Bush's vice president. Bromberg parrots the defector's defense, that he did not leave the Democratic Party, the party left him. "I've never voted *for* a Republican," he says. "I voted *against* Jimmy Carter."

Bromberg thinks of himself as a "Scoop Jackson Democrat" after the late Washington State senator who was known for his hawkish views on foreign policy. Bromberg backed Bob Dole for the Republican nomination for president in 1988 and volunteered to work on behalf of Dole's 1996 candidacy. Bob Packwood, the Oregon senator forced to resign in the wake of sexual harassment charges, is a friend and one of the regular guests at the Brombergs' biannual treasure hunt, where fifteen power couples spend an evening speeding around the city in limousines rented by the Brombergs in frenzied pursuit of clues. "The adults act like children for a night," says Bromberg, who with his wife devises the brain-teasing clues. An easy one:

> When the world was young, they were free.
> Much later, they found a home in D.C.
> Their keeper's asleep,
> But across the street
> Is a clue for you
> At a joint in full view.

The clue describes the animals in captivity at the National Zoo and the tavern across the street from the zoo's Connecticut Avenue entrance that is known affectionately as "the Zoo Bar."

Bromberg does not do anything halfway. His intensity is evident in his rat-a-tat conversational style and his dislike of small talk. To get her husband to relax, Marlys Bromberg confiscates his watch on weekends in the country. They recently built a 2,200-square-foot country home in rural Rappahannock County, Virginia, where the view out their window is of hayfields for as far as the eye can see. But Bromberg can't leave his work behind. He tells friends invited for Sunday brunch to bring *The New York Times*—or else.

The Brombergs live in the pricey Kalorama neighborhood of Washington, where they host $1,000-a-plate fund-raising dinners for key players on health care issues, Democrats and Republicans. Before stepping down following the 1994 elections, Bromberg was among the highest paid trade association heads, drawing $300,000 a year in salary plus another $150,000 in benefits.

Bromberg still spends most mornings as a consultant in his old office on 19th Street, between L and M Streets. "It's where the good restaurants are," he says. Pictures on the wall show him with presidents, presidents' wives, members of Congress, and Winston.

"I've had two wives, five daughters, and four female dogs," he says. "He's the only other male who's ever been in the house." The Brombergs adopted Winston after their last child went to college. Their dedication to the dog is exemplary, especially since Winston suffers from a skittish bowel and, like a true city dog, insists on being walked on a leash even in the country.

On Sunday, January 9, 1994, Bromberg was exercising on his NordicTrack while watching *Meet the Press*, when he heard Sen. Pat Moynihan declare, "We don't have a health crisis in this country." Bromberg let go of the ropes on his exercise machine so he could applaud. This was not just another senator mouthing off. As chairman of the Senate Finance Committee, Moynihan could make or break the President's health care bill. Although the mercurial chairman frequently was at odds with the White House, Bromberg did not regard him as a reliable ally. Moynihan was not on a first-name basis with lobbyists. When Bromberg needed something from the Senate Finance Committee, he went first to Packwood, then the ranking Republican member. But Moynihan's public declaration that the U.S. health care system was not in a crisis would be a selling point to use with other senators.

The health care industry exerts influence on Capitol Hill in various ways. It buys access to senators and congressmen and their staffs with generous campaign contributions, guaranteeing that it will at least have the chance to tell the hospitals' side of the story on any major issue. Even more important, however, is the vast network of hospitals that Bromberg can call on to apply pressure at home on a reluctant lawmaker by means as varied as a personal visit to the lawmaker's office, a letter to the editor published in the local newspaper, or local sponsorship of Harry-and-Louise-style TV ads giving the hospitals' point of view. The least valuable approach, in Bromberg's mind, is the one the public tends to think of first—a lobbyist schmoozing a senator or congressman over drinks at a Capitol Hill bar.

"One of the perceptions about lobbying is that you go out drinking, and the guy's your buddy so he does you favors," Bromberg said. "Those days are long gone. That sort of thing may work on tiny things like a technical amendment to a bill, but on big, important issues personal friendships don't mean a thing. It doesn't work that way. I'll bet we could have done just as good a job as we did this year [on influencing health care reform] without ever going to the Hill or ever talking to a member of Congress. It is knowing when and how to ask the troops in the field to do it. My job is like being a general . . . dealing with the strategic planning and timing, but the people out there did the work. How many times can I run up and say to Bob Dole, 'Hey, Bob, do me this favor, do me that favor,' as opposed to having one of my members—the biggest hospital in the state of Kansas—call him once in a while to remind him that when I do talk to him, I'm talking for that hospital. So it's really not me. . . ."

Bromberg described how his office organized grassroots interests into community teams to approach members of Congress in their districts. "If we have a congressman on our [target] list, we put together a team in that district," he said. "Is there a Mayo Clinic? Is there an Aetna,

CIGNA, Prudential office? Is there a VHA nonprofit hospital system? Is there one of my hospital systems? Is there anybody who is a member of the Healthcare Leadership Council? If so, they become part of the local team. Then we say to that team, 'Can you add people from the Chamber of Commerce, civic leaders, community leaders, so it's not just health people?' Then we say, 'Go as a group and meet with your congressman, and keep meeting with him. Go to his forums. Sit in the front row, and speak up. And your message is the same message you'll see in our ad: Price controls and caps on spending are going to reduce quality. Keep doing it over and over again.'"

In the grassroots lobbying effort, every opportunity is exploited to win converts to the hospitals' cause. Thus, patients, while hospitalized, find "tent cards" on their meal trays laying out the issues involved in health care reform from the hospitals' point of view. Doctors and nurses are briefed, so that they can respond to patients' inquiries.

Every hospital in Bromberg's network is given a one-page checklist of items ranging from assigning a hospital representative to speak at the local Rotary Club to inviting the congressman to visit the facility. After the Clinton health care plan was introduced, Bromberg advised his client hospitals, "We want you to picture that it is August 1994, and there's about to be a vote on the floor of the House or the Senate on a motion to strike global budgets and price controls and substitute a monitoring mechanism. Your congressman is called to the Oval Office. He walks in and finds the President there with the Speaker of the House and the Majority Leader, and the President says, 'We've got to have your vote on this.' And he goes on to offer an agricultural subsidy, a bridge, or a highway in exchange for the congressman's vote. And the congressman says, 'I can't. I'm committed to the people back home.'

"Now, what must happen between now and August 1994 to bring that about?" Bromberg asked. "What do you have to do back home in your district today and nine months from now to enable that congressman— or force that congressman—to look his own party leadership in the eye and say no? Then we work backwards. In the first month, we did this. Then we did that. We added the Chamber of Commerce and the Restaurant Association. We had the congressman in. We showed a film to our employees. We had a couple of meetings. We called all the doctors and nurses in. . . ."

Rep. Jim Cooper, an earnest Rhodes scholar who represented a rural district in eastern Tennessee, was an early ally of Bromberg's in his fight to influence the course of health care legislation. Several hospital chains are based in Nashville, including the Hospital Corporation of America, a founding member of Bromberg's federation. Cooper, who planned to run for the Senate in 1994, needed millions of dollars to wage the campaign and he needed to distinguish himself from Clinton and the national Democratic Party. Aligning himself with the health care industry would help build his campaign war chest, and standing up to Clinton was a way for Cooper to look tough and independent. A study by the consumer organization Citizens Action revealed that Cooper led the House in contributions from the health industry: $668,182 between January and September 1993. Cooper was the first Democrat to break ranks with the President on health care. Cooper drafted an alternative health care plan, dubbed "Clinton Lite" because it relied less on government.

Bromberg quietly helped round up co-sponsors for the Cooper plan, knowing it would never pass Congress because it called for taxing employer-provided health benefits, a provision both Republicans and Democrats opposed. Nevertheless, from Bromberg's perspective, it was a way to slow momentum for the Clinton plan.

The Tennessee-based National Federation of Independent Business also watched Cooper's every move. Privately, Cooper told the White House that he eventually would be dragged kicking and screaming to support an employer mandate. The NFIB's main concern was the employer mandate portion of Clinton's bill, which would have required some businesses to pay for employees' insurance. Cooper told the White House that his condition for backing off his bill and supporting the Clinton bill was a "carve-out" that would exempt small business, allowing him to look as though he had gotten the White House to back down.

Cooper did not reveal his close ties to the hospital industry. He told Bromberg that being linked to health care providers was "the kiss of death" among his constituents, who blamed exorbitant hospital costs for exacerbating the health care problem. Behind the scenes, Cooper gave a pep talk to "team leaders" installed by Bromberg's group to work against the Clinton plan in fifty-seven congressional districts around the country. In the November election, Cooper lost his bid for the Senate to Republican Fred Thompson, a former Hollywood actor and Washington lobbyist.

Lobbyists sometimes hire other lobbyists. Nominally, Bromberg was a Democrat, but he did not know anyone in the Clinton high command the way he knew, say, Dole or Packwood, so he bought his way in. The day after Clinton was elected, Bromberg put Democratic superlobbyist Thomas Hale Boggs on retainer. Boggs, a heavy contributor to Democratic causes, is a member of one of Washington's most prominent political families. His father, Hale Boggs, was a powerful member of the House at the time of his death in a plane crash. His mother, Lindy Boggs, became a respected member of Congress in her own right after assuming her husband's seat. Boggs's sister and brother-in-law, Cokie and Steve Roberts, are nationally known political commentators. Boggs introduced Bromberg to Jack Williams, a Little Rock lawyer who had been Clinton's law partner during the two years Clinton was in private practice after losing his first reelection race for governor.

With Williams greasing the way over the next year, Bromberg met with Clinton's top advisers: Mack McLarty, Dave Gergen, George Stephanopoulos, and Harold Ickes. Bromberg had been prepared to ignore Stephanopoulos as "an arrogant young kid" not worth his attention. Then Rostenkowski told him how much he liked Stephanopoulos, who had worked for Majority Leader Richard Gephardt before joining the Clinton campaign. Bromberg soon was convinced that Stephanopoulos, with his links to important Democrats on the Hill, would be the one who cut the deal on health care reform. Stephanopoulos was cordial, but gave Bromberg no indication he was willing to deal.

It was different with Harold Ickes, a fiftyish New York lawyer, whose father had been Interior Secretary under Franklin D. Roosevelt. Ickes, who had a long history in Democratic politics and a reputation for toughness, had joined the White House staff as a kind of enforcer. Bromberg said he expected "some flame-throwing liberal friend of Hillary's who represented labor unions." It turned out that Ickes's law partner, a Long Island political leader named Jack English, was the same man who had gotten Bromberg into politics thirty years earlier. The two New Yorkers connected. Bromberg liked the fact that Ickes did not take "fake notes." In other meetings, there was always furious scribbling. "These people take more notes than anybody I've ever met. I mean Hillary and Ira must have reams of notes somewhere," Bromberg said.

Even as he was cozying up to Clinton's inner circle, Bromberg took steps to cut off a potential money supply for the White House. Money matters in a public policy fight. Tipped off by friends in the business community who had been approached for contributions, Bromberg leaked a story to *The Washington Post* about a plan developed by the Democratic National Committee to bankroll a health care reform campaign. Then, in the strange sort of professional courtesy that prevails in Washington, Bromberg called David Wilhelm, chairman of the DNC, to give him a heads up that the story would be running. Wilhelm claimed not to know about the scheme, which Bromberg believed would have allowed the party to raise money from big donors without disclosing the source. *The Washington Post* story raised enough ethical questions that Wilhelm was forced to kill the plan. Pleased by the development, Bromberg dismissed the DNC's ability to influence the debate.

Hillary Clinton was in a defiant mood on January 21, 1994, when she strode into the Madison Hotel to confront thirty CEOs, all members of Bromberg's Healthcare Leadership Council, seated around a conference table. She said the "so-called pros" in Washington had advised her and her husband to claim victory no matter what sort of health care reform plan emerged from Congress, and that the public would not know the difference between "universal coverage" and "universal access."

Universal coverage meant guaranteed health care for everyone, whereas universal access only meant health-care coverage was available to all who could afford it, which already was true for most Americans. No matter what the terminology, the Clintons believed the public's support for health-care reform was based on a guarantee of coverage for every American.

"Bill and I didn't come to Washington to play those kinds of political games," the First Lady declared. "Our place in history is contingent upon universal coverage."

When Dr. Robert Waller, CEO of the Mayo Foundation, told Mrs. Clinton that his board would not let him accept federal price controls, she denied that price controls were in the administration's plan. At issue was the White House proposal to limit the annual rise in insurance premiums.

"If we can't even agree on the terms, how can we find a solution?" Bromberg asked, not hiding his anger.

Glaring, the First Lady challenged Bromberg, "Well, what are you *for?*"

Over lunch later at the Hay Adams Hotel, across Lafayette Park from the White House, Bromberg briefed Dave Gergen on the meeting, sneering at the First Lady's all-or-nothing position. He told Gergen that Clinton's place in history was not linked to universal coverage, but to his ability to govern as a New Democrat, as he had promised. "This is the guy who has the chance to make the Democratic Party the majority party for fifty years," Bromberg said. "He can prove to every Reagan Democrat like me and to every Perot Democrat that it's okay to come back now. The party's centrist again. And *she* thinks his place in history is out there somewhere. That's the two governments we've got."

Gergen, a Republican who had been brought in to improve the Clinton administration's dealings with Washington's power brokers, was sympathetic. Inside the White House, he, too, had advocated step-by-step reform, rather than the bold overhaul the First Lady wanted. But her resolve drove the debate, and Gergen, his loyalty in doubt, was soon frozen out of the health care deliberations. "We know how to run a populist campaign if we have to," Mrs. Clinton told friends and foes. "We are not going to sign just any bill." Bromberg took to calling Mrs. Clinton "Big Sister" behind her back, a mocking allusion to George Orwell's "Big Brother." In Washington, people shook their heads and said that Bill Clinton was pragmatic and ready to deal, but Hillary would not let him.

At the White House, Hillary's people were no fonder of Bromberg than he was of them. He was known, not affectionately, as "Mr. Strong-arm" for his take-no-prisoners manner. Younger staffers scorned Bromberg's macho style. "He struts," said one, who suspected Bromberg goaded Mrs. Clinton less to make a point than to impress his colleagues. "If Bromberg were an animal, he would be a lizard," an aide to the First Lady said defiantly.

In his State of the Union Address on January 25, 1994, Clinton held up his veto pen and dared Congress to pass any health reform bill without universal coverage. Bromberg was at his home with a *Washington Post* reporter watching the speech on a forty-six-inch television screen. He had arranged for several other journalists to call him for reaction: "It was a great speech. . . . I agree with ninety-nine percent of it. But we don't vote on speeches in Washington."

Knowledgeable, accessible, and always ready with a pithy quote, Bromberg is a favorite source for reporters. He frequently talks "on background," which means he is not identified by name. "It's a weapon," he says. "We spend a lot of time trying to help even if we're not quoted."

In the opening stages of the health care fight, the Healthcare Leadership Council helped steer the debate by posing a "Question of the Week" and faxing it on blank paper to selected reporters: Who will pay for reform? Do the numbers add up? What is the impact on consumer choice of doctor and health plan? How much government control? Bromberg knew that his industry would win if the debate stayed focused on issues that made the public anxious, such as limiting a patient's choice of doctors, the threat of health care rationing, and the budget-breaking cost of covering everyone. He had a bumper sticker in his office: "If you think health care is expensive now, wait until it's free."

Bromberg still regarded himself as a friend of the reform effort and viewed his actions as part of a larger strategy to gain a compromise that his industry could accept. In fact, he was helping to kill the plan.

About that time, in January 1994, Louise Caire Clark, the actress in the Harry and Louise ads, was in Washington having dinner at the Old

Ebbitt Grill, a popular eatery on 15th Street, a block from the White House. By coincidence, the Clintons were there, too. They invited the actress to their table. "I have never been so nervous meeting anyone," Clark later recalled. "I've been around Hollywood stars, and I don't bat an eye. But I was nervous with them. I just kept babbling, 'I voted for you, I voted for you.' He seemed very interested in that and the fact that my sons had campaigned for him. He wrote a note to my sons, which we have framed. It says, 'Dear Matthew and Michael: I'm glad I met your mother. Thank you for your support.' He was charming. He didn't even raise the ads."

Positions hardened, but no one yet dreamed the Clintons would be so inept politically that they would end up with nothing. The President had started out so much in command of the issue that even his opponents assumed that the debate would be at the margins and that some sort of health care bill would become law. Everyone wanted to be at the table when the deal was struck. Bromberg realized that the only way to stop the Clinton plan was to make it politically risky for lawmakers to support it. Bill McInturff, the Republican pollster who worked with Bromberg, said, "We had to create political danger. Members of Congress are driven by public opinion, and if public opinion becomes unsustainable, they change. There are no profiles in courage."

Grassroots pressure had to be applied to reverse the Clinton plan's momentum. Bromberg targeted one hundred "swing Democrats" in the House, those who were not committed to vote for or against the plan. Most were southerners, members of what Bromberg called the "Southern Guts List" because they had stood up to the Democratic leadership on previous votes. The list included Democrats who had voted against Clinton on the 1993 budget and on the parental leave bill, another Clinton priority. If these Democrats had voted against their president once, they could be persuaded to do so again, Bromberg figured.

This was the political climate in Washington leading up to the election of November 1994 in which voters threw out the Democrats, a climate in which "guts" could be defined with no apparent cynicism or sarcasm as a willingness by Democratic lawmakers to cave under pressure, to desert the Democratic Party and the first Democratic president in a dozen years. "Guts" was the term Bromberg ascribed to those members who could be gotten to.

The House Energy and Commerce Committee was a critical battleground. Headed by Chairman John Dingell, whose father had championed health care in the House of Representatives more than fifty years earlier, the committee's handling of the Clinton plan would signal Congress's determination or lack of it on the issue. Bromberg's group zeroed in on nine members of the committee and besieged them both in Washington and at home. Every hospital in the nine districts was contacted. CEOs and other important figures in the districts were flown to Washington at the federation's expense to meet with their congressmen.

The lobbying campaign was in full force when Bromberg bumped into Kansas Rep. Dan Glickman, waiting to see the movie *Schindler's List.* As they stood in line, Glickman told Bromberg how hospital representatives had badgered him about "this damn health bill." Bromberg pretended he did not know anything about the lobbying campaign that he had, in fact, organized in Glickman's district.

"Did they have any impact on you?" Bromberg asked.

"Yeah," Glickman said, sighing. "I've got to get out of Congress. I've got to figure out what else to do. I mean, there must be another job."

Glickman was defeated for reelection in November 1994. Clinton named him secretary of agriculture.

Ultimately, Chairman Dingell fell one vote short of getting a bill out of his committee. The Democratic holdout was Kansas Rep. Jim Slattery, who was running for governor. The White House had hired one of Slattery's senior people as a legislative lobbyist. She and others held long, anguished conversations with him. But Slattery was more persuaded by visits from representatives of Pizza Hut and Hallmark, businesses headquartered in his district. Bromberg knew that running for governor, Slattery could not afford to offend the business lobby in his state by supporting employer mandates to pay for health care. When Slattery got pressure from labor union leaders who wanted universal health care coverage, Bromberg supplied "a quick and dirty paper" on why the Clinton health bill would be bad for the state. Bromberg's office, in fact, churned out position papers for several members of Congress who needed help justifying their stand against the bill.

Clinton went to Kansas to campaign for Slattery. A week later, Slattery rebuffed him on health care. To Slattery it seemed better to disappoint the President than to offend the small-business lobby in his state. Slattery lost the governor's race anyhow.

Opposition was building against the Clinton plan, but there was a moment in March when a bipartisan compromise still seemed possible. Over dinner at the White House, Clinton won the promise from a handful of Republicans, including Dole and Packwood, that they would work for universal coverage. There was such a spirit of good will that Sen. Tom Daschle, a South Dakota Democrat, did not distribute an alternative plan, one he had drafted with White House blessings.

Packwood called Bromberg the morning after the White House dinner. "Thank God, Gramm wasn't there," Packwood said. The GOP's right wing was represented by amiable Oklahoma Sen. Don Nickles. He did not undercut the spirit of the evening the way Phil Gramm, an abrasive conservative, surely would have. Bromberg was also pleased to learn that Mrs. Clinton had said very little during the dinner meeting.

"There is a window here," Bromberg said, cheerily. "Dole is willing to cut a deal. But the window won't stay open very long. I'm not sure the Clintons understand that."

Bromberg wanted to compromise, but partisan politics had begun to undermine any chance for cooperation. The Whitewater scandal was eating away at Clinton's popularity, and the Republican right was growing bolder about denying him a health care bill. Gramm, who would challenge Dole for the Republican presidential nomination in 1996, vowed that health care would pass "over my cold, dead, political body."

The White House let the moment pass. Hillary Clinton and the other strategists thought it was too early to compromise. Clinton had a reputation for folding at the first sign of resistance. His political advisers counseled him to wait. In April, frustrated by the Clintons' insistence on universal coverage, Ways and Means Chairman Rostenkowski called for a tax increase to pay for the ambitious plan. He explained, sarcastically, that he had not yet found "the health care fairy." Bromberg was in Rostenkowski's office when House Speaker Tom Foley called to complain about being blindsided on the sensitive tax issue. Rostenkowski replied: "I was just sending a message to the White House to lower their expectations. I wasn't serious."

By May, Bromberg put the odds of a health care bill making it to the President's desk at no better than fifty-fifty. Morale was low at the White House. Magaziner was battling walking pneumonia and a lawsuit against the special task force on health care for conducting its business in secret. A Providence, Rhode Island, television station reported that Magaziner could be cited for contempt of court. Magaziner got a call from his eleven-year-old son, who was in tears.

"Daddy, are you going to jail?" the boy asked.

Magaziner assured him and his nine-year-old brother, who was too shaken to come to the phone, that this was not the kind of thing that would send their father to jail. Nevertheless, the call troubled him so much he could not sleep that night. In a groggy stupor the next morning, he stumbled going downstairs and bruised some ribs.

Magaziner went to work anyway, but the bruised ribs ached so much he went home early to rest. No sooner had he arrived home when the phone rang. One of the administration's allies on Capitol Hill called to say that moderate Democrats and Republicans whose support the White House was counting on had begun to defect.

"That was the lowest day," Magaziner recalled months later. "I made myself a plate of spaghetti, which is what I always do when I am depressed."

Bromberg himself was stunned by the sharp decline in support for the President's plan. Democratic pollster Mark Mellman had made public brutally negative numbers on how public sentiment had shifted away from the Clinton plan. Bromberg knew that the Health Insurance Association of America had similar polling data, but had kept its findings quiet. The insurance industry did not want to encourage the growing clamor on Capitol Hill and on editorial pages to pass insurance reform and put off the tougher question of universal coverage. Hospital and insurance interests believed that this patchwork approach would result in higher insurance premiums and the likelihood that young, healthy people would choose not to be covered.

The conventional wisdom in Washington was that those in Congress would not dare run for reelection without passing a health care bill of some kind. "That's bullshit," Bromberg said, offering poll numbers to prove it. Republican pollster McInturff had revealed poll results on May 26, 1994, showing that a majority of women, ages thirty-five to fifty-four, opposed the Clinton plan for the first time since it was introduced the previous September. "The window of support for dramatic change is beginning to close," said McInturff. Two years earlier, forty-five percent of the electorate thought the health care system should be "radically changed." Now the count was twenty-seven percent and falling.

Dole was the key to any deal. Almost every day, Bromberg called Sheila Burke, Bob Dole's chief of staff, to ask, "Is it time?" Her answer was always, "Not yet." The reform process had come down to waiting while Dole checked the political winds. Bromberg and other Washington insiders anticipated a moment when Dole and Pat Moynihan, the Finance Committee chairman, would work out a compromise bill. After Nebraska Sen. Bob Kerrey joined Republican Sen. John Chafee as a co-sponsor of a progressive GOP alternative, Bromberg thought a breakthrough was in the making. He urged Kerrey to call Dole. "Then on Sunday, I turn on the tube and Dole says, 'Yeah, Bob Kerrey called me about that,'" Bromberg said, savoring his role as facilitator.

Kerrey called Chafee's proposal "the best deal in town" and urged Clinton to embrace it. Chafee and Clinton met in May and said nice things about each other's health care plans. But Chafee's bill, which called for mandating individuals, not employers, to pay for health insurance, was not acceptable to Clinton. Later in the summer, Kerrey, at Bromberg's urging, attempted again to be the human bridge between Dole and the Democrats. Kerrey praised a modest health care plan that Dole belatedly had put forward. Other Democrats ridiculed the measure, and the political climate for any compromise chilled so rapidly that Dole in the end did not even back his own bill.

With an eye on the Republican presidential nomination in 1996, Dole was less and less inclined to deal with Clinton if it meant angering the GOP's right wing. In a memo to the President, dated June 10, 1994, Ira Magaziner warned of "a deadly chain whose links threaten any deal short of a presidential surrender." Magaziner portrayed Dole as eager to placate the Republican right. "He now smells blood and also wants to defeat the President," Magaziner wrote. "He convinces moderate Republicans to hold back. Moderate Democrats want Republicans for cover."

The health care reform coalition was crumbling. The only alternative, Magaziner said, was "a fighting strategy." Diehards in the White House still believed that by holding firm they could force a debate on the Senate floor that would galvanize the nation in the way that the Persian Gulf debate had three years earlier. They thought Republicans would not dare filibuster a historic health reform package and Democrats would not desert their president.

By July, Bromberg rated the chances for health care reform at thirty-five percent and dropping daily. A *Wall Street Journal* editorial under the headline "Three Blind Mice" castigated three moderate Republicans as "traitors" for continuing to work for health care reform. In a meeting Bromberg had with Dole and other Republican senators, Dole talked about the value of a bipartisan approach, but was outnumbered.

"These other guys started jumping down my throat," Bromberg recalled later. "Phil Gramm, who I had known since he first came here as a Democrat, started in on me, saying, 'Goddamn it. . . .'" These Republicans wanted to pull the plug on reform. They wanted Dole to punish the three defectors. They did not want to hear a presentation from a lobbyist about the virtues of compromise. After the others left, Dole confided to Bromberg: "They weren't looking out for Bob Dole."

"Dole can't afford to be Mr. Negative," Bromberg said sympathetically. "Those guys were out for blood." The Republican right had given Dole no maneuvering room. If he wanted to be the party's standard bearer in 1996, he could not let health care reform go forward. On September 26, 1994, with Bromberg's odds at a hundred to one against passage of a health care reform bill, the Democratic leadership, acknowledging defeat, withdrew the legislation from further consideration.

The Republican takeover of Congress in the November 1994 election killed the chances of any health reform plan with the name Clinton on it. Shortly after the election, instead of popping champagne Bromberg was curiously gloomy. From his point of view, the defeat of national health care reform coupled with the Republican victory in Congress had created fifty state nightmares. The Republicans promised to slash spending and "devolve" responsibility for massive federal programs to the states. That meant deeper cuts in Medicare and Medicaid and less money for hospitals. A national organization like Bromberg's would be less effective dealing with individual state capitals, a job better handled by Bromberg's competitors at the state level. Even before the Republicans sealed their takeover, Bromberg envisioned a coalition with the American Association of Retired Persons to fight Medicare cutbacks. The AARP had been on the opposite side in the debate over Clinton's health reform plan.

"This is a town where you change sides very quickly," said Bromberg. "The definition of friendship is who can help you in the next hour. Republicans philosophically are with us and Democrats aren't. Then you switch to a fight over cutting Medicare, and it tends to be liberal Democrats who bail us out. I can't say more Republicans are good for us or more Democrats are good for us. I don't trust anybody."

Bromberg was in New Orleans on election night preparing for a board meeting the next day. The Senate going Republican was not much of a surprise. The GOP's sweep of the House, on the other hand, was startling. At 7:30 the next morning, Bromberg delivered a breakfast speech to the New Orleans Chamber of Commerce Health Committee. "Some of the faces have changed, but the issues are the same," he said.

Bromberg examined the political revolution from the viewpoint of his industry's self-interest. Although Rostenkowski was a friend, his defeat in the election was a victory for Bromberg's for-profit hospitals. As Ways and Means chairman, Rostenkowski had protected the interests of nonprofit teaching hospitals in Chicago. With their protector gone, the nonprofits would take their share of cuts, lessening the burden on Bromberg's clients. The Democratic leadership in the Senate spoiled that small victory by awarding Illinois Sen. Carol Moseley-Braun a seat on the Senate Finance Committee. She, like Rostenkowski, would be in a position to protect Chicago's inner-city hospitals.

Prospects were bleak for health care reform in the new, Republican-controlled 104th Congress. A slowdown in medical inflation prompted by fear of government intervention lulled some policy-makers into believing the system would fix itself. As Bromberg had feared, Republicans concentrated on slowing the growth in Medicare and Medicaid in order to achieve their primary goal of a balanced budget. The emergence of contentious social issues—welfare reform and affirmative action—took the spotlight away from health care reform.

In a way, Bromberg emerged both victim and victor in the year-long health care fight that produced no improvement in coverage for Americans. After helping to derail the Clinton bill, Bromberg ended a quarter-century of working full-time for the Federation of American Health Systems to go into private practice as a lawyer and lobbyist. His age and triple bypass would make it prohibitively expensive, if not impossible, for him to buy health insurance on the open market. As a well-connected lobbyist, Bromberg had alternatives that the average person does not have. The federation created a vice chair's position for him to advise on "strategic matters," a position that continued to reward him financially, but, more importantly, provided health care benefits.

The word "lobby" dates back at least to the mid-seventeenth century when the large anteroom off the floor of the English House of Commons where members of Parliament could be approached by special pleaders became known as the lobby. According to H. L. Mencken, in 1829 petitioners for special privileges in Albany, New York, were called "lobby-agents." It was not a complimentary term.

Walt Whitman characterized "lobbyers" as "crawling serpentine men, the lousy combings and born freedom sellers of the earth." James Buchanan wrote President-elect Franklin Pierce in 1852: "The host of contractors, speculators, stockjobbers and lobby members which haunt the halls of Congress . . . are sufficient to alarm every friend of his country." In the 1800s, lobbyists had attained such influence over the legislative process that they were called the Third House of Congress.

In its purest form, lobbying—the ability of citizens to redress grievances and petition the government—is a form of free speech protected by the First Amendment, although subject to some prohibitions, limitations, and disclosure requirements. The Sierra Club and the Salvation Army wear white hats in the public's mind, yet they lobby just as ferociously. Where there is a cause, there is a lobbyist. The breakdown occurs when the narrow interests overwhelm the national interest. John F. Kennedy once said, "The consumer is the only man in our economy without a high-powered lobbyist in Washington."

Lobbyists rival lawyers as the professionals everybody loves to hate. Democrats in Congress—out of power and consequently out of favor with lobbyists—rose to their feet to applaud President Clinton when he called on lawmakers in January 1995 to stop taking lobbyists' perks. Bob Dole, leader of the new GOP majority in the Senate, pointed out the hypocrisy of Clinton's demand, noting that the President accepted money from lobbyists for his legal defense fund created in the wake of Whitewater. The next day, the White House issued a statement that Clinton would no longer take contributions from lobbyists; neither would he return lobbyists' contributions that had already been collected.

Scrutiny of lobbyists has escalated, along with their numbers and their power. In 1973, during Gerald Ford's confirmation hearings as vice president, it was revealed that, as a member of Congress, he had never written a check for cash. This was before ATM machines, when writing checks for cash was common. The fact that Ford had never written such a check suggested that he, like many lawmakers at the time, had lobbyists pay for everything.

Contrast that laissez-faire atmosphere to the current climate that has prompted legislation that bans gifts, all but ends lobbyist-paid meals, and treats fruit baskets as contraband. "It would be great if congressmen bought us dinner for a change," said Bromberg sarcastically. "I don't care. It's a stupid proposal. Campaign finance reform probably isn't going to pass, but if it did, I wouldn't care about that either. If they abolish PACs or reduce them too much, these politicians are still going to call me and they're going to say, 'Find ten guys to send me a thousand each.' If bundling is illegal, then we'll send the checks separately."

Bromberg declared lobbying-reform efforts a waste of time. Restrictions only spur a search for loopholes. When Congress abolished payments for speeches, for instance, lobbyists gave money to the members' favorite charity, which made them look good at home. Free trips were limited to two nights and three days, but that's the perfect amount of time for a getaway weekend at a fancy resort, Bromberg said.

Modern campaigns cost a lot of money. In 1994, House and Senate winners spent a record $393 million, almost a third more than the $297 million spent to win all congressional seats in 1990, the previous midterm elections. The price of a seat in Congress is set by an economy of its own, independent of the general rate of U.S. inflation. When an unlimited amount of cash is available to buy a finite number of congressional seats, a bidding war ensues and prices rise.

Washington lobbyists who fund campaigns will not take a candidate seriously unless the campaign hires professionals for polling, message development, and broadcast advertising. Holding fund-raisers and going to fund-raisers is a staple of the lobbyist's life. "I hate it," says Bromberg, who offers this novel alternative: Why not rent RFK Stadium one night a year and set up 435 booths, one for each member of Congress. "Just go from booth to booth, instead of going to five fund-raisers a week," he says.

What would he call it? Buy Your Congressman Night?

"Rent," he says emphatically.

Congress traditionally has coddled lobbyists. The 1946 Federal Regulation of Lobbying Act stood practically untouched for half a century until the Disclosure Act of 1995 closed a large loophole that had allowed thousands of lobbyists to escape registering. When Tommy Boggs, one of Washington's superlobbyists, first registered in 1967, he says he was only "the seventeenth person to do so." As of 1995, there were at least twelve thousand lobbyists in the nation's capital, but fewer than half were registered. By definition, lobbyists attempt to influence some aspect of public policy. So many people are promoting narrow and inevitably competing self-interests that the common good frequently gets lost.

The role money plays in the birth and death of legislation has changed in form if not substance. Hill veterans remember the days when a doddering committee chairman had to be accompanied by an aide to keep track of cash donations thrust at him by lobbyists attempting to influence legislation. Bromberg entered politics in 1964 working for a New York Democrat running in a Republican district. When a poll four weeks before the election showed the Democrat could win, Bromberg got a call to come to a hotel room at the Waldorf-Astoria late at night. The man in his underwear who opened the door handed Bromberg a bag stuffed with $5,000 in small bills, the equivalent of roughly $25,000 in inflation-adjusted 1995 dollars.

Such blatant transactions were not unusual. "When I first came here," says Bromberg, "there was a Seafarers' Union lobbyist who sat at his own table at the Democratic Club writing checks. Everybody loved him. He was called Uncle Phil. The day my boss told Uncle Phil he was going to retire from Congress, Phil said, 'Don't be silly.' He pulled out his checkbook and wrote a check. My boss ripped it up."

A turning point in the relationship between Congress and lobbyists came in the 1970s with the so-called Watergate reforms. Public revulsion at the money abuses revealed in the Watergate pressured Congress to pass the Federal Election Campaign Act (FECA) in September 1974, just after Richard Nixon's resignation and before the elections. This, coupled with further reforms two years later, would have a dramatic effect upon power relationships on the Hill.

By 1974, all over the country, a decline was evident in political organizations like the famous Daley machine in Chicago that had put Dan

Rostenkowski in Congress in 1958 and kept him there since. The 1968 and 1972 Democratic conventions had been disasters for party bosses. If the Democratic Party apparatus hit its low point before Watergate, Gerald Ford's ascent to the presidency marked the beginning of the end for the GOP's moderates.

Activists driven by anti-war, civil rights, and environmentalist concerns were knocking down the Democratic Party walls. In the GOP, where a rightward drift that began with the 1964 presidential campaign of conservative Arizona Sen. Barry Goldwater had been checked by Nixonian pragmatism, a vacuum existed. Republicans who survived the Nixon debacle unsoiled tended to find refuge in the more conservative ranks of the party and began to define themselves as polar opposites of their Democratic opponents.

Ford barely survived a challenge from within the party by Reagan, exposing the weakness of the party's old guard. Republicans who did not position themselves on the right had nowhere to go. Some fell to old-age attrition. Democrats defeated a few, but most were done in by the wave of resurgent conservatism. Prominent industrial state Republicans with voting records to the left of most Democrats, like Senators Jacob Javits of New York, Ed Brooke of Massachusetts, Clifford Case of New Jersey, Charles Percy of Illinois, Charles (Mac) Mathias of Maryland, and Richard Schweiker of Pennsylvania were purged, all but the last two by crippling primary challenges from the right.

Less visibly, Republican moderates and liberals in the House were also being supplanted by new right-wing blood. The changes were not so noticeable beacuse minority members in the House are far less powerful than in the Senate, and the more conservative newcomers were relegated to the back benches until their numbers increased, culminating with the 1994 election of seventy-three Republican freshmen. Moderate pragmatist Republicans with strong party ties like John Anderson, Paul Findley, and Tom Railsback of Illinois, Millicent Fenwick and Harold Hollenbeck of New Jersey, John Rhodes of Arizona, Bill Frenzel of Minnesota, Pete McCloskey of California, and Stewart McKinney of Connecticut were vacating their seats for a variety of reasons. Ideological upstarts like Newt Gingrich, with a radically different agenda, began arriving.

Liberal or conservative, most of the more ideological members had a national constituency and funding base, and were less reliant upon local party organizations. Elections hinged less upon what candidates could accomplish in Washington for the voters and more upon what candidates advocated ideologically. With voters thus distracted from bread-and-butter by such issues as abortion rights, combating communists, and a new emphasis on moral values, economic special interests could play at will. Why should a corporation care whether a politician supports or opposes the Panama Canal Treaty or school prayer, as long as he or she will support a special tax break?

Post-Watergate changes in campaign finance laws opened a new sluice for cash: political action committees, or PACs, comprised of individuals with common interests pooling their money to contribute to candidates who share their views. The result was that representatives found it easier to raise most of their campaign funds from sources outside their districts. Lawmakers turned to lobbyists, who dispensed PAC money at the rate of up to $5,000 per election, as opposed to the $1,000 limit for individual donors.

Corporate America, trade associations, and organized labor cranked up their PACs to the point that by 1980 PACs were providing half of the campaign money for House members, a pattern still true today. The $1,000 limit on contributions from individuals made impossible the kind of envelope-full-of-cash kingmaking that Bromberg recalled from 1964. Local fat cats, even local party organizations, could no longer finance local elections.

Representatives today raise most of their money by themselves, not through the party. Far more than clean government, the class of 1974 bought itself a measure of independence from party leaders—and from the voters—by limiting individual contributions and legitimizing national PACs.

Prior to the changes in the campaign laws, the Corrupt Practices Act of 1934 had prohibited contributions by corporations, or by anyone with a federal contract. The advent of PACs provided a way for these interests to legally play the game. A politician could stay in office by helping a company on the other side of the country fix its problems with a federal contract or regulation or investigation, instead of by helping a local community get a new federal courthouse.

At least at the outset, many representatives felt liberated from the tyranny of the party bosses and the committee chairmen. But like runaway children who fall into the thrall of street pimps, members of Congress would soon discover that their new benefactors exacted a price for security.

Newt Gingrich had been Speaker of the House for just a week when lobbyist Paul Equale, senior vice president of governmental affairs for the Independent Insurance Agents of America (IIAA), toured the Speaker's well-appointed suite in the Capitol. Democrats had controlled the House for the previous forty years, when the back rooms of the

Speaker's suite were off-limits to Republicans. Equale recalls the wide-eyed wonderment of the Gingrich aide accompanying him, who said, "This feels like we're opening King Tut's tomb."

Lobbyists like Equale are always welcomed by Republicans and Democrats alike because money is vital to politicians, and lobbyists control the purse strings. Equale lobbies on behalf of the association's 300,000 independent insurance agents. He is a Democrat who once worked for George McGovern, which brands him, in Gingrich's words, "a counterculture McGovernik." But Equale saw the Republican wave coming. In the six months before the election, he "reoriented" a lot of the money that ordinarily would have gone to Democrats and gave it to Republicans. Equale was in a celebratory mood when Gingrich emerged from an inner office to greet him.

"You guys have been great all along," Gingrich told him. Equale confided that he took "some spears in my chest" from Democrats who thought he did too much for Republicans. Now, gazing out from the Speaker's balcony in the Capitol, he had no regrets. "Great balcony, great view," he said, savoring the moment.

Access is the lifeblood of lobbyists. Gingrich wanted to know whether Equale was getting in to talk with the new committee chairmen.

"Is it working?" the Speaker probed.

"It's going great," said Equale, treating the question as friendly small talk.

"No, I mean is it working?" Gingrich persisted. "I want to know if people who should be taken care of are able to operate in the new system."

Whatever anxiety Equale had about operating under the new Republican regime was defused by the Speaker's obviously sincere concern. Musing later about the episode, Equale said, "For all the talk about term limits and reforms, it's the same old thing. You always take care of your friends." Although Equale's view on this seems to contradict Bromberg's assertion that personal friendships "don't mean a thing" in today's world of lobbying, the two actually hold similar views. Bromberg is right that friendships alone do not close a deal, but a member of Congress is more likely to respond favorably to a friendly lobbyist who wants to drop by with a client for a visit.

During the campaign, Gingrich had told lobbyists that for those who did not financially help Republican candidates "it's going to be the two coldest years in Washington." That meant uncooperative lobbyists would lose the one thing they could not afford to give up—access to the agenda setters in the House—not to mention all the little ways the Speaker had to punish those who failed to enlist for the Republican revolution. "Let's say I need Speaker Gingrich to give a speech to my association or I want to impress my client by taking him over to the Speaker's office," Equale said. "There are lots of ways for a politician to screw someone. Benign neglect is the worst thing that can happen in politics."

Republican control of the House and Senate allowed the corporate community to put its money where its heart is. Previously, business PACs supported Democrats because they were in the majority, not because they necessarily liked Democratic policies. The Clintons' health care bill tapped into long-standing resentments and made it harder for Democrats to raise money for the 1994 midterm elections.

"If people screw you long enough, you screw them right back," said Equale. "Gingrich is exploiting an attitude that is already there. [Former House Whip] Tony Coelho taught Democrats how to be a permanent majority by, in effect, blackmailing business groups—in a nice way, but it was still blackmailing. The jig is up. Gingrich is saying, 'You better start playing ball with us.'"

The Republican reformers did not see any contradiction between their pledge to clean up Washington and their embrace of lobbyists. The new Republican majority flaunted its ties with the lobbying community. During the first hundred days of the new Congress, Ohio Rep. John Boehner, head of the House Republican Conference, was pictured in *Time* magazine holding his regular weekly meeting with lobbyists who support the pro-business provisions of the Republican Contract With America. Republicans, smoldering from decades in the minority, leaned on their corporate contacts to replace allegedly Democratic-leaning lobbyists with card-carrying Republican lobbyists. GOP strategists believed that weeding out Democrats from the lobbyist ranks would make it easier to raise money and maintain their majority.

The governmental affairs office of "The Big I," the nickname for the Independent Insurance Agents of America, is just two blocks from the Capitol, close enough for busy lawmakers to duck in for a quickie fund-raiser almost anytime. "It is the political equivalent of waterfront property," Equale boasts. On Valentine's Day morning, 1995, Equale's group held the first private sector fund-raiser for Speaker Gingrich, raising well over $50,000. Gingrich stirred the insurance agents with the promise of legal reform, one of ten elements in the Republican Contract. Trial lawyers were attacking "with both guns blazing," he reported. He needed the agents' help. They, in turn, outlined the kind of legal reforms that would help their industry.

"Three hours later," Equale marvels, "I was up on the Hill having lunch in the Members Dining Room, when Newt waves me over. He says, '[California Rep.] Chris Cox is going to introduce the bill that we discussed. I want you to start rounding up Democrats.'"

The insurance agents Equale represents are mainly white males, many of whom listen to Rush Limbaugh and vote Republican. Equale is a child of the 1960s. He was one of the student organizers of the 1970 mobilization against the Vietnam War. Now he is surprised to find himself in sympathy with the Republicans' emphasis on old-fashioned values. How Equale crossed the divide from his counterculture McGovernite days to become the IIAA's lobbyist is a tale familiar to baby-boomers who came of age in the 1960s. Conservatives call it growing up; liberals call it selling out.

Equale grew up in the Sunnyside section of Queens, New York, the kind of blue-collar, working-class neighborhood that Archie Bunker popularized in the television sitcom *All in the Family*. When George McGovern ran on an anti-war platform in 1972, Equale was enrolled at the State University of New York at Buffalo. He earned independent study credit for working in McGovern's campaign. "I cut my hair for McGovern," he says. It was the first of many accommodations he made before becoming part of what he once thought he hated.

Politicians tend to remember those who helped them win, and McGovern remembered Equale as the young man who helped him carry the Buffalo area. Three years later, in December 1975, wearing his new interview suit, maroon "sincerity" tie, and wing tip shoes, Equale met with McGovern in his Senate office. They reminisced about the campaign. When a bell rang summoning senators to vote, Equale asked if he could come along. He had never seen the Senate in session. On the short walk to the Capitol, McGovern introduced him to Ted Kennedy and Frank Church, two prominent liberal senators. Seated in the front row of the Senate gallery for the vote, Equale was in awe just being that close to Hubert Humphrey and Birch Bayh—"giants of the Senate," in his mind.

Frank Church unexpectedly sat down next to Equale and started one of those chance conversations that would change a life.

"George tells me you did a great job for him up in New York," the senator said. Then, after a pause: "What do you think of Senator Humphrey?"

"He's a giant of American liberalism," Equale replied, meaning every word.

Church turned to Equale and said, "Hubert Humphrey hasn't had a new idea in thirty years." It was Equale's first exposure to the rivalry between politicians that he now takes for granted.

"I was twenty-four years old," Equale said, recalling the day. "He grabs my arm. He leans in as close as he can get, gives me that famous politician's grin and says, 'Do you want to help make me the next president of the United States?'

"'Sure,' I said."

On the last day of 1975, Equale moved to Washington, where he became one of the legions of young people who every election cycle stake their future on a political candidate. If Church's candidacy had taken off, Paul Equale could have been the George Stephanopoulos of his day. Instead, when Church dropped out of the primaries, Equale went to law school and got a job as a government lawyer in President Jimmy Carter's newly created Department of Energy. Equale's job was mainly to keep Carter's Democratic allies in New England happy by cutting bureaucratic red tape when they needed heating oil. When the Travel Industry Association of America offered him a job as a lobbyist, Equale took it. Gasoline rationing was the hot issue.

Ronald Reagan's election ended the reformist zeal that had marked the Carter years. The day before Reagan was inaugurated, Equale quit his job and left Washington. "I had a very dogmatic, noncompromising, unabashed view about Republicans and Democrats. I have since moderated that tremendously. Some of my best friends are Republicans."

Equale's decision to leave Washington was not all political. His personal life was in a tailspin. He had turned thirty years old and had just gotten a divorce. He dropped out for a year and became a beach bum. "I was living on the beach, literally, all over the country, just following the sun. The first time I put on a suit to go for an interview, my legs broke out in a rash. It had been so long since I had a pair of long pants on."

Darkly handsome and smooth-faced, Equale could pass for an Italian film star. Bright, charming, and blessed with the gift of gab, he is "camera ready." That makes him a catch in image-conscious Washington. "When the lights come on, I can do anything," he says. Following one interview, Equale was asked whether he would be interested in a job representing the tobacco industry, an overture he did not pursue despite the six-figure salary that went with the job. Both his parents had been heavy smokers; his father had died of lung cancer when Equale was only ten years old. Equale had not left all his principles and idealism on the beaches, but he had turned a corner. He joined the governmental affairs office of the IIAA in 1982 and has been there ever since. The conservative Republican who hired him is now godfather to one of Equale's children.

Equale transformed the IIAA from a sleepy one-issue office into a legislative affairs powerhouse. It took more than his good looks and charm. Equale has a dynamic personality, but his real strength is the organization he represents. Independent insurance agents are everywhere. They tend to be pillars of the community: serving on the local hospital board, as members of the Rotary Club, or leaders of the United Way campaign. When they speak, members of Congress listen.

No amount of campaign money or expenses-paid junkets can equal the influence of a personal connection. To illustrate the point, Equale tells the story of George Frazier, an insurance agent in Hope, Arkansas, who has known Bill Clinton since he was four years old: "The first time I ran into Bill Clinton during the campaign, I said, 'Governor, George Frazier says hello.' He literally stopped and turned around. He walked over and said, 'I love that man.' And every single one of these guys in Congress has a George Frazier. My guys work in campaigns. They serve in state legislatures. They are Kiwanis Club presidents. My guys are the guys back home in real America that these guys pay attention to."

Similarly, when the Democrats controlled the Senate, the man to see was Majority Leader George Mitchell. His brother was a past president of IIAA's chapter in Maine.

The Clinton health care plan preserved the role of big insurance companies, but the mandatory purchasing alliances specified in the plan would have driven the independent agents that Equale represents out of business. When Hillary Clinton and administration officials held town hall meetings around the country, Equale made sure his members were out in force. There were thirty-five IIAA members at one public forum where Mrs. Clinton took a question from an agent, who happened to be a woman. Women still are uncommon in an organization that an observer characterized as "a bunch of pale, stale males." The female agent asked Mrs. Clinton for advice on what she should do if she lost her job.

"I'm assuming anyone as obviously brilliant as you could find something else to market," the First Lady quipped. The flattery worked in the context of the town hall meeting. When the quote showed up in *The Wall Street Journal*, however, it sent shock waves throughout the IIAA network. Soon after, CNN anchor Charles Bierbauer reported on *Newsmaker Saturday* that an unnamed White House official in a closed-door briefing for reporters had identified Equale's independent insurance agents as the biggest stumbling block to health care reform.

"Top officials on the President's health care task force seem to have focused on the independent insurance agents as the strongest opponent," Bierbauer said. "At a background briefing this week, one top administration official declared the insurance agents see health care as a 'cash cow.' The official insisted on a cloak of anonymity, but masked no feelings: 'There's no compromise with them. They're going to have to go into another line of work.'"

Equale sprang into action. He phoned around to find out who at the White House had singled out his agents. The culprit, he determined, was Hillary Clinton herself. He then called the White House to protest. Equale was told that the First Lady had confused his group with another group, which he assumed was a convenient cover story. Equale eventually received a letter of apology from the White House for maligning the motives of the insurance agents. Apology or not, agents still believed that Hillary Clinton was out to get them. They were ready to go to war. Equale did not think a high-profile offensive was smart, at least not yet. Public support for health care reform was still strong. If the agents went on the attack, they would look like the heavies.

"I don't want to go to DefCon Five until I have to," Equale explained, using a military analogy. "The perception of power is power. It's like nuclear weapons. If you have to use them, you're lost." The threat of tens of thousands of agents working their contacts in district after district acts as a deterrent for members of Congress. Besides, other groups were out front on the health care reform issue. The Health Insurance Association of America was providing "air cover" with the Harry and Louise spots on TV. The National Federation of Independent Business was doing the dirty work on the bill itself. Let them be the bad guys, Equale reasoned.

Independent agents had a lot to lose in the Clinton health plan, but Equale never had to go to DefCon Five or anything even close because others quickly attacked and defeated the Clinton plan. From Equale's perspective, it was not even a good fight. His party, the Democrats, at last had the White House, only to conduct themselves in the most amateurish way.

Clinton's people did not know how to play the game. In Washington, there are things said for public consumption and then there are things said in private, where officials quit posturing and get down to business. The White House health care operation did not work that way. "You would go to private meetings with these people, and it was the same as going to meetings with the communists," Equale complained. "You'd hear the same rhetoric privately that they were using in public. After a while you'd say, 'What the hell am I doing this for?' There was no use meeting; there was no second track."

Equale's frustration was personal as well as professional. He had friends in the White House, and they were blowing their opportunity. Equale had worked with several Clinton aides, Stephanopoulos among them, in Majority Leader Dick Gephardt's 1988 bid for the presidency. Equale had cultivated Gephardt from the time he was a freshman congressman as the embodiment of the new blow-dried reformer wave. "I was the first volunteer in his campaign," Equale said. "When Dick traveled, I sat in the plane next to him. The first penny to his Effective Government Committee came from IIAA. I'm a true believer." Equale was one of the many lobbyists whose backing undercut Gephardt's attempt to pose as a Washington outsider in the primaries.

What is different about Equale in the secretive world of lobbying is his openness and his insistence that what he does is honorable. The IIAA typically sponsors forty-five or fifty congressional and administration staffers for opening day of the baseball season at Camden Yards in Baltimore. "He hollers, 'I'm going to do this. I don't think there's anything wrong with it. I've got nothing to hide,'" says a House Democratic staffer, cupping his hands to his mouth to mimic Equale shouting his innocence.

"And by the way," the aide adds, "the seats he had were the farthest away from home plate. We were all the way out in left field." How does this staffer repay Equale? "When I have a document coming down, and I know it won't hurt my boss if I leak it, I call Equale. I say, 'Check this shit out,' and I send it over on a fax machine." This aide works for a key committee member working on health care. He shipped quite a bit of useful information to Equale during the debate.

Equale went on *PrimeTime Live* in January 1994 to defend taking congressional staffers on a paid junket to a Florida resort after the show's hidden cameras caught them cavorting in the sun. Equale pointed out that Sam Donaldson, the show's co-host, had accepted a $30,000 speaking fee from the same insurance industry that *PrimeTime* was criticizing. ABC subsequently imposed a ban on correspondents speaking to trade groups for money. Equale succeeded in shifting the focus to Donaldson and away from the congressional staffers, who remained anonymous.

"I think I covered their cookies very well on the air—that was my job," says Equale. "My constituents in that interview were the people I work with on Capitol Hill. I can't tell you how many members of Congress and staffers who were not on the trip called me and said, 'I'm glad somebody had the guts to go on the air.'"

Beneath his bravado, Equale felt queasy about the whole episode. He knew that it looked awful. Some of the younger staffers had visited a topless bar; it was rumored that *PrimeTime* had hidden cameras there as well. The fact that lobbyists underwrite trips to resorts for members of Congress and their staffs is incomprehensible to the average citizen. At best, it is a perk that is undeserved; at worst, it looks like legal bribery.

A companion piece on the same *PrimeTime* broadcast showed two senators, Democrat John Breaux and Republican Thad Cochran, at a celebrity tennis tournament sponsored by the Tobacco Institute. "It's the kind of thing, even if you did nothing wrong, the American people don't quite understand that it's okay," said Equale. Given the material, the senators got off relatively easy, Equale said. "If I were the producer, I'd show people freezing in the East, digging out from the snow, with Jimmy Buffett in the background and members playing golf," he said.

In the 1992 presidential campaign Ross Perot had pounded away at lobbying abuses, stoking the public fire for reform. Bill Clinton in his inaugural address vowed to "break the stranglehold the special interests have on our elections and the lobbyists have on our government." On March 24, 1994, the House passed, 315–110, a lobby reform bill that would ban registered lobbyists from treating lawmakers to dinner or a ball game. Insiders regarded the legislation as mostly cosmetic. A loophole, promoted by veteran members accustomed to living off lobbyists, would have allowed other company officials or trade organization members to pay the bill.

The Senate followed on May 11 with overwhelming support, ninety-five to four, for legislation forbidding lobbyists from giving any gift to a member or staffer, including paying for travel expenses, tickets to sports and entertainment events, and even fruit baskets, unless shared within the recipient's office. The bill also required all lobbyists to register, disclose their fees, and declare whom they were representing and on what issues.

Tempers flared on Capitol Hill the week the legislation was debated and passed. Members felt trapped. They hated the gift ban, thought it was unfair, but did not dare reject it in the face of mounting public cynicism. The primary sponsors in the Senate—New Jersey Sen. Frank Lautenberg and Michigan Sen. Carl Levin—were said to have introduced it as an election year ploy. Both were running for reelection. Attending a sold-out Barbra Streisand concert at the USAir Arena, where tickets cost $350 apiece, Lautenberg, who is one of the Senate's many millionaires, volunteered to other VIPs at a backstage party, "I paid for them!"

Equale said he could work around whatever rules Congress passed, but he was miffed at Congress's duplicity on the issue. When Equale encountered Sen. Carl Levin and his brother, Michigan Rep. Sander Levin, in the locker room of the Washington Sports Club on Capitol Hill, he let his feelings be known.

"I can't play squash with you," he said, his voice heavy with sarcasm. The bill did not rule out joint recreating, but Equale, whose PAC had given generously to the Levin brothers, wanted to make a point. "The real problem is that *you* sit around in locker rooms and cut deals and schmooze," Equale accused the lawmakers. "You wrap yourself in plastic and act holier than thou. It's pathetic."

Members of Congress have fewer perks than most lobbyists, a disparity that is responsible for the growing sense of deprivation that many lawmakers feel. If Equale wants a car and driver, he can have them. If he travels on business related to the association, his wife often accompanies him at IIAA expense. And lobbyists do not have to worry about keeping up a populist front. "Don't tell anybody I don't drive an American car," he grins, heading for his BMW.

Le Mistral Restaurant, on Pennsylvania Avenue a few blocks east of the House office buildings, is a typical lobbyists' haunt. Equale's favorite table by the window on the second floor is up a flight of stairs lined with black-and-white, signed photos of members of Congress. From that vantage point he can see everyone entering and leaving, in case someone he needs to talk with passes by. He is on a first-name basis with the restaurant owner. This is a place where he enjoys doing business—"until they make it illegal," he says, laughing.

With Congress in recess, Equale dressed as if he were auditioning for a Dewar's scotch ad: white sports shirt with Boca Raton Resort Club gold logo on the pocket, blue blazer, jeans, and moccasins. While the members of Congress flew home for the obligatory "district work period," Equale planned to knock off early to swim with his children.

When Geraldine Ferraro left Congress to run for vice president in 1984, Equale briefly considered running for her seat, which was his district in Queens. "I thought about it overnight and realized that I already had the job that I wanted," he says. As an aging beach boy, Equale did not relish explaining in the context of a political campaign why he once thought Timothy Leary had the key to the universe. Then there were the financial constraints. Members of Congress earn $133,600 a year, well below what most top trade association lobbyists are paid. Having remarried, Equale had sold his townhouse on Capitol Hill and moved his growing family to a house with a pool in Potomac, Maryland, an upscale suburb. "I can barely pay my bills now," he says. "I earn this huge salary, but I have a huge mortgage. I have no second thoughts."

The lobbying reform legislation died in the final days of the 1994 congressional session. Professional lobbyists never even bothered to lobby against it. Groups like the Christian Coalition and the Family Research Council, headed by former Reagan aide Gary Bauer, worked against it in league with radio talk show host Rush Limbaugh, claiming it would have a chilling effect on grassroots lobbying. Equale ridiculed the bill, which, among other things, attempted to impose strict limits on members of Congress accepting meals from lobbyists. "Stop me before I take another Big Mac," Equale said, mockingly. The bill addressed relatively minor gifts, not the huge flow of special interest money that influences legislation.

Members of both parties colluded to stop action on the bill. Republicans wanted to deny Democrats any victory that might help them in the November 1994 election. Veteran Democrats, jokingly dubbed "the golf and tennis caucus," waited so long to bring up the bill that they guaranteed its failure. House Speaker Tom Foley publicly called for reform. Privately, he stalled. He thought the bill was silly. "The American people just don't understand," he complained privately.

In the Republican landslide of 1994, Foley, who also had strenuously resisted the people's desire to impose term limits on members of Congress, became only the second Speaker of the House to be defeated for reelection. This time responding to the public clamor for reform, the Republican-controlled Senate voted in July 1995 to prohibit senators and their aides from accepting any gift worth more than $50 or gifts totaling more than $100 from any source in a year. Four months later, the House voted overwhelmingly for an even tougher gift ban, prohibiting expense-paid trips, free meals, and any other gifts from outside interests. Congress also imposed stricter registration and disclosure requirements for lobbyists, the first serious attempt to plug loopholes in the 1946 lobbying law. As a final indignity, House Republicans stopped assigning lobbyists parking spaces on Capitol Hill and took away the special blue cards that had granted lobbyists after-hours access to the Capitol.

Equale expressed concern not for himself—he said the reform measures would have "zero impact" on his ability to lobby—but for the members of Congress, who, he said, had further degraded themselves and the profession of politics by giving in to the public clamor. Equale said only a few members were willing to say it publicly, but most expressed the view privately, that the lobbying reforms were a sop to the voters, not a substantive attempt to clean up Washington. "The unfortunate thing is that this *looks* like something they had to legislate because something was wrong," Equale said. "They have created the impression that members and staffs are so prone to temptation they can't even accept a T-shirt or baseball cap. This was legislative masochism. . . . Next they'll hermetically seal themselves in plastic wrap so they are completely insulated from the real world."

In its zeal to quiet the public's fears about the influence of money, Equale thought Congress probably would do away with the system of political action committees, which Equale described as "a 1970s solution that turned into a problem." Doing away with PACS would also be the perception of reform, not real reform, Equale said. He explained, "The money is going to somehow get to these politicians who are candidates for public office. If they do away with PACS, the members will come to us and ask us to get individual contributions from our people. They'll want us to play bagman for them." Equale, like Bromberg, thinks that whatever restrictions are put on lobbyists' contributions, members of Congress will find a loophole to keep the money flowing.

Equale's answer to the charges that money breeds political corruption is not new rules and limits, but fuller disclosure: paid ads, if necessary, in local newspapers listing who gives how much to members of Congress. He also would provide free or subsidized access to television for federal candidates. As for lobbyists gaining advantage from gifts, golf games, and lunches with elected officials, he said, "We tend to cancel each other out. If I take a staff member out to lunch on Monday, the bankers will take him out on Tuesday. It's a wash." What Equale did not mention is that the men and women who pay the insurance premiums and maintain savings and checking accounts at the banks are the ones who never play golf or have lunch with a congressman.

Lobbyists are embedded in the congressional culture. They have lines out to places the public has not even thought about. An example is the Rules Committee, the arm of the House leadership that decides which bills are to be voted on and whose amendments considered. It is a procedural killing ground. Until the Republicans took over in 1995 and forced a vote on term limits, the Democratic-led House Rules Committee had prevented bills to limit members' terms from coming to the floor. Under the iron grip of Speaker Gingrich, the Rules Committee acts as a rubber stamp for the GOP leadership. Under former Speaker Tom Foley, a passive and enigmatic leader, the committee exercised more independence and was thus worth cultivating. Equale's group had a relationship with everyone on the committee, and one senior Democrat, South Carolina Rep. Butler Derrick, was a member of the IIAA.

The Rules Committee was expected to play a central role in crafting a health care bill. Each bill that emerges from a committee must "get a rule" before it goes to the House floor for a vote. The House Rules Committee limits debate and amendments and serves as a gatekeeper to the floor. The gate swings open as well as shut. Depending on the assigned rule, some amendments may be in order, but amendments to those amendments may not. The Rules Committee grants or denies all sorts of narrow or broad requests. It is one committee where even a fifth-ranking member has real power.

The most assiduous courting was of course reserved for Rules Committee Chairman Joe Moakley of Massachusetts. On a sunny spring Saturday, Equale explained how the process worked to a class of college students studying public policy who had gathered in a lobbyist's office on Connecticut Avenue.

"Mr. Moakley spent some good time a couple of weekends ago with some of my members on a boat," Equale said. "Many activities that our members do are to make sure Joe Moakley is enjoying himself."

The young men in the George Washington University class wore jackets and ties; the women wore business clothes. There were some amused smiles at Equale's candor in discussing the social etiquette of lobbying but no Marxist outrage at the system. Many of these students were, after all, aspiring lobbyists.

Equale talked about the mechanics of fund-raising. Every year, when Chairman Moakley addresses the crowd at his annual fund-raiser on the pier in Boston, he sees a swarm of two hundred insurance agents, each pinned like a prom date with the IIAA logo and the words "Go for Joe." Each agent is worth $100 to the Moakley campaign, a good deal for everyone, Equale declared.

"Inside Washington, it is maybe a thousand bucks to have dinner with Joe Moakley; frankly, I would rather be home with my kids. If you go to Boston, for a hundred dollars, you can go to that fund-raiser." The agents contribute their own money. This is an advantage for members of Congress who are attacked for accepting PAC money and want to show they have grassroots support.

Lobbyists are shadow players. Their lives mimic the lives of the members they influence, yet they are not directly accountable to the voters. They have the fun of the game with none of the risk. "It sounds arrogant, and I understand that it sounds arrogant, but if you consider the size of the constituency I represent and the size of this office and the way that it's organized, it's very, very similar to a member of Congress's office," Equale says. He has a legislative staff, a political staff, a support staff, and a grassroots person who is the equivalent of a caseworker in a congressional office. He is at home on Capitol Hill and far more likely to be around after the next election than many members.

"I get to play with the fire without getting burned," he says. "They have to vote, which is the worst part about being a member of Congress. It would be a great job if you never had to vote."

Equale thinks of himself as different from the hired-gun K Street

lobbyists who represent moneyed corporate interests. He says his constituents, the independent insurance agents, are "real Americans," who
exercise influence through him in the same way that in an earlier time
people were represented through participation in churches, labor
unions, and political parties. He omits the true tie that binds all varieties
of lobbying, and that is a willingness if need be to subvert the national
interest to special interests, which is why they are so named.

Most of the time, Equale is a modest man. But living and working in
the shadow of history's greats does things to people. Equale unabashedly
explains that he reaches consensus in his organization "the same way that
an effective politician like Franklin Roosevelt could gather together the
different strands of those people who wanted us to stay out of the war in
Europe at any cost and those who were trying to get us in at any cost . . .
to pull that together in a politically effective way and harness the power
of a nation. It's my responsibility to do the same thing within my trade
association."

Equale can activate thousands of agents with the touch of a computer
key. Before he generates a "grassroots action call," he warns the lawmaker who will be on the receiving end. It is a matter of professional
courtesy. "It's sort of like discovery among two lawyers in a courtroom
where you have to show each other your evidence," he says. "My job is
to make life as easy as possible for a member of Congress. If I have to
make life tough, I can do it, but it's with great reluctance."

Congress has grown wary of fax attacks and postcard blitzes generated
by special interests. The premium is on "grasstops," the buzzword for quality contacts made by prominent people or personal friends. "It's the difference between getting five thousand postcards from people you don't know
and getting twenty-five handwritten letters from people you do know or five
phone calls from people you went to college with or a personal visit in your
office by the best man in your wedding," Equale explains. This is the strategic placement of artillery, to use one of Equale's military metaphors.

Convinced that the Clinton health care plan would collapse of its own
weight, Equale never resorted to "carpet-bombing," another military
term for the kind of all-out assault where agents are unleashed on every
member of Congress.

Then there are "surgical strikes." Equale told how he might fly in fifty
members of his association for instruction on how to talk to representatives who serve on the House Energy and Commerce Committee. He
offered a sample of the kind of instructions he dispenses:

"When you ask a member of the committee for his vote and he says,
'I'm okay on that,' that's not a commitment.

"If he says, 'I'm with you,' that's not a commitment.

"If he says, 'You don't have to worry about me,' that's not a commitment.

"What they have to say is, 'I will vote with you.'"

Grooming insurance agents to close a legislative sale is not hard. Equale reinforces his advice with this true story. When Tony Coelho, a master at political hardball, ran for majority whip, he asked his campaign manager the night before the election if he planned to vote for him. "For Christ's sake, I'm your campaign manager," California Democrat Vic Fazio exclaimed. "Vic, that's not an answer," Coelho replied. It was not real until he heard him say it.

Equale hands out a press packet of his clips that includes a March 29, 1988, profile and a March 18, 1990, fashion spread in *The New York Times,* both of which portray him as an ambitious insider with a flamboyant style. "There's a picture of me and a story about how I one-upped [Florida Sen.] Bob Graham on the Senate floor. And I'm the greatest thing since sliced bread. Then I went to my board meeting and got questions from guys who don't read *The New York Times.* These are the people who pay my salary, and I really need to remember when and where I came from."

The IIAA board members did not see any value in having their association's legislative tactics publicized in the elite media. It was a sobering moment that kept Equale out of the spotlight for a millisecond. He cannot help himself. He is a political junkie. He likes reporters. He thinks that what he does is a legitimate part of representative democracy. He believes, perhaps naively, that the more the public knows about what lobbyists do, the less stigma there is to being one.

"I am very aware that I am candid in the extreme," he says. "It's my style. It's who I am. It's how I am. It's how I got where I am today."

Equale's tendency to say more than he should causes him headaches. "Bullet in the heart," he groaned at a *National Journal* article on him titled "Wired." The article credited Equale with a first-rate lobbying operation even while independent agents are losing market share to insurance giants like State Farm. By Washington just-spell-my-name-right standards, it was good publicity. "I can't tell you how many people have called and said, 'What a great piece,' but they haven't read it," said Equale, who was inconsolable. "This is going to cost me—it's already cost me," he said gloomily. "I've had to talk to [Michigan Democratic Rep. John] Dingell. [New York Republican Rep.] Bill Paxon will be in my office tomorrow."

Equale had mentioned his close ties to both lawmakers, and members of Congress do not like being cited by name in an article about a lobbyist's political clout. It offends their cherished image of independence from favor seekers. Equale also had to pacify his board members over the accompanying photograph of him in a three-piece suit, which the article said cost $1,450. "What it doesn't say is that it's not my suit," he says. The photo was taken from the "Men's Fashions of the Times" spread several years earlier in which Equale was shown modeling a three-piece pin-striped suit.

The *National Journal* interview had been innocent enough. The reporter had asked Equale to explain the bipartisan way that he operates. Equale had pointed out that, unlike a lot of groups that had to "refocus" after the GOP takeover, he had had good relationships with Republicans.

"His first three paragraphs are me sitting there gobbling M&M's like some lout and bragging about my contacts," says Equale. "That's the reason lobbyists say 'no comment.' I feel like someone pulled my pants down. Like when you're robbed or mugged, you feel violated. Until it happens to you, you don't understand the feeling."

As the November 1994 election drew near, Democrats in Congress felt their world closing in on them. Predictions that the Republicans would capture the Senate, and possibly the House, had the lobbying community hedging its bets. PAC contributions were down; so were Democrats' poll numbers. During one of the spring recesses, Equale found himself on a flight to Florida with Pennsylvania Sen. Harris Wofford, a courtly academic whose upset victory in 1991 signaled the power of the health care issue.

"He's the kind of guy who knows he knows me, but he's not sure where," says Equale. "He's running for the Senate, needs the 300,000 members I have and the PAC contributions. Unlike some of these other guys, he doesn't even know enough to say to his staffer, 'Who is that over there?' He looks at me with a blank look. I'm not supporting him this time around." Wofford, too gentle and diffident for politics, lost his reelection bid to Rep. Rick Santorum, a Gingrich protégé whose macho conservatism would bolster the Gramm wing of the GOP in the Senate. Equale's organization did not support Wofford because of his role in the health care issue, a decision that was made easier by Wofford's aloof unwillingness to play the game.

Republican challengers streamed through Equale's Capitol Hill office in search of money. The heat was on the business community to back Republicans now that they were within reach of the leadership. After a decade of contributing heavily to Democratic incumbents, the PACs were on notice to change their pattern of giving.

One evening event took on the feel of a revival meeting when a business lobbyist, Barry Gottehrer of Massachusetts Mutual Life Insurance Co., stood up waving a $15,000 check and cried out, "I've been making a mistake! I've been supporting incumbents, not my business interests!" Gottehrer was speaking for many in the room who had contributed to Democrats because they were in power, not because they endorsed Democratic policies.

GOP consultant Brad O'Leary followed up with a "PAC List of Shame" that named the lobbyists and trade groups backing Democrats with their contributions. He published the list in his newsletter, *The O'Leary Report*, which circulates among lobbyists and Republican law-makers. In the newsletter, O'Leary praised Gingrich for "laying down the law with certain PAC executives who have been consorting with the enemy." The hegemony that Democrats enjoyed over PAC money had come to an end.

Two weeks before the November election, Equale got an agitated phone call from an aide to Richard Gephardt. The Democratic leader had just received a list of lobbyists who had contributed substantially to Democrats in the past but were now backing Republicans. Equale's name was at the top.

"What are you doing?" the aide implored.

"What I'm doing is representing my members' interests," Equale replied.

"We want Dick to be the next Speaker, not Minority Leader," the aide declared.

"It's my duty to keep my job before I can help anyone," Equale shot back. "This is what you get for the fun and games of the last two years."

As Equale saw it, the fund-raising arm of the Democratic Party had become totally disconnected from the policy arm. Maybe that was the way the civics textbooks said it was supposed to be, but Equale groused, "A lot of people who had given money to Democrats, myself included, had to live through a torrent of political initiatives that were deadly to the people we were raising the money from. It was difficult for me to go back to my members and say, 'They're screwing us.'"

Equale ascribed the Democrats' supercilious attitude to arrogance—"as if they were ordained by God to always be in control, and we had to keep giving them money even if they weren't working with us." Equale also knew that Tony Coelho's strategy to create a permanent Democratic majority by raising money from business PACs was an unholy alliance for some Democrats, who continued to see themselves as allies of labor, not business.

Democrats moving from the majority to the minority after the 1994 election no longer had easy access to PAC money. Special interests gave Democratic incumbents money because they were in power, not necessarily because they did their bidding. "For the most part it was a case of my good Democratic friends taking our money, smiling at us, then going off and screwing us," says Equale. In Newt's world, politics had become meaner, faster, and more deadly. Equale likened it to rollerball, a futuristic sport that combines the worst of football and hockey. If you lose, you die.

"Politics is live or die now," he said. "It's no longer just playing hardball. You don't just get respect for playing the game rough and tough. Now you have to actually impale your opponent. This year was by far the worst."

In the final weeks, Equale avoided calls from Democrats who wanted to hit him up for money. But he picked up the phone when Rep. David Bonior, third in the House Democratic leadership, came on the line.

"Dave, are you in mourning because of this baseball strike?" Equale asked breezily. He and Bonior, a baseball enthusiast, had been to many games together.

"I'll tell you, in a way, if I get reelected, maybe it's because of the strike because now I have some time on my hands at night," Bonior replied, making the segue from sports talk to money talk.

"I'm going to help you. I'll make a few calls for you," Equale said. "But I have to tell you that the climate for Democrats in my community is the worst it's ever been in my history. My members think that the Democratic Party used to wake up in the morning and phone Moscow, but now Moscow is too right-wing. Now they think the Democrats are phoning Beijing. It's disaster out there. You guys have some serious problems. I'll do everything I can to help you, David, but I think we're in for some serious shit come November."

Bonior, a dour liberal, but significantly not a liberal on abortion rights, managed to win reelection with sixty-two percent in conservative Macomb County, Michigan, against an exceptionally weak opponent. He went on to lead the Democratic effort to expose Gingrich's alleged ethics violations. That put him at the top of the hit list of Democrats targeted for defeat by the GOP in 1996.

Equale saw the 1994 debacle coming for Democrats. "When I'm talking to these people, it's not just, 'Oh, yes, congressman, of course I'd like to send you the money,'" says Equale. The power of the purse gives him leverage. Equale was privy to the Democrats' succession strategy to elevate Gephardt to Speaker should the Democrats retain control of the House and Speaker Tom Foley be defeated. In the closing weeks of the campaign, when Gephardt's office called and pleaded on behalf of this or that endangered Democrat, Equale, for the most part, responded. It was an investment in the future. Few people envisioned the Republicans winning outright control of the House.

Equale was home with his family on election night with two televisions going, phones ringing, and a fax machine humming. He had known the scope of the Democratic defeat by midafternoon; now he was tracking individual races to see who had fallen and which of the challengers he had put money on had made it.

Equale's association is "an equal opportunity giver" on Capitol Hill. "We do Republicans and Democrats, challengers and incumbents," he said, "but we don't do both sides of a race. The dumbest thing to do is give a check to each side. It's like arming both sides in a war. Nobody appreciates you because they know you're helping the other guy. If you pick the loser, then help the winner retire his campaign debt and help him in his next race. Only sometimes do I get emotionally involved, like with Dick Gephardt. But I have a good relationship with Gingrich. Professionals understand you have to do what you have to do. We should never ever fall in love with any of these people. Every one of them has a defective gene somewhere. Whether they're very conservative or liberal, I judge them as people on their credibility. Do they keep their word? That's what counts."

Many PACs guessed wrong. They scrambled after the election to get in the good graces of the new Republicans. Helping successful candidates pay off their campaign debts is known in the trade as "catching the late train." Republican fund-raisers combed the financial reports of defeated Democrats for names of corporate donors who might welcome a second chance to curry favor with Republicans. Some Republican lawmakers put heat on their corporate buddies to replace lobbyists deemed too friendly to Democrats with true-blue Republicans. Like many other Washington firms, Equale's team adjusted its lineup by giving a more prominent role to Bob Rusbuldt, a Republican Equale had hired ten years earlier.

The joke circulating among lobbyists had a worried Democrat saying to superlobbyist Thomas Hale Boggs, "Jesus, Tommy, what are we going to do? The Republicans have taken over. They control everything. All committees have new Republican chairmen. There are more than seventy new freshman Republicans in the House. What's going to happen to us?"

Boggs replies, "I don't know. I've only been a Republican for two weeks."

The day after the election, Equale got twenty calls from senior Democratic staffers hunting for jobs. Democrats raged at the White House: Bill Clinton blew their reelection. It was Hillary's fault. Health care reform was a disaster.

"We fucked you so bad you had to redirect your money," a surviving senior Democrat, Vic Fazio, told Equale, excusing the lobbyist for supporting the GOP.

Equale commiserated with the old-guard Democrats, blaming Clinton: "Vic, if you run with the President at the top of the ticket in 1996, the President will lose and you'll lose more seats. You may not get it back in your lifetime."

It was an emotional time for the newly disenfranchised Democrats. John Dingell, for decades one of the most powerful men on Capitol Hill, begged off when Equale asked him to take the lead on a bill he had championed in the last session. "I'm not the right man," Dingell demurred. "I'm going to be a big target." Equale tried to flatter Dingell into taking on the task, telling him how important his leadership is even if he is in the minority. He was astounded at Dingell's response. "He was very emotional about his role in the next Congress. These men, the bigger and tougher they are, the softer they are. For forty years they've gotten all the attention and ass-kissing; now they're insecure."

Lobbyists were too busy making new friends to mourn the loss of the Democrats. "It's wonderful to be a high-paid observer of democracy," said Equale. "When the train comes to take the dead away, we wave."

Equale moved on to the next big fight: proposed banking reform, which would have expanded the portfolio of services that banks provide. If banks could sell insurance, Equale's agents might be driven out of business. A friend in the White House tipped off Equale on the administration's proposal the day before Treasury Secretary Robert Rubin unveiled the plan publicly. The insider tip allowed Equale to position himself with the media. Three major newspapers (*The Washington Post, The Wall Street Journal,* and *The New York Times*) quoted Equale and reflected his concern that banks would gain too much concentrated power. "The day after Bobby Rubin announced, we were everywhere," said Equale.

Equale's strategy to keep banks out of insurance was to frame the issue as a heroic battle of the "little guys" against centralized power, although the little guys in this scenario were, in fact, four of the most formidable lobbies on Capitol Hill—representing small business, Realtors, senior citizens, and the independent insurers. The proposed coalition was a fine idea, except for one thing: "If you put them in the same room, they break out in hives," Equale said. Only months earlier, the National Federation of Independent Business and the American Association for Retired Persons had been enemies during the health care debate, each pursuing its narrow special interest. Equale's association contemplated a television spot modeled after the Harry and Louise ads. It would show an elderly woman approaching an ATM machine, fumbling with her glasses, barely able to follow the instructions. Then a voice would intone, "Now they want us to buy insurance out of this machine too."

It only takes a few election cycles on Capitol Hill to feel you have seen it all before. Politicians raise issues year after year that attack various special interests, which then contribute heavily through their PACs to the same politicians. There is often less a genuine desire to resolve issues than there is to use them as fund-raising vehicles for one party or another. Banking and insurance issues are perennials. Even if the legislation is worthy, the lobbies are so strong that they cancel each other out.

"I'm going to complicate this process so damn much that I'm going to make sure nothing passes," Equale vowed at the onset of the banking reform fight of 1995, knowing he would not get a bill that would satisfy his organization.

He kept his word. The legislation that emerged repealed a Depression-era law barring mergers of banks and securities firms, but it left untouched the federal prohibition against banks selling insurance. In an interview published in the September 18, 1995, edition of *Fortune* magazine, Gingrich candidly explained why he had backed Equale's insurance agents over the bankers: "In a typical town, there is one bank president and 130 independent insurance agents. I do not believe you can ask your freshman congressmen to vote against independent insurance agents and hope to survive. It's that simple."

Equale could not have put it better himself.

CHAPTER THREE

THE CHAIRMAN

The Last Man Standing

The C-SPAN camera focused on Sen. Daniel Patrick Moynihan of New York, catching his mumbled "Yes." In the same frame, the camera caught the look of disbelief on the face of the aide standing immediately behind him. The aide leaned forward and gently asked Moynihan if he had meant to vote the way he did.

"That's right," Moynihan snapped back, clearly irritated.

Never before had a mere aide questioned his vote. A Roman Catholic, yet a staunch supporter of a woman's right to choose an abortion, Moynihan had just aligned himself with the anti-abortion bloc on the Senate Finance Committee.

Had Cardinal O'Connor of New York gotten to him? The Cardinal was threatening to shut down Catholic hospitals if the Clinton health plan covered abortion services. Had Moynihan undergone a conversion? Or was he simply being perverse and once again sticking it to the President?

None of the above.

As chairman of the Senate Finance Committee, Moynihan was doing what chairmen do: searching for a compromise that could get a majority of votes in committee and allow health care reform to move onto the floor of the Senate. A contentious debate over abortion could halt the entire process.

"Abortion awaits us," he had warned President Clinton in an Oval Office meeting just weeks earlier.

Pro-choice groups assailed Moynihan for seeming to abandon his commitment. But Moynihan was not listening to them. He was playing to an audience of one man: Missouri Sen. John Danforth, a moderate

Republican and an Episcopal priest, whose vote he needed, and who opposed abortion.

Danforth had developed a "conscience clause" that would allow employers to forgo coverage for abortion services. The Danforth amendment was so broadly written that opponents feared some employers would use it to refuse coverage for employees with AIDS. That concern would have to wait. Moynihan had one goal, and that was to keep Danforth's support for health care reform. Without Danforth and a handful of other moderate Republicans, Clinton's attempt to overhaul the health system was doomed.

Abortion advocates and antagonists were mobilized. Lawrence O'Donnell, Jr., staff director for the Senate Finance Committee and Moynihan's closest adviser, had invited representatives from both sides to his office to explain their positions. Neither side was in a mood to compromise.

During one of these sessions, O'Donnell found himself wondering why a procedure like abortion should be covered by insurance anyway. His prescription eyeglasses, he reasoned, cost about as much as an abortion. Women who wear glasses will need many more pairs than they would ever have abortions, yet no one had come to him demanding that glasses be covered under the health care plan.

For most women who have an abortion, it is a one-time expense. So why should the decision to include or not to include abortion coverage be allowed to derail an attempt to extend health benefits to millions of people?

O'Donnell stifled a smile in deference to the earnest pro-choice woman making her case on the other side of the desk. She might not appreciate his prescription glasses analogy. But he knew the idea would appeal to Moynihan.

Did he raise it with the senator?

"Shit no," said O'Donnell. "He would have been so captivated he'd have gone out and said it, and been killed politically."

Moynihan did what he had to politically. He voted with Danforth and against his own conscience to advance the overall goal of health care reform. That is the essence of compromise, to give up something in order to achieve a greater good. Finessing the abortion issue in committee turned out to be a wasted gesture on Moynihan's part. Before abortion could become a deciding issue in health care reform, the bill drafted by the White House was withdrawn by the Democratic leadership, a casualty of internal Democratic divisions as much as Republican opposition.

Washington is a city of titles and few outrank "The Chairman." In the House or the Senate, the reward for outmaneuvering or simply outlasting one's rivals is a committee chairmanship. In the hierarchy of committees, few are the equal of Senate Finance, which has the power of the purse and through which all major social reform involving taxation must proceed. When it comes to ideas and historical grasp, Moynihan has no peers in public life. But could he lead? Translating the activist promises of Bill Clinton and Hillary Rodham Clinton into successful legislation would require skillful leadership. That was the challenge Moynihan faced when he ascended to chairman.

Moynihan's chairmanship coincided with—or, more accurately, collided with—the Clintons' push for universal health care. Moynihan was skeptical of the government's ability to engineer the needed reforms. The White House tried to engage him, but he kept a disrespectful distance. When Mrs. Clinton asked Moynihan why he did not regularly send a staffer to White House meetings on health care, he replied that he was too busy with the budget. "Just keep us briefed," he said breezily. In fact, he and his staff had concluded the meetings were a waste of time.

Publicly, Moynihan kept up a thin veil of support. Privately, he regaled visitors to his office by holding the 1,342-page Clinton plan aloft and, with great dramatic effect, dropping it with a loud thud.

"You could murder someone with this," he declared with his famous puckish grin.

Moynihan has the advantage of always being the most intimidating person in a room. His aura of superiority puts others on the defensive, a mismatch he seems to relish. From the President down, no one at the White House knew how to handle Moynihan, if, indeed, anyone could. "Every time we had a meeting, it would disintegrate into a how-do-you-please-Moynihan meeting," recalls a top White House aide. "How do you kiss his ass? He was so changeable in his views that every time we solved one problem, there would be another impediment."

At bottom, Moynihan did not believe the Clinton health plan was workable, politically or substantively. That was evident in his body language. He stopped just short of rolling his eyes at the President's earnest entreaties. Moynihan may have seemed mercurial to the White House, but he was unshakable in his view that for any plan to pass, it would require sixty votes, enough to overcome a likely Republican-led filibuster. And attracting sixty votes would require substantial compromise, a presumption that the White House refused to accept.

It did not take much for the suspicion to take hold among the President's aides that Moynihan's response reflected deep animus towards Clinton. O'Donnell thought that was ridiculous. He took to calling the White House staff "the children."

It is true that Clinton and his boy army have never understood Moyni-han. And Moynihan, with his sense of history, could not conceal his dis-dain for Clinton's impetuous nature and his ragged way of doing business. At a deeper level, Moynihan's cranky behavior during the year-long health care debate went to the core of his suspicion about government.

He is an incrementalist. He does not believe that huge social over-haul should be forced through Congress by one vote. He told Clinton from the start that he should move slowly, and put together a bill that could win seventy votes in the Senate, a fitting majority for such his-toric legistation. That was like telling Hillary Rodham Clinton that she should go back to the kitchen and bake cookies. Mrs. Clinton, who headed her husband's reform effort, regarded incrementalism as a moral failing. She had a mission, and that was bold change. In her view, any legislation so watered-down that it could attract seventy votes was not worth having.

Clinton's young aides did not appreciate Moynihan as the great char-acter he is. They thought his excessive politeness was mannered and phony. The Senate Finance Committee was not *Masterpiece Theater.* The aides spent many hours debating how to deal with him, and how to go around him.

"What is the reasonable half-life of a favor?" a senior aide exploded after watching Moynihan on television in early January 1994 agree with Republican Sen. Bob Dole that health care was "not a crisis." Clinton had attended a fund-raising dinner in New York for Moynihan the previ-ous October and lavished him with praise, saying he belonged in "the public service hall of fame." To further ingratiate himself, the President stayed to have his picture taken with each of Moynihan's big givers. "And he's back on the Sunday talk shows kicking the guy with imperfectly dis-guised disdain," said the aide. "Where is the other side of the coin?"

Moynihan's eccentricities are excused by many because of his over-riding intelligence and the image he has crafted as a public servant, unswayed by money or power. Health care was one of the few issues that Moynihan knew little about, and he did not want to learn. A better atti-tude on his part might not have changed the ultimate outcome for Clin-ton's reform effort, but Moynihan's dilatory approach contributed to the disarray.

"When the history of this two-year horror is written, much of the trail of responsibility will lead to the Senate Finance Committee," said a Democratic senator, who asked to remain anonymous since he continues to work with Moynihan.

As chairman, Moynihan was more professor than power broker. He conducted business in the Socratic way, questioning rather than lecturing. He waited for consensus to emerge, and it never did. Democrats on the Finance Committee were angry over the way Moynihan handled his job. Some privately accused him of "appeasing" the Republicans in the lengths he went to court their votes. In the end, Moynihan could not save the Democrats from the divisions among themselves, which were equally responsible for defeating Clinton's reform efforts.

The critical question is whether Moynihan acted responsibly out of his knowledge of political reality in the Senate or whether he knowingly sabotaged the Clintons' efforts out of his own perversity. Even the White House was not sure. Asked midway through the process whether Moynihan was doing "a brilliant job" in cultivating potential Republican votes or "blowing it," a genuinely puzzled senior Clinton adviser shrugged, "Which is it?"

The Senate Finance Committee drafts legislation on taxing and spending, two of Congress's most critical functions. The majority party has a narrow edge with eleven members to the minority party's nine. A single defection creates gridlock, effectively handing each member of the ruling party a veto. The committee is dominated by senators from rural states and from states with industries, like oil producers, accustomed to special tax breaks. As a group, they do not naturally flock to solve social problems associated with cities. The committee has traditionally been a haven for moneyed interests looking for tax breaks, a bias that the White House refused to fully grasp.

The Clintons had an optimism about health care that took the place of a strategy. Who would dare oppose universal coverage? They felt that what they were doing was so noble and good that it would succeed on blind faith alone. Moynihan had none of their zeal. When it came to health care, he was an agnostic. "What we can get legislated is what we're for," O'Donnell said.

The era of iron-fisted chairmen is over. The post-Watergate class of reformers elected to Congress on pledges to clean up government demanded that chairmen exercise power more democratically or risk mutiny. Some of the old guard were still around when Moynihan arrived at the Senate in 1977. Louisiana Democrat Russell Long, son of the fiery populist Huey Long, exacted loyalty on the Finance Committee through intimidation and fear. The results did not always please President Jimmy Carter, who was often at odds with his fellow Democrat. "I never know what he's going to do—except screw me most of the time," Carter once said.

Long made it clear that if a member wanted anything for his state, he better vote with the chairman on the big votes. Moynihan set aside whatever impulses he may have had to challenge Long and was a loyal member of the committee. Not coincidentally, the benefits flowed to New York.

When Moynihan became chairman, he did not follow the Long model. He recognized that times had changed, and that there were fewer federal goodies to trade away for votes. Even if he wanted to, he could not persuade members with promises of pork. He tried to guide the committee through the force of intellect and ideas and have it function through accommodation and compromise. Long had lots of eleven-to-nine, party-line votes. Moynihan wanted twenty-to-nothing votes if he could get them. The White House wanted Moynihan to be like Russell Long and ram the health care bill through the committee.

Moynihan's immediate predecessor, Lloyd Bentsen, might have been more temperamentally suited to the task. A Texas patrician, Bentsen maintained an outward gentility, but he ran the Finance Committee with the discipline of a drill sergeant. Hearings began at 9:00, not 9:01. Witnesses were given a prescribed number of minutes to testify, and each member had an allotted time to speak. Bentsen would read his opening statement and then ask the questions that his staff had prepared for him. The questions were printed in large type in the briefing book before him, and Bentsen would ask them word for word. There was rarely anything a witness said in response to, say, question number 2 that would in any way change the next question or prompt a question 2a or 2b.

The regimentation enhanced Bentsen's control. Louisiana Democrat John Breaux had already served fourteen years in the Congress when he was elected to the Senate and joined the Finance Committee. "It was like walking into federal court for the first time to try a case," he said. "It was intimidating—and I loved the guy." Bentsen was an autocrat, but he was popular. Members liked knowing exactly what to expect.

On December 10, 1992, President-elect Clinton named Bentsen his Secretary of the Treasury. Many analysts came to believe that the appointment was the first mistake Clinton made in pushing his reform agenda. As chairman of the Senate Finance Committee, Bentsen would likely have been a trusted ally of the administration. But this revisionist view overlooks the fact that Bentsen, from his perch at Treasury, was among the harshest critics of the Clinton plan, and would likely have incurred the White House's wrath just as Moynihan did by urging compromise. Nevertheless, when Bentsen went to the Cabinet, the fickle Moynihan, as the next-longest-serving Democrat on the Finance Committee, ascended to the crucial chairmanship.

Moynihan likes to be courted and made to feel important. Yet after he became chairman, it took four phone calls to Little Rock before the President-elect got back to him. Staff appointments that Moynihan pushed for were not made. Then shortly after Clinton took office, *Time* magazine quoted an administration official saying of Moynihan that the White House was ready to "roll right over him if we have to."

Upon reading the remark, Moynihan was livid. Clinton had to personally apologize for the ill-considered words of an anonymous staffer. At the same time, Clinton was embroiled in an uproar over his nomination of Zoe Baird to be Attorney General and her failure to pay Social Security taxes for an illegal alien nanny. The young Clinton presidency showed a lack of discipline that Moynihan found appalling. Some of it was generational. Clinton's informal style seemed to Moynihan to indicate a lack of respect, not only for himself as Congress's reigning intellectual but for the presidency, an office that Moynihan revered.

Soon after his inauguration, on January 25, 1993, President Clinton announced that his wife would head the administration's health care reform efforts and that she and her team would have legislation ready to introduce in Congress by the end of April. Mrs. Clinton and Ira Magaziner, the brilliant but politically challenged staff director of the project, worked feverishly, discussing ideas with hundreds of academics and health care experts. They fell months behind schedule.

Moynihan watched the elaborate process first with bemusement, then with irritation. Normally, congressional committees write legislation with broad guidance from the administration, and with an understanding of what can pass. Hillary and Ira were producing a monster, and how he handled it would determine his standing as a chairman and as a loyal Democrat. He thought the debate should be less about loyalty and more about truth in advertising. And with that in mind, he dropped the first of many bombshells on a Sunday morning, September 19, 1993. Appearing on NBC's *Meet the Press*, he remarked almost casually that the numbers underlying the Clinton health plan were "fantasy, but accurate fantasy." What he meant was you could make the numbers add up on a computer but paying for the broad reform the Clintons called for, and still reducing the deficit, as the plan promised, was not achievable in the real world.

Moynihan did not think his analysis was unique or particularly insightful, and so he did not consider its impact. Like the little boy at the parade in "The Emperor's New Clothes," he merely remarked upon what he saw, oblivious that others would be shocked by his observation.

The withering aside shattered the buoyant mood at the White House.

All week, aides had been persuading academics and economists that the plan was credible. "I thought we had beaten this down," a senior White House aide recalls. "And then BOOM! Moynihan comes out and destroys the whole thing. That was devastating to us, absolutely devastating. We never recovered." What the White House found especially galling was that Moynihan had delivered his broadside without warning. "No one from his staff ever came to us and went through the numbers," says the senior aide. "No one asked us a question. Every other committee did."

Moynihan made his assessment based on a rough draft that was believed to have been leaked by Democratic Rep. Pete Stark of California, head of a House subcommittee on health and a critic of the Clinton approach. The book-length draft of the health plan went on to become a *New York Times* best-seller, but a legislative flop.

Moynihan is an unscripted politician. He did not enter the NBC studio on Nebraska Avenue that Sunday morning with a "fantasy" sound bite in mind. He was asked a question about whether the savings that the Clinton plan projected were realistic. He simply said what he thought.

"I tell him afterward that at the White House they're crying their eyes out about it," says Lawrence O'Donnell. "It's the biggest, most serious blow that this bill has suffered, and they've never had a day like this. They can't believe it happened. And he says to me, 'Well, what would they like me to do, just sit there and look like a fool?' You see, he believes that everybody out there watching the show knows it's fantasy, so if he tries to say anything else he looks absurd."

Moynihan was vindicated months later when a Congressional Budget Office analysis confirmed that the Clinton plan had substantially overstated the amount of deficit reduction that could be achieved through health care reform.

Any study of Moynihan as chairman has to assess honesty as a technique. Is there room for it in public affairs? The accepted forms of leadership are arm-twisting, giving away pork, and accumulating IOUs. Michael Kinsley, the writer and commentator, once wrote that a gaffe in Washington is when a politician inadvertently tells the truth.

On the wall of the spacious office he occupied in Moynihan's cluster of rooms in the Dirksen Senate Office Building, O'Donnell hung a poster depicting the Clinton health care reform plan. Drawn in Rube Goldberg style, the poster showed a bureaucratic maze of dozens of boxes marked with the names of programs, sub-programs, and sub-sub-programs connected by lines that converge and cross like the train tracks at Grand Central Station. The mock flowchart is signed by Senate Majority Leader Bob Dole, who used it to illustrate his televised response to President Clinton after Clinton's address on health care to Congress and the nation. Dole's top aide, Sheila Burke, presented it to O'Donnell as a gesture of friendly combativeness.

O'Donnell's wall hanging was a statement of independence. Like Moynihan, O'Donnell's attitude toward the White House ranged from hostility to condescension, despite the fact that a Democratic administration was in power. In turn, O'Donnell, no less than Moynihan, was distrusted and disliked by the Clinton White House.

Ira Magaziner, who headed the White House Task Force on National Health Care Reform with Hillary Clinton, had put in two all-nighters to get the draft health care plan ready, and he took any attack on the integrity of the numbers personally. A terminally serious individual, Magaziner had more than the usual difficulty adjusting to Moynihan's eccentricities. This time, he thought to himself, "When in Rome. . . ." If he could not persuade Moynihan through ordinary means, he would resort to the extraordinary.

Moynihan was fond of citing "Baumol's disease" as the intellectual rationale for his skepticism about health care reform. The theory, developed by economics professor William J. Baumol, states that in certain fields, particularly the performing arts, productivity cannot be increased because the human input cannot be mass-produced.

"It takes as long today to play a Mozart quartet as it did two hundred years ago," Moynihan would declare with a flourish. "You cannot play the Minute Waltz in under a minute. . . ." Pause for effect. "Therefore, you cannot make these savings in the health industry."

Magaziner knew that in order to convince Moynihan, he would first have to convince Baumol. He corresponded with Baumol, who is on the faculty at New York University. He understood the professor's intellectual argument. Service industries, such as health care, cannot be forced into the same productivity as manufacturing. Magaziner explained that he was proposing some one-time changes to make the system more efficient. He did not think he was being disingenuous.

Mozart could not be speeded up, Magaziner agreed. "But what if your Mozart quartet has to stop after the first five bars to make a phone call to an 800 number to play the next two bars, and then stop again four bars later to fill out five forms?"

Baumol and Moynihan were old friends, and Moynihan relied on his judgment. They had known each other for more than four decades, since they were students together at the London School of Economics. The White House welcomed Baumol's involvement as a bridge to the otherwise unreachable Moynihan. Like the Henry Kissinger of health care, the professor shuttled between the White House and Moynihan's Senate office to broker the changes that would secure Moynihan's grudging support.

The White House did what it could to win over Baumol. Hillary Clinton phoned the professor several times. He sent her materials to read, which she would recite back to him in subsequent conversations. "She was not going about it in any superficial manner," Baumol said. "She was hoping to get the senator to give unqualified support to the bill as it was drafted. And we were hoping to persuade her to take a more measured position on the cost estimates. I thought, perhaps naively, that with more plausible numbers the plan would fare better."

The Clintons' contention that they could expand health coverage without incurring substantial new costs was improbable on its face. Baumol tried in his courtly way to get beyond the antagonism that had developed between the two camps. At one meeting in Moynihan's office, he referred to an old *New Yorker* cartoon in which an architect is meeting with two clients. The caption says, "You realize this is only an estimate. Of course, the actual cost will be higher."

"I don't think I'm telling tales out of school to say the senator broke up, and Mr. Magaziner looked rather glum," Baumol recalls.

President Clinton won praise from Congress and the country when he outlined his plan before a joint meeting of Congress. But it would be several more weeks before the White House would send legislation to Capitol Hill. Moynihan opened hearings before he actually had the Clinton bill. Health and Human Services Secretary Donna Shalala was the first to feel his scorn. Shalala, testifying before Moynihan's committee, observed that "a few people" would pay more under the Clinton system.

"Oh really, how few?" Moynihan asked.

"Forty percent," Shalala said.

"Forty percent!" Moynihan sputtered. He had not heard that before. Neither had the rest of America. Shalala's remarks reverberated across the country on that evening's network news shows. She was not prepared, and felt Moynihan had trapped her. Indeed, the White House calculations were still being disputed internally. Treasury Secretary Lloyd Bentsen had refused to testify before Congress because he felt he could not convincingly defend the numbers. The White House tried to explain that the forty-percent figure was misleading, that the actual percentage of those who would pay more was lower and that some people who paid more would receive better coverage. The correction, lame as it was, could not undo the damage.

"Professor Moynihan is having a good first term," a top White House aide wisecracked, his sarcastic tone conveying the unspoken addendum: "at the President's expense."

The White House continued to adjust its numbers in an effort to placate Moynihan, knowing that failure to win his approval would insure defeat. The bill was finally delivered to Congress on November 20, 1993. The day before, Hillary Clinton and Shalala went to Capitol Hill to privately brief Moynihan. He issued a statement saying the new figures were "more realistic" and announced that he would sign on as a co-sponsor of the Clinton bill.

Hillary Rodham Clinton tried to connect with Moynihan through his wife. The week after the inauguration, she invited Elizabeth (Liz) Moynihan to lunch at the White House. Here was a political wife with whom she could identify. Mrs. Moynihan runs her husband's campaigns and happily acknowledges that she is the political arm of the Moynihan operation. "I am it," she says. "He hasn't made a call to raise money since 1987." Mrs. Clinton had just been named health care czar, the first "real job" ever undertaken by the spouse of a president.

"There are not too many political partnerships of the kind we enjoy with our husbands," the First Lady mused over lunch, likening her new title to the political influence that Liz Moynihan so elegantly wields.

The two women had a pleasant time together, but Mrs. Moynihan would later remark to friends, "No one ever called me a co-senator." It was her way of differentiating her reserved style from Hillary Clinton's public image as co-President. Mrs. Moynihan rarely grants interviews. She believes a political wife, even a powerful political wife, should work in the shadow of her husband.

Liz Moynihan is an architectural historian. Her heart is in sixteenth-century Central Asia. She handles the day-to-day politics for the same reason she runs the household—her husband isn't very good at it.

The First Lady was on the telephone to Liz Moynihan regularly, trying to use her as an intermediary. Treasury Secretary Lloyd Bentsen, a contemporary and a former Senate colleague, was dispatched to talk to Moynihan. "We tried everything," said an exasperated White House aide. Moynihan was unfailingly cordial with Clinton, but it was clear that he felt there was no one of sufficient stature for him to deal with in the White House—"not even the President," said the aide. Still, there was a conviction in the White House long past the time it was warranted that Clinton would get a health care bill, maybe not in the time frame that he wanted, but at least a commitment to put universal coverage in place over a number of years.

No one confronted Moynihan about the way he was behaving and the corrosive effect it was having on Clinton's standing in Washington among the intelligentsia. "When you have people who are loose cannons in positions of power, it's difficult to tell them to go to hell because you need them," a senior White House official said. Another top aide called Moynihan's insistent undermining of the Clinton health care plan "pathologically destructive."

For his part, Moynihan felt the Clintons were operating in a dream-world. He knew what his committee would accept and what it would not. In addition to the overall cost of the plan, members were rebelling against the Clintons' insistence that employers pick up the bulk of costs for employees. In the real world, a president and his first lady would have quit talking about an employer mandate months earlier, Moynihan knew. The business lobbies had too many senators in a choke hold for employer mandates, in effect a tax on business, to be a real option.

Joseph Califano, Lyndon Johnson's domestic policy adviser, told O'Donnell that LBJ demanded to know how every senator and representative was going to vote—in committee and on the floor—before he allowed a bill to be sent to the Hill. Johnson could tolerate a certain margin of error on the floor votes, but not in the committee.

"There are only twenty people on that committee, you know, and we own thirteen of them," Johnson would remind his head-counters.

January 1994 was a turning point for health care reform. Clinton's moral authority was being eroded by questions surrounding the Whitewater episode, and there were fresh allegations in a conservative magazine from two Arkansas state troopers about his much-rumored womanizing while governor. Moynihan, appearing on one of the Sunday talk shows, was asked whether he thought a special counsel should be named to investigate the Clintons' Whitewater investment. "Yep," he said. Other Democrats quickly followed suit. While the appointment of an independent counsel was probably inevitable, having the call come from Moynihan further strained his relationship with the White House.

During this period, Senate Minority Leader Bob Dole ventured the opinion that health care was "not a crisis." Democrats seized on the remark as a major blunder, an interpretation that was backed up by polling data. The public took it to mean the Republicans would do nothing to address the health care problem, which reinforced the perception that the party did not care about ordinary people. The Democratic National Committee quickly produced a television ad showing several Republicans echoing Dole's sentiments.

Then Moynihan spoke out, and not only endorsed the Republican view, but challenged the White House to confront the real crisis in America: the welfare system. "Everybody on welfare is in crisis; that is how you get there," Moynihan said. "You are in crisis when you are on it, and probably some time after that." He called for a welfare reform bill by spring and suggested he might hold health care hostage if the Clintons did not respond to his demand. Moynihan said that the President, by talking about welfare reform without offering a legislative remedy, was merely using the issue as "boob bait for bubbas."

How did Moynihan come to challenge his party's president this time?

Republican strategist William Kristol, the first to venture openly that health care is not a crisis, took credit for Moynihan's outburst. The son of neoconservative thinker Irving Kristol, a Moynihan buddy, William Kristol had been one of Moynihan's teaching assistants at Harvard. He had emerged from four years in the White House as Vice President Dan Quayle's chief of staff to establish himself as one of the GOP's leading thinkers. A week earlier, Kristol had bumped into Moynihan in the lobby of the Carlyle Hotel in New York City, where the Moynihans stay when they are in Manhattan. Kristol says that Moynihan volunteered his agreement on the "no crisis" issue.

"Of course, you're right," the senator said upon seeing his former protégé.

"Why don't you say that publicly?" Kristol ventured.

The next Sunday, Moynihan told the nation that the Clinton White House was addressing a phony crisis, not the real one.

O'Donnell tells a slightly different version of the story, having debriefed Moynihan. He questions, for example, whether Moynihan was as definitive in his agreement as Kristol remembers. But O'Donnell was nervous enough about where it all might lead that he turned down a request from Kristol to meet with Moynihan to discuss health care.

Several weeks later, Moynihan and other congressional leaders met with the First Lady at the White House. Moynihan spoke gently and indirectly, yet his message was unmistakable: "I told you so."

"The worst, the most corrupting of lies are problems poorly stated," Moynihan said, quoting Georges Bernanos, a French essayist. He commended Mrs. Clinton for the "exquisite" job she had done in stating the problem of the uninsured. Then he read aloud from a press clipping quoting the First Lady on how the United States has the best health care in the world. The frozen smiles around the table indulged Moynihan in his need to once again demonstrate he was right.

When her turn came, Hillary Clinton retreated from talk of a health care crisis. As if following a script written by Moynihan himself, she declared that American medicine was in the midst of a heroic age. The real crisis is not in health care, she said, but in insurance coverage.

Analyzing the exchange later, O'Donnell mused, "You'd better be very, very precise if you're giving him the words of the day. You can't wire him that way. And you can't tell him what language means."

Moynihan believed that bipartisan support would be essential to pass as sweeping a measure as health care reform, but the Clintons did not trust Republicans or believe them essential to success. The Clintons counted on the power of moral hubris to prevail over partisan politics.

Early in 1994, Ira Magaziner drafted a memo titled "The Ultimate Congressional End Game—Or Is There Life After Dole?" His conclusion was a tentative maybe.

Dole commanded enormous loyalty among Republicans in the Senate. "Republican senators do not operate on their own," Magaziner's memo warned. He said Nancy Kassebaum, a fellow Kansas Republican, would stick with Dole. So would Bob Packwood, who faced ethics charges and would not want to offend the Republican leader. "The others might break with him, but it will be a wrenching decision which might occur only if Dole quietly assures them of no sanctions," the memo said.

Magaziner envisioned three scenarios, none of which materialized. The first scenario proposed a meeting with Dole in February "to sound him out. If by May we're not talking seriously, move to Scenario Two or Three."

The second scenario had the White House splitting off enough Republicans to combine with most of the fifty-six Democrats to gain the necessary sixty votes to head off a GOP-led filibuster. Magaziner rated this option "a good alternative, but not a likely one."

The final fallback position anticipated losing moderate Republicans like Packwood and Kassebaum, but assumed, naively, that Democrats could pass a bill in the House and move forward with fifty to fifty-five votes in the Senate. Let the Republicans filibuster. The assumption shared by Hillary Clinton and other White House strategists was that the GOP could not sustain a filibuster for very long on such a popular measure.

Magaziner's memo epitomized the flaws in the White House strategy. Heavy on assumptions and light on tactics, it relied in the end on Clinton, "the comeback kid," somehow pulling out a victory against all odds. The optimism about Clinton's resilience suggested an ivory-tower isolation from realpolitik. And the willingness to gamble and lose a singular moment for health care reform because of such misplaced confidence revealed an arrogance Magaziner and the others did not even know they had, much as fish do not know they are wet.

*   *   *

In the late spring of 1994, Clinton's second year in office, Liz Moynihan invited Hillary Clinton to lunch. Health care reform was tottering. Liz thought a nice lunch and conversation with her husband and Professor Baumol would give Hillary the right perspective on the real cost of reforming one-seventh of the country's economy. In addition to being brilliant, Baumol was sweet and gentle, "a die-hard old liberal," Liz said.

Lunch for four was set at the Moynihans' eleventh-floor apartment on Pennsylvania Avenue. Liz's bold sense of color and design sets off the space, chosen for its spectacular view of the Capitol dome. A life-size sculpture of a butler stands in the foyer, a gift from their artist son, Tim, and a whimsical reminder of the period when Moynihan, as U.S. ambassador to India from 1973 to 1975, had real servants.

While the building was still under construction, Liz went up in a hard hat with the workmen to select the best apartment. Having settled on their dream location, the Moynihans promptly sold their Capitol Hill home. Told their apartment was months away from completion, Moynihan protested that he would be homeless. The contractor relented and the Moynihans moved into the model apartment. When potential buyers came around, they were shown the Moynihans' living quarters.

Liz knows what she wants. She can be as direct as her husband is oblique. Any power directory of Washington has Liz's phone number. She is much easier to deal with than her husband. On this spring day, she had an agenda. She wanted to gently introduce Hillary to reality. Baumol was the one to do it. He admired Mrs. Clinton, and he supported her husband's goals.

"I am so pleased you are in the White House," he told the First Lady. He had found her an eager student in their earlier telephone conversations, and he was happy to finally meet her. Of course, he still had reservations about what she was doing, and he was not reluctant to share them. Baumol warned Mrs. Clinton that if she did not present the economics of the plan correctly, it would not be accepted.

Liz Moynihan concurred. "If you don't get this straight, they're going to hang this on you," she warned.

Hillary smiled. She was gracious. And she revealed nothing about what she was thinking.

"She was the apogee of discretion," said Baumol, who respected the First Lady's steely resolve. She was as impenetrable as a prisoner of war reciting name, rank, and serial number, and nothing more.

"I admired the fact that she did not react, nor did I expect her to disagree violently or say she discovered the beauty of my argument," said the bemused professor.

Liz found Hillary's attitude frustrating, but not unexpected. The Clintons, she had discovered, simply do not hear what they do not want to hear. They filter out even constructive criticism from friends. "They think you're being hostile," Liz said.

That perceived hostility is an undercurrent in the Moynihan-Clinton relationship. Moynihan felt compelled to point out over lunch that when Richard Nixon was President, there was a health care bill *and* a welfare bill. As Nixon's urban affairs adviser, Moynihan had participated in their development. Did he intend an unspoken jab at Clinton for stalling on welfare reform?

"As a matter of fact," Mrs. Clinton smiled sweetly, "Mr. Nixon was just at the White House. He met me outside the Oval Office and said, 'Mrs. Clinton, if I had had my way, you wouldn't be working on health care today.'" A return jab perhaps? The health care bill that Moynihan helped fashion a generation earlier had been blocked on the Hill by congressional Democrats.

Although health care reform remained alive on a political life support system well into September, its obituary had been written by Memorial Day. Liz was at the Moynihans' farm in upstate New York when she took a call from George Stephanopoulos.

"What do you think is happening?" Stephanopoulos asked in his earnest choirboy manner.

"If you mean on health care," Liz responded, coyly, "you know more than I do."

Stephanopoulos knew that Liz was the key to her husband and her husband was the key to health care reform legislation in the Senate. Moynihan had not yet moved a bill through his committee.

"In general, what do you think?" Stephanopoulos pressed.

"You mean the politics?" Liz replied, as though she only now realized what he was getting at. "I don't think you're going to get a bill."

As Liz Moynihan recalled it later, Stephanopoulos giggled.

"He thought it was very amusing," she said. "He wanted to know why I would say that. I told him, 'Because it's not bipartisan, and you won't have time to pass anything.' He giggled again."

Maybe it was the nervous laugh that got to her. All the hurt and anger came tumbling out.

"Last February, when Pat told the President it had to be bipartisan, you thought it meant he was against you," she lashed out at the young aide.

"When people told you what you wanted to hear, that you could get a bill with all Democrats, you listened to them. It's never going to happen, and what's more," she said, almost triumphantly, "Pat felt it shouldn't happen."

On June 14, 1994, a little before nine o'clock on a steamy morning, Moynihan's dark blue Jeep Cherokee rolled up to the White House. Moynihan was dapper in a beige suit and colorful bow tie. He had come to deliver some bad news to the President: There were only six Democratic votes in the Senate Finance Committee for the employer mandate, which was the heart of the Clinton plan.

Moynihan was accompanied by Sen. Bob Packwood, then the ranking Republican on the committee, who arrived in a light blue van with Oregon plates. Packwood was an authority on health care. Twenty years earlier, he had introduced Nixon's plan, which contained an employer mandate and a guaranteed benefit package, features attacked as too radical in the Clinton plan. Some of the language in the Clinton bill had, in fact, been lifted, word for word, from the Nixon plan. White House aides thought, foolishly it turned out, that borrowing from the former Republican president would insulate them from the charge they had produced a liberal, big-government plan.

Clinton stepped out from behind his desk to sit closer to his guests in the Oval Office. Moynihan took the seat closest to the President. Vice President Al Gore, Treasury Secretary Lloyd Bentsen, and other top aides filled two couches. Another layer of aides and hangers-on occupied the outer ring in what O'Donnell mockingly referred to as the "geek chairs." This is where he and other staffers sat prepared to furnish information if needed, and to take notes.

After the initial pleasantries, Moynihan invited Packwood to speak. At the time, Packwood was the butt of jokes on late-night television for making inappropriate sexual advances to more than two dozen women. But in the Oval Office, he commanded respect.

"You can't sit on a barstool and talk to people out there about what's going on in the country and not know there's a passion against employer mandates," Packwood told the President. "People think it will add a dollar an hour to the minimum wage."

"That's not true," Clinton protested.

"It doesn't matter if it's true," Packwood continued. "Restaurateurs, large and small, think it's true. We do not have the votes . . . and I say that as someone who supports mandates. I think you have to back off."

The discussion turned to "hard" and "soft" triggers," Washington euphemisms for postponing tough choices. Clinton favored the certainty of a hard trigger. In this case, if the reform plan did not generate the expected savings, price controls would be automatically triggered. A soft trigger created more maneuvering room before imposing price controls.

Moynihan interrupted to correct the terminology. He pointed out that, with guns, it is the soft trigger that fires easily.

"There was a little lag in getting it, and then the President really laughed," O'Donnell observed later, as he dictated an account of the meeting to his assistant. "It's not clear Gore ever got it," he added wickedly, a shot at Gore's earnest, Boy Scoutish demeanor. The oblique sexual reference may have passed others by as well.

Packwood cited a study showing that more than ninety percent of the country could be covered without imposing an employer mandate. It would cost $300 billion.

"I don't know where in hell we're going to get $300 billion," said Clinton, impatiently. He urged his Capitol Hill visitors to "outline the things we agree on." First, there is no majority on the Finance Committee for any plan; second, there is no majority on the Senate floor for any plan; third, twenty-three Republicans and more than fifty Democrats are on record saying every American ought to be covered.

"And number four," Gore interjected. "If there's some way to duck this decision, they will." Gore's comment had an angry edge to it.

"I still think we should try to pass something this year," Clinton said. "I want intense consultation with minimum rhetoric on all sides, including the White House."

"Do you feel we've let you down?" Moynihan asked Clinton. "Do you feel we're going too slowly?"

If Clinton felt any animosity toward Moynihan for his handling of the health care reform bill, he did not take Moynihan's invitation to show it. Instead, he furnished Moynihan with an alibi. "You've got a more conservative committee," the President said.

"More representative," Moynihan corrected. Clearly, the White House was seeing bogeymen where none existed. If anything, the membership of the Finance Committee was more moderate than the Senate as a whole.

"Could Social Security pass?" Vice President Gore asked sarcastically. It was a charged question, designed to make the President's point that conservatives were blocking progress.

"You could pass anything in 1935," Moynihan replied.

Clinton was uncharacteristically quiet while Gore noisily pushed for a more confrontational posture with Congress. Gore called Congress's failure to pass universal health care "a national embarrassment."

"Maybe the Senate Finance Committee should say, 'We've busted our pick on this,' and give up, and have health care taken up on the Senate floor," Gore said.

Back at his office on Capitol Hill, O'Donnell flipped through his notes to compose an account of the meeting for Moynihan to look over later, and to have in his files. Staffers routinely do this for their bosses, and O'Donnell always reconstructed as much of the dialogue as he could in order to provide an accurate play-by-play report. He then would dictate an additional and more colorful memo that was embellished with little asides only he would appreciate. The Vice President was a favorite target. "Gore at every turn makes speeches, doesn't try to talk to senators," O'Donnell noted. "It's as if C-SPAN's in the room when Gore talks."

White House reporters waited outside to question Moynihan and Packwood about the meeting. Gore suggested that before the senators confronted the media, "We should agree on how we're going to characterize the meeting." After a few minutes, they settled on "a good, candid discussion that moves health care forward."

Clinton urged that they avoid mentioning "universal coverage." The phrase had taken on too much baggage, the President said. Focus groups conducted by presidential pollster Stanley Greenberg had discovered that middle-income voters interpreted "universal coverage" to mean that they would have to give up something to cover the poor. Greenberg suggested the President promise instead to provide "guaranteed insurance for all." It meant the same thing but it did not scare middle-income people into thinking they would be the losers.

As the meeting broke up, Gore pulled Moynihan aside: "The President is introducing his welfare bill today in Kansas City. It would be nice if you could say something outside about that."

"Oh sure," Moynihan replied.

It was midmorning, but already sweltering outside. Moynihan joked about how a Panama hat would come in handy on a day like this. The whir of Clinton's helicopter lifting off the South Lawn for Andrews Air Force Base was heard in the background. Moynihan never mentioned the President's welfare plan.

Lawrence O'Donnell, forty-three, brushed a lock of thick, graying hair off his forehead. His blue eyes were intense, but his face was expressionless as he stood behind and slightly to the side of Moynihan in the press gaggle, like a human antenna monitoring the questions and answers for signs of trouble. O'Donnell's first child, a daughter, had been born that weekend in New York, but that did not stop him from boarding an early morning shuttle flight to Washington so he could accompany Moynihan to the White House. "I abandon my family after one day in true Irish fashion," he joked.

Congressional staffers frequently operate under a cloak of anonymity when dealing with the press so as not to deflect attention from their bosses. O'Donnell's caustic view of politics, combined with his literary talents, make him an exceptionally rich source for reporters. It is hard for him to hide (not that he wants to). Even his unattributed quotes are recognizable to the practiced eye.

"We're climbing down the mountain of sanctimony into the valley of compromise," he confided to reporters after the meeting in the Oval Office. The political climate had begun to shift markedly in favor of the Republicans. Polls showed public support for the Clinton plan plummeting. The Clintons could have gotten a better deal if they had compromised two months ago, O'Donnell told reporters. In the end, of course, the Clintons got nothing.

O'Donnell is not one who sees public policy disputes in shades of good and evil but in terms of what is achievable. He thinks of himself as a meteorologist. He does not just wish for snow. He predicts how much there will be and measures it when it arrives.

With the possible exception of Stephanopoulos, who valued though rarely heeded O'Donnell's forecasts, White House aides thought O'Donnell was the devil incarnate. "A nightmare," one young aide fumed. "The most arrogant man in Washington. He is contemptuous of every other human being except for Moynihan."

True, O'Donnell did not hide his disdain for the amateurish way White House aides conducted themselves. But that judgment was widely shared in Washington. O'Donnell annoyed these young staffers in a way that no one else could because he was supposed to be one of them.

"The long hair, the motorcycle, that's his thing, his shtick, to detract from his being your normal Ivy League guy," the White House aide concluded in disgust. O'Donnell had graduated from Harvard, but he did have working-class roots. His father was a Boston cop who went to night school and became a trial lawyer. Of the four boys in the family, Lawrence was the only one to attend Harvard, and the only one who did not become an attorney.

Under Moynihan's direction, the Senate Finance Committee drifted like twenty graduate students on independent study. He had more credibility with Republicans, especially Packwood, than he had with many

Democrats. Those in his own party thought he went to ridiculous lengths to gain Republican support, with no apparent result.

"Do you think the Republicans are using you?" *Wall Street Journal* reporter David Rogers asked, referring to O'Donnell and his boss collectively.

"Of course not," O'Donnell replied. Lying awake that night, he realized that of course they were.

By making it clear from the start that he wanted Republican votes, Moynihan had ceded too much power to the GOP. His strategy revolved around Bob Dole, the Minority Leader. Moynihan believed that without Dole's support, or at least his benign neglect, the Democrats could not get the sixty votes in the Senate necessary to head off a filibuster.

All that remains of that unrequited dream is a note that Moynihan kept in his desk drawer. Scrawled in Dole's handwriting, the note says, "Is it time for the Moynihan bill?" One evening in his office, weeks after all hope had been lost for a health care reform bill, Moynihan waved the piece of paper like a prosecuting attorney brandishing telltale evidence.

"Dole passed me a note in April," Moynihan declared. "[The Clintons] would have killed for it in September." The note signaled Dole's willingness to make a deal, but the White House, fearing a trap, concluded it was too early to move toward a compromise.

No one can know whether the note Dole wrote in April could have borne fruit in the poisonous political climate of 1994. With Clinton weakened by the Whitewater scandal and Republican control of the Senate within reach, Dole would have been constrained from making a deal by the forces within his own party who equated compromise with betrayal. Texas Sen. Phil Gramm, a hard-right conservative and Dole's chief rival for the Republican presidential nomination, had vowed that health care reform would pass "over my cold, dead, political body."

Yet Gramm had secretly visited Moynihan early in the process to talk about the various proposals. A former economics professor, Gramm told Moynihan he had no problem with the provision calling for an employer mandate. Later, as Gramm took increasingly more radical positions to court the GOP's right wing, aides to Moynihan wondered how Gramm's backers in the business community would react if they knew he was not taken in by their sky-is-falling rhetoric about an employer mandate. Not that Gramm would vote for it, mind you, but as an economist, he knew that the opponents of a mandate were exaggerating its negative impact.

By the time hearings were completed and the committee met to fashion its version of health care reform legislation, the members were hopelessly split. Republicans who opposed any bill knew that victory was in the air. Lawmakers of both parties who favored substantial reform smelled defeat. No one wanted to go through the arduous process of writing a bill. The atmosphere was strained.

Moynihan's airy humor was still able to break the tension. On one occasion, as committee deliberations over health care stretched into the night, an exasperated Senator Breaux said, disgustedly, "We've talked about health care until we're sick. We've talked about everything."

The normally genial committee members glowered at each other. Then Moynihan chirped, "Acupuncture. We haven't talked about acupuncture."

The hearing room erupted in laughter. "I met with a group of acupuncturists," Breaux retorted, his anger vanishing like a summer rain, "and laugh therapists, and music therapists."

"There you have it," Moynihan smiled.

Moynihan soldiered on in public. But intended or not, there was the occasional smirk or a mischievous smile or a wink that let everyone know he was not really aboard this runaway White House train. He was indulging "the children" at the White House. When a pair of moderate southern Democrats, Rep. Jim Cooper and Sen. John Breaux, broke with the Clintons to offer their own compromise plan, Moynihan took to chanting to colleagues in committee and on the Senate floor:

> Cooper, Cooper, Cooper, Breaux,
> That's the way we've got to go.

Moynihan believed that compromise was the Clintons' only hope. Yet his jauntiness gave the proceedings the aura of an Irish wake. He was dancing on the grave of health care reform.

Hundreds of interest groups wanted to meet with Moynihan, so it had taken months for the New York State Health Care Campaign, an advocacy group, to arrange an appointment. They wanted it to go smoothly, so they practiced what each of them would say when they met with Moynihan to lobby for expanded health coverage. Moynihan is so enigmatic that ordinary mortals who are granted an audience spend much of their time worrying they are not up to his standards.

Moynihan was late, arriving at a quarter to six for the scheduled five o'clock meeting. He apologized and then launched into a series of anecdotes.

"I learned that Frances Perkins was a great Labor Secretary," said Donna Kass, who had traveled from Long Island to make her pitch for a single-payer plan. "He gave us a history lesson."

An hour and ten minutes later, Moynihan looked at his watch. John Carpenter, a Suffolk County co-chair and an activist with the Gray Panthers, was seated next to Moynihan and, realizing time had run out, said, "Excuse me, sir, I haven't said what I came down here to say."

"What do you want to say?" Moynihan asked.

"I want to talk about senior citizens," Carpenter replied.

Moynihan then clapped his hands over Carpenter's and said in a loud, jocular tone, "People like you and me!"

Determined to say his piece, Carpenter pressed ahead. "When I talk to seniors, I tell them that one in three end up in nursing homes."

"You don't tell this to them. I wouldn't," Moynihan replied impishly, trying to keep the mood light.

The group's after-action report of the session ranged from "a disaster" to "weirdest meeting ever." Carpenter, British by birth and as mannered as Moynihan, judiciously summed up the phenomenon. "Moynihan," he said, "is charming at first, but then you wish he'd answer."

The bill that Moynihan finally mustered out of the Senate Finance Committee with eleven Democratic votes and three Republican votes was the Clinton bill practically unchanged, except it had no employer mandate. Far from being hailed as a great achievement, the bill was given no chance of passing the full Senate and became a footnote to the long health care reform process. Moynihan believed there was no longer a majority in the Senate in favor of a bill, any bill. In effect, the chairman had raised the white flag of surrender.

In an effort to salvage something that could pass, a rump group of moderate Democrats and Republicans from the Senate Finance Committee picked up where Moynihan had left off. Calling themselves "the Mainstream Group," they labored for several weeks to produce a scaled-down bill combining insurance reform with expanded medical coverage for women and children.

Democratic Majority Leader George Mitchell, who had tired of Moynihan's antics, acted as the committee's shadow chairman. The relationship between Moynihan and Mitchell, a disciplined, by-the-book former judge, had never been good. Moynihan resented the intrusion on his turf. He privately predicted Mitchell would fail in this last-minute scramble for a face-saving deal. And fail he did.

After informal vote counts showed the mainstream version would not fare much better than the Clinton original, Mitchell announced on the Senate floor on September 26 that he was pulling the health care bill off the Senate calendar. That meant health care reform was officially dead in the 103rd Congress.

The subject of health care reform had obsessed Washington for more than a year. When it was over, a lot of people went through withdrawal.

O'Donnell no longer compulsively clicked on the *Today* show when his alarm went off. One morning, he spent an hour transfixed by a rerun of a 1970 Frank Sinatra concert. "That's the kind of thing you can do now that everything's collapsed," he said, unapologetically.

The finger-pointing began in earnest. White House aides grumbled that Moynihan had let down his President and that he did it intentionally. A top official called Moynihan "Machiavellian."

O'Donnell said the only Machiavellian decision that Moynihan made was to stop telling people what he thought. "You can't tell those children what you think is going to happen because then you are the enemy— they have a list," O'Donnell said. "So, we just won't tell them anymore. We just won't. It's not like we were working against them or something. It wasn't like that. It was just there's no sense talking to them. They're just silly people."

From Moynihan's vantage point, O'Donnell said, the choice was simple: compromise or accept defeat. On legislation as sweeping as this, compromise had to be reached early or not at all. Dole's note passed across the table to Moynihan in April was the end of the compromise season, not the beginning. From that point, all that was left was defeat with honor, and the White House could not even manage that.

"The White House made every mistake it could find to make, and then went out and found more," O'Donnell fumed.

Moynihan's comments on Sunday morning television were "microscopic nothings" in the course of the debate, said O'Donnell. "Everybody up there in that incredibly childish, unprofessional, silly shop thinks that the use of the word 'fantasy' was decisive on a fucking show that's on Sunday morning. It airs at seven A.M. in Los Angeles and no one in America sees it."

O'Donnell was right that Moynihan alone was not responsible for the failure of health care reform. But he was disingenuous when he argued that Moynihan's words did not have a decisive impact. Washington is an echo chamber. When the chairman of the most important committee in the Senate belittles his President's plan, the opposition gains not only great comfort, but legitimacy.

The truth is that Moynihan never believed in the Clinton plan. He thought it was a dangerous social experiment. Moynihan is an incrementalist, a consensus-builder, a conciliator. That is why he could work for four presidents, only two of them Democrats.

In his scholarly way, he prepared for the debate over health care reform by reviewing the history of the enactment of Social Security and Medicare. He reread *The Politics of a Guaranteed Income*, a book he himself wrote in 1973 about how the right and left combined to kill the family assistance plan.

"This is what is going to happen to the health care bill," Moynihan told friends early on. "The Left will think it's not good enough and the Right will say it goes too far. And we're going to wind up with nothing."

Moynihan pointed out that he was not alone in failing to build a coalition that could sustain the attacks from the special interests. Rep. John Dingell, in his thirteenth year as chairman of the House Energy and Commerce Committee, was widely regarded as the quintessential chairman—tough, in control of his committee, and able to ram through legislation at will. He could not muster a majority on his committee for the Clinton bill, or any alternative bill for that matter, even though he regarded the legislation as the most important of his career. Yet nobody said that health care reform died in John Dingell's committee.

The critics' case against Moynihan turns entirely on his handling of Clinton's Health Security Act in committee and ignores his substantive accomplishments, from pushing through Clinton's deficit reduction package in 1993 to two massive trade agreements. But that is to be expected. Health care reform was more than a piece of legislation; it was a searing emotional experience, and its failure set the stage for the Republican takeover.

Moynihan will be remembered for many things other than his chairmanship of the Senate Finance Committee. His career spans more than forty years of post–World War II history. He is one of the last great pretelevision personalities. He talks in a nineteenth-century cadence and with a brilliance that forces the world to slow down and pay attention. He has been an ambassador to the United Nations and to India and a visionary on social problems as diverse as auto safety, out-of-wedlock births, and ethnicity.

Moynihan was a thirty-six-year-old assistant Secretary of Labor in 1963 when John F. Kennedy was assassinated. When he heard the news, Moynihan went immediately to the White House. Stopping at the empty Oval Office, which was undergoing renovation while the President was away, Moynihan picked up a framed picture of Kennedy that was lying on a secretary's desk. When a security guard objected, Moynihan replied dejectedly, "What difference does it make?" He left with the picture, which now hangs in his Senate office above a typed explanation of how he obtained it.

Next, Moynihan rushed out to Andrews Air Force Base to beseech returning Cabinet officers to have the federal government take custody of the assassin, Lee Harvey Oswald. Moynihan did not trust the Dallas police, or local police anywhere for that matter. He worried that if Oswald escaped or was killed, people would think there was a conspiracy and they would lose faith in the government and their country. He stood on the tarmac at Andrews and yelled at the returning officials, "Get Oswald into federal custody! If something happens to him, for generations there will be talk of conspiracy."

With everyone else caught up in the tragedy of the moment, Moynihan could not get anyone to take him seriously. He later attributed the inability of the Kennedy liberals to act on his advice to class differences. None of the people he shouted at to take action had ever been struck by a policeman's nightstick. They had no reason to suspect the worst.

By Moynihan's own account, he had only one real conversation with Kennedy. While he admired Kennedy's charisma, he was not impressed with his intellect. "There was a disparity between the aura of the man and what he could produce at any given moment," Moynihan said in a 1977 *Playboy* interview. The evidence he cited for this indelicate observation went back to the first time he was introduced to Kennedy, at the 1960 Democratic Convention. Told that Moynihan was at Syracuse University, Kennedy remarked, "Oh, I have an honorary degree from Syracuse University."

"A perfectly sensible thing to say but rather disappointing to me," Moynihan admitted. "I wanted him to say something brilliant, never to be forgotten. An exchange of incomparable lucidity and prophetic clairvoyance, instead of 'Guy from Syracuse; I'll stick him with this, press the flesh and get on with it.'"

Kennedy's death opened the legislative floodgates on Capitol Hill for civil rights bills, the War on Poverty, and the Great Society. Lyndon Johnson was stylistically Kennedy's opposite, but liberals still ran the government. Moynihan helped fashion the Job Corps program. But he lost an important battle over the direction of the anti-poverty effort. Moynihan wanted the emphasis to be on job creation and income assistance for the working poor. Instead, the focus was on giving the poor a greater voice through community action programs, which liberals favored. The results, analyzed years later, suggest the federal government succeeded in creating a class of community activists while doing little about overall poverty.

Moynihan was so certain that jobs were the key that he launched an internal study, intended for the President, the Secretary of Labor, and their staffs, to prove he was right. "The Negro Family: The Case for National Action" was supposed to establish the link between unemployment and unstable families in black communities. Instead, Moynihan discovered that black male unemployment was actually falling while new welfare cases were rising. Until then, unemployment and marital separation had seemed to be parallel phenomena with family breakups directly linked to job losses. But beginning in 1963, the separation rate moved upward even as unemployment dropped sharply, causing the once-parallel lines to cross. Professor James Q. Wilson called it "Moynihan's Scissors." Moynihan did not know what to make of his findings. Until then, he thought any problem could be solved with a full employment budget.

On June 4, 1965, President Johnson gave an address to the graduating class at Howard University, a historically black college. The President, basing his remarks on Moynihan's research, called for a greater commitment from white America to overcome the historic wrongs that had led to the breakdown of the Negro family. The final draft of the speech was read to civil rights leaders Martin Luther King, Jr., Roy Wilkins, and Whitney Young, who privately approved.

That summer, Watts erupted. The riot in the black ghetto of Los Angeles and the urban unrest that it set off around the country proved Moynihan's thesis that Johnson's legislative initiatives had done little to improve the lives of black Americans. But when Moynihan's seventy-eight-page report on the Negro family became public in the immediate aftermath of Watts, civil rights leaders were in no mood for dispassionate analysis. James Farmer, head of the Congress of Racial Equality, called the Moynihan Report "fuel for a new racism." The other leaders followed suit, branding Moynihan a racist.

The Moynihan Report accurately diagnosed the problem of the rising illegitimacy rate in the black community and how it was driving up the welfare rolls. But Moynihan's failure to offer a solution invited cries of racism from black leaders and white liberals. This was the 1960s, a time when faith in government was high and people looked to government to solve problems.

Moynihan had not intended to write a political document, but one of observational social science. He had more than a dozen charts and twenty-two numerical tables illustrating what he called "the tangle of pathology" in the Negro community, the rising illegitimacy, divorce rates, delinquency and crime, and the impact of negative social behavior on achievement. One table compared the higher rejection rates of blacks by the armed forces for failure to pass the mental test; another compared national median IQ scores with those of children in Harlem, who in the third grade tested almost ten points lower.

"At the heart of the deterioration of the fabric of Negro society is the deterioration of the Negro family," Moynihan wrote. He blamed three centuries of injustice for the distortions that he saw, particularly in the role of the black male. First slavery, then segregation kept the Negro "in his place," Moynihan wrote. "These events worked against the emergence of a strong father figure. The very essence of the male animal, from the bantam rooster to the four-star general, is to strut. Indeed, in nineteenth-century America, a particular type of exaggerated male boastfulness became almost a national style. Not for the Negro male. The 'sassy nigger' was lynched."

Moynihan predicted there would be "no social peace" in the United States for generations if blacks as a group did not fare better. "It made it so agonizing for Pat," says James Q. Wilson. "He thought he had done the right thing."

Moynihan was badly beaten in his first try for public office, a 1965 run for president of the Manhattan City Council, and was back teaching at Harvard when his report on the Negro family was leaked to columnists Rowland Evans and Robert Novak.

They reported in their August 18, 1965, column that the White House, sobered by a summer of violence, had begun to examine ways to bolster the black family. Proposed solutions ranged from using men instead of women to deliver welfare checks to lowering military requirements as a way to get more black youths into the army. The latter was immediately assailed as "preferential treatment."

"The implicit message of the Moynihan Report is that ending discrimination is not nearly enough for the Negro," the columnists wrote. "But what is enough? The phrase 'preferential treatment' implies a solution far afield from the American dream. The white majority would never accept it. . . ."

The debate over the Moynihan Report foreshadowed today's controversy over affirmative action. Democratic liberals were fiercest in rejecting the Moynihan Report as familiar dogma that blamed the victim. "People were very shaken up," Moynihan recalls. "And they said, 'Go away. Who the hell are you?' The worst were the Presbyterians, white Presbyterians from churches in upper New York." Liberals treated Moynihan like a pariah. The experience left him with a visceral distaste for his party's left wing and contributed to his decision to take a leave of absence from Harvard to join the Nixon administration in 1969 as an urban affairs adviser.

Moynihan did not speak out publicly in his own defense for two years. When he did, in an article in the neoconservative opinion magazine *Commentary*, he blamed liberals for halting the progress of blacks. The refusal of liberals to confront the rising illegitimacy rate in the black community, he wrote, shows what a "destructive" and "rigid" force liberals are in American society. No amount of criticism could sway Moynihan from his convictions. "He's not arrogant," says columnist Mark Shields, a Moynihan admirer. "He just believes there is no human problem that can't be solved if people would just do what he tells them."

The controversy launched Moynihan as an authority on issues of race and poverty. A framed copy of *Time* from July 28, 1967, with Moynihan on the cover hangs on the wall in O'Donnell's office. Moynihan had come to a lot of people's attention, including that of President-elect Richard Nixon.

Nixon had just won the 1968 election when he summoned Moynihan to his transition headquarters in the Hotel Pierre in New York. Moynihan did not know what to make of the invitation and called his friend, Stephen Hess, for advice. Hess had been Nixon's speechwriter in 1962 when Nixon ran for governor of California and knew him well. Hess assured Moynihan that the purpose of the meeting was for Nixon to explore domestic policy ideas with him.

After the meeting, Moynihan told Hess, "I couldn't believe he knew so little about domestic policy. I would have bluffed it."

As oblivious as Nixon was to policy concerns, he knew every nuance when it came to politics. Ten days before the 1962 California election for governor, which was to be his comeback after losing the presidency to Kennedy, Nixon announced to Hess, "I've lost the election." Nixon knew before the polls and the pundits that his campaign had peaked.

On election morning, with the outcome still very much in doubt, according to polls, Hess asked, "Dick, do you still think you're going to lose the election?"

"Yes," Nixon replied. "But at least I'll never have to talk about crap like drug addiction again."

Once in the White House, Nixon compensated by recruiting Moynihan, who churned out a rich trove of creative domestic policy: national health insurance, higher education reform, creation of the National Institute of Higher Education, experimental schools, welfare reform, and the family assistance plan. None were enacted by the Democratic Congress. Still, domestic spending rose under Nixon, which Moynihan continues to point out to disbelieving liberals.

"When a Democrat is elected, he has to go to the right," Moynihan says. "When a Republican is elected, he has to move left. The key is to get them when they're in the center."

Moynihan stood out like a boutonniere on a pin-striped suit in the Nixon White House. His staff were all former students of his at Harvard, young men bursting with enthusiasm and energy. Hess, one of the old-timers at thirty-six, was Moynihan's deputy and acted as general chaperon. "I felt like I was sitting on a nest of hummingbirds," he says.

Assailed as a racist within his own party and then defecting to a Republican administration should have been enough to end Moynihan's career as a Democratic politician. But he would survive that and more. In 1970, another leaked Moynihan memo suggested that the country could benefit from a period of "benign neglect" on matters of race. The phrase itself was taken from Canadian constitutional history. Moynihan was calling for a lowering of political rhetoric, not a lessening of commitment, but his liberal critics seized upon the memo as further evidence that he was unsympathetic to black Americans.

Republicans did not trust him either. As the most visible Democrat in the Nixon White House, they blamed Moynihan when quotes critical of Nixon appeared in the media. Reporters who covered the White House confirm that Moynihan and his domestic policy aides took the heat for things that were said by card-carrying Nixon loyalists. Moynihan's White House colleagues rarely missed an opportunity to embarrass him. "Moynihan in to see me, disturbed about staff leaks designed to screw him," Chief of Staff Bob Haldeman wrote in his diary on March 31, 1970. "Made point he's ruined in Democratic Party because of the 'benign neglect' memo. He's really distressed, mainly because he has nowhere left to go."

Moynihan was a man without a party, "the Dave Gergen of his day," Mark Shields joked at a Washington dinner. (Gergen became a counselor to President Clinton in 1993 after serving as a White House aide under Presidents Nixon, Ford, and Reagan.) From this fragile partisan base, Moynihan went on to become one of the most enduring members of the Senate, winning elections by wide margins. "He's been left for dead several times, but he's still around," Liz Moynihan observes.

That searing personal history puts things in perspective, she says, when unnamed White House aides younger than her adult children make disparaging remarks about her husband. "Those are gnat bites after you've been called a racist because of the Moynihan Report. Who in hell cares what they say? When he was in the Nixon White House and they leaked his memos, I went berserk."

Moynihan left the Nixon White House well before the 1972 election to avoid taking sides, but continued to speak kindly of the President. After Nixon's landslide reelection, he rewarded his former adviser with an ambassadorship to India. Moynihan was out of the country when Watergate destroyed Nixon's presidency. Liz Moynihan's archaeological studies flourished during the family's three years abroad. But Pat Moynihan had minimal tolerance for Third World inconveniences. When people inevitably asked if he got sick on the food or water, his answer was, "[I got sick] the day I arrived, and I stayed sick for three years."

Moynihan does not like being out of the loop, and India was not exactly on the fault line of U.S. foreign policy. "When India ceased to be a democracy, our actual interest there just plummeted," Moynihan said in his 1977 *Playboy* interview. "I mean, what does it export but communicable disease?"

The condescending comment reflected Moynihan's irritation toward countries that sought U.S. aid at the same time they denounced the United States as a capitalist devil. Appointed ambassador to the United Nations by President Gerald Ford, Moynihan quickly dubbed the U.N. "the theater of the absurd."

Moynihan's skepticism of government largesse is so deep-seated that in 1977, his first year in the Senate, he ventured this caustic opinion: "There is just one social program of which its sponsors have said, 'That works.' And that is castration as a treatment of sexual offenders."

Moynihan's ideology is impossible to categorize. Framed on the wall of his private Senate bathroom are covers from *The Nation* and *The New Republic* proclaiming, within weeks of each other, that Moynihan was a neoconservative and a neoliberal.

His election to the Senate in 1976 was a fluke. He lacked a constituency among the liberals who dominated New York politics at the time. But the liberal vote was split in the Democratic primary among three candidates, including feminist icon Bella Abzug. In a bitter primary contest, Moynihan won by a single percentage point over Abzug. Traditional political labels were rendered meaningless when the conservative *National Review* made Moynihan its Man of the Year after he beat incumbent Republican James Buckley, brother of the magazine's founder, William F. Buckley, in the November 1976 election.

Al Shanker, the crusty head of the American Federation of Teachers, was no great fan of Moynihan's when Lane Kirkland called from the AFL-CIO to enlist Shanker in a campaign to convince Moynihan to run for the Senate. Moynihan had just published an essay in the magazine *Public Inter-*

est, titled, "Qui Bono—In Whose Interest?" He argued that federal aid to education is supposed to benefit poor children, but that it actually ends up benefiting teachers. And if one teacher is married to another, their combined salary puts them in the top five percent of earners.

Moynihan had not yet said anything about tuition tax credits but seemed to be leaning in the direction of public assistance to parochial schools. Moynihan was then U.S. ambassador to the United Nations. He invited Shanker to lunch in the penthouse apartment at the Waldorf-Astoria hotel in New York that served as the ambassador's residence.

"He served a marvelous wine, a great burgundy," Shanker recalls. Moynihan reassured Shanker that he was not trying to "break the wall" between church and state. "I was there when the deal was made," Moynihan exclaimed, citing legislation signed by President Lyndon Johnson that restructured federal aid to education along a formula of the money following the child.

"It didn't sound very ominous to me," says Shanker. "So we not only supported him, we made the difference."

Bella Abzug, the other leading candidate, had earned the union's enmity by supporting a community control movement that advocated parents taking over schools to teach their children. Using a crowbar to physically break in, she led delegations of parents into schools that had been locked and ruled unsafe in the Ocean Hill and Brownsville neighborhoods. "So we had a particular score to settle outside of our general liking for Pat Moynihan," says Shanker.

The AFT mobilized its 187,739 members in the state with an aggressive telephone polling operation. This display of old-fashioned political muscle helped Moynihan edge out Abzug. Shanker stayed at the victory party past 3:00 A.M., until the results were certain. After only a few hours sleep, he boarded the earliest Eastern Airlines shuttle to Washington.

"Who gets on the plane? Bella," Shanker recalled. "Everybody applauds. She walks down the aisle, shaking hands on the left and the right. I was in the middle of the plane. When she got to me, she put out her hand. And when she saw it was me, she said, 'You'll get yours, dearie.'"

Moynihan was the poster boy for the fledgling neoconservative movement. Norman Podhoretz, then the editor of *Commentary* magazine, the neoconservatives' house organ, saw in Moynihan the first charismatic leader since John F. Kennedy. He would be president someday, Podhoretz predicted.

In Washington, Moynihan surrounded himself with bright, young aides drawn to the intellectual ferment embodied by the neoconservatives. Elliott Abrams, Charles Horner, Chester (Checker) Finn are now all Republicans and played major roles in the Reagan administration. Tim Russert, bureau chief for NBC in Washington and host of *Meet the Press*, was the house liberal.

New York senators typically ask for appointments to the most prestigious committees, Foreign Relations and Judiciary, which handle war and peace and confirm Supreme Court justices. But Moynihan wanted Finance and Public Works. He was interested in urban design. He wanted to save New York City's Penn Station. "That's where the money is," he told his staffers. "That's how you help the state."

For an unabashed intellectual, Moynihan understands the nitty-gritty of politics. In 1977, he had just been elected when he shocked the liberal Democratic Party establishment by backing Robert Byrd, the West Virginian who had once been a former member of the Ku Klux Klan, over Hubert Humphrey, the party's happy warrior, for Senate Majority Leader. Moynihan had done a realistic calculation and concluded that Byrd would win. So he met with Byrd and endorsed him. While the photographers clicked away, Moynihan quietly mentioned the committees he would like to be on. "I understand," Byrd said.

With Moynihan's endorsement, Byrd won the Majority Leader's job. Their picture appeared on the front page of *The New York Times*. Soon after, the committee assignments were made, and Moynihan was on Finance and Public Works. Byrd had delivered.

Moynihan's signature issue in his first term was vouchers for Catholic schools. He introduced a bill to provide tuition tax credits for parents who wanted to send their children to parochial school. It passed the House but was defeated in the Senate, thanks largely to the leadership of Republican Sen. Jacob Javits. President Jimmy Carter threatened to veto the bill on the grounds that it violated the separation of church and state and would siphon off much-needed resources from public schools. Championing school vouchers cost Moynihan the support of the powerful teacher's union in New York. "He knew he was doing something he said he wouldn't do," says Shanker. The AFT did not endorse Moynihan again until 1988, by which time he had dropped the issue. "I want to maintain my good relations with labor," Moynihan explained. Philosophically, he supports school vouchers; pragmatically, he stays silent.

Moynihan's neoconservative friends believe he made a calculated decision he could not survive in New York as one of them, that Bella Abzug or someone like her would pick him off. They love him as a human being, but they are disillusioned. "He's a very charming guy, but [long pause] very flexible," says one.

*   *   *

Moynihan likes dealing with only one person, who serves as alter ego, buffer, and adjunct wife. This is common on Capitol Hill, where many powerful politicians rely on a single, usually anonymous, staffer. Lawrence O'Donnell played that role for Moynihan from 1988 until after the 1994 election. It is a job description that he realizes has limited applicability outside the Beltway. "The minute I walk out of here, I'm no good to society," he quips. "My skills are not transferable, unless Moynihan has a brother running a movie studio."

When O'Donnell took over as staff director of the Senate Finance Committee, lobbyists went into shock. O'Donnell was their worst counterculture nightmare. He ended the easy access they had enjoyed under the Bentsen regime, letting it be known that schmoozing with lobbyists was not his style any more than it was Moynihan's. Moynihan continued to raise hundreds of thousands of dollars from political action committees with an interest in legislation that he controlled as chairman of the Senate Finance Committee. But he kept his personal contacts with lobbyists to a minimum, as did O'Donnell.

O'Donnell grew up in the same cauldron of ethnic Irish pride and rage as Moynihan did a generation earlier. He had avoided Moynihan's class at Harvard because he hated writing and Moynihan required a twenty-page paper on top of a midterm and final exam. After college, O'Donnell drifted for a year. He was working as a parking lot attendant when his father, the former cop who was now an attorney, took on the Boston Police Department on behalf of a widowed black mother, from the Mission Hill housing project, whose husband had been shot and killed by two Irish-American police officers. The father successfully prosecuted the case, and the son who hated writing wrote a book about it, *Deadly Force,* which became a television movie and took him into circles in Hollywood and New York that changed his life.

He met the Moynihans through their daughter, Maura, who was married to (and is now divorced from) John Avedon, son of fashion photographer Richard Avedon. O'Donnell became a tenant of the Moynihans, renting the apartment they own at 35th Street and Madison Avenue in the Murray Hill section of Manhattan. Liz loved him. He was the only tenant they ever had who paid his rent on time, she told him.

Moynihan's 1988 reelection campaign was looming and Liz, the campaign manager, wanted this enterprising young man on the staff. She took him to dinner and presented it as a great opportunity for him. "I responded politely," says O'Donnell, who had no interest in politics, or so he thought. But at her request, he went with her to Sawyer-Miller, a media firm, to talk about campaign commercials.

Everyone sat around a table in a big boardroom. Moynihan was there. The meeting had been called for read-throughs of ten television commercials. They would choose four and use three. David Sawyer read each script in his broadcast-quality voice. O'Donnell remembers a commercial designed to pander to each constituency except maybe the fishermen in Montauk, Long Island. The killer ad was one on Social Security.

"Pat Moynihan saved my Social Security," Sawyer said in his salesman baritone. Flash to an elderly woman. Moynihan listened quietly. Then he said, slowly, each word formed like a musical note: "She's an actress?"

The answer, of course, was yes.

"Then it's a lie," Moynihan said. "I didn't save anybody's Social Security. Does anybody have a typewriter here? It takes ten minutes to write one of these things."

There was no typewriter. This was the computer age. So they gave him a yellow pad and ballpoint pen. O'Donnell checked his watch. Moynihan came back in eight minutes with a script telling how he *and Bob Dole* had helped shore up the Social Security trust fund. The revised script said, "Cut to Bob Dole saying, 'Pat Moynihan did this. . . .'"

Moynihan did not ask anybody whether it was okay to quote Dole. He assumed no one would object, least of all Dole. And he was right.

Moynihan also insisted on substituting a spot about his efforts to ban cop-killer bullets for one the media advisers had proposed about his securing federal money for the Harlem Boys Choir. "That's computers giving money to other computers," he said stubbornly. "I'm not going to do a commercial about grants. I get thousands of grants, almost literally in my sleep, but that's not what I want to take credit for in this setting."

The whole procedure took about an hour. Not only did Moynihan leave with a fresh set of campaign ads, but with a convert. O'Donnell was so intrigued by the performance he agreed to sign on for a month, time enough to help Moynihan head off a challenge from Rudolph Giuliani, who was hinting that he might run for the Senate.

The thought of facing Giuliani unnerved Moynihan. A latter-day Eliot Ness, Giuliani had a tough-guy image that was a political marketer's dream. Moynihan was so intimidated, he wondered whether to run again. What depressed him was fund-raising. He hated it. He knew that running against Giuliani meant raising big bucks. Besides, Giuliani's credentials were impressive, despite O'Donnell's protestations of his provincialism, "He's never been to Paris! He's never been to Israel!"

Ultimately, it was Giuliani who lost his nerve and dropped out of contention without ever mounting a campaign. Moynihan spent $4.8 million on his 1988 reelection race, winning a two-to-one victory over unknown attorney Robert McMillan, who spent just $529,000, one-ninth as much as Moynihan. The comparison that Moynihan prefers to make is with Alfonse D'Amato, the state's bulldoggish junior senator, who two years earlier had spent $13 million on his Senate race. "We've been good at the politics, but not because we're good at raising money," Liz says. "If we had had a serious challenge, we might not have made it." Actually, the record suggests otherwise. Moynihan's shortcomings as a campaigner are legion, and he has been far more successful as a fund-raiser than he would have people believe.

With Liz's imprimatur, Moynihan took O'Donnell to lunch and offered him the job of senior adviser. "A lazy government job is one of the things I abhor the most," he says, only partly in jest. "I figured it was genetic coding, that as an Irish kid I should look for the no-show job, then go to the golf course and work on my swing. Most importantly, I don't know anything he doesn't know. What advice would I give him? The smartest guy in the world wants advice from me—on something he's been working on for thirty years?"

The Senate Finance Committee is a magnet for special interests seeking to influence tax legislation. Packwood remembers Russell Long telling him, "We've put in and taken out the investment tax credit six times since I have been here, every time in a tax reform bill. One time we put it in and took it out under the same president. Now you tell me when it's reform." Serving on Senate Finance means never having to beg for money again. Bentsen offered lobbyists a chance to have breakfast with him once a month if they would contribute $10,000 to his 1988 reelection campaign. Three days after the breakfast club, dubbed "Eggs McBentsen," was revealed in a *Washington Post* story, Bentsen acknowledged he had made a "doozy" of a mistake, and ended the practice.

Moynihan was similarly caught exploiting his chairmanship. The corporate lobbyists scheduled to attend a reception at the Rainbow Room in New York's Rockefeller Center in July 1993 received an invitation that emphasized Moynihan's elevation to chairman of the Finance Committee "where he will oversee fifty-five percent of all federal spending and ninety-eight percent of all revenue raising as well as health-care reform and trade." An embarrassed Moynihan canceled the event after a story in *The New York Times* questioned the timing of the invitations, which were sent out the week before the Senate Finance Committee began work on the Clinton budget.

The chairmanship gave Moynihan financial security at campaign time. He collected more than $200,000 in contributions from health care

PACs alone in 1993–94. But the greatest impact of the title was the attention that went with it. Things he had been saying for years were now suddenly news. The morning that Moynihan's proposal to impose a stiff new tax on ammunition made the front page of *The New York Times,* O'Donnell marveled at the newfound power. In the past, Moynihan received polite condescension when he raised the issue. "An ordinary member of the Senate is like a fucking illegal alien," O'Donnell exclaimed. "He's only been saying it for ten years. It's on page one because he's the chairman."

Moynihan performed heroically in his first year as chairman. He pushed through Clinton's budget, which included a controversial gas tax and unpopular cuts in Medicare spending. "Moynihan Passes Test as 'Kingpin,'" *The Washington Post* trumpeted on June 19, 1993, the morning after the eleven-to-nine, party-line victory on the budget. When Democratic Sen. Bob Kerrey threatened to vote against the package on the Senate floor, saying it did not go far enough to curb the federal deficit, Moynihan stepped in to save the budget from defeat. He had endorsed Kerrey, a war hero, in the 1992 presidential primaries, and admired the younger man, a quirky thinker much like himself.

Clinton cursed his fellow Democrat when Kerrey called to say he could not support the budget. "My presidency is at stake," Clinton cried. Kerrey's vote meant the difference between winning and losing, and losing a critical vote so early in his presidency would undermine Clinton's authority, perhaps irreversibly.

White House aides turned to Moynihan. Do whatever it takes, they told Moynihan. But Kerrey was not the type who could be swayed by the promise of a bridge or a dam in his home state. Kerrey invited Moynihan to his office, and they talked in broad, historical generalities about the end of the Cold War and its impact on U.S. budget-making.

Kerrey's anguish was evident, and Moynihan determined that it was fruitless to ratchet up the pressure. Kerrey emerged sometime later to tell the media clustered outside that Moynihan had told him to lighten up. Go see a movie. Off he went, reporters in tow, to the Tina Turner story, *What's Love Got to Do with It.*

That evening, Liz Moynihan phoned Kerrey at home. He was still leaning against voting for the Clinton budget. "People understand when you do something because of principle," he said stoutly.

"I told him he couldn't get away with that," says Mrs. Moynihan, recalling the conversation. She engaged Kerrey in a rambling, soulful conversation that touched on everything from the Cold War to the hopes and dreams of future generations. She was incensed at a report that later suggested she simply called in a chit, a quid pro quo for her husband's earlier political endorsement. "I told Kerrey he ought to do it, but I didn't say he should do it for Pat," she insists.

"I told him the reason he should be for the budget, even though it was flawed, is the same reason Pat was: It was the end of the Cold War, Russia was on the edge of collapse. It was important that the U.S. look like it could govern itself. And if you can't get a budget, you can't govern yourself.

"That was one argument. The other was personal. Bob Kerrey is a person of strong character, a person who has courage about speaking out. People like that are needed, and I would like to see him continue to be a national Democrat. If he had cast the vote that killed the budget, he would have been silenced. He was tortured over this. He wanted to be talked into voting for the budget. He never regretted the vote." Kerrey's vote for the budget on August 6, 1993, created a tie, which was broken by Vice President Gore, acting in his capacity as president of the Senate.

Thus, Moynihan got credit for saving Clinton in the first of the near-death experiences that characterized Clinton's term in office. Moynihan had proved his loyalty. The White House thought the next big challenge—health care—was also a test of loyalty. Delivering the biggest social program since Social Security would solidify the Democratic Party's hold on the tenuous coalition that had put Clinton in office. From the start, Moynihan felt that he had been handed an impossible task.

When black activist minister Al Sharpton announced that he would challenge Moynihan in the Democratic primary in 1994, Liz secretly explored how to get Sharpton out of the race. "This is a distraction to Pat while he's trying to pass health care," she explained in a meeting with two Democratic Party operatives, whose help she had enlisted. Her idea was to have the Rev. Jesse Jackson approach Sharpton with the offer of a role in New York Gov. Mario Cuomo's reelection campaign, conditioned upon Sharpton's withdrawing from the Senate race. "I felt it out a little," said one of the party officials. "But I knew if we went to him [Sharpton] with any kind of overt proposal, he would blow us up in the press. He would talk to us, and then he would go to *The New York Post*." To Liz's chagrin, nothing was done.

Though Sharpton was given no chance of winning, he was an irritant. His presence in the race forced Moynihan to go back to New York on the weekends to campaign. Most senators routinely return home, especially during an election year. But Moynihan had been spoiled. As a high-minded intellectual, he behaved as though he should be above the ignominy of a commoner's campaign.

Sharpton also revived the ugly charges of racial insensitivity that had dogged Moynihan for almost thirty years, ever since the controversy over the Moynihan Report. With Sharpton in the race, Moynihan tempered his insistence that the White House press ahead with welfare reform. He did not want to talk about his concern about the rising illegitimacy rate in the black community in the context of a primary fight with Sharpton. It would only provide ammunition for Sharpton to raise old fears about Moynihan. The racism label is Moynihan's herpes. It subsides, but it never goes away.

Meanwhile, Cuomo courted Sharpton. A photograph of the two of them smiling and collegial at a church rally in Buffalo made the front page of *The New York Times*. "We heard from Mrs. Moynihan," said the Democratic official. "She felt that Cuomo was giving aid and comfort to the enemy by cozying up to Sharpton."

Dutifully, the DNC official phoned one of Cuomo's top aides to lodge a complaint on behalf of the Moynihans. The Cuomo aide could not believe what he was hearing. "Pat Moynihan is the most popular pol in the state," he exclaimed. "He's worried whether he'll win with seventy-eight percent or seventy-four percent [of the vote]. Give us a break. We're fighting for our lives."

Moynihan ran for his third Senate term against a Republican tide that would ultimately sweep away Mario Cuomo and many other Democratic stalwarts, including House Speaker Tom Foley, the first Speaker defeated in 132 years. A fund-raising letter signed by Moynihan and sent to his New York constituents claimed that Moynihan was high on the GOP hit list and that the Republicans were prepared to spend a lot of money to defeat him. The letter said that gun owners had targeted him because of his proposal to impose higher taxes on ammunition. In fact, the National Rifle Association did nothing of the kind.

California Rep. Maxine Waters's press secretary, Patrick Lacefield, who used to live in New York and received a copy of the letter, was so incensed at the exaggerated threat that he sent back a note (and no donation) saying, "Look, anybody who knows anything knows this is a totally safe seat."

Behind the scenes, Moynihan is far more political than his image suggests, and a skillful inside player when it suits his purposes. One example comes from Democratic Sen. Tom Harkin of Iowa. Once, after getting the better of Moynihan on a minor issue, Harkin later went to him for help on getting funds for a highway project. Moynihan responded with a lengthy story that seemed off the point. "I was sitting there thinking this is inter-

esting, but, well, why is he telling me this?" Harkin recalled. "Then I realized I was the central character in the story. It was Moynihan's way of letting me know he hadn't forgotten."

Moynihan views every issue through the prism of what is good for
New York. When Clinton needed to raise tax revenues in his first budget, Moynihan favored a gasoline tax, which would have had minimal
impact on his constituents. In fact New York ranked last among the
states in the per capita expense of a gasoline tax. One survey showed it
would cost the average citizen $58 more a year in New York versus $64
more a year in Montana, the hardest-hit state. While the actual difference was minuscule, selective use of the statistics allowed Moynihan to
say that the tax increase in the Clinton budget would impact New York
the least.

Not shy around presidents, Moynihan goes to the top when he has a
complaint. In October of 1994, Clinton was in Manhattan to address the
United Nations. Given the President's shaky standing in the polls, the
speech was designed to shore up his image as a leader. Clinton needed to
do well. In a receiving line moments before Clinton was due to speak,
Moynihan whispered to the President, "The GATT is dead."

The news unsettled Clinton. He accepted Moynihan's statement at
face value, not suspecting the senator was intentionally exaggerating the
difficulties that the GATT—the General Agreement on Tariffs and
Trade—faced in the Senate. The GATT was still very much alive, but
Moynihan, one of the world trade treaty's biggest backers, wanted to
shake up an administration that he thought was dangerously complacent
and could squander the seven years of negotiations that had produced
the treaty.

Moynihan felt that Clinton had to be scared into understanding how
close he was to losing the treaty. South Carolina Sen. Ernest Hollings
had warned the administration in April that he intended to use the full
ninety days allotted for debate, and if Clinton wanted the treaty to pass,
he had better send it up early in the year. Preoccupied with health care
reform, the White House did not forward the treaty to Congress until
June. Hollings, who objected to provisions concerning textiles, his
state's major industry, kept his promise to stall the vote. In the end, Clinton was forced to call for a special, lame-duck session of Congress to vote
on the GATT.

Wielding the power of his committee chairmanship never really
meant much to Moynihan, although he thoroughly enjoyed hearings that
he treated as educational seminars. Ideas matter to Moynihan. If an
interviewer does not ask questions that interest him, he does not bother

to conceal his boredom. He is at his best analyzing social trends. His research on the black family was groundbreaking. The welfare plan that he designed for Nixon, cash assistance combined with work, is a model that, according to many, could succeed today.

Whether Moynihan's academic collegiality might have worked is a moot point. The Democrats are unlikely to take back control of the Senate in 1996. And Moynihan, who will be seventy-three in the year 2000, is unlikely to run for a fifth term.

His biggest legislative achievement is the intermodal transportation bill that he shepherded as a subcommittee chairman in 1991. He congratulates himself on its futuristic title, which made the intellectual point that transportation should be integrated, that air, land, and sea should all be part of a single system. But critics say he never translated his intellectual insight into serious policy, and the bill became a classic exercise in pork with the title "intermodal" on top. Moynihan started out as the great intellectualizer and ended up as a kind of absentee landlord who looked the other way while other senators bought each other off with various favors.

Moynihan is not above such gamesmanship himself. Once, trying to get some pork for his constituents, he inserted language into a bill to earmark money for the renovation of a Brooklyn courthouse. The Office of Management and Budget, headed by Bush appointee Richard Darman, produced a cost-benefit analysis that eliminated Moynihan's courthouse project. Darman's relationship with Moynihan, which had been longstanding and friendly, suffered permanent damage.

Moynihan does not like to think of himself as playing pork politics. He saw the incident as a usurpation of power by the executive branch. He did not argue his case in terms of whether he had a worthwhile courthouse project or not. The difference between Moynihan and Sen. Robert Byrd, known as the "Prince of Pork" for the federal largesse he has won for West Virginia, is that Byrd is more up front about what he does.

Moynihan thought of himself as a forward-looking legislator on transportation, but he became almost irrelevant as the process disintegrated into traditional horse-trading and late-night legislating. Other people gradually took over the endgame. Moynihan dropped out. He initially sought funding for Maglev, magnetic levitation for high-speed trains. When he could not get the support, he lost interest.

Yet Moynihan is still regarded as a visionary on transportation issues. A 1959 article that he wrote on auto safety said accidents should be treated as a "disease" and appropriate action taken. The piece predated Ralph Nader's seminal work, *Unsafe at Any Speed*, by seven years.

Nader wrote the book that Moynihan wanted to write, indeed, thought he was *entitled* to write. Moynihan had "discovered" Nader and brought him to Washington as an assistant in the Labor Department after commissioning the bright, young consumer advocate to write a study on federal employees' occupational safety. Moynihan is sensitive about the fact that his protégé upstaged him. Yet he remains captivated by Nader's unorthodox views, inviting him to testify before the Senate Finance Committee against the GATT, a courtesy it is unlikely either of his recent predecessors, Bentsen or Packwood, would have extended if they were in charge.

The Senate, like the Harvard Club, is a closed society. Ritual is everything. And its members close ranks when threatened by outsiders. It pained Moynihan to vote against Sen. Bob Packwood.

"Give me something," he commanded O'Donnell when the issue of Packwood's diary first surfaced. Moynihan was clearly hoping for a reason to support Packwood and the constitutional issue that he had raised to resist turning over his personal diaries to the Senate Ethics Committee. But when a Justice Department investigation was launched into Packwood's behavior, introducing the possibility of criminal charges, Moynihan could no longer defend his friend.

"There is nothing we can do," O'Donnell told him.

Moynihan and Packwood have been close since 1977, Moynihan's first year in the Senate. They fought on the same side for tuition tax credits. They whispered to each other during hearings like schoolboys at prep school. They share a mutual love of history. On the floor one day, Moynihan said, "Have you read Putnam's new book?"

"Well, I didn't even know who Putnam was, let alone Putnam's new book," Packwood says, laughing. "I have to confess probably the first thing that would have caught my eye on books would not have been *Making Democracy Work: Civic Traditions in Modern Italy*. He says, 'You've got to read it; the conclusions are amazing.' So I got the book."

Packwood was the Finance Committee chairman for two years in the 1980s during the six-year period the Republicans controlled the Senate under Ronald Reagan. Aware that a shift in the political fortunes of the Senate is never more than an election away, Moynihan playfully acknowledged the likelihood that they would trade places again by referring publicly to his friend as "the future chairman," a prediction that was to come true as a result of the Republicans regaining the Senate in the 1994 election.

"He's a great guy to have in that job," Moynihan says. "We don't try to fool each other."

With regret, Moynihan joined ninety-three other senators on November 2, 1993, to defeat Packwood's attempt to conceal his diary with its graphic accounts of sexual encounters, real and imagined. Packwood did not hold it against him. It was political, not personal.

"I understand political correctness, and I understand why people voted the way they did on the Senate floor," Packwood says. "When I explained to Pat how they wanted all of the diary, and not just the relevant parts, he said, 'The end of democracy comes when the government tries to take away privacy.' Pat put his arm around me. He is very understanding."

Other senators were less understanding. Moynihan was the only Democrat who voted to support an Ethics Committee decision not to hold public hearings into the charges against Packwood. He did it out of friendship. He had also recently been reelected to his fourth six-year term, which would probably be his last, and he had nothing to lose. When more charges surfaced after the Senate vote, including one that accused Packwood of harassing a minor, the six-member Senate Ethics Committee voted unanimously on September 6, 1995, to recommend Packwood's expulsion from the Senate. He resigned less than twenty-four hours later.

Capitol Hill lore abounds with tales of autocratic chairmen who behaved more like barons than democrats. Former Ways and Means Chairman Dan Rostenkowski, for one, seldom paid attention to the views of his committee members, least of all the junior ones. During conference committee meetings, where differences between House and Senate bills are resolved, Rostenkowski would grant members ten minutes to make their points, then would look the other way or otherwise occupy himself while they were speaking. Moynihan was not like that as a chairman. He was collegial; he liked compromise and consensus.

In the days leading up to an important vote, Moynihan scheduled private meetings with each member, Democrat and Republican, in the fabled "back room" of the Finance Committee offices, where serious business is done. The purpose of these confessionals was to extract every member's bottom line. Except for O'Donnell, no staff members were present.

As a prelude to the 1993 budget vote, for example, Moynihan invited each member of the committee to write down on a piece of paper how much deficit reduction should come from cuts in Medicare, how much from a gas tax, and how much from increased taxes on corporations. He let them see how hard it is to come up with a formula rather than tell them how hard it is. As the final product took shape, if any member wanted to make a change, Moynihan would say, "Well, all right, but first show me where the votes are."

"Toughness is passé," says O'Donnell. "It's trickery. Compromise enough in someone's direction and then you have them."

The media flocked to Moynihan's hearings. He was invariably entertaining and quotable. Impeccably polite with his colleagues, praising them to excess, he could at the same time verge on being abusive with witnesses. The cruelty is disguised as intellectual combat, so not everybody realizes what is happening.

At his best, Moynihan is an intellectual who dazzles and entertains with his command of ideas and language. At his worst, he is a sophist who harasses and embarrasses anyone who offends his refined linguistic sensibility. Woe to the witness appearing before Moynihan whose sloppy syntax or, even worse, sloppy thinking provokes the chairman's ire.

Moynihan has an intimidating intellect, and he uses it to intimidate. Years after he humiliated her, Catherine Ann Bertini remembers every painful minute. Bertini was the acting assistant secretary for family support when she appeared with Under Secretary of Health and Human Services Constance Horner on May 15, 1989, to testify before Moynihan's subcommittee on Social Security and family policy. Moynihan had wanted to grill Health and Human Services Secretary Louis Sullivan about the department's progress in implementing the Family Support Act of 1988. Sullivan had begged off to deliver a commencement speech, which annoyed Moynihan.

The hearing room in the Dirksen Senate Office Building was filled with the usual collection of administration and congressional staff members, lobbyists, and reporters. Those who had witnessed previous performances by Moynihan no doubt expected to be entertained as well as informed. They were not disappointed.

Horner was an old friend of Moynihan's and he addressed her as "Connie." Bertini, on the other hand, was just another bureaucrat, target practice for Moynihan, the rhetorical sharpshooter. She had barely begun to speak when she made the mistake of using social workers' jargon, an offhand reference to "intake workers."

"'Intake workers'? It sounds like a valve, sort of a complex hydraulic system," Moynihan said mockingly. "Do you mean welfare workers?"

"Yes, sir," Bertini replied.

Moynihan was not about to let up: ". . . I don't mean to be in any way critical, Ms. Bertini, but you said, 'This is an aspect of the program.' I think those are your words. No, it isn't; it is the law. It is the law. How many people, how many fathers, have you taken to court in the last year, saying, 'You are breaking the law. You owe us money'?"

"Well, I am afraid our reporting process does not directly include that information, sir," Bertini said.

"You lost me," Moynihan chided. "'Our process does not directly do it'? Do you do it indirectly?"

Bertini, flustered: "I am sorry. Are we discussing the AFDC [Aid to Families with Dependent Children] program specifically?"

Moynihan: "Yes."

Bertini: "When a mother comes in, and it is established who the father is, if it is, what kind of parameters for child support—"

Moynihan: "'Parameters'? Now, what is a 'parameter'? Describe a parameter to me in mathematics. What is a parameter?"

Bertini: "I don't mean it in mathematical terms, but rather—"

Moynihan: "In what sense do you mean it? What sense has it got?"

Bertini: "Has that particular father, if he is—"

Moynihan: "No, 'parameter.' I want to know about 'parameter.'"

Bertini: "If I could use the word 'scope,' that may be a better word to use."

Moynihan: "That is good. 'Parameter' is a fake word. It acts like you know a lot of algebra, which most of us don't know. Maybe you do; I don't. It is a word to be avoided unless you know what it means. 'Scope' is good."

Bertini: "The scope, in each individual case, or what specifically is being done by that father, if he is named, in order to pay for the support for that child. That is asked of the welfare mothers who come in to apply in any office. As the process goes forward, there is a court order undertaken. If there is child support to be paid—"

Moynihan: "Court order 'undertaken'? Court orders are issued."

Bertini: "Yes, sir. If there is a court order issued, and support has been paid, then obviously that would be added to the state's collection process."

Moynihan: "'Collection process'? How do you add to a process?"

Bertini: "The state undertakes the process of collecting child support dollars for those people."

Moynihan: "It 'undertakes the process'? You mean, what? The state collects the money from the father?"

Bertini: "Yes, sir."

Moynihan: "And then what happens?"

Bertini: "In the case of AFDC mothers, the state uses that collection to offset the AFDC payments at the same rate that the state pays for the AFDC collection."

Moynihan: "By 'offset,' do you mean it gets to keep some of the money?"

Bertini: "Some of the money. That is correct."

Moynihan: "What is the rest of the money?"

Bertini: "Well, fifty dollars is a passthrough that goes to the mother."

Moynihan: "Why say 'passthrough,' when you say the fifty dollars goes to the mother?"

Bertini: "Those are just the common terms that are usually used to discuss it, the fifty-dollar passthrough."

Moynihan: "And that is why we don't know anything about the subject. May I say, quite gently, we don't know one damned thing about the subject—passthrough, parameters, all of those words, which avoid meaning. Remember, that mother and child get an extra fifty dollars per month—not just once in a while, per month. And the federal government gets some, does it not? How much?"

Bertini: "The federal government takes the money that the state otherwise uses and—"

Moynihan: "'The federal government takes the money which the state otherwise uses'? That does not make any sense, Ms. Bertini."

Bertini: "Sir, if you don't mind, Mr. Bob Harris is here, who is the head of our child support enforcement office, and if I could ask him to respond more thoroughly to your questions, I would like to do that."

Moynihan: "Sure."

Bertini had testified before congressional committees two dozen times, but never before had she been so unnerved. At the end, she stood up to her full five foot two and with all the dignity she could muster walked out of the room.

"It was absolutely awful," Bertini said, "the most humiliating moment of my life."

An aide rushed up to her and apologized, saying, "The senator does that about once a year to someone."

Washington is a city where everyone is expected to play his or her assigned roles. Moynihan is one of the few exceptions. The only thing that is predictable about him is his unpredictability. He can be charming, coy, and cutting, often at the same time. He is hard to read and harder to get to know. An interview with Moynihan proceeds under his unwritten rules: Ask whatever question you want and he will answer whatever question he wants, even if totally unrelated to the one you asked. The blanks will be filled in by Lawrence O'Donnell, Moynihan's aide and alter ego.

O'Donnell was as improbable a staff director for the stuffy Senate

Finance Committee as Moynihan was its chairman. With his long hair and laid-back attitude, he let everybody know he was just passing through and would not dream of making a career out of something so ostentatiously careerist as a congressional staff job. His attitude was that of an archaeologist who had stumbled on a great dig, or a Hollywood screenwriter doing research for his next movie. Politics was theater, and he could not imagine a more fascinating central character than Moynihan.

O'Donnell did not come to Washington to change the world, or to make public policy, or even to bolster his résumé. He came because Liz Moynihan asked him to. He was about as ideological as a brussels sprout. When White House aides anguished over health care reform, O'Donnell stepped back and reminded himself, "Washington is a great place as long as you have no vested interest in the outcome."

Bill Clinton is not the first president to become exasperated with Moynihan, whose stubborn individualism makes him an unreliable team player. A favorite Moynihan expression is "white shoe fuck." He uses it to deride people who, in his view, are "above it all." The phrase captures his deep-rooted feelings about class. Anyone who has worked for Moynihan can recite the lines: "These guys have never been in a city jail. They don't understand what it's like. I have been there. They don't understand how people live. They don't know what it's like to [have to] meet a rent payment." Moynihan's brush with the law occurred when, as a college student, he resisted arrest after arguing with a cop over a minor traffic infraction. The cop whacked him with his nightstick, and the future senator spent a few hours in a Massachusetts jail.

Moynihan came of age in Hell's Kitchen, a Manhattan slum. His father walked out and the family was on welfare for a brief period. Patrick and a younger brother and sister moved with their mother into a succession of cold-water flats. In exchange for signing a new lease, they often got a free month's rent. Now it is all part of the Moynihan mystique, that he shined shoes in Times Square, worked as a stevedore on the West Side piers, and tended bar in the corner pub owned by his mother on West 42nd Street.

But Moynihan knew there was a better life out there. He was ten years old when his father left, just disappeared, never to be heard from again. Until then, his childhood had been comfortably middle class. The abandonment thrust the family into poverty. John Moynihan was an itinerant journalist, personally engaging but weak, with a taste for alcohol and a love for gambling that finally overwhelmed him. His son was driven to regain what in his mind's eye rightfully belonged to him. Moynihan graduated first in his class from Benjamin Franklin High School (now the Manhattan Center for Science and Math) on 116th Street and FDR Drive. The yearbook predicted he would become a bank president, "cussing out the labor unions and durn radicals."

Moynihan's patrician manner belies a past that is seared in his memory. His trademark handkerchief in the pocket and hand-knotted bow tie project a drawing-room nonchalance that he has worked hard to achieve. He rarely talks about his growing up, now more than a half-century ago.

"He would occasionally blurt out something to me," says a friend. "And I'd try to engage him, and he'd wave his hand and say, 'That's enough of that.'" Moynihan would never discuss the pain he must have felt at his father's abandonment, the way Clinton and other baby-boomer politicians poured out their feelings.

Moynihan's struggles as a youth surface in his attitudes about class. He is class-conscious in the best and worst sense. "Class, that's why he despises Clinton" says the wife of a southern Democratic senator. When it is pointed out that Moynihan comes from Hell's Kitchen, she huffs, "No more." Moynihan's critics say he has become what he hates, an uppity patrician whose horizons end at the Harvard Club. After the 1994 election, when Democrats looked to Moynihan for leadership on his pet issue, welfare reform, they discovered his highest priority was being renamed regent to the Smithsonian Institution.

At the same time, Moynihan recoils from the habits of the rich. As a young man, he worked for Averell Harriman, one of the "Wise Men" who shaped the post–World War II world. He saw how Harriman never carried money and let others pay for minor expenses. "He watched aristocrats," says a friend. "While he would have liked their financial independence, he didn't like some of their personality characteristics."

Moynihan's class consciousness surfaced during a 1990 Senate debate over curbing speaking fees and other outside income that senators could collect. Under pressure from their House colleagues, who had already voted to ban honoraria, senators voted overwhelmingly to abolish the practice as well, and to cap the amount of outside professional income they could earn. The measure left untouched the fortunes of the Senate's many millionaires while restricting the ability of those like Moynihan who are not independently wealthy to supplement their salary.

Infuriated by the unfairness, Moynihan introduced a surprise handwritten amendment to extend the new limit on outside earnings to unearned income, the money that millionaire senators draw from family businesses and stock investments. Texas Sen. Lloyd Bentsen, the product of oil money, dismissed the maneuver as "class warfare." Moynihan had waited to spring his amendment until very few senators were on the floor, and as they streamed back to cast their vote, they joked about how they were voting according to their financial situation. The wealthiest members voted against the amendment; the less endowed were for it. As the vote stalled in a fifty-fifty tie, Moynihan stood in the center aisle, waving his arms aloft like a desperate auctioneer. "One more vote," he pleaded.

Laughing, Alaska Republican Frank Murkowski stepped forward and switched his vote. He had nothing to lose, really, because everybody knew that when the fun and games were over, the leadership would make sure the amendment died in committee and never reached the President's desk.

Moynihan spends every summer churning out a book. He has published eleven, and edited or co-edited five more. The advances he receives are modest, pegged as they are to sales. One of his books, Moynihan notes with some bitterness, sold four thousand copies, which barely puts it above a vanity press publication. His books are treated as important and have been kindly reviewed, but they do not sell well, in part because he does not have the time to do them justice. "His books are much less than he," says a friend. "What he will tell you is that he is poor. He has a senator's salary, but that is all he has. He is operating at breakeven. He is frustrated because he takes the advance because he needs the money, but he has to agree to a short deadline."

While they may be commercial failures, the books Moynihan has written and edited on public policy and social issues add to his reputation as an intellectual. Columnist George Will once wrote that Moynihan "writes more books than some political people read."

Moynihan is a workaholic who will die over his 1960s vintage Smith-Corona electric typewriter. He does not own a single tool of recreation. He is in the office on Saturday and Sunday and has been there on Christmas Day. When Congress is not in session, he and Liz retreat to the farm in Pindars Corners in upstate New York that they bought more than thirty years ago. Moynihan writes in a one-room schoolhouse located on the property. A short distance away is the imposing but gracious pre–Civil War house that Liz has painstakingly restored, and that the Moynihans call home. Liz's mother is buried on a hillside on the seven-hundred-acre farm, beneath a huge cedar tree.

Handling Moynihan is high art. "You're absolutely right," is a good way to begin. That creates the proper climate for slipping in the ifs, ands, and buts that must be introduced for Moynihan's own good. O'Donnell has perfected the technique. "The first word out of my mouth is absolutely total agreement—even if I think it's a bad idea, and I know we can never do it," he says. "And maybe just as I go out the door, I do this little Columbo-like moment and say, 'Al Sharpton might run against you—if you do whatever that thing is.'"

All politicians are self-involved; Moynihan, especially so. Aides joke that the basic construction for a Moynihan speech is, "I said, I did, I am. . . . I said, I did, I am. . . ." One does not really interview Moynihan. You give him a forum to quote himself. And he talks about whatever is on his mind. He is masterful at self-quotation. Over the course of an hour, he will get up from his chair three and four times to pull a book from the shelf and read aloud a favorite passage. It turns out that they are books he has written, so he is reciting with great fondness his own words.

For an Irish street kid, Moynihan sure can put on airs. He wants recognition as an eminent pundit. His conversation is sprinkled with, "I projected . . . I foreshadowed . . . I alerted. . . ." People who want his help flatter him by referring to his "prophetic skills." He has become a parody of himself, the prince of posturing. He talks as if his visitor is not there, as though he is addressing some distant audience.

A former aide offers instruction on how to deal with Moynihan: "The first impression is critical because he is quick to judge people. If you can be not merely conveniently sincere, but legitimately so, that's a good thing," she says. "How you first get on with him can mean life and death for the relationship. Then you should know that the light of his life is his grandson, that his mother had a bar in Hell's Kitchen, and that he has a farm in Pindars Corners. Also, do not make an appointment in the morning. He's not good in the morning. He's grumpy. You would not want to have breakfast with Pat. He's in a better mood at three in the afternoon."

O'Donnell refined the former aide's advice, warning against any mention of Moynihan's mother's bar, the farm, or three-year-old grandson, Michael Patrick. "He'll think you're trying to ingratiate yourself."

O'Donnell was eating dinner at the Morrison-Clark Inn on Massachusetts Avenue one night when his cell phone beeped. It was Liz Moynihan calling. She was on her way to New York and worried that Pat would not get a proper dinner without her. A bowl of Cheerios is the outer limit of his culinary skills. Moynihan is inept at life's ordinary tasks. They fall to Liz. In return, she says, "He's good to me. You don't make any money on sixteenth-century India." A scholar in her own right, Liz has written one book and published a number of academic articles on archaeological finds in India. Their marriage of forty years is modeled after the traditional arrangement where the man is the thinker and breadwinner and the woman handles the house and children.

"It was frustrating when we shared things," she says. "He takes too long to make decisions. He didn't go to schools. He doesn't buy houses. But he's a person who's made a difference. I didn't set out to make a difference. By freeing him to do all this, I have made a contribution. Besides, he's lousy at it."

Elizabeth Brennan Moynihan is her husband's buffer in politics and in life. She handles what he hates and what he is no good at, from asking people for money to operating the dishwasher.

"He's a miserable bachelor," she says. "Once this summer, he soloed on the dishwasher. I came back to two weeks of dirty dishes in the kitchen sink."

Pat and Liz met in the Averell Harriman campaign for governor of New York in 1954 and married the following year. Their similar Irish Catholic backgrounds drew them together in Harriman's world of wealthy WASPs. They became good friends, and Moynihan proposed marriage before they ever had a formal date.

She is absolutely crucial to his career. She is his campaign manager, not his campaign wife. Get to Liz, and you've gotten to Pat. "It's the same person; you can't even distinguish them," says O'Donnell. "Like the nuns say, 'Pray to the blessed Virgin Mary because her son can't deny her.' The nuns were teaching you strategy with God." The same strategy is useful when dealing with the Moynihans.

Liz is an elegant woman with silver, shoulder-length hair. She and Pat are like matching bookends. He has his bow tie and impish manner. She has an artistic funkiness about her. But she is practical. Part of being practical is accepting what she cannot change. A friend recalls having dinner with the Moynihans when they lived on Capitol Hill. The conversation and the drinks were still flowing when Moynihan gazed at his watch and announced, "Ten o'clock, off to bed!" And he ambled upstairs. Liz, long accustomed to his unpredictable ways, sighed, "I guess the evening's over."

Her dream is that someday she and her husband will write a book together about their favorite places in New York. She has not read all his books. "But I can recite them all," she adds dryly, a wicked reference to Moynihan's tendency to quote himself.

Protective of her family life, Liz rarely gives interviews. "A lot of people don't know we have children," she says. "We never used the kids." She was furious when New York Times reporter Todd S. Purdum wrote that Moynihan went out of his way to introduce his black daughter-in-law, Tracey, at the New York State Democratic Convention. The implication was that Moynihan, faced with a challenge from an African-American, had his son's wife on stage to curry favor with blacks. She points out that the couple had been with them throughout the day, and had appeared at other events. "It was such a nasty thing to do," Liz said. "I wrote him a note. I thought that was a cheap shot."

The incident upset Purdum, who likes and admires the Moynihans and feels he handled the facts fairly. The extent of Liz's fury stunned him. She fired off the handwritten note on Hotel Carlyle stationery. It was full of underlinings and capitalized words to convey the full extent of her outrage. Purdum phoned her at the hotel, but she refused to take his call. "She thinks I'm the devil incarnate," he says.

"You know I really don't have the energy left for this anymore," Liz sighed. "We've been through three generations of reporters, and I don't have the energy for it. If you don't use your kids for political purposes, they're not fair game—and these bastards don't play by those rules."

Liz is one reason why Moynihan has never been a serious contender for president. "I wouldn't allow it," she snaps. Then she adds, "He's never been interested. People have come in the past to talk to him about it. I would absolutely never let him do it. It's a terrible job. He couldn't stay interested in politics long enough to run for president. Jimmy Carter went to Iowa ninety . . . or some absurd amount of times. I'm happy to say I've never been there."

The political professionals dismissed Moynihan as "another Adlai Stevenson," an egghead ill-suited to the campaign trail. If Moynihan felt passed over, he never let on. The system demands a degree of blandness and adaptability that is beneath him.

A recently retired Democratic senator, asked why Moynihan was never a serious presidential contender or even a vice presidential prospect, replied, "Flaky—and then, in the past, he's had a problem." The senator then made a motion as if he were chugging a drink. In the past? "Oh, I don't know," he replied, "but I've seen him when it was embarrassing."

Compared to some of the headliner drunks, Russell Long among them, Moynihan's indiscretions are minor. The tales that Washington insiders collect about Moynihan are more like after-dinner jokes—comedy not tragedy. They are a throwback to an earlier time when hard drinking was a way for men to prove themselves.

Whatever pain Moynihan has caused himself and his family, his public life has been unscathed and to some extent even enhanced by his prodigious thirst. It has made him more of a character, which, after all, is his real place in the political firmament. George Will, paraphrasing President Lincoln's response when told that General Grant drank too much, wrote, "Find out what Moynihan drinks and send a case of the stuff to the other ninety-nine senators."

Age and wisdom have conspired to impose moderation, so the most outlandish stories about Moynihan's drinking go back a while. Midge Costanza, the former vice mayor of Rochester, New York, and then assistant for public liaison to President Carter, recalls waiting in a holding room at a Manhattan hotel with other guests, including Moynihan, to be seated at the head table for a political dinner.

"The senator was known to imbibe a bit," Costanza recalls. "I came walking in, in my trim, size-six-at-the-time body, and I was wearing a red dress. We were doing photo-ops, and Moynihan—I'm five feet for Christ's sake—comes at me, all red-faced and smiling. 'Midge, Midge, Midge, what we need is more cleavage here, and less cleavage in the party'—pointing to my top. He did not plunge his hand into my dress, but because of the difference in our height [Moynihan is six foot five] it looked that way in the picture."

Moynihan's aides managed to kill the photo. It was never published. But the story got out, and a *Doonesbury* cartoon strip portrayed Moynihan as the dinner guest from hell. "To be on the safe side, I'd put him with the extra man," the host is advised.

When a reporter called Costanza for comment, she made light of the incident, quipping, "I hope he enjoyed it more than I did." Moynihan was furious at her for the wisecrack. He thought it implied that he really did plunge his hand down her dress. He wanted her to defend him. She told him that humor was the best defense.

Many of the stories about Moynihan's drinking conclude with his performing heroic intellectual feats when lesser men would have been under the table. At a stag going-away party for Frank Shakespeare, a former CBS executive whom Reagan named ambassador to Portugal, Moynihan did not show up at the seated dinner in the Madison Hotel until after the food was served and the toasts had begun. He staggered in, visibly drunk, and proceeded to drain what was left in Ed Meese's wine glass. Round-faced and jovial, Meese was one of the more ideologically conservative Californians who had come to Washington with Reagan. Other guests say they will never forget the look of astonishment on his doughy face. The room fell quiet. All eyes were on Moynihan, who lurched his way to the podium.

Several people had been assigned to speak. Moynihan was not one of them. The audience sat transfixed, expecting the senator from New York to make a monumental fool of himself. Instead, Moynihan delivered a brilliantly crafted testimonial to Frank Shakespeare based on quotes from William Shakespeare. His voice was thick with alcohol, but his command of Shakespeare was clear and on point. When he finished, Moynihan lurched his way back across the room and out the door, leaving the stunned diners with a story they would repeat for years.

Preparing to review one of Moynihan's books for the July 9, 1984, issue of *The New Republic*, journalist Morton Kondracke scheduled an interview with Moynihan for the late afternoon. Moynihan offered Kondracke a drink, which he declined. Moynihan then filled a large tumbler with ice and poured straight scotch over it. He had three of those and by the end of the session was quite expansive. Kondracke quoted him saying, "You'll find I've never been wrong about anything." Moynihan says the quote was "a simple joke as we began an interview on my life and times. I belong to a Church which believes in forgiveness but consigns infallibility to the Pope."

With his ebullient manner, flushed face, and unruly white forelock, Moynihan could answer a casting call for an Irish pol. Some people wrongly connect his unusual speech pattern and his sometimes unsteady gait with drinking. They actually result from two unrelated problems.

To compensate for a childhood stammer, Moynihan devised an elaborate, Edwardian way of talking to avoid certain words and to cover up his hesitation. It is easy to attribute his exaggerated pronunciation and dramatic pauses to his being a little tipsy, yet he sounds the same first thing in the morning.

He also has trouble standing upright for extended periods. He suffers from peripheral neuropathy, the degeneration of nerves in his legs. He turned down a coveted invitation to speak at the 1994 Gridiron Dinner, an annual spoof of politicians staged by Washington journalists, because he could not stand long enough comfortably to deliver a speech.

Moynihan and his wife sleep in separate bedrooms because he is such a fitful sleeper. He gets up in the middle of the night and reads for hours. He is cranky in the morning and prone to displays of ill temper throughout the day. His staff bears the brunt of it.

"My predecessor in the job gave me a good piece of advice," recalls a former staffer. "When Pat gets on one of his tears, imagine you're watching television. Throw a TV screen around his head and have the same emotional response you would have watching television."

There is a side of Moynihan that is irrational, and those who love him, or who work for him, say it is best to just let him rant. "His anger is not personal," says O'Donnell. "He's more angry about the situation. But it's there, and it can scare people to death."

O'Donnell copes with the boss's tempests better than most. He grew up in a boisterous Irish Catholic working-class family that he cheerily describes as dysfunctional. "What he does doesn't even pass for anger in my family," says O'Donnell.

Moynihan is a snob when it comes to associating with street politicians. When Mayor Ed Koch, a voluble self-promoter, called one day to discuss efforts to save a museum for the city, Moynihan hung up the phone and declared, "That guy has never been in a museum except to step out of a parade into a museum to take a piss."

Moynihan's lofty approach works, especially in juxtaposition with the junior senator from New York, Alfonse D'Amato, who is often referred to as "Senator Pothole." New Yorkers seem satisfied with the division of labor. Mayor Koch, who now hosts a radio talk show, often says, "You would go to D'Amato if you wanted to get your passport expedited, but if you want a discussion on policy toward the People's Republic of China, you'd go to Moynihan." The remark rankles Moynihan. "I'm not running for county sheriff," he retorts.

D'Amato hustles in a way that Moynihan finds distasteful. On a slow campaign day, D'Amato will do morning television, stop at a couple of fund-raising breakfasts, then board a plane and do airport press conferences in Buffalo, Rochester, and Syracuse. With Moynihan, forget morning television. Given his wake-up mood, it would be a disaster. He prefers meeting with editorial boards, where he can pontificate and dazzle. Then he might take a break for a walking tour to indulge his interest in architecture and history, followed by lunch with the mayor and local officials. After lunch, nap time. Then a fund-raiser. Then fly home.

This deceptively leisurely style does not make it any easier on staffers. Moynihan has a reputation for being one of the most demanding bosses on Capitol Hill. Everybody who works for him becomes adept at mimicking the boss's unique patter. "You never forget those 6:30 in the morning, 'Have you checked the newspapers today, lad?'" chuckles Michael McCurry, a Moynihan alumnus who is now White House press secretary. "He expected you to be up to speed."

Moynihan's bible is *The New York Times*. He has always had a pipeline to the editorial page, and he uses it. The relationship is best summed up as one of Olympian camaraderie. Moynihan keeps in touch with editors and columnists at other publications as well, sending them notes and often attaching something he wrote years ago that they might find relevant today. Conservative columnist George Will is a favorite, as is *U.S. News & World Report* writer Michael Barone, whose command of historical details rivals Moynihan's.

Beneath the veneer of scholarly discussion, Moynihan is a player in the hard-news game. "He would always say, 'Real time, real time, real time,'" says McCurry. "He knew that you have until noon before the editors make a judgment on the day's news."

It is rare to find a member of Congress who is not dedicated to constituent services, which covers everything from meeting with visiting Boy Scouts to untangling government red tape. In election years, Moynihan gets defensive about this and works up pages of all the things he has done for New York. Moynihan thinks of himself as a civilized man in an uncivilized business. That is his strength politically. He is New York's special senator.

His newsletters, which he writes himself, are flights of erudition about whatever happens to strike his fancy. He has shared his memories of joining the navy as a young man in 1944, educated the voters on the history of the Social Security Act, and revealed his tips for delivering commencement speeches (he delivered five one year). The newsletters were one of his favorite ways to keep in touch. When the new Republican majority in Congress moved to eliminate them after the 1994 election, Moynihan reminded the Republicans they were tampering with an ancient institution. The first newsletter had been sent out from Philadelphia in 1791.

"I don't think we should destroy two-century-old institutions," he wrote. "But then, there are a lot of things I think with which others around here differ."

Campaigning for reelection in 1994, Moynihan was not the least bit defensive about the collapse of health care reform. That was Bill Clinton's problem. He had a triumph of his own to talk about that played well in Manhattan's silk-stocking district, and in the suburbs: the infamous nanny tax. The issue arose when Zoe Baird, a corporate attorney from Connecticut, was withdrawn by the White House as a potential Attorney General because she had not paid the Social Security taxes for her nanny. "Someone said she came down with a great reputation and left with the name of a problem," says Moynihan. "And it broke on this man's watch," he says, jabbing his finger to indicate President Clinton. "We never got a bill from them to do anything about it. We wrote our own bill and we passed it. Passed it unanimously. . . . And the House passed it unanimously. And the President signed it in the dark."

True, Clinton did not celebrate the elimination of the nanny tax for part-time household help the way he would almost any other piece of legislation. He did not want to draw attention to the "yuppie from hell" problem that was a sore spot of his presidency. Moynihan happened to be meeting with a newspaper editorial board in Syracuse when he learned that Clinton had signed the bill. "We have decriminalized baby-sitting," Moynihan announced abruptly, as if it were an urgent news flash. The editors were accustomed to Moynihan providing the odd sort of fact, but this one landed without any context. Half the people in the room said, "What?"

So Moynihan explained how he had worked it out so that anybody under eighteen is not required to pay Social Security taxes, and that part-time workers who earn under $1,000 are also exempt. "And I realized about half the people in the room had been thinking, 'Jesus, will the IRS be after me? What was her name? Alice . . . Alice what?' And the federal government was going to be after them, and now it wasn't going to be. So I would stand up and say, 'Incidentally, don't worry anymore about baby-sitters. It's very simple now.' My God, there was much more anxiety out there than anybody ever knew."

As staff director of the Senate Finance Committee, O'Donnell commanded the highest salary, $130,000, that a congressional staffer can be paid. "Statutory maximum, top of the show, as they call it in show business," he quipped. The figure is set by federal statute, and O'Donnell never thought it was anything to boast about. Compared to what he could make on the outside, the money was not a reason to stay, but to leave. His salary was public record, so why be coy about it, he thought. He delighted in keeping an ironic distance from the politics of the moment. He was there to observe, and this was great material, but he had no vested interest in the outcome. Then he discovered on November 8, 1994, that there was something at stake after all—his lifestyle as a member of the Democratic majority.

The first call came from Sheila Burke, Bob Dole's chief of staff. In a cheery mood, she wanted to congratulate Moynihan on his reelection. It was only two o'clock in the afternoon, but exit polls conducted by the television networks were a reliable predictor of the probable results. Burke, a former Democrat with a sharp intellect, admires Moynihan, and he dotes on her. But his reelection was only a tiny part of her merriment. "We've definitely won eight," she told O'Donnell. In one day, the Republicans had gone from a minority of forty-five seats to a majority of fifty-three seats. With the transfer of power, all the committee chairmanships shifted from Democrats to Republicans, and so did the highest ranking staff positions. Moynihan had lost his chairmanship, and O'Donnell would no longer be top of the show.

At the time, however, O'Donnell was just glad to have some news to pass along to Moynihan. "She saved me," he says. He had been on the phone to his friends at the networks without much success. Burke's sources were clearly better. Already, there were subtle shifts in power.

Moynihan spent election night 1994 in the presidential suite of the Hyatt Regency in New York. There was a party for him on the terrace. He won handily with fifty-five percent of the vote against Republican Bernadette Castro, an heir to the Castro Convertible Sofa fortune. She complained that her fellow Republican, Senator D'Amato, had sabotaged her fund-raising efforts. D'Amato and most senior Republicans did not want to expend time, energy, and money on a futile effort to displace Moynihan. His share of the vote was down substantially from sixty-seven percent the previous election, but he had survived the Republican blitzkrieg. He was not at all surprised that the Democrats had lost the Senate. And his chairmanship? "That's all right at my age," he said quietly. "I have been there."

The next day, Moynihan and O'Donnell walked to a little Italian restaurant on Lexington Avenue for lunch. People offered congratulations, but O'Donnell could see that Moynihan was depressed. He felt that he had proved himself as a leader, and it irritated him that many would judge him in the context of a failed health care reform effort. "You wouldn't want this job for the next two years," O'Donnell assured him.

O'Donnell argued that the loss of the Senate "saved" Moynihan from a presidential legislative agenda that would be unachievable. "And we would know it," he declared between forkfuls of pasta, "and we would begin with that same dynamic and that same set of phone calls about *why isn't this happening*—and them not understanding why it isn't happening."

The official White House explanation for not getting a health care bill was forty-four Republicans in general and Bob Dole in particular. If the Democrats had clung to the Senate but with a narrower margin, Clinton would still have been checkmated. "There would be no functional point to retaining this chairmanship," O'Donnell told Moynihan. "We are out from under the pressure of all that for these two years."

Moynihan understood that he was better off not having to carry the Clinton agenda. "You've made me feel a lot better," he said. And after a time, he realized how relieved he was. As chairman, it was not enough to just make rhetorical points. He was accountable. The Republican takeover freed him to be a voice of opposition, a role that has defined him for better or worse throughout his career. He could sit back, pontificate, and criticize without having to worry about producing legislation. Moynihan has always been more comfortable describing society's ills than offering a cure.

Liz was thrilled to be free of the White House.

"If you are chairman and it's a president of your party, it's a lot of fun if you and the President have the same views," she explained. "If you and the President *sound* like you have the same views, and it turns out you don't, or you have a White House as difficult as this White House to deal with, it's no fun. Still, Pat did a lot. He handled the budget, NAFTA, health care, and GATT—and they've been pretty rotten to him. Let them deal with Bob Packwood—and Pat's back may get better. It gets worse with stress."

O'Donnell implied in his pep talk that Moynihan would be sentenced to the minority for two years. An assessment of the Senate seats at stake in 1996 and 1998 subsequently led O'Donnell to conclude that the Democrats' first chance to win back control is the year 2000, when the Republican freshmen elected in 1994 are up for reelection.

O'Donnell thought life in the minority would be a dramatically easier job. He was to learn quickly that being in the minority is never easy.

"I have to fire people, and I have to cut everybody's salary very dramatically," he said. "I don't mind that in theory. There's no indignity in it for me. Welcome to democracy. . . . It's just that the more I've thought about it, as I stare at how to make the budget work, cutting everybody's salaries, my salary. . . . And I have this baby in New York. Maybe I can watch the C-SPAN version of this."

The angst among Democrats was understandable. O'Donnell's budget as staff director for the Senate Finance Committee was cut in half. He went from having $1.9 million to spend and fifty-four staffers reporting to him to having $880,000 and seventeen staffers. The Senate committees divide their resources, two-thirds majority and one-third minority. The fact that it was expected did not make it less painful.

O'Donnell despaired at the task ahead: "I'm dealing with staff where I have to say, 'You're going to get a $10,000 pay cut, at least. I very much want you to stay. I don't know if we can do this without you. You'd be crazy not to look for another job.'" He would cut his own salary by $15,000.

O'Donnell found the change in his own status stunning. He could be gone for over an hour and come back to no phone calls. In his majority days, a stack of pink phone messages always awaited him, a third of them marked urgent. This time, he watched President Clinton's State of the Union address on television.

His dance card for 1995 was empty. He was not invited to the traditional "Salute to Congress" black tie dinner, sponsored by the Washington Press Club Foundation, which marks the beginning of a new Congress and a new social season. He watched on C-SPAN as freshman

Rep. Sonny Bono wowed the audience of insiders with a Beltway version of a Las Vegas lounge act. The previous year, O'Donnell went as the guest of *New York Times* reporter Adam Clymer, who was honored at the dinner for his coverage of Congress. O'Donnell had turned down several other invitations to accept Clymer's. With the Republicans in charge, O'Donnell was no longer a hot guest. "I'm watching myself slip into absolute oblivion," he said.

O'Donnell's new place in the pecking order was made clear in many ways. On the phone one day with journalist Morton Kondracke, he could hear Kondracke being loudly paged in the background. "Lindy Paul on line two," the pager said. Lindy Paul was O'Donnell's replacement as staff director of the Senate Finance Committee. "And in the less than a billionth of a second that it took, I'm thinking, 'Does he know that I heard that? And if he does know, what's he going to do?'" O'Donnell recalls.

"Lindy Paul's calling me back," Kondracke said forthrightly. "Can I get you later?"

"And he never called back," says O'Donnell with a wry laugh.

When he moved to the smaller minority quarters, O'Donnell never unpacked a single box. He wrote a letter to the Moynihans early in the new year with his resignation. He said he had missed the first year of his baby daughter's life, and that he needed to live in the same city as his wife. That meant Los Angeles, because O'Donnell's wife, actress Kathryn Harrold, had established a career in Hollywood. "Liz would say in so many words, 'I think that a wife's most important job is to make sure the husband is happy in his work,'" O'Donnell said. "There aren't any of those people left. I'm not going to get that deal. She is up-to-date in her way of thinking on everything else, but her solution was for Kathryn to move to Washington so I can comfortably do this work."

O'Donnell was gone by summer. "You have to break this addiction," he said. "It's spectator stuff for us now. The Democrats are not in the game. I'd have to have a real good justification to stay."

At times, being in the minority would not be any easier for Moynihan than it was for O'Donnell. The country was in a convulsion over welfare reform, Moynihan's issue, and he unhappily found himself on the outside looking in. The Republicans' pledge to balance the budget by 2002 required draconian cuts in spending. Polls showed that voters by a substantial majority thought too much money was being spent on welfare. As the country's leading critic of the welfare system, everyone from the press to his Democratic colleagues looked to Moynihan for answers.

"Thirty-two years of welfare reform is more than I can bear," Liz

Moynihan sighed. "Why don't they implement what he passed?" She was referring to the Family Support Act of 1988, authored by Moynihan, which passed the Senate with ninety-six votes. It had never been fully funded. The legislation bolstered work requirements with job training and child care. Once regarded as a conservative reform measure, it now appeared generous in contrast to Republican proposals.

Sen. Tom Daschle, the earnest South Dakota liberal elected as Minority Leader, sought Moynihan's advice on welfare reform. How should the Democrats frame the issue? And how would that thinking translate into legislation? Daschle assembled a welfare reform task force. Months went by. Moynihan did not take the task force seriously.

A *Newsweek* "Periscope" item noted that Senate Democrats were wondering what had happened to Moynihan.

"He's still talking about the Family Assistance Plan," grumbled a Democratic senator, referring to the measure that Moynihan had drafted a generation earlier for President Nixon.

The country's preeminent scholar on families and children stood on the sidelines. Some of his moderate Democratic allies from the health care reform fight could not understand why he did not join them this time in their rush to the middle. He did not believe in legislating social policy on hopes. Cutting off unwed mothers from welfare in the hope that some Darwinian impulse would take hold, and that they would suddenly pull themselves together, struck him as the ultimate folly in social engineering.

"Tell me what we ought to do about it," a leading Democrat recalls pleading with Moynihan.

"I don't know—maybe nothing," Moynihan said. "All we can do is understand it."

During congressional hearings, Moynihan pulled out charts on out-of-wedlock births that showed skyrocketing rates throughout the North Atlantic nations. One expert testified that European countries had begun to tackle the problem by making contraceptives more available. Asked if there was a lesson in that for the United States, Moynihan quipped, "You start by being born a Norwegian."

Moynihan's supercilious attitude grated on his colleagues. Tired of the taunts that he was AWOL on welfare reform, Moynihan requested a meeting with Clinton shortly before the 1995 Easter recess. The question on the table: What do we do now? Ten senators were present in the Cabinet Room late that afternoon, including Moynihan and Daschle. Clinton wanted to know if Democrats should get together on a single bill in the Senate as they had done in the House. While the House measure failed, it demonstrated a rare unity among Democrats.

"I have the Clinton welfare bill from last year," Moynihan volunteered.

"Oh, no, no, something everyone can agree on," Clinton responded, as if such a thing existed among Democrats.

In the end, only three of the ten senators thought the Democrats should offer an alternative bill, and they lacked real conviction. Connecticut Sen. Chris Dodd, whom Clinton had recently named co-chairman of the Democratic National Committee, led the opposition to a separate bill. "It would only invite stories that Democrats can't get together," he said. His wry argument won out.

"I hate the House bill," Clinton declared. The legislation passed by the Republican House transferred control of welfare programs to the states in the form of block grants frozen at 1994 spending levels. The measure would end the sixty-year-old federal entitlement for poor children and allow states broad discretion on how to spend their dollars. The nation's least powerful citizens would have to fight for a shrinking share of state budgets under the new arrangement.

Moynihan strongly opposed turning over Aid to Families with Dependent Children to the states, and had pressed Clinton without success to promise that he would veto any bill that did not protect the federal entitlement to welfare. "It is beyond belief that in the middle of the Great Depression in the 1930s we provided for children a minimum benefit to keep them alive, and in the middle of a successful 1990s, with a $7 trillion economy, we're going to take that away," he declared. Moynihan suspected that in the Age of Gingrich, with Clinton scrambling to conform to the new Republican ethos, welfare reform would be difficult to veto. Senate Democrats, even liberals like Majority Leader Tom Daschle, were not going to fight for the entitlement. Daschle said privately that Democrats could never explain to voters why it was so important to oppose shifting welfare programs from one set of bureaucrats to another.

Moynihan noticed on that lovely spring day in April 1995 in the Cabinet Room that Clinton avoided using the word "veto." Hating a bill is not the same as vetoing it. So Moynihan pointedly inquired of the President, "Would you veto the bill that came out of the House?"

Clinton said yes. O'Donnell was sitting along the wall with other staffers and made note of the President's commitment. Did it mean anything? Clinton had gone further in his term without wielding a veto pen than any previous U.S. president since Millard Fillmore, 142 years earlier. "I have to admit that my mind immediately went to, okay, if they change a sentence, would you veto it?" O'Donnell recalls. "'Now, now,' I said to myself, 'Don't be so suspicious.' Any normal person hearing what Clinton said would expect a veto."

In the van driving back to Capitol Hill, Moynihan was jubilant. He had finally extracted what he wanted from Clinton. "He said that he would veto the *House* bill," O'Donnell quietly reminded his boss.

"Ah, c'mon, don't do your thing of always trying to figure out what card he's trying to hold back," Moynihan replied.

Within weeks, it became obvious that Clinton, who as a candidate had vowed to "end welfare as we know it," wanted badly to sign a welfare reform bill.

Moynihan's role in the Senate now has forced him back to his roots as a Democrat and as a liberal. He is one of the few politicians of stature willing to defend welfare as an entitlement. His longtime nemesis, Rev. Al Sharpton, the civil rights activist who had opposed him in the Democratic primary the previous year, faxed Moynihan a letter commending him for his position on welfare. In May of 1995, Moynihan introduced an updated version of his Family Support Act as a historical marker of where he is thirty years after he launched the debate about family breakdown with the Moynihan Report. He did not bother to seek cosponsors. The bill, when it was put to a vote in the Senate, failed, fifty-six to forty-one.

Moynihan realized he could not stop the Republican approach on welfare reform. All that remained in the Democratic arsenal was Clinton's veto. Moynihan's grim task was to serve as pallbearer for the doomed legislation. Days before the Senate passed its version of welfare reform by an overwhelming eighty-seven to twelve, Moynihan accused the Clinton administration of standing by "passively," and predicted that if the legislation became law, "Children will be sleeping on grates in ten years."

Moynihan had one strategy all along, and that was to exact Clinton's veto. He would do nothing to make the legislation more palatable even though he was one of the conferees named to resolve the differences between the House and Senate. It was a useless exercise, he told an aide. "In eighteen years, I've never been to a conference that wasn't completely orchestrated before I walked in the door. As a minority member, you're just there for a quorum." He might even support the most punitive measures the Republicans proposed, he said petulantly. If the bill closely resembled the House version, there was a better chance that Clinton would veto it.

Within the administration, there was fierce infighting over what Clinton should do. One set of advisers, headed by political consultant Dick Morris, who until joining the Clinton reelection team had worked mainly for Republicans, wanted Clinton to sign a welfare reform bill to prove he was a centrist. Another group of advisers, which included Health and Human Services Secretary Donna Shalala and Children's Defense Fund president Marion Wright Edelman, a good friend of Mrs. Clinton's, urged Clinton to veto what the Republicans were proposing. "This is about everything we believe in," they told the First Lady, pleading with her to intervene.

Mrs. Clinton refused to be drawn into the fray. Scarred by the health care battle, she had stepped back from an activist role in domestic policy. Despite a lifetime of having been an advocate for children, she refused to take a public stand. And whatever she did privately was kept private.

White House aides leaked word to reporters that Clinton, in his regular weekly radio address on Saturday, September 16, 1995, would announce his support for the welfare reform bill that would be voted on by the Senate the following week. Chief of staff Leon Panetta had not even read the bill. "Those guys don't care about anything but positioning," said one of the bill's opponents. On Friday, Shalala went to Clinton with some preliminary numbers drafted by HHS that showed the Senate welfare reform bill would put 1.2 million more children into poverty. The President, shaken by Shalala's assessment, backed away from the ringing endorsement his aides had predicted. The Sunday *New York Times* headline declared, "President Voices Optimism on Hopes for Welfare Bill." But the story noted that Clinton stopped short of calling the Senate bill a measure he could sign.

Shalala had agreed to keep the ominous numbers confidential, but Clinton, characteristically, wanted to know what others thought. He mentioned the study in a private conversation with Al From, executive director of the Democratic Leadership Council, the centrist Democrats who had been his most fervent backers in 1992. From believes that Clinton must stand up to his party's liberals if he is to win reelection, and when *The Wall Street Journal* cited the HHS study as evidence Clinton was resisting pressure from the left, From was fingered as the leaker.

Moynihan called Shalala. "Is this true?" he asked. "Is there a study?" Shalala replied that the numbers were preliminary, but that was enough for Moynihan. He then publicly demanded a full-blown study, saying that he knew the President would not knowingly sign anything that would hurt children. He was only faintly patronizing.

When the formal study was released some weeks later, it confirmed the early estimate that 1.2 million more children would be pushed into poverty by the Senate's welfare reform bill. White House aides now confided to reporters that Clinton would almost certainly veto welfare reform when it reached his desk. Moynihan had trapped the President.

*   *   *

Presidents come and go, but Moynihan endures. Asked what his secret is, he replies, "Don't ever get to be known as a politician." He smiles as he says it, savoring one of the contradictions of his career. "I've spent my life in politics," he says. "Liz and I are married forty years in May, and we met in the Harriman campaign in Albany. For forty years New Yorkers have been saying, 'He's a nice guy, he's real smart, you know, but he doesn't understand politics.' And they're [other politicians] all defeated or in jail—Ouch!—and I'm the last man standing of my generation."

A streak of anarchy runs through Moynihan's dark Irish soul. He wants to tear down everything he has built. As a young aide in Lyndon Johnson's Labor Department, his research helped create the Great Society, but after several glasses of wine, he will expound on what is wrong with Head Start, the one program from that era regarded as an undisputed success. He has been a leading critic of the welfare state for thirty years, but, at other times, one of its strongest defenders. He does not see any inconsistency in this; it is simply social relativism. If the alternative is to plunge into the unknown, and to make assumptions about human behavior for which there is no empirical data, Moynihan would rather keep the status quo. "What do we *know?*" he asks.

He hates orthodoxy in any form. He follows his own impulses and cares little about party loyalty. Otherwise, he could not have served two Republican Presidents. Too erratic and undisciplined himself to seek the presidency, he has a need to assert his superiority over the mere mortals who gain the office.

One symbol of the contradictions roiling within Moynihan is a mammoth new federal building on Pennsylvania Avenue between the White House and the Capitol, which is second in size only to the Pentagon. One of the last meetings Moynihan had at the White House with President Kennedy was over tea to discuss the redevelopment of Pennsylvania Avenue, Washington's main downtown thoroughfare. First Lady Jackie Kennedy wanted a more Parisian look, and Moynihan made it his crusade. Moynihan championed the construction of the monumental building, the last link in the redevelopment project that has spanned three decades.

The resulting behemoth of a building looms as a target for critics of big government, which Moynihan professes to be. Originally expected to cost $362 million, its ultimate cost is expected to be at least $656 million. Anticipating attacks from the new breed of budget-conscious Republicans in Congress, Senate Majority Leader Bob Dole, a friend and colleague of Moynihan's for almost twenty years, quietly proposed that the structure be named "The Ronald Reagan Building." The Reagan family gave its approval. Moynihan, one of Reagan's harshest critics while he was President, welcomed the shrewd proposal as another of those delicious ironies that have marked his career in politics.

CHAPTER FOUR

THE SPEAKER

Stranger in Paradise

Just before midnight on January 9, 1995, less than one week after he
had achieved his childhood dream by being sworn in as Speaker of
the House, Newt Gingrich faced the unenviable task of firing the
very first person he had hired for the new Republican team that was taking charge after four decades of Democratic rule.

Gingrich winced at the recollection of his jovial mood before Christmas when he had called Christina Jeffrey at Kennesaw State College in
Georgia, where she was an associate professor of political science, and
informed her, "I have spoken to your college president. I told her she's
losing a professor. And you have a new job. You are the House historian."
He remembered being a little miffed at the time when Jeffrey said she
wanted to think it over. What was there to think over? He was offering
her one of the most prestigious jobs for a historian in the country, a position he himself had insisted years earlier that the House create.

Now he wished that she had turned him down so that this moment
could have been avoided. He called Christina Jeffrey and her husband,
Robert, also a political science professor, while they were in the process
of moving into their new apartment in suburban Virginia. He had to tell
them to go back to Georgia. Their Washington adventure was over
before it had started.

That afternoon, Gingrich had been told by his press secretary, Tony
Blankley, that reporters were asking about a controversial incident in
1986 involving Jeffrey. As a volunteer grant reviewer for the Education
Department, she had recommended that funding be denied for a proposed junior high school curriculum on the Holocaust. She wrote, "The
program gives no evidence of balance or objectivity. The Nazi point of

view, however unpopular, is still a point of view and is not presented, nor is that of the Ku Klux Klan."

Blankley told Gingrich that *The New York Times* and others were set to publish the story that the historian the new Speaker had hired was an anti-Semite and a racist. If he acted swiftly by firing her, the controversy over her past statement could be contained and his blunder could be transformed into news reports of how he had acted decisively.

Gingrich had hired her with great gusto, as though he could wave a magic wand and make anything he wanted happen in Washington now that he was Speaker, but when it came to firing her he had one of his aides call. "The Speaker wants your resignation," the aide said. "Well, if the Speaker wants my resignation, you just tell the Speaker to call me," Jeffrey snapped.

An hour later, Gingrich called. As the Jeffreys remember the conversation, Gingrich never actually said she was fired, but only that she would have to resign. Later in the conversation, which went on for over an hour, Gingrich corrected himself, saying, "I think we've already said that you've resigned." The Jeffreys subsequently learned that the resignation announcement was timed to meet *The New York Times*'s 9:30 P.M. deadline. "I'm really sorry," Gingrich said. "I feel really awful. I hope you guys aren't going to hate me over this."

Jeffrey tried to explain that she had answered the allegations of anti-Semitism and racism when they first came up in 1986, and was sure she could do so again. She could not believe that Gingrich, a fellow historian who had been a visiting professor in her classes, was going to dismiss her without so much as a hearing.

Gingrich's mind was made up. The press had already been told. "I've got to pick my fights," he told the Jeffreys. "There are some battles I cannot win. If I went ahead with this, you'd become the poster child for the Democrats. I've been here sixteen years. I know how these things work."

The Jeffreys argued that the politics of the situation would work in Gingrich's favor if he would stand firm and defend her. Knowing Gingrich was the son of a military man and was obsessed with military strategy, Christina Jeffrey said, "Look, I'm an army brat, too. As the minority whip, you've got to pick your fights and be on the offensive all the time. But when you're the Speaker, you're on the defensive. . . . This is the first fight of the new regime. You don't get to say, 'Well, I think I'll pass on this one.' Your reputation is tied up in this appointment. This is the House historian position that you fought to get. . . . If you fire me, you'll rue the day."

Gingrich argued, "You have to do this, Christina, for your family. You're going back to a better place." He pointed out that he had checked with the college before he had called her to make sure she had not forfeited her health benefits in the abortive move. It especially annoyed Jeffrey, the mother of five, that Gingrich was resorting to a family values argument. "Stand by your man—unless she's a woman," she thought. As for the health benefits, she had seen to that herself and knew that she was covered.

After hanging up, Jeffrey thought how different the Gingrich she had just encountered was from his image. He had gained power by challenging his enemies and never backing away from a fight. Now, it was different.

Christina Jeffrey did not sleep that night. She remembered Gingrich, soon after he was elected Speaker, ruminating about the era of Speaker Sam Rayburn and imagining himself as a Speaker in the Rayburn tradition, as if all the vicious politics Gingrich had played to get to the speakership could be obliterated and he could start over with a clean slate. Jeffrey had been reading *Rayburn: A Biography* by D. B. Hardeman and Donald C. Bacon and thought, "The more you know about Sam Rayburn, the less similarity you can find to Newt.'"

Rayburn was a disciplined, orderly man, who believed in lying prone on his back with eyes closed for nine hours a night, whether asleep or not, because a man needs his rest. Gingrich hardly slept at all between his long days of furious activity. Rayburn was a lonely man, who shied from publicity—another trait not shared by Gingrich. In *The Years of Lyndon Johnson: The Path to Power,* Robert A. Caro had quoted one of Rayburn's fellow legislators saying, "You could always swear by anything Sam told you." Months later, when Gingrich failed to follow through on a promise to apologize publicly for his treatment of Jeffrey, she said, "Like all Newt's promises, it was written in air."

There was one thing that Newt Gingrich had in common with Sam Rayburn. They both loved to take long walks. Each weekday morning, Rayburn walked the two and one-half miles from his apartment near DuPont Circle to the Capitol, and on weekends, alone, without family or friends, he walked around the city, usually unrecognized. Gingrich liked to get up early and walk from his apartment on Capitol Hill to the Washington Monument and back before starting his workday. On weekends, too, he liked to take long walks. Once he walked from Capitol Hill to National Airport, a distance of about five miles, to meet his wife, Marianne, who was flying back to Washington.

On a crisp morning in March 1994, Gingrich stepped out of his apartment building and began his stretching exercises. It was 6:00 A.M. The sun would not make an appearance for another nine minutes. Gingrich wore a white sweatshirt celebrating *Cheers,* the TV sitcom set in a Boston bar, off-brand jeans, and ankle-high walking boots. The decidedly untrendy exercise outfit seemed a perfect match for Gingrich's pudgy physique.

It was still more than seven months before the November election that would introduce Gingrich to millions of Americans who were aware of him only vaguely, if at all, despite his eight terms as a congressman from Georgia and his persistent presence on television. Polls showed that those who did know of him split between admirers and detractors. Few people were neutral about Gingrich.

After loosening up with a requisite number of toe touches, Gingrich headed off on a morning walk that would take him past the Library of Congress and the U.S. Capitol, down the hill to the Mall, past the National Archives, the Air and Space Museum, and the other Smithsonian museums, up an incline to the Washington Monument, then back again, three miles in all. At the start, it was cold enough for gloves and a hat, but Gingrich stuffed his hands into his pockets and let his thatch of silver hair warm his head. He wore thick glasses, not the contact lenses he wears in public.

None of the bicyclists, joggers, or other walkers seemed to recognize Gingrich. None of the cars streaming into Washington from suburban Virginia honked hello. If, as then seemed probable, the Republicans were doomed to continue as the minority party in the House of Representatives, Gingrich's ambition to be Speaker of the House was no more than a dream.

As usual on these walks, Gingrich had company that March morning. Unlike most people who at that hour prefer solitude, he was gabby and congenial. Marianne had joined him once—and only once—on a daybreak walk. She kept asking, "Where's the coffee?" There was none. Gingrich does not rely on caffeine to get him started. He prides himself on his ability to snap awake instantaneously. "I don't know how much of it is genetic and how much training," he said, explaining that his stepfather was a career infantryman and that combat readiness was drilled into him.

Gingrich had been up late the night before doing his weekly viewer call-in show on National Empowerment Television, a cable network started by conservatives to recruit like-minded viewers to their cause. The network is not even available in many parts of the country, including Washington, but Gingrich did not mind. Audience share was never the most important thing to him as he traveled television's back roads from C-SPAN to CNN and, finally, to the major commercial networks. Anytime two or more voters gathered in front of a TV set, Gingrich saw possible converts to the Republican cause.

In the past, those who rose to prominence in Congress were those who excelled at compromise, and who set aside their partisan rhetoric in order to make deals in the back rooms. Gingrich understood that in the television age, being deft at compromising would not get you airtime. Good television demanded conflict, and Gingrich provided that. He stated extreme positions, and defended them in colorful, often outrageous language. He was one of the most polarizing figures Washington had seen in some time.

The Democrats regarded Gingrich as a rabble-rouser who lacked the stature to pose a serious threat. Hard as it was to imagine the Republicans ruling the House after four decades of Democratic control, it was even harder to picture Gingrich as Speaker. He was a bomb thrower, a big mouth, a slick operator who, under the guise of reform, had done more than anyone else to discredit the Congress. His ascendancy had been marked by vicious and slashing attacks on the Democratic leadership, and on the moderate establishment of his own party. He had all but burned down the House while insisting that he only wanted to save it. Twice, he had nearly perished himself, narrowly escaping defeat in his Georgia district in 1990 and 1992.

If Gingrich's public posturing was all the Democrats had to fear, their nonchalance might have been justified, but the made-for-TV grandstanding was only one side of Gingrich. The side unseen was Gingrich the military strategist, pursuing his political enemies like Grant hounding the Confederates or Patton rampaging across Europe. Although he never donned a uniform himself, Gingrich studied war well enough to lecture at the National War College, and he applied the lessons learned from his military heroes to the battlefield of politics.

Reaching the Washington Monument, the halfway point of his morning walk, Gingrich stopped to admire the familiar marble and granite monuments. When he was feeling low, the sight of the White House and the Lincoln Memorial against the morning sky never failed to revive his spirits. "I had a couple of winters when I was fairly depressed and things were just very hard and not working very well," he said. During these periods of gloom, he had considered quitting. "I found that if I walked this particular walk while the sun was coming up it was almost impossible not to feel optimistic by the time I got to the Washington Monument."

Turning toward home, Gingrich squinted into the sun glinting off the Capitol. He picked up the pace, breathing in big gulps of cold air and sniffling between machine-gun bursts of words. He described the Republicans' struggle to take over the House as "the long march"—Gingrich's version of Mao's long and ultimately successful military campaign to take over China. In his mind, the question was not whether the Republicans would prevail, but when. If not this election, then the next one or the one after that.

Few people could have been found that day in March 1994 who would have bet much on the Republicans' chances of taking control. Gingrich was in line to succeed Bob Michel of Illinois, the party's long-serving leader in the House, who had announced his retirement. Asked what he was doing to prepare for his new job, Gingrich replied that the idea of getting ready to be Minority Leader is "like running to be third at the presidential nominating convention." He played to win. "Frankly, all of my current planning is designed to be Speaker."

Gingrich was born Newton Leroy McPherson on June 17, 1943, in Harrisburg, Pennsylvania. His biological father was a stormy Celt, whose fits of temper and drinking led to a divorce when Newt was three years old. Newt's mother, only seventeen at the time of his birth, found refuge in Bob Gingrich, a stoic military man of Germanic descent. The exacting discipline that came naturally to Gingrich had to be grafted onto Newt, who was by nature impulsive and gregarious.

Growing up with this authoritarian father-figure instilled in Newt Gingrich an enormous desire not only to succeed, but to rebel against the existing order. He once remarked that he was not able to get through *The Great Santini*, Pat Conroy's autobiographical novel about an overbearing military father. "I grew up living this stuff," he said. "We practiced being ready to go to Switzerland as refugees. I kept a foot locker by my bed of the things we would take if the balloon went up." Bob Gingrich did not physically abuse the son he adopted, but he inflicted a great deal of emotional pain. As a child, yearning for approval, Newt found his stepfather silent and unresponsive. "The Colonel," in turn, looked upon this bookish boy with his thick glasses and flat feet as a sissy.

What Gingrich missed in his family life, he sought from a series of mentors throughout his childhood and young manhood. He was, he says, like the young Arthur in T. H. White's whimsical book *The Once and Future King*, who, standing between two adults, would leap up every so often to grab a very large word. "That was my childhood," Gingrich said. "I had all of these wonderful people who would reach in and teach me and protect me and shelter me and encourage me."

That is why Gingrich, unlike many traditional conservatives, has a broader view of family than the two-parent nuclear unit. He talks about extended families as a positive thing. He was adopted, as were both his biological father and his stepfather. "And so I come out of an environment where when people walk up to me and say, 'You want to bring back Norman Rockwell,' they haven't got a clue how chaotic my background is."

Under the media scrutiny that comes with the speakership, some clues have emerged. For one, Bob Gingrich remained seated and unsmiling during the wave of standing ovations that greeted his son's inaugural address as Speaker, an image that conveyed the tension between them. For another, former aides have talked about everything from Gingrich's extramarital sex life to his relationship with his mother. Gingrich has dismissed them as "disgruntled former aides," but he has not disputed their stories. Kip Carter, who taught with Gingrich at West Georgia College and worked in his early campaigns for Congress, recalls a scene from 1978 with the congressman-elect and his first wife, Jackie, sitting at the dining room table while she sorted Christmas cards and he, typically, was speed-reading his way through a stack of books and paying only partial attention. Jackie put the cards into different piles, one for major contributors, another for important personages, and so on. Occasionally, when there was a card of interest, such as one from Vice President Mondale, she would hand it to Gingrich. "Oh, Newt, here's a nice Christmas card from your mother," Carter recalls Jackie saying. Gingrich, who was sitting to Jackie's right, took it with his left hand, pivoted the card one-quarter turn, and dropped it in the wastebasket.

Gingrich was almost fifteen in the spring of 1958 when he visited the World War I battlefield at Verdun, France. The sight of the gangly teenager wordlessly striding around the hallowed ground was recorded by a family friend on eight-millimeter film and later transferred to videotape. An orchestral version of the song "Stranger in Paradise," dubbed onto the film's soundtrack, lends an oddly dreamy aura to the black-and-white footage. The experience made a profound impact on an adolescent steeped in military mores, yet singularly unsuited for a career in the military. Returning home on a ship to the States later that year, Gingrich decided that he had a moral obligation to take up public service. His stepfather had been trained for combat with guns. Newt Gingrich would fight his wars with words on the battlefield of ideas. Maybe then he would be worthy in his stepfather's eyes.

Gingrich came of age during the war in Vietnam, but there was never even the possibility that he would serve. If his flat feet and poor eyesight were not enough to keep him out of the military, his family obligations were. By 1966, when the Vietnam buildup was at its height, and young men were being drafted all around him, Gingrich was married with one child and another on the way. His wife, Jacqueline Battley, seven years his senior, had been his high school math teacher. Gingrich's stepfather, disapproving of the union, had refused to attend the wedding, and his mother, deferring to her husband, stayed away as well.

Their reaction only stiffened his resolve to succeed on his own terms. He had set his goal: to win elected office and help create a majority Republican party. Jackie had taken a job in Atlanta and Newt had enrolled as an undergraduate at Emory University. Gingrich became active in the Young Republicans and methodically set out to make himself known. As a ten-year-old boy, Gingrich had written a story for his local newspaper pleading for the town to create a zoo. He liked the attention he drew to himself and his cause. From then on he would hang around the newspaper office the way other kids spent time in the schoolyard. In Atlanta, Gingrich used his cachet as a budding political activist to cultivate contacts at the city's newspapers. He knew a college kid would have a hard time getting in to see anybody important, so he found out which bus *Atlanta Constitution* political editor Reg Murphy rode to work and made sure he bumped into him. "He figured out where I lived, too," says Murphy. "He would come over and baby-sit my children." Murphy found Gingrich to be an engaging young man who took his daughter, Susan, to the zoo, and was also a good source on what was going on inside the Republican Party—which in the South was not much in those days.

Gingrich would spend hours at the *Atlanta Constitution* office, fascinated by how the newspaper worked and how politics and the media fed on each other. "If he saw something in the paper he was halfway interested in, he'd either be in the office or on the phone," says Murphy. Those early contacts paid off. When Murphy became editor of the *Constitution* in the early 1970s, Gingrich would come by and they would have coffee together at a cafeteria across the street from the paper. "He was so damn full of energy, and so damn full of ideas," says Murphy. "He could talk to you all day about an idea or about a dozen ideas."

Mel Steely was on the search committee for a new history professor at West Georgia College when Gingrich's application arrived in 1970. What struck Steely was not Gingrich's credentials, which were good enough—he had a master's and soon would have a Ph.D. from Tulane University—but the long, eclectic reading list that he had attached "so you'll know more about me." It included books on business management, zoology, history, government, international politics, some novels, "and even something on yoga," Steely recalled.

Gingrich got the job, and with his typical passion, plunged into teaching "the twentieth-century world" to undergraduates in the sleepy south Georgia community of Carrollton. Floyd Hoskins, who shared an office with Gingrich, remembered how his new colleague bounded into work each morning enthusing about a book he had just read or a new theory, as if he had just discovered the ultimate answer to one of life's conundrums. "We used to call him Mister Truth," Hoskins said.

Being a professor taught Gingrich the value of provocative speech to rouse students and get them to pay attention. He liked to flatly assert a statement he knew was preposterous, such as, "In the next century, Brazil will dominate the Western Hemisphere," just to make students think, Steely said.

Gingrich teamed up with Steely and Hoskins for a course that taught World War II with twisted facts meant to provoke the students. They reversed battles and had the Russians and Germans joining to conquer the United States. "Most of the students just took notes faithfully," said Steely. "When we had the U.S. losing Guadalcanal, Hoskins objected. He had won a Silver Star in that battle. We told him, 'You don't know what was going on—you were in the water.'" Seeing their professors arguing over a historical event forced students to take notice, achieving what hours of academic lectures could not. It was a style that Gingrich later adapted to politics.

Admiring students surrounded Gingrich constantly. His professed love of animals and the environment made him a Pied Piper with the Earth Day generation. "He had all the freaks following him," recalled Lee Howell, then the editor of the school paper. Gingrich lived across the street from the campus and on weekends would often host faculty and students for a pig roast. He would dig a pit in his dirt-and-gravel driveway and talk while turning the pig on a spit over the fire. "We were starving for intellectual discussion around here," said Myron Arons, a member of the psychology department. "He represented everything I thought education could be. He was eclectic, idealistic, held good discussions, and was extremely modest in his living."

Newt was a Republican in solidly Democratic Georgia, but in the South party affiliation did not necessarily signal where you were on the conservative to liberal continuum. Gingrich called himself a moderate conservative and emphasized the moderate. He liked to tell people that when he was a graduate student at Tulane in 1968, he helped coordinate Nelson Rockefeller's campaign against former Vice President Richard Nixon, a politician Gingrich openly disliked. Much later, when he was poised to become Speaker of the House and news reports pointed out that his résumé omitted this phase of his political life, Gingrich noted sarcastically that since Sen. Ted Kennedy did not mention Chappaquiddick on his résumé, why should he have to dredge up Rockefeller?

Equating his support of a moderate and moneyed Republican with Chappaquiddick was typical of the rhetorical excess in which Gingrich indulged.

Gingrich had only been at West Georgia College a year when he began to talk about going into politics as a Republican. "There were so few of us then, you more or less had to wear six-shooters," recalled Hoskins. When the Committee to Reelect President Richard Nixon wanted Gingrich to be Georgia state chairman, he said no. He only wanted to run his home congressional district because he had his future in mind more than Nixon's. When CREEP replied that there was no need for local chairs in the state, Gingrich held out. "You'll have one in the Sixth District if you want me," he said. The Nixon campaign agreed to Gingrich's terms, and he used the position to begin building a network in the district where he knew he would eventually run.

Lee Howell was one of the first students Gingrich recruited to help him advance his political ambition. Only three years younger than Newt, Howell was part of the generation that did what it could to avoid serving in Vietnam. Howell had left West Georgia College to join VISTA, the domestic version of the Peace Corps and a way to sidestep Vietnam. Having returned to campus in the fall of 1971, he remembers vividly the night that Gingrich, the magnetic young professor, strolled into the college newspaper office, where Howell was the student editor, carrying a six-pack of beer. "You got a refrigerator? Put this in and let's talk," Gingrich said.

It was against the rules to have beer on campus, but the ban was rarely enforced. The staff at the weekly paper, which was self-supporting, joked that if they ran out of beer, they could simply increase the size of the local beer store's ad and collect payment in kind.

Gingrich came by almost every Wednesday evening when Howell and the others put the paper to bed. He would bring beer with him or go out to get some during the long deadline night. "He probably had an agenda, but as far as I knew, he just wanted to talk," Howell recalled. Much of the talk made good copy. And years later, when Howell went back and looked at the columns he wrote during that period, he realized how the bull sessions got translated into flattering coverage for Gingrich.

Gingrich had an old red Volkswagen Bug, which Howell drove when the two rode across the district promoting Richard Nixon's candidacy and simultaneously introducing Gingrich to Republican audiences. It did not seem to matter that Howell was president of the campus Democrats and on George McGovern's state campaign committee. They were an odd pair in other ways, too. Gingrich was intense and nerdy, with thick glasses, long sideburns, and eyes that glowed with missionary zeal.

Howell's beard and shaggy hair marked him as a member of the counterculture. Gingrich used him as a prop to inflame Republican passions. "I'd sit in the back of the room while he was doing his thing up front," Howell recalled, "and he'd point to me and say, 'See that bearded hippie in the back—that's what a McGovernik looks like.' And I'd smile and flash my peace symbol. It was all a big joke."

When Gingrich ran for Congress two years later, some Republicans wanted to know why he had hired a peacenik, Howell, as his press secretary. Others wondered what he was doing with a Jewish campaign manager. Charles H. (Chip) Kahn had met Gingrich at Tulane and, like the others in Gingrich's orbit, was captivated by the professor's reformist crusade. Gingrich was pro–civil rights and pro-environment, and extolled the benefits of a strong two-party system. He had the backing of liberals and environmentalists in his losing 1974 and 1976 races against Democratic incumbent John Flynt, an avowed segregationist. Progressive Democrats offended by Flynt's stand on civil rights flocked to Gingrich. "Republicans were so few and far between then, we didn't figure one Republican would hurt that much," said Howell.

After each loss, Gingrich was "real low," said Howell, but within days he would bounce back and start planning for the next campaign. He figured he would have won in 1974 if it were not for Gerald Ford's pardon of Nixon, which hurt all Republicans. And in 1976, he was hurt by Georgia native Jimmy Carter's race for the presidency, which generated a huge Democratic turnout in the state. Three days after the 1976 defeat, Gingrich met with his coterie of advisers, who, like him, were mostly academics who reveled in spinning out political theories. After assuring Gingrich that he would win the next race in 1978, the strategizing turned to Gingrich's presidential prospects in the year 2000 or 2004, after he had made his mark in Congress. They calculated the likelihood of a Democratic president being in office then, along with the odds of an economic turndown, which would enhance Gingrich's chances. Then they factored in Gingrich's age to arrive at the optimal year. They even came up with a slogan: "A new president for a new age." Kip Carter, who taught Classical Chinese history at West Georgia College, and who led the discussion that morning, recalled, "Newt liked the sound of that."

Indeed, Gingrich acted more like an aspirant for national office than a defeated congressional candidate from a rural district in Georgia. He attended political gatherings in Washington and around the country, tirelessly promoting himself and building a network of contacts. At these events, he sought out prominent journalists like Jack Germond and David Broder, pressed his business card into their hands, and invited them to call when they were in Atlanta. "Everyone comes through the Atlanta airport," he would say, cheerily.

With Carter in the White House, Gingrich took up the cause of conservatives who were resisting the President's attempt to negotiate new treaties that would eventually yield U.S. control over the Panama Canal. Gingrich wanted to run a full-page ad in the Sunday *Atlanta Journal-Constitution*, but he did not have the $3,500 it would cost. Howell's mother had recently passed away and left him some insurance money, which he offered to contribute. "Newt was shedding all these alligator tears and promising to pay me back," Howell recalled. "I figured I'd never see the money again." Gingrich eventually repaid Howell for one-half the cost of the ad.

Waiting for the next congressional race to begin, Gingrich tried his hand at writing a novel about the Russians invading Western Europe. The result was clunky and sophomoric. He sent six chapters to futurist author Alvin Toffler's agent, who wrote back, "I trust you are better at shaking hands than at writing fiction." The brutal critique dissuaded Gingrich from writing fiction again for a decade.

Gingrich was never on a tenure track at West Georgia College. His unconventional ecology courses and futuristic history lessons lacked the appropriate academic gloss. Besides, his real interest was a career in politics. Yet Gingrich was so hungry for upward mobility that when the presidency of the college came open unexpectedly, he applied for the job. The quixotic move said more about Gingrich's state of mind at the time than his chances of being selected.

Then Jack Flynt announced he was retiring, which created an open seat in Georgia's Sixth District and a new opportunity for Gingrich. A hotly contested Democratic primary was followed by a runoff between the two leading vote-getters, state senators Peter Banks and Virginia Shapard. Georgia does not require party registration, and the Gingrich forces turned out their people to vote in the runoff *for* Shapard, whom they regarded as the weaker candidate. "It's much easier to run against a woman in a rural district," explains Kip Carter, pointing out this was 1978, and women had made little progress in Georgia politics. Indeed, Shapard was the first woman elected to the state legislature in her own right, as opposed to those who took over the seat of a deceased husband.

Shapard held moderate to liberal views, particularly on civil rights. In the mid-1960s, when the town fathers in Griffin, Georgia, where she lived decided to fill the local pool with concrete rather than allow integration, Shapard opened the pool at her home and provided transportation and lifeguards so children, mostly black, could swim. Shapard's presence in the race presented a whole new dynamic. Running against Flynt, Gingrich was the progressive new face. With Shapard opposing him, he would have to reposition himself to wage a campaign from the right.

Jackie did not want her husband to run a third time. She had just come through an operation for ovarian cancer and the prospect of another grueling campaign was simply too daunting. She was happy being a college teacher's wife and did not share Gingrich's vaulting ambition. But her husband's mind was made up, and she dutifully threw herself into the campaign effort.

This time, Gingrich had to win, and he was prepared to do whatever it took. He told his friends at the *Atlanta Constitution* that by running twice before, he had become "the shadow incumbent." Abandoning the good-guy image of previous campaigns, his rhetoric took on a hard edge. He told a group of college Republicans that the way to get ahead in politics was to be "nasty" and to "raise hell." He spoke mockingly of establishment Republicans, such as Presidents Nixon and Ford. "They have done a terrible job, a pathetic job," he said, rolling out the ad hominem adjectives that would come to characterize Newtspeak.

The new slashing style was born in part of desperation. Lacking tenure, Gingrich was told in August, just as the campaign was heating up, that he could no longer teach at West Georgia College, and was, in effect, being fired. "We were scared to death," recalls Kip Carter. "Newt had no job and two small children. We had our names on all these loans at the banks. This was his third time. We had to win, and we did things that we ought not to have done."

The idea was to portray Shapard, who was originally from New York, as a meddling Yankee who would force her pro–civil rights views on the district. Gingrich campaign workers spread the false rumor that Shapard had met her husband, who was from a wealthy Georgia textile family, when she came south as a freedom rider battling for integration. A television spot exploited the fear among whites that Shapard might be too favorably inclined toward minorities and the poor. The spot showed mostly black and some white hands grabbing checks from a mail slot. It was based on Shapard's vote against a bill that would have required welfare recipients to physically come to a welfare office to pick up a check. The measure was presented as an effort to combat fraud, which was dubious, and it would have presented enormous hardship to the poor, some of whom would have had to travel substantial distances. The bill was defeated, but it made a chillingly effective campaign ad.

In the final two weeks of the race, Shapard mentioned almost offhandedly that she would commute to Washington if she won. Her husband's business was in Griffin, and she had four children between the ages of seven and thirteen. Gingrich seized on the comment to launch an attack on Shapard's family values. He ran an ad that said, "If elected, Virginia will move to Washington, but her children and husband will remain in Griffin. When elected, Newt will keep his family together." Gingrich's aides smirked at the emphasis on family values from a man who they knew had been having discreet, but regular, sexual encounters with women other than his wife.

At the same time, a rumor surfaced that Jackie Gingrich was more seriously ill than had been made public. A sympathy vote began to take hold for Gingrich. Shapard's campaign could never prove it, but those involved believe the rumor was spread by the Gingrich camp, which wanted to "win one for Jackie."

Shapard regarded herself as a mother first and foremost, and did not take seriously Gingrich's assault on her character. She later told friends that if she had it to do over, she would have gathered her four children in front of a camera and made a commercial that showed their closeness as a family, to counter Gingrich's ridiculous assertions. Candidates would later learn from experience that negative charges have to be answered immediately, or they will take hold. But with polls showing Shapard comfortably ahead, fifty-four to forty-six percent, her aides advised her not to respond to Gingrich. In the closing days, the polls flipped and Shapard lost, fifty-four to forty-six percent.

Shapard ended the campaign with a substantial debt, which, under Georgia law, she could not repay with assets listed under her husband's name. "After the election, we watched her like a hawk," Kip Carter recalled. "If she tried to use her husband's money, we were prepared to file criminal charges as a warning to the next candidate who took on Newt." Shapard was forced to take a job outside the home to pay her campaign debt. Years later, as Carter reflected on that race, he said, "I've spent many years sending messages to Virginia Shapard trying to apologize."

As for Shapard, her name has become the ultimate trivia question. After Gingrich became Speaker, a friend spotted a reference to her in a news story and sent her this wry note: "You're now going to be in the league with the pitcher who threw the ball that Hank Aaron hit for his 715th homerun." Shapard, an avid baseball fan, replied, "At least that makes me feel good. I know Al Downing's name."

When Gingrich won in 1978, the town of Carrollton rallied around its new favorite son. The town fathers and local academics were determined to send him off in style. "We all helped," recalled Hoskins, Gingrich's colleague from West Georgia College. "We bought him a suit.

Another family paid for furniture, which they sent up to Washington. And then the tragedy happened—the divorce—and we were in it up to our ears. He called at 11:30 one night, and he was crying. I told him, 'You can't do that. It will ruin you. You've just gone up there.' I knew there had been problems for a long time. They had had counseling. He said, 'If I don't get a divorce, I'm going to either kill myself or go crazy.'"

Gingrich had been a congressman for less than six months when Jackie and the girls and the donated furniture came back to Carrollton. "There was a feeling of great resentment after all we had done for him," said Hoskins. In the years ahead, Jackie would go to court repeatedly to get more support money. The congregation at the First Baptist Church took up collections for her "to keep the electricity on and buy canned food to feed the kids," Kip Carter said.

There is no way to sugarcoat the abrupt and brutal way that Gingrich ended his marriage. "He said he couldn't take it anymore," Lee Howell recalled. "He said it was like a growth that you have to get rid of, that you have got to cut out." This was an especially poor metaphor given Jackie's cancer.

A new chapter of Gingrich's life was beginning. He was in Washington now, surrounded by button-down, hyperactive, super-ideological Republicans drafting statements of "mission" and strategizing how to make him a national figure. Howell had not worked in the 1978 campaign and did not expect a job in Washington. But Gingrich urged him to talk to his chief of staff. The interview did not go well. A fat, rumpled Democrat who smokes cigars did not fit the new Gingrich ethos. "I was a little too common for him," Howell said. Later, over dinner, Gingrich assured Howell he could get him a job on the staff. "But I can't promise it will be a major job."

"I told him I don't want to be a flunky," Howell said. "I guess I was too much of the old Democratic image for them. We drifted apart."

Then, two or three years after Gingrich had been in Washington, he called Howell to say he had a check for him. Howell had almost forgotten that Gingrich still owed him money. The check was made out to Georgians Against the Panama Canal Treaty, and it was signed by Joseph Coors. "I guess I could give it to you, but I better do it right," Gingrich said. He deposited Coors's check in the account of the now defunct Panama Canal committee, and wrote out another one for Howell. Ties with conservative industrialists like Coors would help Gingrich bankroll the various political enterprises that came to be known as Newt, Inc.

There is still enough fondness in the way Howell recalls his friendship with Gingrich that some people "get the idea I really respect and admire the guy," Howell said. "I tell them I respect and admire him like I would a snake. I admire his pretty colors and his skin, but I don't turn my back on him." Gingrich's rise to power is littered with the dashed dreams of family and friends who trusted and believed in him, only to be discarded when they no longer fit into his grand scheme.

Kip Carter saw a difference soon after Gingrich's election to Congress. Carter remembers being dispatched to meet Gingrich at the Atlanta airport. "He looked my way and I raised my hand. When we reached each other, he chewed my butt out. He said, 'I'm a U.S. congressman and I don't want to have to look left or right for the person picking me up. I want to be looking at an aide straight on.' He was arrogant beyond belief."

Carter continued to work for Gingrich in the Georgia office for several months until one day, when Gingrich was visiting the district, the two had what would become a permanent falling out. Gingrich had just voted to support a federal holiday to honor Martin Luther King, Jr. and some of his supporters were angry, including a local Chevrolet dealer who had supplied Gingrich with a free car for his campaign. Carter told Gingrich, "He's a redneck. You know he's wrong and I know he's wrong, but he at least is entitled to talk to you and tell you what he thinks."

Glaring, Gingrich held out his hand and, with his pinkie finger raised, he said, "I've got the power of the office." Raising his ring finger, he said, "I've got the money from the PACs." Digging his right index finger into his left palm, he said, "I've got the news media in the palm of my hand. Fuck you guys. I don't need any of you anymore."

Gingrich came to Washington convinced that the route to power in the Information Age was through the public forum provided by the media, not in the back rooms of legislative compromise. He had read David Halberstam's book *The Powers That Be* on how the modern media operate and was fascinated by the long chapter about House Speaker Sam Rayburn's avoidance of television coverage as a way to keep the House a collegial institution insulated from a probing and often predatory press. Gingrich would use television to break down this collegiality. He had first appeared on television when he was sixteen years old, displaying ocelots and snakes on a local show in Harrisburg. He was at home in electronic reality.

Within two weeks of his swearing-in, Gingrich zeroed in on his first symbol of "corrupt Democratic rule." Charles Diggs, a black Democrat from Michigan, had just been reelected despite having been sentenced to three years in prison for mail fraud and filing falsified congressional pay vouchers. Gingrich rallied Republican freshmen around what he called the "double standard of justice that permits a convicted felon to vote in Congress." The House overwhelmingly rejected Gingrich's resolution to expel Diggs, voting instead to assign the matter to the ethics committee for investigation. At the same time, Gingrich added his name to a bill that would make Martin Luther King's birthday a federal holiday. "It was vintage Newt—I'm not anti-black; I'm anti-corruption," Frank Gregorsky, a former aide, recalled. Diggs eventually resigned to serve his prison term and Gingrich had his first scalp.

Gingrich had demonstrated, for those who had not heard, that he was no ordinary freshman member of Congress, to be seen but not heard. He staffed his office with Newt clones, whose first assignment was to read and apply the tenets of Peter Drucker's *The Effective Executive,* one of a long list of Gingrich's recommended readings. While other freshmen offices worked on writing their congressman's maiden speech or drafting legislation, the Gingrich team spent hours concocting a mission statement.

They asked each other, "Why are we here? How will we know we've been a success? What is our fundamental purpose?" They decided their overriding mission was to advance freedom, but there was a division between those who wanted to extend human freedom and those who wanted to give *meaning* to human freedom. Gingrich came down on the side of extending freedom.

"Freedom for its own sake?" a young aide probed. "What is the substance of freedom?"

Gingrich just scoffed. "What do you want me to be, a bishop?" he retorted. "I'm working on the politics."

As far right as Gingrich went, he stopped short of fully embracing the righteousness of social conservatism. Given his own checkered personal history, his reluctance was partly pragmatic, but he also had a strong streak of libertarianism—live and let live. Freedom meant the right to swing your fist if you want as long as you don't hit someone else's nose.

The mission statement they finally settled on was as grand as it was meaningless: "Saving the West and Extending Freedom." Who could oppose that?

Reconciling Gingrich's ambition to create a Republican majority that he might someday preside over with the practicalities of politics was the next step. Gingrich assigned projects to his aides as though he were still teaching college students. "Who's going to read the book on what Hoover did, and how Roosevelt gained seats in 1934?" he would ask.

The relationship between the charismatic young congressman and his staff was of the sort that when the staff thought Gingrich was wrong they did not hesitate to tell him so. "You're selling out, Newt!" they cried when he voted to increase funding for food stamps. When he supported a measure to protect the Alaskan wilderness, his coterie of right-wingers was appalled. "There was an energy crisis, and we wanted to see oil barrels up there," said Gregorsky, who had served as Gingrich's driver in the 1978 campaign and then came to Washington as an "LBJ Intern," notwithstanding that Gregorsky's view of the role of government was diametrically opposed to Lyndon Johnson's Great Society.

After Gingrich was one of only thirteen Republicans to vote for the Democrats' budget resolution in April 1979, Gregorsky and others chided, "You did not come up here to vote for the Democrat tax-and-spend budget. It goes against all your highfalutin rhetoric about change." Gingrich tried to defend his vote. He set up an easel and flip chart to illustrate forty different reasons why he was right. A day or two later, he relented and gave his staff instructions to design a Republican alternative budget. "He defends himself to the death just before caving in," Gregorsky said. That ended whatever nascent impulses Gingrich had toward compromise and accommodation.

From his first day in office, Gingrich was a legislator with no interest in legislating. He introduced dozens of commemorative bills creating such obscure observances as "National Quilting Day," "American Wine Appreciation Week," and "Country Music Month." (One of the first acts of the new Republican majority in 1995 banned commemorative legislation as a waste of taxpayers' money.) He also drafted a few offbeat bills on topics that interested him, such as one that would entitle U.S. space colonies to apply for statehood—if and when there actually were space colonies. To this day, there is not one piece of major legislation that bears his name as a prime sponsor.

When his aides anxiously asked him, "How can you be a congressman and ask to be reelected when you haven't passed a bill?" Gingrich calmly replied, "There are other ways to change the debate." As for concerns that he was not paying enough attention to his committee duties, Gingrich said most committee hearings were staged by the Democratic majority to showcase interest groups and were not worth his time. They were, he observed pungently, "just dog shit."

The seeds that would grow into the 1994 Republican takeover of the House of Representatives were planted fifteen years earlier, on Wednesday, May 23, 1979. That afternoon, Gingrich convened the first meeting of the Project Majority Task Force, an organization which, to that point, had existed only in his mind. Gingrich had been a member of Congress for barely five months, yet he had the audacity to invite the top Republican leaders and the ranking Republican members of the House committees to his matchbox office in the Cannon Building for a seminar on learning to think positively.

That morning, workers removed the standard-issue couches and chairs from Gingrich's office and put in a large conference table surrounded by a dozen chairs. At each place, Gingrich staffers put notebooks with neatly compiled informational sheets and poll results from elections in England and Canada, where conservatives had won recently. Then they waited to see who would come.

The announcement distributed to key Republicans said the meeting would start at 1:00 P.M. and asked them to be prompt. When the time came, two staff members were the only ones in their seats. Between 1:05 and 1:15, four senior Republicans sauntered in one by one, as if to declare by body language that they had more important things to do. They were Barber Conable of New York, the ranking Republican on the Ways and Means Committee, Clair Burgener of California, who sat on the Appropriations and Budget committees, Ed Derwinski, a twenty-year House veteran from Illinois, and Bob Livingston of Louisiana, a member of the Public Works and Transportation Committee.

Gregorsky, the intern, took notes. He recorded that Gingrich opened the meeting fifteen minutes late by saying, "We need to begin developing a plan for the process of causing a Republican majority in the House."

Gingrich introduced Darryl Connor and Don Jewell, who were to serve as facilitators for the discussion. Connor, a psychologist, described himself as an organizational expert specializing in how to change institutions. Jewell said he concentrates on "the human end of the continuum"—how people interact to plan major changes in institutions. During their presentation, Conable doodled on the white notepad provided for him.

Gingrich said the facilitators were there "to teach us how to plan effectively" by first "defining the desired state," then taking "a resource inventory," and finally deciding how to use the resources to reach the goal of majority. "The tendency is first to go straight to solutions and skip the first two stages," he explained.

Looking up from his own idle doodling, Derwinski said, "We can do it your way if that's important. I suppose it would bring on some mental discipline. But I've sat through half a dozen of these type meetings. . . ."

Derwinski told how twenty years earlier, when he was a freshman in Congress, he, too, had scolded his elders for not being more aggressive in going after Democrats. His reward was to be put in charge of a committee to change things. He said he was tired of meetings and wanted "to jump right to the point—how do we get votes?"

He waved a beefy arm in the direction of Connor and Jewell, and said, "We could use their *mythology,* if that has to be done. . . . I'll go along with anything you want to do, Newt."

Gingrich tried to flatter his elders. "We could have gotten a group of freshmen filled with piss and vinegar, but we wanted a representative group of Republican congressmen with experience," he said. "I've thought intensely about this process for five months. . . . Running a national campaign for president is easier than running for Speaker of the House. If we're going to hammer home our message and get a majority, we have to have a comprehensive plan for doing it."

Bob Michel, the Republican whip at the time, came in at 1:36 P.M., and Gingrich motioned for Michel to sit next to him. Trent Lott of Mississippi arrived at 1:43 and David Stockman of Michigan at 1:54. The meeting was dragging and Gingrich knew it. Derwinski continued his pleasant pouting: "Well, Newt, if you'll just plan the way, we'll bite our tongue until we see exactly where you're taking us." Conable offered whimsically snide support: "Well, it helps to know what Newt's doing, doesn't it?" The meeting had the feel of a high school algebra class waiting for the bell to ring.

"If I thought I had enough credibility with you all, I would've brought in a movie projector and showed the first segment of *Patton,*" Gingrich said. He described Patton commenting to a fellow officer about a motley crew of GIs: "They don't dress like soldiers. They don't act like soldiers. They don't think like soldiers. Why in hell would you expect them to fight like soldiers?" Making the analogy to the business at hand, Gingrich said, "The Democrats are more rigorously political than us. They gut us whenever they have to. Our guys are too nice."

There was laughter around the table.

"No, we really are," said Gingrich. "That's part of our problem."

At last getting their attention, Gingrich went on, "There are two ways we can become a majority. A catastrophe can cause the nation to kick them out and put us in. Or we can nibble away at their majority and finally destroy it."

"Or we can collapse ourselves," Burgener interjected.

"Yes, that might happen," Gingrich played along.

"If we did, how will anyone know?" Burgener delivered the punch line.

More laughter.

After that, the discussion was animated. If they were still not sold on Gingrich's fancy facilitators and their jargon, the old bulls at least were glad to be sharing the frustration of spending their careers subservient to the Democrats.

"I know everyone is busy," Gingrich said in closing. "If I didn't think you were busy, I wouldn't have asked you here. We only have one serious problem—building a majority. All else is secondary."

"Newt's right," Burgener said. "We've got to have that effort. I'm willing to devote an hour a week for openers. It's got to do some good."

The others agreed. They accepted Gingrich's proposal for a ninety-minute meeting every two weeks.

As his colleagues got up to go, Gingrich said, "I want you guys to be co-chairmen in the moral sense as well as officially. If I'm wasting your time, not being clear, or don't know what I'm talking about, say so."

"Your only problem, Newt," said Conable, "is that you're too god-damn humble."

The room burst into laughter.

"Barber," said Gingrich, "you're the only one who has told me that in my entire political life."

The year 1979 was a propitious time for Republican revolutionaries. Jimmy Carter's achievement in negotiating a treaty between Israel and Egypt was overshadowed by bad news. Carter was battling double-digit inflation, American hostages held in Iran, oil shortages, gasoline rationing, and long lines at the pumps. A near meltdown at the Three Mile Island nuclear plant near Harrisburg, Pennsylvania, gave credence to the prophetic movie *The China Syndrome* and added to the country's anxiety and gloom. The stage was set for Ronald Reagan, the ex-actor, who preached the politics of optimism.

The election of two prominent conservatives—Margaret Thatcher in England and Joe Clark in Canada—buoyed the spirits of the fledgling task force Gingrich had formed. John Rhodes of Arizona, the Republican leader, showed up for the second meeting along with Michel and the others. Gingrich invited former Nixon pollster Bob Teeter to analyze the Republicans' prospects for winning the House. Teeter said Clark had overcome a fifteen-point lead by Canadian Prime Minister Pierre Trudeau by making full use of television's coverage of the Canadian Parliament. Nightly footage of Clark and other Conservatives challenging Trudeau and the Liberals closed the gap.

"Republicans should rethink how we act and react on the floor of the House," Teeter advised. TV cameras had been allowed in the House chamber for the first time a few months earlier, in March 1979, and Teeter encouraged the Republican insurgents to make full use of the medium.

Teeter said the key to reclaiming the House was targeting voters who had entered the electorate since John F. Kennedy's election in 1960. These voters, between eighteen and forty years old, made up almost half the electorate, Teeter said, and their numbers would continue to grow rapidly for the next half-dozen years. People over forty who were not already Republicans would be hard to recruit, but the younger ones, many of whom voted sporadically if at all, were ripe for the picking. For the first time since the 1930s a large block of eligible voters was up for grabs, Teeter said. The difference between white-collar and blue-collar workers was no longer rooted in economics but in social issues. Teeter said history teaches that a party, an issue, or a candidate could shape this silent electorate into a new coalition.

It was Gingrich who put the two ideas together. He proposed using the television coverage of floor debates as a way to reach the impressionable younger voters. He proposed "structuring events" to get the media's attention. The agenda for the next task force meeting listed, "How can we maximize the benefits of TV coverage of the House?"

Hoping to capitalize on Reagan's growing popularity, Gingrich wanted Reagan and his running mate, George Bush, to appear with Republican incumbents and challengers for Congress at a preelection extravaganza on the steps of the Capitol. Gingrich's staff privately referred to the event as "the making of the GOP national contract," foreshadowing the September 27, 1994, event ten years later where the Republicans would sign their Contract With America.

Political columnist David Broder said of the 1980 gathering, "Junior House Republicans concocted the notion and sold it to a somewhat reluctant Reagan campaign." Reagan's advisers reduced months of work by Gingrich's team to a standard campaign event with the Capitol as a backdrop. Reagan promised that electing him and a Republican Senate and House would result in 1) substantial cuts in spending by Congress to set an example for the rest of the government, 2) selective cuts in government spending to reduce waste, fraud, and abuse, 3) an across-the-board individual tax cut, 4) an effort to encourage more private investment and more permanent jobs, especially in the inner cities, and 5) increased defense spending to restore "our margin of safety" in an increasingly turbulent world. All the promises would be kept within one year, Reagan said.

This is what Reagan had been saying on the campaign trail and, since nobody thought the GOP could overturn the Democratic majorities in both the Senate and the House, the event passed largely unnoticed. Major newspapers played the story inside. Television gave it scant attention except to note a disruptive protest by backers of an Equal Rights

Stanley Greenberg on election night 1992. (© 1992 David Burnett/Contact Press Images)

Frank Luntz conducts a focus group. (© 1995 Martin Simon/SABA)

Michael Bromberg testifies before the House Ways and Means Committee.
(© 1994 Annalisa Kraft)

Michael Bromberg and Winston. (© 1995 Marlys Bromberg)

Paul Equale
inside the Capitol dome.
(© 1995 Barbara Ries)

Paul Equale with presidential candidate George McGovern in 1972.
(Photo courtesy of Paul Equale's personal archive)

Senator Daniel Patrick Moynihan appears on NBC's *Meet the Press* in November 1995.
(AP/Wide World Photos)

Senator Daniel Patrick Moynihan.
(© 1994 Brad Rickerby/SIPA)

Newt Gingrich. (© 1994 David Burnett/Contact Press Images)

January 4, 1995—Newt Gingrich prepares to be sworn in as Speaker of the House.
(© 1995 Ray Lustig/Washington Post Photo)

Governor Bill Clinton tours South Central Los Angeles with Representative Maxine Waters. (© 1992 Allan Tannenbaum/SYGMA)

California Assembly Speaker Willie Brown celebrates the passage of a bill by Waters to divest California of stocks in companies dealing with South Africa.

(© 1985 Rich Pedroncelli)

Sheila Burke.
(© 1995 Richard A. Bloom/SABA)

Senator Robert Dole with Sheila Burke at a Senate Finance Committee hearing.
(© 1995 Walter P. Calahan)

Amendment, which Reagan drowned out by leading the singing of "God Bless America."

The *Chicago Tribune* reported, "Several GOP congressmen had suggested that senators and representatives raise their hands and pledge their 'sacred honor' and even their lives to Reagan's policies. But Reagan's camp thought the Boy Scout–type ceremony was 'idiotic,' according to an aide, and it didn't take place."

In the election that year, the Republicans captured the Senate, but gained only thirty-three of the fifty-nine seats they needed to win the House. What impact, if any, the September event on the Capitol steps had on the results was not measured, but Gingrich learned some lessons he incorporated fourteen years later: Do not try to compete with a presidential election; make promises specific enough to be memorable and accountable; attract media coverage by presenting a ten-part contract (like the Ten Commandments); and add drama by imposing a deadline of one hundred days.

One thing Gingrich kept the same was the post-event get-together with representatives of political action committees to sweeten the campaign coffers of Republican candidates.

Gingrich worried about the impact of his divorce on his 1980 reelection. When he won with a surprisingly strong fifty-nine percent of the vote, he decided it was a good time to introduce his new woman friend, Marianne Ginther, to his staff. "She means a lot to me," he said. "I want you all to try and get to know her. I'm not sure what role she's going to play." Ginther, a straightforward Youngstown, Ohio, native with strong Republican ties, went out for hamburgers with the staff. She was cheerful, friendly, and laid-back. She was everybody's big sister. There was nothing not to like about her. They married in August 1981. At thirty, she was eight years younger than Gingrich, and fifteen years younger than his first wife, Jackie.

For all her surface affability, Marianne bristled at having to play the role of a Washington wife. She disliked being in the public eye and she hated being totally in her husband's glow and at the mercy of his schedule. She regarded her husband's professional life as something she could share, and Gingrich accommodated her when he could. Her name was on the briefing papers along with Newt's that were handed out at a Republican retreat in Racine, Wisconsin, in December 1981.

Frigid winds blowing off freezing Lake Michigan reminded the eight men and three women gathered at the Hotel Racine, a block from the lake, why they had had reservations about traveling to this godforsaken place that seemed more like the North Pole than the heart of America. Racine happened to be Paul Weyrich's hometown and it was Weyrich who had issued the invitations to a representative sampling of his conservative allies at the request of Gingrich, who wanted to enlist their help in forming something he called the Conservative Opportunity State.

Weyrich, whose physique is as soft and round as his views are hard-edged, was the New Right's grand panjandrum. He founded the Heritage Foundation, the think tank that provided the intellectual underpinning of the Reagan administration, and he had helped start the Moral Majority, which evolved into the Christian Coalition. Weyrich was running the Committee for the Survival of a Free Congress (now the Free Congress Foundation), when he met Gingrich in 1974 during his first run for Congress. That year, Gingrich flooded Weyrich's office with campaign literature and position papers, then came to see him personally. Weyrich met with a lot of first-time candidates that year, but Gingrich stood out because he had not even been elected, and he already was talking about how he wanted to reform Congress.

After losing on his first try, Gingrich had come to Weyrich's campaign school in Milwaukee where he was the star of the class. Gingrich organized the other trainees and, at the final session, stood up on behalf of the others and gave Weyrich unsolicited advice on how he and his organization could best help conservative candidates by adopting a team approach, nationalizing the election around a set of issues that Republicans could agree on.

Weyrich remembered thinking, "Where did this guy come from?"

When Gingrich finally did win in 1978, Weyrich invited him to address a meeting of conservatives in Washington and, in Weyrich's words, Gingrich "dazzled them with a great performance."

"He said we should do this, we should do that," Weyrich recalled. "We agreed to a number of projects. We spent some of our resources, as did other organizations. It took several weeks before we were able to give him the results of the work. By that time, he was on to something completely different. Our work went into the wastebasket."

Weyrich was irritated and he let the young congressman know it. "I told him, 'See here, you don't waste other people's time and effort unless you are serious about it. If you're not serious about it, don't expect us to take you seriously.'" Weyrich said other conservatives had been similarly disappointed. Weyrich said the word on Gingrich was, "This guy's an interesting fellow and he has a lot of good ideas, but he doesn't follow through. He has a short attention span."

After his reelection in 1980, Gingrich said he had learned his lesson about floating too many ideas and not seeing any of them through, and the Racine retreat is where he would prove it to Weyrich and the others. Gingrich focused on a single idea: how the Republicans could regain control of the House for the first time since 1952.

"If we play our cards right, we'll take over the House in ten years," Gingrich told the group in Racine.

"Sure, Newt, and before that the Soviet Union will collapse," Weyrich said.

Everybody laughed. A Republican takeover seemed as improbable as the fall of the Soviet empire. The laughter irritated Gingrich, who could not have been more serious.

Gingrich believed that President Reagan would be so popular that his legacy would be at least another eight years of Republican rule. In 1992, the first election after redistricting, Republicans had a chance to break the Democratic lock. "But the only way we can do it is if we turn the congressional elections into a national race on national issues," Gingrich said. He ignored the conventional wisdom that although the public held Congress in low esteem, voters liked their own representatives. Democrats delivered constituent services, from tracking down late Social Security checks to funneling federal grants, which provided an insurance policy against defeat. Gingrich insisted that national issues would bring Republicans the House of Representatives, just as it had brought them the White House.

Gingrich proposed pitting the "conservative opportunity state" against the "liberal welfare state." One of the retreat participants, a Racine businessman named Fritz Rench, objected to using the word "state," saying it reminded him of "Big Brother centralism—[and] gives me bad vibes." Paul Ogle, a Denver businessman, proposed substituting "society." That was the beginning of the Conservative Opportunity Society (COS), the vanguard of the Gingrich-led revolution.

Polling of the phrase word-by-word showed that it was popular. Republican pollster Richard Wirthlin reported that voters overwhelmingly chose conservative over liberal, opportunity over welfare, and society over state. Knowing nothing else about two candidates for the House, the candidate associated with "COS" was preferred, four to one. Gingrich was convinced that he had found the marketing tool that would allow Republicans to seize control of the House.

Over the next two years, Gingrich dreamed up so many projects to advance his goal of a Republican majority that he wore out his staff. Aides privately referred to him as "the Newtron bomb."

"I make leaps so fast that I confuse myself occasionally, but more often other people" Gingrich confessed to his exhausted staffers at a meeting in April 1983. "I'm constantly scanning and then, when I get an idea, most of the time . . . I don't do anything with it. I only actually generate about fifteen percent of the ideas I could. The rest of them I just hide— the rest of them would destroy this system."

Gingrich invited a dozen like-minded conservative young lawmakers to join the Conservative Opportunity Society. At the outset, the group was so inconsequential that it drew more ridicule than respect. The COS members met regularly, but had little influence on public policy, not even with Reagan, their ideological soul mate. If the White House courted conservative votes, it automatically lost moderate Republicans and gave Democratic critics ammunition. Gingrich probed for ways to expand the Reagan Revolution to Capitol Hill. One way was to go over the head of members of Congress, as Reagan himself had done, and communicate directly with the American people through television.

"Let's talk to a bigger audience, let's educate America," Gingrich urged his fellow insurgents. The perfect vehicle was C-SPAN, the cable channel that broadcast House proceedings gavel to gavel. A single camera trained in on a congressman allowed the kind of unfiltered communication that the commercial networks denied.

"What's the point? Who's watching?" COS colleagues objected. The Nielsen ratings did not estimate viewers of fledgling cable channels like C-SPAN, but surely its audience was infinitesimal, compared with that of the major networks. That did not deter Gingrich. He had a teacher's faith in his ability to educate and persuade and ultimately to change minds—one at a time, if necessary.

"My test was very simple," Gingrich said. "How far would you go to speak to five thousand people? The average politician would go around the planet." He figured that even in the early days, between a quarter of a million and a half million people were tuned into C-SPAN at any given moment.

Like a general tutoring a second lieutenant, Gingrich spelled out for Gregorsky his strategy for breaking through enemy lines, that is, the Democratic stranglehold on Capitol Hill, to communicate the Republican message: "Once you start to see a breakthrough, you push and push and push and push to get as many resources into that zone as you can until you've broken through. A lot of the time . . . I am intuiting. . . . An instinct for being at the decisive point in battle is not waiting for accidents to happen. It is getting up in the morning and actively *planning* accidents. I do that all the time."

Gregorsky was working at home shortly after noon on May 15, 1984, when he got a call telling him, "Turn on your TV. The fur is going to fly." Gregorsky tuned to C-SPAN as Gingrich rose on a "point of personal privilege" to rebut remarks by Speaker Thomas P. (Tip) O'Neill the previous day. O'Neill had accused Gingrich and Rep. Bob Walker of "challenging the Americanism" of Democrats by reading into the *Congressional Record* a long foreign policy paper portraying Democrats as incompetent, defeatist, blind to history, and willing to gut U.S. allies to appease avowed enemies.

Burned out and feeling unappreciated, Gregorsky had left Gingrich's staff months earlier to work for the Republican Study Group, the policy arm of the GOP members. As a final assignment, Gingrich asked Gregorsky to write a paper showing how the Democratic House's vote to cut off funding to rebels in Nicaragua fit a pattern of Democrats appeasing communists. The idea was to raise the communist issue in a new way, not challenging Democrats' motives, but challenging their comprehension of the way communists think and act. Gregorsky produced a 29,000-word document with two hundred footnotes backing up charges that key congressional Democrats had misread every confrontation with the communist world, from the shooting down of KAL 007 to Vietnam.

Hoping to goad the Democrats into reacting, Gingrich held a news conference to discuss the paper and, with Walker, read it aloud before an empty House chamber and the C-SPAN camera. The tactics worked when O'Neill publicly denounced the paper and Gingrich for publishing it. That night, Gingrich called Gregorsky to say he intended to answer O'Neill on the floor the next day. Savoring the idea of it all, Gingrich told Gregorsky that this was the most exhilarating moment of his political life.

O'Neill glowered as Gingrich defended the analysis of Democrats as defeatists and accused Democrats of resorting to "McCarthyism of the left" to avoid a legitimate debate. When O'Neill's turn came, his voice rumbled with rage as he once again accused Gingrich of impugning the Democrats' patriotism, adding, "It is the lowest thing that I have ever seen in my thirty-two years in Congress."

Mississippi Rep. Trent Lott, the Republican whip, objected, saying that O'Neill had violated the House rule that members must never personally attack each other. He called for a ruling from the chair. Rep. Joe Moakley, a Democrat from O'Neill's own state of Massachusetts, who was presiding, had no choice but to rule against O'Neill. For the first time since 1797, a Speaker's words were "taken down," or struck from the record.

That night, unable to sleep after the excitement of the day, Gregorsky sat at his computer writing a letter to his stepmother, Cedalia:

"The most astonishing series of events has taken place in a sequence that has not yet run its course. I sit here with my phone unplugged, having been enjoined by my superiors not to talk to any press people, should they call. Something I've written produced an explosion today on the House floor, an explosion which tonight made all three network newscasts, plus MacNeil-Lehrer. . . ."

Gregorsky described the reaction when Gingrich finished his hour-long oration:

"The Republicans gave him a standing ovation and applauded for twenty seconds. This was a great day for our side. We were united. . . . A complete victory is the time for maximum caution. Nearly everything cut the GOP way today. Some members are unhappy about the ruckus. GOP Leader Michel refused to applaud Newt with the others. He has lost control of his own membership. Our guys are fed up with being in the minority. . . ."

Until that day, Democrats had ordered the C-SPAN camera to remain fixed on the individual speaking. Lawmakers did not want constituents to see that they were not in the chamber for every debate. On the night Gingrich and Walker read Gregorsky's paper on the House floor, Gingrich had paused during the intense criticism of Democratic foreign policy as if to invite a rebuttal from the Democrats. He knew, of course, that the chamber was empty, something the audience watching at home could not know. O'Neill then ordered that the C-SPAN camera periodically pan the empty chamber to expose Gingrich's game. For all his political savvy, O'Neill had not understood what Gingrich had grasped instinctively, Marshall McLuhan's dictum, the medium is the message.

The story line was especially pleasing to Gingrich: Obscure Republican takes on powerful Speaker. It was a benchmark in terms of giving Gingrich national visibility. The fact that Lott, the second-ranking Republican in the House, had protected one of the young Turks conferred legitimacy on Gingrich.

To reach his goal of a GOP takeover of the House, Gingrich had to maneuver around Michel and the other elders who held leadership posts without appearing to undermine their authority. Working with the risk-taking activists in the Conservative Opportunity Society, Gingrich pursued a "wedge" strategy designed to draw attention to the conservative agenda. COS sponsored an all-night legislative session on school prayer, celebrated the first anniversary of the U.S. invasion of Grenada, and focused on family values to block the Equal Rights Amendment. The reward, Gingrich promised, would be big electoral gains in November 1984.

Gingrich's disrupt-and-conquer strategy failed. President Reagan won fifty-nine percent of the vote and forty-nine states, but House Republicans picked up only fourteen seats. "It was shattering," recalled Gregorsky. "Most of us spent the whole month of November in shock. We did everything Newt wanted and it didn't work."

The Republican leadership took revenge by stripping the COS rebels of desirable committee assignments and cutting them out of party deliberations. The election results had vindicated the GOP veterans' initial judgment of Gingrich as a renegade. To be a failed visionary at forty-one was more than Gingrich could bear. He was depressed, but rather than retreat, he went into overdrive. He told *The Washington Post*, "I have an enormous personal ambition. I want to shift the entire planet. And I'm doing it. I am now a famous person. . . . I represent real power." He may have been the only one who thought so at the time.

Gingrich, like so many players in Washington, has a hard time seeing the value of anything in life that does not relate to his work. During the psychological slump that followed the 1984 election, friendships suffered, and so did his marriage. In his "Style" section interview for the *Post*, which reflected his despair at the time, Gingrich put the odds on his marriage surviving at fifty-three to forty-seven percent, explaining that Marianne, unlike himself, "doesn't gear up every morning to be a Viking—I mean, that's not her world."

Gingrich once told a friend, "I am the world's best date, but not necessarily the world's best husband." He would take Marianne out for an evening, or away for the weekend, and they would have a great time. Every so often they would hide out like a couple of teenagers, watch videos and eat popcorn. But figuring out how to fit her into his day-to-day life was a lot harder.

Marianne kept her distance from the Washington whirl. Sitting and grinning at everything Newt said was not her idea of fun. He could see that she was not happy. One of the people he sought advice from was Illinois Rep. Lynn Martin, who had arrived in Congress in 1980. If women lawmakers had trouble being taken seriously in the male-dominant Reagan 1980s, the message to political wives was even more chilling. This was the era of the "Nancy gaze," the look of unconditional adoration that First Lady Nancy Reagan had perfected.

"I hadn't met Marianne," Martin recalled. "And I—how shall I put this—I expected this femme fatale the way he built her up. And he wasn't being twitty—the little woman and stuff like that—it was more like, 'I can't tell you how important she is in my life.' He really wanted to make that marriage work. He wanted to reassure her that he thinks she is bright and able. Unlike many political husbands, he's not willing to see his wife pushed around. Most political husbands say, 'That's life.'"

Gingrich wrote his first book, *Window of Opportunity*, as a collaboration with Marianne. She felt she had made a real contribution and it infuriated her when critics suggested she was a glorified secretary. "It went to the core of what she believes about herself," said Martin. "She felt it wouldn't have been said if she was not a woman." After congressional Democrats raised questions about the book's financing, the House Committee on Standards of Official Conduct, popularly known as the ethics committee, launched a probe that eventually exonerated Gingrich of any ethical breach. But the picture of a tearful Marianne storming out of a Capitol Hill press conference when reporters pressed her on her role defined her uneasy relationship with Washington. Martin advised Gingrich not to force Marianne into his public life. "Marianne is tough enough to say, 'This is what I am,'" she told him.

Marianne Gingrich herself confirmed Lynn Martin's analysis of her and her sometimes strained marriage to Gingrich in an interview on a Saturday afternoon in the fall of 1995. While Marianne answered questions on the marble balcony known as "Newt's Porch," adjoining the Speaker of the House's office, Gingrich was inside at his desk catching up on correspondence and autographing copies of his book, *To Renew America*.

When she is being questioned, whatever thought crosses Marianne Gingrich's mind first is the one she is likely to express out loud. This delightful candor, rare in a city where most people in public life have learned to censor their real opinions in favor of banal platitudes, has occasionally stirred controversy, such as when she playfully told writer Gail Sheehy that if her husband decided to run for president, "I just go on the air the next day, and I undermine *everything*. . . . I don't want him to be president and I don't think he should be." After Sheehy's profile of Gingrich appeared in *Vanity Fair*, Marianne said, "I was kidding." Acknowledging her tendency to say too much, she now refuses most requests for interviews.

As if to protect herself, she borrowed a tape recorder to record her own copy of this interview. She struggled unsuccessfully to get it to run, finally giving up without asking her husband to help. Although she smokes ("I keep quitting and starting again," she said), she did not smoke during the interview, which lasted more than an hour.

"What do I do for Newt?" she mused, rephrasing the first question. "Well, I'm from a small town. I have small-town opinions of things. . . . Washington talks to itself to the point where it begins to believe whatever it says. With the politicians and the media all based here, it's the nature of the city to go in its own direction. The country watches and says, 'What are you doing? This makes no sense to me out here.' I think I come in with that sense of 'small town' watching things and just having very commonsense opinions."

Asked for an example, Marianne thought for a while, then recalled a time years earlier when she had heard the government intended to destroy stockpiles it had of cheese and other foodstuffs that were still edible. "I said, 'Are you kidding? Give it to poor people. This is not that hard. You have fifty states out there. You can offer it to each state. If they take it, fine. If they don't, fine. You either destroy it, which is crazy, or give it to people who can use it.'" Her husband liked the idea. "He talked to people and it happened within about a week," she said.

Many political wives adopt causes, such as literacy in Barbara Bush's case, or music lyrics and, later, mental illness in the case of Tipper Gore, but Marianne Gingrich said she rejected that course because "I feel like I should be doing a lot of things as his wife. To pick one issue is to say, 'Okay, this is mine, but Newt has the whole world.' Well, why does Newt get the whole world and I get one issue?"

If she had to pick just one issue, she said, it would be the treatment of congressional spouses, who, if their needs and feelings are considered at all, are dealt with as an afterthought under the laws that protect congressional members themselves. When Marianne's collaboration with her husband on *Window of Opportunity* became an issue, she said she went through "a legal nightmare" because the House ethics committee treated her as a nonperson over whom it had no jurisdiction to either prosecute or exonerate. She was, however, vulnerable to civil or even criminal prosecution and responsible for the costs of defending herself. When she bolted in tears from the news conference that Gingrich had called to answer the charges, it was because she was angry, she said, and still is.

With one of the frequent nervous giggles that punctuate her speech, Marianne described her spouse-of role: "You know, you end up in life with some things you didn't really choose. All of a sudden, I'm married to this congressman. I didn't want to be married to a congressman. That wasn't why I married Newt. I married him for the person he is. When he began working harder and harder, I said, 'No, no, I didn't want to marry a congressman. I wanted to marry you. . . .' I would have married a paleontologist or a professor in a heartbeat.

"When we first got married, he'd get ready to take off and do something and I'd say, 'Wait, wait, Newt. We haven't figured out who's doing the dishes and the cooking here, you know. This is not you walk away and I do it, and when you're gone it gets solved. . . . I left ironing or dishes or cooking—you know, he could do these things. He can do wash once in a while. I was busy, too. . . . People came up to me and said, you know, 'Make him a wonderful wife.' And I would say, 'What about him making me a wonderful husband?' There are two sides to this."

Marianne Gingrich said she was not aware until much later of *The Washington Post* interview in which her husband put odds on the chances of their marriage lasting. She said she was not bothered by it because that was so in character for Newt. Besides, he was not wrong in saying the marriage was under great strain. "We were having difficulties. I was complaining. I was saying basically I wasn't happy with the life I was living. . . . Newt was happy and I wasn't. I said, 'As important as this job is, and it is, you have to keep your priorities straight.'"

When they are together they behave like teenagers in love. She calls him "Newtie." He calls her "Ginthie." They are photographed holding hands and looking lovingly at each other. These meetings are infrequent. Most of their contacts are by phone and always, she said, when they are in separate cities, before they go to bed at night. "We talk about whatever we need to talk about—sometimes ten or fifteen minutes, other times an hour and a half—otherwise you begin to lose touch."

Marianne said she frequently does not recognize her husband as he is portrayed by the media. "They try and make out like he's a bad guy," she said. "I read about him and I say, 'Oh, my gosh, who is that?' Newt is very easygoing. Newt is easy. . . . Years ago there was an article—I kid him about it—that called him Dennis the Menace. It fits him. He's very positive, very happy—and he's mischievous. He gets himself into trouble."

Twice during the interview, Marianne declared that she is not a feminist. Her hobby of doing makeovers for friends and acquaintances fits into her definition of a more traditional role for women. As for her politics, she said she comes across as more moderate than her husband because his boisterous style "confuses people." He gets the media's attention with outlandish rhetoric, she said, but stressed, "Newt's not hard-right. Newt is not for telling anybody what to do. He's more into the idea that people can solve their own problems if government doesn't get in their way." She said she is more likely than her husband to publicly declare that she is a Christian.

On the question of abortion, the issue that more than any other remains emotional and divides Republicans, Marianne Gingrich said she is guided to some extent by the views of her mother.

"I have an older brother and sister who are adopted because my mother was told she could never have children," Marianne said. "She lost one at seven months. That devastated my mother. After that, she adopted. Then I came along and my younger brother came along. My mother is eighty. She had my brother when she was forty. The first thing she ever told me was, 'If you get pregnant, you keep that child because somebody wants it. You remember that.' I recently asked her, 'Mom, what's your stand on this issue of abortion?' She said, 'I'm pro-choice. I really don't see how government can regulate it. I'm not for abortion, but I really think we could be doing more as a society because unless children are really wanted. . . .'" Marianne let the sentence trail off, adding, "She really is a conservative Republican. Her position was she was pro-choice."

Giggling nervously, she went on, "I'm pro-life with a lot of concerns. I say I'm pro-life because I want to go in the direction where adoption is an option and there are fewer abortions in this country, but it's hard to argue if somebody's pregnant they shouldn't have an abortion. How can you take that right away from them? And they're going to do it. If they don't do it by the doctor, they are going to get butchered."

Marianne Gingrich said her husband's spirits seldom sag. An exception was after the disappointing 1984 congressional elections when the Republicans' gains fell far short of Newt's expectations. "Whenever he's talked about quitting, my advice has always been, 'There was life before Congress and there is life after Congress. Winning isn't everything. You are here for a reason, and that reason has to be bigger than winning. You have to believe in what your cause is.'"

Paul Weyrich, who remained Gingrich's friend and political ally despite sometimes being disappointed with his performance, describes that period as "Newt's blue funk."

"I'd seen him upset from time to time for a couple of days, but he went into a funk that lasted for months—doubting himself, maybe his premises were wrong," Weyrich said. "I was very concerned about him in that period because psychologically he was absolutely off balance. Suddenly he didn't have any enthusiasm for anything."

Weyrich discussed Gingrich's melancholy with Vin Weber, a Minnesota Republican who was close to Gingrich. As Weyrich recounted the conversation, he told Weber, "Look, we have here a brilliant fellow. The key is to get him practical. If he goes around zigzagging all over the place, he's not going to have an impact."

"You're right," Weber responded. "The role I can play is to organize him. I will tail him. Whenever there's a meeting, I'll see to it that a practical application comes from the meeting and that we have follow-up."

As Gingrich began emerging from his funk, he set up a meeting with

Weyrich, saying he had something personal he wanted to talk about. Weyrich invited him to his office. Gingrich asked, "If you had to give me advice, how can I make the greatest impact? I know the things we have to do and all that, but I want to know about me personally. What should *I* do?"

Weyrich told Gingrich about a former senator named John Williams, a nondescript Delaware chicken farmer who nevertheless built a larger-than-life reputation by becoming the Senate's point man in celebrated corruption cases involving Bobby Baker and Billie Sol Estes.

"If I were you, I would look at some of the corruption in this town and I would go after it," Weyrich advised. "Frankly, Newt, your problem is that while you are brilliant and while you come up with a lot of innovative ideas, you're not taken terribly seriously. You're an interesting person to spend an evening with, but when it comes to the power centers of Washington, nobody says, 'This guy Gingrich is really going to be something.'"

Gingrich had shown a penchant for ferreting out corruption early in his freshman year by going after Rep. Charles Diggs, but Weyrich chided him for reinventing himself every time a new idea popped into his mind. Weyrich said he does not know how much his lecture had to do with it, but when Gingrich later spearheaded the investigation that forced the resignation of Democratic House Speaker Jim Wright, Gingrich got the attention he had craved.

Gingrich emerged from his depression with a new and even more improbable game plan to achieve a Republican majority. He would forge a "stealth coalition" with moderate Republicans. He invited members of the mainstream '92 Group to meet with the Conservative Opportunity Society. The '92 Group, like the COS, was dedicated to achieving a Republican majority by 1992. Fortuitously, its members had come to the same conclusion, that they could not achieve a majority without reaching out to their ideological opposites. Connecticut Rep. Nancy Johnson and Wisconsin Rep. Steve Gunderson were part of a core group who accepted Gingrich's invitation to attend COS meetings.

The moderates shared the conservatives' frustration with the GOP leadership and its passive acceptance of permanent minority status. They were drawn to Gingrich because he was a fighter with seemingly inexhaustible energy. He persuaded them that even if they did not support him ideologically, the fact that he would do *something* was better than the status quo. Every Wednesday morning, from 7:00 to 8:30, they assembled in Johnson's office. The sessions were freewheeling and therapeutic.

The two factions tried to "work through" issues that divided them to find areas of common ground. At Gingrich's urging, Johnson, who headed a Republican task force on day care, met with conservative leaders Phyllis Schlafly and Gary Bauer to hear their concerns about how government discriminates against stay-at-home mothers. The result was a proposal that included a "Homemaker's IRA."

At the same time, Johnson remained firmly in favor of abortion rights. Gingrich made no attempt to dissuade her and appeared untroubled by the division within the party on the contentious issue. "My idea of success is you and Henry Hyde debating abortion," he once told her. "Why shouldn't we have both sides of that issue?" Hyde, one of the GOP's fiercest critics of abortion, authored the original 1976 Hyde Amendment which first prohibited federal funding for most abortions. "That's Newt's idea of fun," Johnson said, grimacing at the idea of such a debate. Gingrich built a coalition that was more generational than ideological, pitting the young and restless against the established leaders.

Extending his reach beyond Congress, Gingrich took over GOPAC, Inc. in 1986 and transformed it from a traditional political action committee into a training institution. GOPAC, a melding of the acronyms GOP, or Grand Old Party, and PAC, or political action committee, had been started seven years earlier by former Delaware Gov. Pierre (Pete) du Pont to fund Republican candidates for state and local offices. The idea was to create the political equivalent of baseball's farm system for congressional candidates. When Gingrich took over, he concluded that spending one or two million dollars a year on local campaigns would not be enough to achieve the long-term objective of electing a Republican majority. But by using the money to recruit and train promising candidates, Gingrich saw that GOPAC could more effectively expand the party's influence—and his own—and create the momentum for a Republican takeover.

Although its name suggested that it was a typical political action committee, GOPAC operated as a kind of pseudo-PAC, not subject to federal contribution limits and reporting requirements as long as it did not spend money directly on federal races. By complying with the letter of the law, if not its spirit, GOPAC was able to operate without revealing the sources of its financing. Donors, in turn, were insured anonymity for the checks they wrote. The law limits contributions to federal political action committees to $5,000 per contributor per election, whereas GOPAC's "charter members" donated a minimum of $10,000 a year. When a list of contributors was leaked to the press, it showed more than a dozen six-figure donors, led by businessman and unsuccessful gubernatorial candidate Terry J. Kohler and his wife, Mary, of Wisconsin, who together contributed almost three-quarters of a million dollars to GOPAC.

In May 1991, the Federal Election Commission announced it had evidence indicating that GOPAC was operating in violation of federal law by failing to register and file disclosure reports for its activities in federal campaigns. Only then did GOPAC register as a federal political action committee. When GOPAC refused to pay a $150,000 fine assessed by the FEC, the agency sued, charging that GOPAC's earlier failure to register created "the appearance of corruption." Gingrich insisted that GOPAC had influenced only state and local races, and a federal judge ruled in Gingrich's favor in February 1996, saying that GOPAC's creation of a "farm team" for Republicans did not subject it to federal regulation. In his deposition before the FEC's lawyers, Gingrich claimed he had little authority over GOPAC's day-to-day operations. He described himself as an ideas generator who left the details to others.

At the least, GOPAC provided seed money to further Gingrich's goal of ending the war between right-wingers and moderates by downplaying issues that divided them, like abortion, and enlisting Republicans in a crusade they could all support—the dismantling of "the corrupt liberal welfare state." To recruit young activists, Gingrich and his allies recorded instructional tapes—more than two thousand of them over ten years—and GOPAC sent them to Republican candidates around the country. The motivational tapes disseminated Gingrich's views and insured that a new breed of Republicans would be created in his likeness. One flyer—"Language: A Key Mechanism of Control"—offered a word list for candidates who wanted to "speak like Newt." It recommended sixty-four words and phrases to define Democrats, such as "pathetic," "sick," "corrupt," "bizarre," and "traitors."

Having rallied Republicans to a reform banner, Gingrich needed to demonstrate the evils of the entrenched Democratic majority. He proposed taking on Texas Democrat Jim Wright, who had succeeded O'Neill as Speaker of the House. It was a huge step and he had almost no support in the party. Republicans worried it would spark a tit-for-tat ethics war that nobody could survive. Gingrich's advisers warned him that he could never meet the standards he was setting for others.

After researching the record of Wright's political career, Gingrich began making public charges against Wright in 1987. He would travel around the country saying that Wright was "a crook" and when his remarks were reported in the media, the mounting pile of clips helped persuade the House ethics committee to investigate. Though Gingrich later confessed that some of the charges he raised were "a fishing expedition," the committee appointed an independent counsel who spent six and one-half months and $8 million uncovering enough ethical improprieties that Wright resigned after a debilitating battle.

Weyrich, who had encouraged Gingrich to pursue the Democrats on ethical violations, said Gingrich's one-man crusade against Wright "put him on the map."

"You bring down the Speaker, and you're going to be taken seriously," Weyrich said. "One could argue, was it just or not? I don't know. I think that Wright had a lot of problems. In any case, it definitely caused Newt to be taken as a serious figure from that point on."

Discrediting Wright set up Gingrich to run for the job of Republican whip, the party's second highest House position. Gingrich had never before shown any interest in being part of the leadership that he despised. He once told Gregorsky, "If you're the whip, all you do is round up votes. You can't run anything. You're tied to the events on the floor." Being in the leadership would crimp Gingrich's free-floating, intellectual style. Still, he was tired of being treated like a backbencher. He had proved that he could be an effective revolutionary, but could he lead?

His chance to answer that question came on Friday, March 10, 1989, when Dick Cheney, the whip under Bob Michel, was nominated to be Secretary of Defense. Within minutes of learning that Cheney would be leaving, Gingrich was on the phone lining up commitments from colleagues for votes in the election among House Republicans that would pick the new whip. Michel had been grooming Cheney as his successor. When President Bush called with the news of Cheney's selection, Michel said he responded, "Mr. President, thanks a lot. Judas Priest!" Michel's list of possible replacements for Cheney did not include Gingrich, but Gingrich had his own power base from which to pursue his ambition.

One of Gingrich's first calls was to Vin Weber, the soft-spoken conservative who was Gingrich's confidant. Weber advised him not to run. "I thought he couldn't win," Weber said. "It was too big a job, and he was still too controversial within the party. If we wanted to have an impact, we should find a candidate who was more acceptable. And Newt very nicely said to me, 'The purpose of this call is not to ask you if I should run. It's to ask you if you'll manage my campaign.' That being the question, I gave him the answer that he wanted."

By Monday morning, Gingrich had spoken personally to all but a few members. Gingrich, the self-styled guru of futuristic high tech, went about campaigning for the job the old-fashioned way, methodically going through a stack of index cards, one for each Republican member, on which he and Marianne had recorded where everyone stood. He would concede hardly anybody to the other side. "He was ready to work on people that I knew would never vote for him," recalled Weber.

But dogged determination would not be enough. Gingrich realized that he could not win if Michel made the vote a test of loyalty. Michel supported a colleague from Illinois, Ed Madigan, to be his number two. "Early one morning, Newt literally broke down," recalled Wisconsin Rep. Steve Gunderson, who was working actively for Gingrich. "He said, 'I can do everything in this campaign necessary to win, but I can't win if Bob Michel comes down hard on people and forces them to vote against me.'"

The image of Gingrich, exhausted and broken, served as a tonic for his troops. A consensus developed that they should confront Michel. So a dozen conservative activists with Gunderson, a moderate midwesterner, as their spokesman, marched to Michel's office in the Capitol. They did not have an appointment, but Michel, always gracious, welcomed them. His broad smile quickly faded when he heard what Gunderson had to say.

"You have every right to support Ed Madigan, but you don't have the right to forcibly impose him on the rest of us," Gunderson declared. "If you do that, you will probably succeed in electing Ed Madigan, but you will also destroy the Republican conference. There will be no conference because we will be so split up." As Michel struggled to grasp what was happening, Gunderson put it in plainer language. "If you try to block Gingrich," he warned, "you're finished."

"It was a difficult speech for me to give, and an even more difficult speech for him to hear," Gunderson recalled. "I often think that in the course of one morning, I have seen both Newt Gingrich and Bob Michel cry—literally, they both did. It was a very painful time for Bob—the pain of the transition, ideologically, personally, and operationally. Bob knew that unless he used his power and influence, Newt was likely to win. He was all of a sudden faced with the reality he would risk losing his kind of party for the sake of party unity now."

Michel was tired of the combat. He had fought his war a generation ago, landing at Normandy and taking three wounds. Gingrich and the others in that conservative society of theirs had never bothered to put on a uniform. The civility and collegiality that men of Michel's era prized in Congress was not there anymore. If Gingrich wants it so badly, let him have it, Michel thought. He backed off, and Gingrich won by two votes.

"Gad!" said Michel, recalling how he was steamrollered. "When you had Nancy Johnson going for Newt and several of the others—Jiminy Christmas!"

Gingrich's victory was what conservative activists had wished for and worked for, yet it left a bitter taste because the credit for providing the winning margin went to the come-lately moderates, not the long-suffering right wing. In recounting Gingrich's winning campaign for whip almost a decade later, Paul Weyrich did not try to conceal the resentment he still feels. Weyrich's testimony against Sen. John Tower's nomination for Defense Secretary had helped defeat Tower, which led to the appointment of Rep. Dick Cheney as Defense Secretary, which in turn left the Republican whip's job up for grabs.

At Gingrich's request, Weyrich personally lobbied two staunch conservatives who had strong grievances against Gingrich. Both had rebuffed pleadings by pro-Gingrich Republican colleagues, but eventually were persuaded by Weyrich that Gingrich deserved their support. Weyrich described his conversation with Rep. Phil Crane of Illinois, who had not forgiven Gingrich for moving to censure his brother, Dan Crane, also a congressman, on morals charges.

"You've got to support Newt," Weyrich told Crane.

"How can you ask me to do that?" Crane demanded. "You know what he did to my brother. Besides, Madigan is from Illinois."

"Look, Newt will get something done," Weyrich argued. "This is not an issue of conservatism versus liberalism. This is an issue of activism versus passivity, and you have complained to me ever since you got here about the passivity of the Republicans in the Congress. This is your chance to change things."

After almost an hour, Crane agreed to give Gingrich his vote in the secret balloting.

"Newt won by two votes," Weyrich said. "I think it's fair to say if he hadn't had those two votes he would have lost. But in Newt's mind those weren't the votes that mattered. The votes that mattered to him were Nancy Johnson and several of those people, who because they supported him have enjoyed a much greater prominence than one would think they should looking at this strictly from a philosophical basis."

For Gingrich, winning the whip's job was as much a victory over Michel as it was over Madigan. From then on, although Michel retained the title of Republican Leader, Gingrich increasingly took charge. But he did so deferentially, at least in public, preserving Michel's pride even as he prepared for his own ascension to the top job.

Gingrich's dealings with Michel and Michel's allies tracked closely the behavior of the characters in one of Gingrich's favorite texts on the art of politics—*Chimpanzee Politics*. Based on painstaking observation by the author, primatologist Frans de Waal, the book gives new meaning to Aristotle's description of man as a "political animal." As one reviewer observed, "Whole passages of Machiavelli seem to be directly applicable to chimpanzee behavior. . . . [There's] an endless series of unobtrusive social maneuvers leading up to the dethronement of the leader. . . . Chimpanzees never make an uncalculated move."

De Waal, a professor of psychobiology at the Yerkes Primate Research Center in Atlanta, said his book is about "a raw sort of power politics," the pugnacious style that characterized Gingrich's politics as an opposition leader, especially his effort to bring down House Speaker Jim Wright on charges of ethics violations. After de Waal's book was published, the hero of the narrative, a chimp named Luit, was viciously murdered by Yeroen, the chimp he had dethroned, and a strong, youthful accomplice. Once gaining power, de Waal warned, a human, like a chimpanzee, must reconcile with his defeated enemies if he hopes to survive long. "If you keep hammering away on the ones you have defeated, you may be eliciting a coalition against you," the professor said. "You need to be reasonably generous."

Gingrich alternated between being polite to Michel publicly and treating him as irrelevant privately. He chafed through much of his five years as whip because he had to answer to a Republican leadership he regarded as hopelessly out of touch. The disdain was mutual. "They looked at me as the guy who was hired to count the votes," he complained to a friend.

Michel would later say that Gingrich never actually performed the job of a whip, which is counting votes, and whipping members into line. Gingrich delegated the day-to-day responsibilities of the job to his friend and ally, Bob Walker of Pennsylvania. The Democrats had such a big majority of seats that counting Republican votes was rarely critical. Gingrich knew that he would lose on anything important. So he pursued his permanent campaign to discredit the Democrats and, when necessary, to undermine his own Republican leadership.

Gingrich's appeal was his claim that the Republican leadership can make a difference. He had cast his election not as a choice between moderate and conservative leadership, but between active and passive leadership. Michel seemed resigned to minority status. He once counseled a freshman Republican, "Every morning I look at myself in the mirror and I say, 'I'm going to lose today.' And that's how you get through the day because you just have to face the fact that you're in the minority." Gingrich challenged "the minority mind-set," the idea that Republicans were consigned to being a permanent minority. And he assailed the go-along, get-along leadership for caring only about "cutting deals with the Democrats and making it to their golf outings on time."

"This is a *battle*," he would exhort Republicans. "Democrats get up in the morning and look in the mirror while they're shaving and say, 'How can I chew up Republicans today?' And Republicans say, 'How can I be a nice guy?'"

Gingrich promised the moderates that if they supported him, he would give them a voice in the leadership. So for the first time, the Republicans had two chief deputy whips—Walker, who did the traditional job of counting votes, and Steve Gunderson, who was in charge of policy development. Gunderson eventually resigned, unable to bridge the differences between Gingrich and Michel and dismayed by the GOP's rightward shift, particularly on social issues. "I spent most of my time trying to play peacemaker," he said. He was not replaced.

After winning the whip's job, Gingrich and Marianne retreated to a cabin in the Colorado Rockies on one of his periodic reassessments of the timetable for creating a Republican majority. The cabin, one of five owned by Georgia textile heir Howard (Bo) Callaway in Crested Butte, Colorado, was without electricity and an hour from the nearest telephone, but the retreat, like Gingrich's early morning walks, was not about solitude. With GOPAC picking up the tab, Gingrich flew in teams of people for a series of three-day planning sessions, interrupted occasionally by a day off for hiking.

The consensus view was that 1992 offered the next best opportunity to seize a majority in the House, and that GOPAC needed to be restructured to make it happen. The only sour note was a clash between Gingrich and GOP consultant Ed Rollins over whether it is better to run congressional campaigns on local or national issues. Rollins subscribed to the dictum that all politics is local. Gingrich believed Republican challengers were doomed unless they framed their individual contests in national terms. Rollins subsequently was hired to head the Republican Congressional Campaign Committee. He and Gingrich frequently disagreed over strategy and tactics.

As the whip Gingrich could no longer portray himself as an outsider fighting the corrupt establishment. He spent 1990, for instance, defending himself against an insider deal on the congressional pay raise. The House had voted to increase members' pay from $96,600 to $125,100 in exchange for banning lawmakers from accepting honoraria for speeches. Gingrich proposed to the Democrats that both parties not fund any challengers who used the pay raise issue against incumbents. Gingrich's Democratic opponent that year, Atlanta attorney David Worley, pounded away at the insider arrangement that showed Gingrich was as corrupt as the system he claimed to be reforming. Because of the deal Gingrich had made with the Democrats, however, Worley got almost no

financial help from the Democratic campaign committee. Not only did
Gingrich outspend Worley, $1.5 million to $342,000, but the FEC's lawsuit alleged that GOPAC provided an additional $250,000 of "Newt sup-
port" in that race in the form of consultants and expense money targeted
to Gingrich's district. With all that, Gingrich defeated Worley by only
974 votes out of 156,000 votes cast.

Gingrich seized on the 1990 budget fight to burnish his reputation as a revolutionary. To prepare himself for the negotiations, he reread *Advise and
Consent*, Allen Drury's 1959 novel about power politics in Washington.
During the long days that members of Congress and the Bush administration spent sequestered at Andrews Air Force Base hammering out a budget deal, Gingrich showed his disrespect for the Democrats and others by
reading magazines. Conservatives referred to the day the compromise was
struck as "the day of infamy." Gingrich was under pressure to oppose the
deal, which violated Bush's campaign mantra, "Read my lips. No new
taxes!" Gingrich thought he could vote no, and that the Democrats would
deliver enough votes to pass it anyway. Instead, the deal collapsed when
Democrats produced far fewer votes than they had promised.

   In the media, Gingrich's revolt against his own party's president took
on mythical proportions. He had challenged the president of his own
party on an issue that many Republicans believe was responsible for
denying George Bush reelection in 1992. Some in Gingrich's circle had
come to the view that winning a Republican majority in the House
would not be possible as long as a Republican—or at least *this* Republican—was president. There is no evidence that Gingrich subscribed to
this theory, but his public opposition to Bush's budget compromise
delivered a blow to Bush's prestige.

   Curiously, the deal Gingrich rejected was a better one from the conservative perspective than what eventually emerged. It had an investment tax cut, which was a capital gains tax cut by another name. And the
tax increase that Gingrich bitterly opposed actually lowered rates for
many people from thirty-three to thirty-one percent, then extended the
thirty-one percent to eliminate the so-called "bubble" for the highest
earners. "Our best growth bill in years was done in by our growth guys,"
Bush's chief of staff John Sununu complained. Sununu, himself a no-
new-taxes conservative from New Hampshire, said, "The President
would have had a great deal less trouble if the original agreement had
become law."

   There was more turmoil, but the second budget deal passed the Congress. It had fewer spending cuts and higher taxes than the original

agreement. The whole sorry episode split the Republicans and exposed the great divide between the Michel loyalists and the Gingrich activists. "The feelings were incredibly passionate," Vin Weber recalled. "It's the only time a colleague in the House refused to shake my hand in the Republican caucus. He thought we were destroying the Republican Party and the Bush presidency."

Bush was so angry at Gingrich that, at a ceremony on the White House lawn, the President retreated every time he saw Gingrich approaching and, finally, ducked into the White House to avoid a meeting. The idea of a junior member of the leadership bucking his president went against Bush's training in the navy during World War II, which had taught him the value of an orderly chain of command and unswerving loyalty. "There was a sense in the White House that the admiral of the fleet had made the decision and I was but a disloyal ship captain," Gingrich said. "I think that is a total misunderstanding of politics. For me to have voted for that compromise would have destroyed my effectiveness."

Weyrich says that Gingrich's stand against his own party's president illustrates both a strength and a weakness. Gingrich is a gut fighter, Weyrich says, but he doesn't really care that much about winning.

"Newt very much likes the approval of the establishment while fighting the establishment," Weyrich says. "His great weakness is wanting to make deals and accommodations with people who disagree with him, even when it's to his disadvantage, just for the sake of having made such accommodations."

When Weyrich called Gingrich to congratulate him the morning after the budget plan Bush negotiated with the Democrats was defeated, he expected Gingrich to be in a happy frame of mind. "Instead I found him in a terrible state of depression," Weyrich recalled.

"What's the matter?" Weyrich asked.

"Well, the Bush people called and they said they are not going to deal with me," Gingrich related. "They're going to deal with the Democrats."

"But you're in a position where if you play it right they're going to have to deal with you," Weyrich pressed.

"Yeah, but they are saying they don't want to deal with me," Gingrich said, glumly.

"Why do you care? You just beat them."

"Well, yes, but. . . ."

To Weyrich, Gingrich's reaction demonstrated that he loves playing the game more than winning. He'll take either side of an issue for the sport of it.

Gingrich did not run for whip to follow Michel's example of blind loyalty to the President. He saw himself leading a frustrated Republican minority whose interests had constantly been undermined by leaders who were unwilling to take a stand. The disunity among Republicans was demonstrated when Gingrich, newly elected as whip, employed the word "we" when talking with reporters, implying he was speaking for the leadership. The usually mild-mannered Michel stomped into a meeting with Gingrich and the others and declared, "There is *one* leadership. We are not going to have people freelancing." Everybody sat up big-eyed and staring, never having seen Michel so exercised. "We are going to be disciplined and responsible," Michel continued, pounding his fist on the table for emphasis.

All eyes turned to Gingrich, expecting a fiery response. But Gingrich was apologetic. "He's right—I screwed up," Gingrich said. "I have not made the transition yet to realize that I have a different responsibility. I hadn't thought about it this way, and he's entirely correct."

Michel noticed how careful Gingrich was to make it continue to appear that he, Michel, was still number one among Republicans in the House, even while distancing himself from Michel's way of doing things. "He'd say, 'Blah, blah, blah, blah,' but eventually he'd say, 'It's Bob's call—it's the leader's call,'" Michel said. "He'd make a special point of saying that. But you knew what he was trying to do. He wanted to stake out a position that was at some odds with me."

Gingrich continued to second-guess the way Michel was doing his job. For example, Gingrich proposed changing the Republican Conference by-laws to give the Minority Leader the power to name the members of the Rules Committee, which controls the flow of legislation in the House. Michel said, "I don't crave that power and I don't need it in the minority." But Gingrich urged, "When we're in the majority, the Rules Committee has got to be an arm of the leadership." Michel balked, telling Gingrich, "It's a tough thing to tell someone who's been around a long time that you're replacing him." Nevertheless, Michel eventually did what he called "the dirty work" by replacing Jimmy Quillen of Tennessee with Gerald Solomon of New York as the ranking Republican on the committee.

Recalling the incident, Michel marveled that Gingrich had had such confidence about the Republicans winning a majority. The genial Michel would never have made the move without Gingrich's prodding. "Of course, Jimmy Quillen has hardly ever spoken to me since that time," Michel said. "But it was the right decision because [Solomon] is much more feisty. Today, he's a heck of a chairman."

Bush's 1992 reelection campaign posed another test for Gingrich in how far he would go to challenge the old order. Gregorsky sent a memo to Gingrich pleading that he distance himself from the White House. "Don't send any more memos to those guys. They make jokes about you. Let them lose. We will start from scratch once they're gone." Gingrich was, in fact, something of a joke around the White House. Top aides received almost daily communiqués, which they dubbed "Newtgrams." These missives were dated and signed as though the author thought that someday they would have historical significance.

Gingrich backed Bush in a perfunctory way, but he was not surprised—and not altogether unpleased—when Clinton won the election. With the Democrats in charge of the White House and Congress, the revolution could proceed without fear of undermining a Republican president.

In December 1992, as both parties were adjusting to the shift in power in the White House, Majority Leader Richard Gephardt called Gingrich and asked him to come by his office for a visit. "You know, we've been through a long decade of fighting," Gephardt began. "It just seems to me that you and I ought to be able to find a way to work together."

"I'll be very up front with you," Gingrich replied. "When you run over me, I'm going to cause you as much pain as I can. I'll help you, but it's got to be based on that kind of honesty, so we're not just sticking thumbtacks in each other to see how much we bleed."

It was the conversational equivalent of smoking a peace pipe. Over the last decade, the level of rancor had steadily worsened with Wright's forced resignation and the House Bank scandal, which tarred the reputations of dozens of members who had not been penalized, as ordinary citizens would have been, for overdrawing their checking accounts. Gingrich seemed sobered by some of the consequences of his rabble-rousing. The public outcry over members of Congress bouncing checks had led to his close friend Vin Weber's decision not to run again. And Gingrich, a month after demanding that a special prosecutor investigate the House Bank, was found to have bounced twenty-two checks himself, including one for $9,643 to the IRS.

Gingrich still had enemies in the Republican Party, but most resistance had turned to resignation. All but a few of the old-style House Republicans had vanished, and the survivors were seen as accommodationists. Feeling the weight of what he had created, Gingrich called together a handful of past and present aides in the summer of 1993 to talk about the challenge ahead. "I'm going to be Minority Leader in another year and a half," he said. "I can't do everything myself." In the mod, baby-boom language that he and President Clinton shared a fondness for, Gingrich declared that he needed to deputize at least fifty "effective change agents" to do the work he once had done by himself.

Gingrich confessed that night that the many theories he spouts about effective management rarely translate into behavior. The gap between his vision and reality is so big, he said, "sometimes I want to walk outside and shoot myself."

Because they met at the Hyatt Regency hotel on Capitol Hill, Gingrich dubbed the five aides present the Regency Group and asked them to report back in a month. The memo that Gregorsky wrote did not fulfill his Regency assignment, but was intended as a psychological guide for those struggling to understand Gingrich. Quoting from Carl Jung's 1923 explication of psychological types, Gregorsky categorized Gingrich as an "extroverted intuitor."

"He seizes on new objects with great intensity, sometimes with extraordinary enthusiasm, only to abandon them cold-bloodedly, without any compunction and apparently without remembering them, as soon as their range is known and no further developments can be divined. . . .

"Think of the operational battle-fatigue around Newt," Gregorsky wrote. "Newt's mission is absolutely consistent—no one in senior GOP ranks has anything to rival it for depth and durability. Beyond that, little else seems reassuring, because NG 'spotlights' endless targets of opportunity."

Gregorsky forwarded the memo to Gingrich's press secretary, Tony Blankley, with a note saying, "If you think this is too crazy to discuss in front of the group, just don't acknowledge it." Blankley, an urbane Englishman, chose not to respond.

When Bob Michel announced in October 1993 that he would leave Congress at the end of the term, Gingrich was able to round up enough support in four days to insure that he would be Michel's successor although the Republicans would not officially vote for another fourteen months. Gingrich boasted that the swiftness with which he positioned himself "startled the connoisseurs of how the game is played." Gingrich had followed a written plan he had prepared months earlier to consolidate his power and make the establishment take notice. In a show of force that scared away potential challengers, he announced his bid to be leader at a news conference surrounded by seventy-five Republicans.

Health care reform was the dominant issue on Clinton's agenda in the fall of 1993 and Republicans were divided over whether to oppose the White House or cooperate. Gingrich wanted a deal. He thought Republicans who said there was "no crisis" risked looking like they were the party of George Bush. He said so publicly, braving condemnation from the Right. The split in the GOP was evident when Hillary Rodham Clinton, speaking for the administration, testified before a House committee on the health care reform plan that she had helped create. Most of the members of Congress were deferential to the First Lady, but Rep. Dick Armey, the Texas conservative, repeatedly challenged Mrs. Clinton's assertions. Armey's unsmiling public persona led Mrs. Clinton to liken him to Dr. Jack Kevorkian, then in the news for assisting terminally ill people in committing suicide.

This was not the first time and would not be the last that Armey's demeanor and hard line on social issues would make Gingrich look moderate by contrast. New York Sen. Daniel Patrick Moynihan, observing the contrast between Gingrich and Armey, recalled in a private meeting at the White House how prostitutes in Renaissance France paraded with a monkey on their shoulder, so that the monkey's ugliness would highlight the prostitutes' beauty. "In Dick Armey, Gingrich has his monkey," Moynihan proclaimed to much laughter.

Gingrich was still open to a deal when Ross Perot called in the fall of 1993 about working together on a positive health care bill. Gingrich later flew to Dallas and secretly conferred with the billionaire industrialist. But when Whitewater, the land scandal dating to Clinton's days as governor of Arkansas, continued to dominate the news, Gingrich felt less need to cooperate with the weakened Clinton. He was both fascinated by and appalled at the White House's inability to contain the scandal. It was like watching a drowning person, he said. No one helped Clinton for fear of getting pulled down with him. Clinton's approval rating was in freefall.

When Republicans gathered in Salisbury, Maryland, for their annual winter retreat in January 1994, Gingrich was emboldened by the incompetence of the White House. Where only months before, he had fretted about Clinton "stealing our welfare policy" and treading on free-trade Republican turf, he was now convinced that Clinton did not have what it takes. He was just not a leader.

"We're going to make history," Gingrich told Frank Luntz, the young pollster he had invited to make a presentation at Salisbury.

Gingrich envisioned nothing less than an "American Renaissance," and wanted to know what Luntz thought of the phrase. "It doesn't work," he replied. "People think it's part of the Marriott chain."

Because Luntz had offended many Republicans by working for Pat Buchanan and Ross Perot in their 1992 bids to unseat George Bush, bringing him to Salisbury was a daring step. Luntz had impressed Gingrich with a presentation about his work for the right-wing Reform Party in Canada, which had used a populist message to go from one to fifty-two seats in Parliament in the 1993 elections. Gingrich encouraged Luntz to lay it on the line with the ninety-five members, including Michel, who had come to the retreat expecting nothing more challenging than a pep talk. Gingrich told Luntz, "We did not bring some brash young guy here for you to pretend you're forty-five. We had forty-five-year-olds who were available. So if you're not going to take the risks of being your age, why are you here tonight?"

The roads had iced over that afternoon, and a car carrying the materials for Luntz's presentation never made it to the retreat. "Without any data, I went overboard because I had nothing to ground me," Luntz said, his books of data and his slides stuck on an icy road somewhere between Washington and Salisbury.

Left to his own devices, and without any quantitative backup, Luntz launched into what many present took as a show of disrespect. "Face it," he said. "The public doesn't like you." He told them they should shed their coats and ties and adopt a more intimate relationship with the voters. As Luntz went through his gyrations, two members got up and left to demonstrate their displeasure. His peroration struck them as so much generational baloney. Others appeared nonplussed. Who was this clownishly dressed youngster to tell them what to do?

Texas Rep. Tom DeLay finally rose to challenge Luntz. How could he denigrate the party when Republicans had won a string of off-year elections that year, even capturing big-city mayoral races in Los Angeles and New York? "No, sir," Luntz replied. "Those were Democratic defeats, not Republican victories." A rising star in the Republican leadership, DeLay did not take kindly to being slapped down in public by someone so obviously his junior in age and stature. He came back at Luntz, who went back at him, and on it went for several rounds. Luntz would later apologize to DeLay.

Gingrich sat in the back of the room watching, but saying nothing. The chill that Luntz left was unmistakable. "Don't worry about it," Gingrich counseled his young protégé, adding some advice that, coming from Gingrich, sounded a bit disingenuous. "From now on, bold, but pleasant."

Gingrich had long believed that the only way for Republicans to win a majority was to nationalize congressional elections and have them turn on the same broad themes that consistently elected Republican presidents over Democrats. The Contract With America would enable every Republican literally to read from the same page in the 1994 campaign.

After laying the foundation at the Salisbury retreat, Gingrich delegated the work of drawing up the Contract to a team headed by Texas

Rep. Dick Armey, and the job of marketing it to another team, headed by Rep. John Boehner of Ohio. Boehner's top aide, Barry Jackson, who had run a family-owned party rental business back in Ohio, said there was not much difference between commercial and political marketing. "In politics, you've got a product and your customers are the voters. You're trying to convince the voters to buy your product and not the other guy's product. It's real simple."

Brainstorming sessions produced sixty-seven different items that could be included in a contract with the voters. Armey's team prepared a questionnaire for incumbent House Republicans and Republican challengers, asking which items they wanted in the contract and which they did not. The challenge was to craft ten bills that all Republicans were willing at least to vote *on,* if not vote *for.*

Gingrich decreed that every element of the Contract had to pass "the Connie Morella test," after the moderate Maryland Republican congresswoman. Morella and other moderates could be persuaded to put things to a vote that they did not actually support. If signing the contract could cause problems with constituents, that, too, could be taken care of. The marketing team drafted a letter for Sue W. Kelly, a candidate in New York, to send to Gingrich and publicize in her district. In it, Kelly objected to the provision denying welfare checks to underage mothers, saying, "I'm proud to sign the contract. I'm glad you're going to give me an opportunity to debate this, but I want to put you on notice that I intend to bring up an amendment that will strike this language."

The only real tension was over social issues, and making sure they stayed out of the Contract. Gingrich sided with Nancy Johnson and other moderates when Armey surreptitiously inserted a "gag rule" on abortion counseling in welfare reform legislation. Johnson and other pro-choice moderates discovered it only after they had signed the contract. She was so furious that she fired off a memo to all Republican challengers, titled "Beware: Gag Rule Problem Real!!" Gingrich intercepted the memo and advised Johnson to tone down her language. "He knew I would make enemies," she said. The memo was rewritten, with Johnson's permission. And the truce held between moderates and conservatives.

The final ten bills were crafted in mock hearings and mark-up sessions conducted by Republicans in the House. This not only allowed greater participation in the content of the legislation, but also gave Republicans practice conducting hearings in the House, something none of them had ever done as members of the minority.

Focus groups conducted by Frank Luntz gave the marketing team feedback on the ad that was to run in *TV Guide* ten days before the election. People said it reminded them of the Declaration of Independence. As for the Contract language, the more words the better, the focus groups said. Don't just promise to "change welfare as we know it," as Clinton had, tell us what changes you intend to make, the focus groups said. Participants in the test group did not draw the distinction between passing the contract items and simply bringing them up for a vote, but they did say that passing two or three of them would at least show the politicians were trying. Disillusionment with Washington ran so deep that three out of ten would do.

A special election in Kentucky over the 1994 Memorial Day break signaled a changed political landscape. Veteran Democrat William Natcher had died, leaving vacant the seat he had held for forty years. In the special election, Ron Lewis, a religious bookstore owner who had no experience in politics, defeated Democrat Joe Prather, president of the Kentucky State Senate. Lewis was the first Republican ever elected to the House from that part of Kentucky. The television ad that morphed Prather's face into Clinton's was shown on network newscasts. It tapped into the country's deepening disgust with the party in power. Raising money for Republican challengers became dramatically easier with the prospect of substantial GOP gains in November.

The day after the GOP's upset victory, Gingrich opened up the usually private meeting of House Republicans to the news media, thus broadcasting across the nation the Republicans' message that the long-awaited realignment of U.S. politics had begun.

Health care reform would soon become hostage to the Republicans' ambition for a majority. Flying back to Washington on June 8 from Miami, where they had made a joint presentation before the Group Health Association of America, Democratic polltaker Peter Hart turned to his Republican counterpart, Bill McInturff, and posed this question:

"It's the day after the election. Bill Clinton, against all odds, only loses seven seats in the House and retains the Senate. What would you do to make that happen?"

"You'd have to have combat troops in North Korea," McInturff replied, on the theory that Americans rally round their commander in chief, at least in the short run. "Or you'd need a trifecta: a crime bill, welfare reform, and health care."

"Flip side," Hart continued. "Clinton loses the House and Senate, suffers record high losses, the biggest since World War II. . . . What would it take to get that result?"

McInturff answered so quickly that he surprised himself. "Health care can't pass," he said. "It's the defining issue to break gridlock." For the Republicans to gain control of the Congress, Clinton had to be seen as unable to bring about the change in Washington that voters had wanted in 1992, and would demand in 1994.

The conversation stuck in McInturff's mind. He called Joe Gaylord, Gingrich's longtime political guru, and suggested they put "the Peter Hart question" to other Republican pollsters. "I said to Joe, 'This is such a good question, tell Newt we should put it on the table: What has to happen to make him Speaker?'"

Once each month, Gingrich presided over a roundtable discussion with the top Republican pollsters. The idea was to listen to a variety of voices so Gingrich would be sure of getting unfiltered advice. There had been so much sustained good news for Republicans that disagreement was rare. Gingrich would usually start off the discussion with something like, "Are things as good out there as they feel to me?" And he would be greeted with a chorus of "Yes, yes, yes."

On this June day, he asked the pollsters what it would take to give the Republicans control of Congress. They answered unequivocally, just as McInturff had, "Block health care reform. . . . It allows the Democrats to say, 'We delivered.' It would give them the middle class."

The notion that Republicans could openly oppose health care reform and not be punished by the voters was a radical thought at the time. The conventional wisdom was that Republicans, however much they wished to kill health care legislation, could not have their fingerprints on the murder weapon. Yet here were GOP pollsters sitting around a confer-ence table at GOPAC brazenly devising a strategy to obstruct progress on health care reform. McInturff found the idea so breathtakingly risky that he exclaimed, "When it goes over the cliff, I'd like to be thirty miles away in a bar, with lots of witnesses."

All heads turned, and McInturff suddenly felt very alone. A moderate by current standards, he was sometimes out of step with his party's new radicalism. Having once worked for Elliot Richardson, former Attorney General, who epitomized old-style patrician Republicanism, McInturff was a marked man in some right-wing circles. The other pollsters accused him of going soft. "Everyone else thought I was queasy, moder-ate, squishy, and gutless," he recalled. "They were proud to be pushing it over the cliff. Their attitude was, 'For Christ's sake, if this is a dangerous bill, and it's the difference between us and them, then we should stand up and say we're against this stupid stuff.'"

The task would not even be that hard. By May or June, it had become clear that health care reform would not proceed in the House unless there was a breakthrough in the Senate. And Democrats were so divided, Republicans could easily stall legislation in the instinctively dilatory Senate. A handful of moderate Republican senators, led by Rhode Island's John Chafee, were the only defectors from the GOP's obstructionist strategy.

Watching the GOP strategy unfold, McInturff tweaked Peter Hart, whose provocative question had unwittingly aided his Republican counterparts in formulating the hardball tactics that would help make Gingrich Speaker. "You're such a good focus group leader," McInturff told the puzzled Democrat.

Throughout the summer, when reporters called Gingrich, they were often told that he was in a planning session. "What's he planning?" they would ask. "He's planning the transition," came the reply.

"People sort of giggled," recalls Tony Blankley, Gingrich's droll press secretary. But Gingrich was confidently developing plans for the opening day of the next Congress, with himself as Speaker, followed by a marathon hundred days designed to rival Franklin Roosevelt's New Deal in style while dismantling it in substance.

At the same time, Gingrich cracked the whip on moderate Republicans in the House who were still flirting with the Clinton White House on health care. Iowa Rep. Fred Grandy told *The Washington Post* that Gingrich had given him and other moderates "marching orders" to vote against any amendments in committee that might produce a compromise. Grandy observed that Gingrich was "on a glide path" to becoming Speaker. A number of House Republicans who had privately told First Lady Hillary Rodham Clinton, "We'll be there at the end," called to say the political climate had changed, and they could not support any reform plan.

It was clear that Gingrich was going to replace Bob Michel as Republican leader, and Gingrich was not afraid to use that as leverage. He warned Republicans that if they accommodated the White House on health care or anything else, they could lose their committee chairmanships in the next Congress. The White House made a halfhearted attempt to engage Gingrich on the idea of comprehensive health care reform. "It's all big government," Gingrich said dismissively. Publicly, he said that Hillary's plan would create "a police state."

Ninety days before the November election, Clinton's poll numbers had plunged significantly. Only thirty-nine percent believed he had the honesty and integrity to be president. The dismal showing emboldened House Republicans to hand Clinton a defeat that would ordinarily be unthinkable in an election year. In an unholy alliance with anti–gun control Democrats and Black Caucus liberals irate about provisions expanding the death penalty, Republicans mustered enough strength on a procedural vote to kill a crime bill that Clinton was touting as a major accomplishment. The defeat sent the Democrats into disarray and convinced many of them to distance themselves from the White House. It also meant that health care was dead. The Republicans had run down the clock. What little time was left in the session would be given over to stitching together a compromise crime bill.

Anger dominated debate on the House floor. Republicans derided money in the bill for crime prevention programs as social welfare pork designed to buy big-city Democratic votes. Democrats assailed Republicans for hiding behind a procedural vote to embarrass the President when their real goal was to prevent a ban on assault weapons from reaching Clinton's desk. Texas Rep. Dick Armey blurted out at one point, "We don't care very much about your President." Gingrich then went to the microphone, but Democrats shouted, "Object!," and he could not speak.

A handful of House Republicans had voted with the White House. Rep. Fred Grandy was one of those he himself called "The Infidel Eleven." Anxious to hold their votes, the White House invited them to meet with Clinton. Gingrich went along as part power broker and part monitor. He wanted to retrieve some of the eleven or at least exact a price for their vote. Those who attended thought Gingrich was surprisingly cordial, almost embarrassingly so. There was no real change in his determination to confound the President, but when he was in a room where the mood was more centrist, he showed his adaptability.

Ultimately, the White House struck a deal to keep the moderate Republicans' votes by agreeing to across-the-board cuts in both social programs and prison construction money. Conservative Republicans demanded that Gingrich punish the members who had voted with the White House. But the moderates had acted in good conscience with Gingrich's support, so he was not going to let his normal allies on the right railroad them. He stood his ground when an angry mob of forty right-wingers confronted him about stripping Ohio Rep. John Kasich of his ranking seat on the Budget Committee. "You'll have to come through me if you want to get Kasich," Gingrich said, defending his friend and budgetary soul mate.

Throughout September 1994, the House floor was a killing field, and Republicans paid no price for blocking everything the Democrats put forward. Gingrich even voted against a lobbying reform bill that he had previously supported. A week later, the Senate failed to pass the bill after Gingrich rallied three hundred radio talk show hosts, the Christian Coalition, and *The Wall Street Journal* editorial page against the legislation. The measure that drew fire from the Right would have required greater disclosure of grassroots lobbying, which social conservatives and the gun lobby—not to mention Planned Parenthood and the environmentalists—relied on to pressure Congress. Six months earlier, Gingrich had written to Democratic House Speaker Tom Foley to ask that the very same provision be included. When he was called on the inconsistency, Gingrich claimed he had not understood the implications when he lobbied for the provision.

Opposing lobbying reform would ordinarily be political suicide. People like lobbyists even less than politicians. Tony Blankley advised against taking on an issue that had no public relations upside. "You're going to have most of the editorial page writers writing that we are skunks," Blankley said. There was no way that he could think of to generate enough repetitions of the Republican message to offset the army of opinion on the other side.

"Lack of courage is never a good reason to do something," Gingrich replied stubbornly. Then he called Rush Limbaugh, the most influential of the nation's conservative talk show hosts, to enlist his support. With Limbaugh on board, Gingrich triggered the mass fax operation that links House Republicans to the radio talk shows. In twenty-four hours, the talk shows generated such a large number of phone calls to congressional offices that Republicans voted against the lobbying reform bill without fear of repercussion. The bill was subsequently revived without the grassroots oversight provision, but died in the Senate.

Making sure the Democrats did not pass anything was one prong of the Republican strategy. Offering a positive alternative in the form of the Contract With America was another. The third prong was money. Typically, GOP challengers had pulled even with incumbents in early October polls, only to fall behind because they ran out of money, whereas labor unions and other interest groups came through for Democrats in the final weeks.

Gingrich's goal was to raise enough money to make sure GOP candidates could keep up with Democrats, TV ad for TV ad, down the stretch. Gingrich had long been disgusted by Republicans in safe seats collecting PAC money they did not need for their own races while doing nothing to elect other Republicans. He invited each Republican incumbent to donate $60,000 of his own campaign funds to the Republican Congressional Campaign Committee. Just in case they were tempted to ignore the invitation, he reminded them that their place on committees in the new Republican majority House would be influenced by their generosity to fellow Republicans. GOP incumbents dutifully transferred $3 million to challengers in the month before the election.

Gingrich also warned PAC contribution managers of the possible consequences if he became Speaker: "For anybody who's not on board now, it's going to be the two coldest years in Washington." He told a gathering of lobbyists that they should contribute to Republicans out of gratitude to the GOP for killing the lobbying reform bill. A *Washington Post* front-page story about the session quoted Gingrich portraying Clinton as "the enemy of normal Americans." Tony Blankley agreed the language was "a little colorful—he should have said 'threat to normal people,' not enemy."

After reading the *Post* account, David Dreyer, a White House aide, said of Gingrich, "He's done Lord Acton one better. He's corrupted by power he doesn't yet have."

In the last month before the election, Gingrich made the rounds of fund-raising receptions to drive home his message that a new day was dawning in Congress. At a $10,000-a-plate dinner for two dozen business lobbyists at the Jefferson Hotel, a few blocks up 16th Street from the White House, Gingrich promised that a GOP-controlled Congress would "go to the core of what you need." The dinner was hosted by Texas Rep. Jack Fields, a ranking member of the House Commerce Committee, and the lobbyists present had an interest in telecommunications, maritime shipping, and other matters before the committee. There were no reporters present, so Gingrich was blunt. He told the lobbyists there would be "no more tinkering at the margins" of their issues and "no more signing ceremonies" at the White House. He meant that, with Republicans in power, lobbyists would not have to settle for watered-down compromises, and that Republicans intended to prevent all pending legislation from reaching the President's desk.

The final days of a congressional session are usually marked by a flood of last-minute bills. Many of the lobbyists present favored compromises that had already been struck and feared that delay would allow their opponents in the environmental community and elsewhere to dig in harder, but they nevertheless applauded Gingrich's remarks. "Nobody wanted to look like a wimp, like we were afraid to go for a bigger piece of the pie," said a lobbyist who was there. "They were thinking that if the Republicans do as well as expected, they'll repeal [job safety] regulations, shut down the Endangered Species Act, and make property rights the core of any environmental legislation. What they're going to get instead is gridlock."

A bright sun and cloudless blue sky welcomed Republican incumbents and challengers who gathered on the steps of the Capitol on Tuesday, September 27, 1994, to sign the Contract With America. Gingrich pronounced it "Reagan weather," recalling how dark clouds had given way to sunshine at the precise moment Ronald Reagan had stood up to take the oath as President succeeding Jimmy Carter in 1981. Reagan weather was the perfect setting for Republicans bent on taking back the House from the Democrats, Gingrich thought as he scribbled notes on a yellow legal pad for the keynote speech he would deliver to this collection of men and women who embodied his own dreams and ambition.

Gingrich composes his speeches off the cuff, weaving in well-worn material with new thoughts "to try to feel the mood of the day and the crowd and be responsive to the moment." His speech this day would range from a homespun metaphor about the country breaking down like the family car with four flat tires to an apocalyptic closing predicting a brutal and savage end to civilization as we know it unless the United States halts its slide into decadence. He ridiculed columnists and TV commentators who had mocked the Contract as a political trick. Afterward, a reporter asked him why he had picked on the press corps. "Because I think the coverage of this so far has been pathetic," Gingrich said. "It's been negative, cynical. . . . One of the reasons this country is cynical is because the press corps doesn't get it."

Having delivered this diatribe, Gingrich strode across the South Lawn of the Capitol to greet the GOP challengers and other well-wishers, who shouted out to him, "Good luck, Mr. Speaker."

"Not yet," he said. "We've still got work to do."

A first-time candidate approached Gingrich for advice on running for Congress.

"Never give up," Gingrich said. "Don't stop. Run seven days a week. Shake hands all day. Sleep in the car. Try to put in at least a hundred hours a week. Be very positive and very firm. When your opponent smears you, come back with the truth. Remember that the Big Truth beats the Big Lie. And don't be afraid to ask for money because this is their country and they have a right to give their money to you rather than a Democrat who is going to raise their taxes and take it from them anyway."

Ever since the anti-Washington mood gripped the nation, political consultants have warned politicians to keep shots of the Capitol out of their advertising. A sea of mostly white men in dark suits did not look like a revolutionary army ready to take back Washington for ordinary people. Indeed, the event competed for news attention with a visit to Washington by Russian President Boris Yeltsin. Republican planners were aware of the conflict but decided to push on, reasoning that the Cold War was over, and the fact that two politicians who were having trouble at home were meeting was not a big story. They were right.

It would have been easy to stigmatize Gingrich and the GOP as obstructionists if it were not for the Contract. Most voters had little or no idea what was in the Contract, but its existence deflected the argument that Republicans were simply naysayers. More important, Gingrich knew that if the Republicans took over they would have very little time to prove themselves to a skeptical public. Fulfilling the Contract in the first hundred days would make a powerful first impression, even if most of the major reforms it promised would either die or languish in the Senate.

That afternoon, Gingrich appeared with Tony Coelho on CNN's *Inside Politics*. Coelho, a scrappy Californian, had held the whip's post for the Democrats opposite Gingrich, and was now advising the White House on its 1994 election strategy. Throughout their partisan battles in Congress, the two men had developed respect for each other and had actually grown quite close. Coelho had abruptly resigned his seat effective June 15, 1989, after *The Washington Post* broke a story about his investment ties with convicted junk bond salesman Michael Milken.

It was widely assumed that Gingrich would go after Coelho on his ethics problems the way he did Jim Wright. "People thought that he was part of what brought me down," said Coelho. "That's not true at all. He came to me and said, 'I hope you're not thinking of doing anything rash. I'll work something out. We want you around here. It's exciting with you here.'" But years later, when Coelho was being talked about as a possible chief of staff for President Clinton, Gingrich was quoted saying that perhaps the reasons Coelho left Congress should be explored. The implied threat permanently damaged their relationship. "He can't help himself," said a Gingrich friend. "Wave the flag and he's ready to fight."

The brief exchange—with Coelho in CNN's New York studio and Gingrich in Washington—previewed the new political order. Coelho, now an investment banker, was out of training for political combat and seemed unsure of himself. Gingrich was at the top of his game.

Moderator Judy Woodruff, jabbing the Contract With America, posed the first question: "Your critics are saying all you've done is run out a string of Republican golden oldies to pander to the public's desire to get something for nothing. What do you say to these people?"

Gingrich ignored the question and delivered instead a prepared barb: "Well, first of all, I couldn't help but be amused by the fact that you have a Republican college teacher and a Democratic investment banker on this show—and what a remarkable change in the two parties that is. I think if you go back twenty or thirty years, nobody would quite believe you'd have this particular match-up. . . ."

Caught off guard, Coelho never regained his composure. He and Gingrich argued, sometimes drowning out each other's words, over who was to blame for the deficit-ridden 1980s, the Republican president or the Democratic Congress. Politically savvy viewers could not miss the message: After forty years in the minority, the Republicans were on the offensive, and it was the Democrats who were forced to defend their record.

The Democrats unwittingly helped the Republicans by attacking the Contract With America without offering any positive ideas of their own. Polls showed that the public saw the GOP as the party of change, a remarkable turnabout in just two years.

When Gingrich sat down for lunch in late September with Bob Strauss, a former Democratic National Committee chairman, Democrats all over the country were bracing for electoral disaster. Vin Weber had arranged the lunch after telling Gingrich that he needed some gray-beards he could turn to and some relationships on the other side of the aisle politically. Strauss gravitated to power and, while still a Democrat, had served as President Bush's ambassador to Russia.

Strauss remembers the call from Weber suggesting he meet Gingrich for lunch. "Why?" he asked. Gingrich was not on Strauss's radar screen.

"Because he's going to be Speaker," Weber replied.

"You're crazy as hell," Strauss said.

But Strauss did not need much convincing that day five weeks before the election. Gingrich arrived with a pocketful of figures that showed the wide lead Republicans had in a number of polls. "He talked the whole damn time," says Strauss. "He didn't learn anything from me; I learned from him. I knew we were in for big trouble. He was so intense and so full of what he was doing."

Gingrich's thinking went way beyond election day. Republican thinker and strategist William Kristol mentioned offhandedly in an interview that even if the GOP won both houses, Congress would not govern the country because, in a democracy, the President governs and Congress legislates. Kristol received a handwritten note from Gingrich that said: "Study your American history—Henry Clay." In the early nineteenth century, Henry Clay as Speaker of the House established a domestic agenda for the country over the opposition of President Andrew Jackson.

Gingrich met with Republican pollsters at the GOPAC office on October 11 to assess the strength of the Republican tide. Clinton had had a string of foreign policy successes, from staring down Iraqi President Saddam Hussein to pulling off a high-risk invasion of Haiti. The pollsters concluded that events in Iraq had temporarily taken the froth off the Republican tide, but that nothing could happen to reverse it. Gingrich was in a particularly ebullient mood. His ego seemed to know no bounds.

Gingrich used these sessions to air his thoughts on issues, and to get the pollsters' reaction. He was looking for a way to debunk the White House claim that Clinton, faced with a Republican Congress, could run against Congress the way Harry Truman did in 1948. What about saying that a Republican-led Congress would use subpoena power to go after President Clinton? Most of the pollsters in the room thought that would be going too far. A few, notably Ed Goeas, who had done much of the work on the Contract, supported Gingrich. In any event, Gingrich made it clear he was not looking for permission.

Some advisers worried that Gingrich was developing "the king mentality." One opinion counted, and that was his. He was going to make the point regardless. The White House was "ridiculous" to think that Clinton could "pull a Truman" and run against a GOP-led Congress, Gingrich said. "Don't think Truman," he counseled. "Think Nixon."

A couple of the pollsters jotted down the line. Truman ran against a do-nothing Congress, but Nixon was impaled by an aggressive Congress. "Clinton's people would have to be lunatics to want a Republican-run House or Senate," said one of those present, savoring the prospect of hearings on Whitewater and other matters that could embarrass Clinton.

Democrats scrambled to distance themselves from Clinton, a futile exercise as it turned out. "You can't jump off the *Queen Elizabeth* between London and New York and swim to safety," said Bill McInturff.

There was one small detail that could derail Gingrich. He was, according to some reports, in danger of losing his own House seat. Former Democratic Rep. Ben Jones had gained traction in his challenge to Gingrich with allegations of ethical misconduct connected to GOPAC's refusal to release the names of its donors. A former actor who once played Cooter in the television series *The Dukes of Hazzard,* Jones posed enough of a threat that Gingrich cut short a national campaign tour on behalf of Republicans and headed back to his Atlanta district for the final weekend before the election. Gingrich's outlandish suggestion that Republicans treat Democrats as enemies of "normal Americans" provoked a humorous response from Jones.

"Me, I've never been normal," Jones quipped. "And if I were normal, I wouldn't be in politics." Jones debated an empty chair when Gingrich refused to show up because he objected to Jones having used foul language in an interview with a local alternative newspaper. Jones claimed it was an offhand remark not meant to be published. He had said of Gingrich, "Oh, fuck him and the horse he rode in on."

On the weekend before the election, Gingrich again raised doubts about his ability to be more than a partisan slasher with an insensitive and, some said, senseless remark about Susan Smith, the South Carolina woman who had drowned her two children. Gingrich said the tragedy "vividly reminds every American how sick the society is" and that "the only way you get change is to vote Republican."

In the end, the contest with Jones amounted to little more than a side show. Gingrich won his ninth congressional term with sixty-four percent of the vote, only the second time he had exceeded sixty percent. Jones shifted his challenge to Gingrich from the political arena to the House ethics committee, where his research on the web of enterprises known as Newt, Inc. formed the basis for the first of a half-dozen ethics complaints filed by him and others against Gingrich in 1994 and 1995.

The fact that Gingrich was worried about losing was astounding since the Sixth District of Georgia is the second most Republican in the country and the third biggest recipient of federal largesse. The home of Lockheed, one of the giants in defense contracting, it is the beneficiary of Pentagon spending by a ratio of sixty-nine to one over the average congressional district.

On election day, November 8, 1994, Republicans gained fifty-two seats in the House, making Gingrich the first GOP Speaker in forty years. Almost half the freshman class of seventy-three Republicans turned out to be Gingrich progeny, trained and recruited by GOPAC. The transformation was complete. The GOP leadership would now reflect Gingrich's activist style and conservative bent and Gingrich would have the power and responsibility for domestic policy that is normally accorded to a president.

Moderate Rep. Fred Grandy, who had given up his seat in the House only to lose his race for governor of Iowa, said conservatives filled a vacuum left by the party's moderates. Grandy calls his fellow moderates, not without sarcasm, "the cocktail coalition."

"They are all those so-called Rockefeller Republican types who love to sit around and listen to one another at a Ripon lunch or a Lincoln Day dinner, who might conceivably get it up for a fund-raiser if a presidential aspirant comes through the state, but get them to drive a senior citizen to the poll on election day, forget it," said Grandy. "These people are going to Florida."

Gingrich had painstakingly built a new Republican Party, and moderates, who had done nothing to stop him, were now a minority within the party. "I'm a boutique Republican," Grandy said sadly. "And Newt is Wal-Mart."

In a hotel ballroom in suburban Atlanta, hundreds of well-wishers chanted, "Newt, Newt, Newt," while the loudspeaker churned out "Happy Days Are Here Again," FDR's favorite song and a traditional Democratic theme song. Gingrich, raising his arms to quiet the crowd, observed with delight, "Chanting the name of an amphibian has got to be one of the weirdest political phenomena."

Long after midnight, when all but the hardiest revelers had gone to bed, Gingrich's staff presented him with a banner that had the names of all the past House Speakers and across the bottom, in big red letters, Newt Gingrich. As an aide snapped pictures, Gingrich said he had spoken with Bob Michel, and that after thirty years in the minority, Michel had no bitterness that this glorious moment was not his. "It shows that politics is not as cynical as people say," Gingrich declared. Then he broke down and cried. It was several minutes before he could regain his composure.

After the election, Gingrich returned triumphantly to Washington and held a press conference in the Capitol. The media that he had manipulated to his advantage on his climb to power now lavished him with the kind of attention that is usually reserved for a new president. While Gingrich pontificated in the Rotunda of the Capitol, Bob Michel was spotted getting a cup of coffee from a carryout window in the basement. He looked the same, dressed in an expensive suit and with a gold chain for his watch. But he was all alone, carrying his own tray.

The sense of exhilaration that surrounded Gingrich's stunning takeover of Capitol Hill did not last long. The bombastic rhetoric that had served him well as a revolutionary did not suit his new role as Speaker, and the policies that he and his fellow Republicans sought to impose to shrink government frightened and angered the beneficiaries of federal programs. As Clinton learned in his losing fight for health care reform, Americans resist change and view with suspicion the agent of change. Like Clinton before him, Gingrich overreached whatever mandate he had been given by the voters in the 1994 election. By the end of his first year as Speaker, Gingrich's popularity had plummeted to a point comparable to Richard Nixon's at the depths of the Watergate scandal.

A year that had begun with Gingrich grinning broadly from the Speaker's podium as he accepted the applause and cheers of the new Republican majority ended with much of the federal government shut down by a budget dispute between the White House and Congress, Gingrich under investigation by a special counsel, and one member of Gingrich's prized freshman class daring to distance himself from the Speaker. Rep. Mark Foley of Florida, one of the GOPAC Generation in

Congress, was quoted in *The Washington Post* as saying, "Newt Gingrich didn't elect me to anything. . . . I know he must be agonizing, but everyone remembers that he attacked the ethics of [former] Speaker [Jim] Wright, and now all this is just coming back to roost."

Gingrich had molded a Republican Congress in his own image, and it rewarded him with shock-troop efficiency. At the end of a hundred days, the House had passed nine of the ten elements of the Contract. Term limits, perhaps the most popular of the Contract provisions, failed, but Gingrich did not see that as a real setback. After all, had term limits been in effect, Gingrich could not have carried out his long campaign to win the speakership. By the time he achieved his goal, he had been in Congress for sixteen years, well beyond the proposed limits. Most of the House-passed legislation fulfilling the Contract stalled in the Senate, where a coalition of moderate Republicans joined with Democrats to kill some measures outright and water down others.

When negotiations over the budget broke down in the winter of 1995, Gingrich convinced President Clinton that he was unable to make a deal because the seventy-three freshmen who had charged into office the previous year brandishing budget axes would not let him. Some thought the Speaker was simply using the freshmen as an excuse to create a confrontation. The result was two government shutdowns, with the Gingrich-led Republicans taking the position that they would settle for nothing less than a balanced budget in seven years, accompanied by a substantial tax cut that would require even deeper cuts in government programs.

Watching these antics from Georgia, Lee Howell was reminded of the times two decades earlier that he and Gingrich would drive across the Sixth District together and Gingrich would spout his revolutionary theories. As Howell recalled it, Gingrich said "You make the situation as bad as can be, and then you pick up the pieces."

Over the years, Gingrich had nurtured and thrived on attention from the media, yet, once achieving his goal, he seemed ill-prepared for the microscope that would examine his every word and deed. Rep. John Kasich, the firebrand chairman of the House Budget Committee and a close associate of Gingrich's, likened being the first Republican Speaker in forty years to being the first to walk on the moon—no one could tell you what it was like. "Newt doesn't like using a script when he talks, but he's starting to see the need," Kasich said in December 1995, after Gingrich's undisciplined public utterances threatened to undermine the revolution he had led.

When questioned about his tendency to start spouting his ideas even before they are fully formed in his own mind, Gingrich would say that he

understood that as Speaker his every word would be dissected and analyzed; yet language had always been his most potent weapon and he
was too accustomed to being on the attack to quit the habit easily. Voters
who knew little else about Gingrich knew that he had suggested children
born to unwed teenage mothers be placed in orphanages, and that he had
blamed the policies of liberal Democrats for a pair of grisly murders in
Illinois, only to have the family of the victims beg him not to use them as
political fodder. The Speaker's public image sank even further when he
suggested that he was prompted to force a government shutdown in
part because Clinton had snubbed him aboard Air Force One on the flight
to and from the funeral of Israel's slain Prime Minister, Yitzhak Rabin.

Frank Luntz watched in horror as Gingrich's standing fell with the
American people. A weakened Speaker would make it harder to achieve
the GOP's ambitious agenda, just as Clinton's weakened presidency had
foreclosed health care reform. Luntz had learned from doing focus
groups for Ross Perot how to introduce an unorthodox politician to the
public in a way that could have buffered Gingrich from some of the
attacks on his character and ethics. But before Gingrich was even sworn
in as Speaker, he flirted with a $4.5 million book deal that the House
ethics committee would later rule, while not illegal, gave the impression
that he was cashing in on his office. There was a recklessness about the
way Gingrich operated that made voters uneasy. "You can't make a second first impression," Luntz lamented.

Under the guise of reform, Gingrich had done more than any other
single individual to discredit Congress as an institution. The web of
interconnecting enterprises that Gingrich had used to raise millions of
dollars to finance the Republican revolution was a late-twentieth-
century version of the big-city Democratic machines of another era,
except that Gingrich's Tammany Hall was nationwide. Now, at the midpoint of the first Republican Congress in forty years, not only was his
reputation damaged, but Congress itself was held in lower esteem than
it had been on the eve of the 1994 election.

One year after the 1994 special election in Kentucky that seemed to
be the harbinger of all things good for Republicans, another Kentucky
election signaled a possible turnabout. In November 1995, Democrat
Paul Patton won the Kentucky governorship, and in the process
reclaimed a Democratic majority in the very district that had given the
GOP its first real indication control of the House was within reach. Significantly, Patton's victory seemed to mirror a milestone of an earlier era.
In 1947, during the last period that a Democratic president faced a
Republican House, a Democrat also won the Kentucky governor's race,

an outcome that foreshadowed a reversal of fortune for the GOP. In the
1948 election, Harry Truman campaigned against the "do nothing Congress" and Democrats took back the House. With only two elements of
the Contract having become law, some Democrats began referring to
Gingrich's House as the "do nothing Congress."

In December 1995, ethical questions that had dogged Gingrich for
years caught up with him, prompting the House ethics committee to
name former prosecutor James M. Cole as special counsel to investigate.
Cole's original mandate was limited to examining whether a college
course taught by Gingrich and financed by tax-deductible contributions
was really a political vehicle. House rules and federal campaign finance
law forbid the use of tax-deductible donations for partisan activity. The
special counsel who investigated Speaker Jim Wright also had started
with a tightly drawn mandate, only to expand his inquiry as new information raised troubling new questions. Democrats predicted, perhaps
wistfully, that the same would be true in Gingrich's case.

Clinton's State of the Union address in January 1996, in which he pronounced an end to the era of big government, marked another turning
point in the dynamics between the White House and Capitol Hill and
exposed the divisions within the Republican Party itself. Just two days
after Clinton's centrist themes envisioning a smaller, but caring government received warm reviews from the press and the public, Republicans
abandoned their all-or-nothing negotiation strategy and conceded that
Clinton had won the public relations game. One astonished Clinton
Cabinet member said, "It's like you wake up the next morning and the
army's gone, when just the night before they were coming over the hill."
Gingrich conceded defeat, and, with talk of revolt in his own ranks,
retreated to revise his strategy.

Gingrich had dared to imagine himself a Speaker in the style of Sam
Rayburn, a man so devoted to the institution he served that he gained
the respect of everybody who dealt with him. For Gingrich to be thought
of as another Rayburn would have required Washington and the nation
to be seized with collective amnesia. Gingrich could not escape his past.
The ruthless way that he had achieved his position would forever color
the way he was perceived. He would not get forgiveness for the sins he
had rooted out and avenged in others.

CHAPTER FIVE

MEMBER OF CONGRESS

Knocking Down the Door

Rep. Maxine Waters and her California political consultant were having a pleasant Saturday lunch in the coffee shop of the Doubletree Hotel in Los Angeles on the weekend before the November 1994 election when several young African-American men dressed in dark suits and bow ties—the distinctive dress of Nation of Islam security guards—suddenly appeared and stationed themselves around the hotel.

"Farrakhan must be in town," Waters said.

"Let's leave," said the consultant, Leslie Winner, unnerved by the prospect of an encounter with Louis Farrakhan. While Farrakhan is popular with many of Waters's inner-city constituents, there is peril for any politician who appears too closely identified with the radical Muslim leader.

"Let's leave," Winner repeated, this time more insistently. "You don't want someone to take your picture."

Unperturbed, Waters calmly finished her vegetarian burger, her eyes fixed on the unfolding drama. More young men lined the walkway, signaling Farrakhan's imminent arrival. "Don't you want to see it?" she asked, gently scolding the anxious consultant. "That's how you learn."

Let other politicians run away from controversy. As a black woman in a white political world, Waters had decided long ago to "give myself permission" to defy the rules and rituals that had kept people like her from having a voice. And she will suffer the consequences if she thinks the point is worth making.

From childhood on, Waters has had to prove herself in an unaccepting world. She is the fifth of her mother's thirteen children and, by her account, "the first child in my family to come out too skinny, too black,

and too looking like they say my father looked." Her father left before
she was two. She has a vague memory of his visiting when she was six or
seven years old, but there was no contact after that. Everybody said she
looked like him. "If my father was someone who had gotten himself
together, fine, but he had not done what he should do—and I was a constant reminder of it," she says.

A fierce determination, and an almost supernatural belief in herself
got her out of the segregated St. Louis neighborhood where she was
born and all the way to the halls of Congress. Unlike many who escape
deprivation, economic and emotional, Maxine Waters was not content to
better her own circumstances. She vowed to use her considerable talents to create opportunities for others.

When she arrived on Capitol Hill in January 1991, one of 435 members
of the House, President Bush was in the White House and the Democratic
barons were firmly in charge of Congress. Unlike most of the freshmen,
who accommodated the entrenched leadership, Waters confronted authority at every step. She quickly acquired a reputation as someone not to provoke, especially on the sensitive issue of race. Getting the all-white
Veterans' Affairs Committee to hire African-Americans was one of her early
victories. She strongly identified with the black community and its grievances, and had been a longtime ally of the Rev. Jesse Jackson.

Yet, while Jackson was still toying with running in the 1992 race, Waters
endorsed Bill Clinton for president. She was not particularly enamored
of Clinton, but had concluded he could win. She was one of the first
nationally known black leaders to support the former southern governor.

Waters commanded more authority than most junior members
because of her closeness to Clinton, and her take-charge style, and she
was just beginning to translate that into real gains for her district when
the Republicans won control of the Congress in November 1994. The
GOP's victory symbolized the rise of the suburbs as a voting bloc and an
end to the kind of government assistance to the cities that sections of
Waters's South Central Los Angeles district relied upon. On the day that
Newt Gingrich was sworn in as Speaker of the House, Waters refused to
stand in his honor. The balance of power had shifted, and Waters saw no
reason to pretend she was happy about it.

As an African-American, a Democrat and a woman, Waters was now a
minority within a minority within another minority in the House.
Women are a majority of the U.S. population, yet they make up only ten
percent of the current membership of Congress. The thirty-nine
African-Americans currently serving in the House set a record in terms
of numbers, but are still less than nine percent of its members.

Waters was the sixth black woman elected to the House, winning her seat twenty-two years after Shirley Chisholm of New York broke the combination gender-race barrier in 1968. Physically and stylistically, Waters resembles the fiercely independent Chisholm, who, in 1972, became the first black woman to seek a major-party presidential nomination. Waters, like Chisholm, is petite and deceptively demure until she opens her mouth and dragon-fire oratory pours forth. Waters champions the interests of minorities and women, as did Chisholm, who retired in 1983 after seven terms.

After the Republican takeover, it took a while for Waters to adjust to her new situation, and the diminished role that Democrats played in the Congress. She resented the long plane trips back from the West Coast only to cast vote after vote with the losing side, and thought her time would be better spent organizing and educating voters to oppose the Republicans in 1996. She understood that in an era of budget deficits and shrinking government, she faced opposition from whichever party controlled the Congress. Indeed, her role as a representative of the neglected inner city was not that different now that the Republicans were in charge than it had been with the Democrats.

"I have to fight and struggle and scratch and claw no matter who's in power," she says. "I do what I do with Democrats or Republicans. I don't know how else to do it."

In elementary school in St. Louis, Maxine Carr had a teacher who graded her pupils on their clothes. "I would get terrible grades," she recalls, "because with my mother and all those children, you got what you got." As the fourth girl in the family, Maxine got the leavings. She grew up feeling like the outcast, the underdog—the kind of person she would later champion politically.

The family shopped at a Goodwill store on Wednesdays when the new batch of clothes arrived. Maxine learned to select the better dresses by their labels, stitching, and linings. The experience left her with a discerning eye for quality, and a determination to never again settle for anything less. At age thirteen, she took a job cleaning tables in a segregated restaurant to earn money to buy her own school clothes.

Today, Waters wears designer suits and shops at Neiman-Marcus, but she still visits used clothing stores. "I know how to pick the best stuff," she says proudly. Other people's hand-me-downs that might have embarrassed her once are now incorporated as flamboyant vintage clothes. "I love clothes," she says. "I love clothes a lot, yes I do."

Growing up in a large, impoverished family, Waters survived by learning how to draw attention to herself in a positive way. "We had to scramble for basic things—for space," she recalls. Add to that the fact that Maxine looked like the husband her mother wanted to forget and you begin to understand Waters's fierce drive to distinguish herself. Gifted academically and athletically, she found many areas where she could shine. She got good grades in school. She took ballet at the community center. She swam competitively. She excelled in the fifty-yard dash and the hundred-yard dash. She played baseball, volleyball, and softball. Away from her family, there was nothing she could not do. "I had to find my own way," she says.

The public schools were Waters's salvation. Here she found a caring community of teachers, notably all strong black women, whose interest in her extended beyond the classroom. Decades later, Waters remembers their names and credits them with helping her build self-esteem. "They weren't teachers who came to the school and said, 'My job is from 8:30 to 3:00, and I don't work overtime, and I don't work the schoolyard.' We had teachers who fed you if you were hungry, who took you on picnics on Saturdays, who spanked you with a rattan, who would come to your home. We had teachers who cared about you. And they told you you could do things."

Waters's high school English teacher was so taken with an essay that Waters wrote about the black opera singer Grace Bumbry, who lived in St. Louis, that she drove Maxine to Bumbry's home to show her and her parents the composition. Maxine had seen Bumbry perform on the Arthur Godfrey show, where the beauty of her voice made the veteran entertainer cry. There were not a lot of blacks on television in the 1950s, so seeing a black opera star on a popular variety show like Godfrey's made a big impression on Waters.

Maxine absorbed the lesson that being poor did not make her a lesser person. When bill collectors came to the door to harass her mother, even as a young child she refused to be intimidated. Waters recalls white insurance men who would come around regularly to collect 15-cent premiums for each child in the family, and who "showed disrespect by walking into your home beyond the living room and asking personal questions about black lifestyles." A friend, Brenda Shockley, says, "She told me stories of people coming to her house and threatening to repossess the furniture. Maxine would say, 'Take it now.' She was a kid, ten or twelve years old. They may have been powerful, and they may have been white, but she wasn't going to let them threaten her. She wouldn't let anybody have that kind of authority over her."

The public facilities that were available even in the poor St. Louis neighborhood of Vashon lessened the impact of poverty on children like Maxine. Almost every day after school, she went to the Vashon Community Center, where she played sports, swam in the Olympic-sized swimming pool, appeared in plays, and rounded out what she calls a real liberal arts education. "This is just amazing when I think about it," she says. "My mother was on welfare, and we had nothing in terms of resources, but I learned to dance the ballet, and I knew about Martha Graham."

The Vashon High School yearbook predicted in 1956 that Waters would be Speaker of the House someday. She was always entering oratorical contests, and had ranked well enough in the city finals to represent St. Louis in the regional competition. "I think they saw Speaker as *speaker*," says Waters.

The Congress was far-off and mysterious in the lives of poor, inner-city families, but local ward politics played a crucial role. When Waters's mother ran out of coal to heat the house or needed money to buy food, she went to the ward captain for help, the man who was responsible for getting out the vote. "And he responded," says Waters. "He must have had a kitty somewhere, that's all I can think of. It was the old chicken-in-every-pot kind of politics." On election day, Waters's mother worked at the polling place.

Maxine wanted more out of life than to just scrape by. While her achievements were noted and even appreciated at home, they added to the sense of estrangement that she felt in the family. Her mother married several times, and the family was on and off welfare. "My mother was basically a very hardworking woman. She was not someone who was mean or who tried to hurt anybody," Waters says carefully. "My mother had a sixth-grade education, and she didn't always understand the needs of her children, necessarily. She *often* didn't understand me."

Waters remembers as a child eavesdropping on her mother's conversations with friends. That is how she learned about abortion and the drastic procedures that women resorted to before abortion was legal. "My mother, obviously, didn't do it because she had thirteen kids, but they were always talking about what somebody else had done. 'She put turpentine on sugar. . . She douched in lye. . . . She fell down the steps.' " Waters literally shudders as she recounts these horrific tales that made her the strong abortion rights advocate she is today. "Even though, when I was very young, I believed the Christian teaching that it was a sin, I kind of thought, well, if you needed to sin, you just had to sin." She laughs long and hard. On abortion, as on issues of race and class, Waters held the hurts and fears of childhood close, but she was determined to change many things as soon as she could.

Waters lived in a lot of places growing up, but the one she calls home is a street in St. Louis called Montrose. "It was like a little town," she says. "We ate food at each other's homes. We knew everything that was going on in everybody's family. We sat out on the stoop in the summertime until late at night because it was always too hot to sleep. Nobody had air conditioning or fans or anything like that." The street is gone now, cut through by a freeway. Waters's family moved into public housing soon after she left home in 1956 to get married. She was eighteen.

Like so many young people seeking opportunity, Maxine and Edward Waters headed west to California. They settled in South Central Los Angeles, where he went to work in a printing plant and she got a job in a garment factory. They were frustrated that they could only get low-paying, menial jobs. By the early 1960s, they had two children to support.

Waters eventually landed a solid middle-class job as a telephone operator at Pacific Telephone, where she might still be today, she says, if a friend had not told her about a new federal program called Head Start. Excited by the prospect of providing an early childhood educational experience to poor children from backgrounds like her own, she left the security of the phone company to became an assistant teacher at Head Start. The experience shaped her life as much as or more than the lives of the youngsters she worked with. She had found her calling, a job through which she could better people's lives. From that moment on, her career and her commitment to improving the lives of families like the one she had grown up in were linked. "Head Start changed my life," she says. "Through Head Start I discovered me."

Head Start launched Waters's career as an activist. In encounter groups led by outside facilitators, community workers such as herself were encouraged to speak honestly about race and relationships. "I really started to state what I thought," she says. "I remember at some point deciding that I had been silenced by this need to be liked and not wanting to step on anybody's toes or hurt anybody's feelings. What I discovered is I really don't care whether people like me or not. It freed me up."

The survival skills that Waters learned as a child had taught her to live within her own world and to mask the anger that she felt. The Head Start encounter groups drew her out and made her see that her anger could be a positive force in the community. Waters became every conservative's nightmare, a liberal activist created and funded by taxpayer money. The very language of that period—"encounter groups," "outside facilitators," "community workers," "speak honestly about race and relationships"—epitomizes what the Right loves to hate about government social programs, which, they say, serve only the bureaucrats.

Waters saw that neighborhood activists like herself were valued at Head Start, but the big decisions were made by people with college degrees. She was learning how the system worked and what she had to do to gain real power. Nearly a decade after graduating from high school, Waters enrolled at California State University in Los Angeles where she earned a degree in sociology. Her choice of major flowed directly from her life experience.

"My first idea of a powerful person was a social worker," she says. "Social workers came to your home if you were on welfare, and they told you what to do. They determined how much money you got. They could ask all kinds of questions. They were perhaps the most important person you saw. They drove a car. Nobody in our neighborhood had a car. They wore nice clothes. They were educated. If they wanted to they could make your life better or easier. So, why not want to be somebody who could do those things?"

"She told us the social worker was the only one who could control her mother," says a friend, Jackie Dupont-Walker. "She thought that was where the power was."

Always looking for ways to make a difference, Waters began to volunteer in political campaigns. That meant more time away from home, and a keener sense of what she wanted to accomplish. Her marriage faltered along the way, a casualty of her growing ambition. "My first husband was not a bad guy," she says. "We were just on two different tracks after a while." Their divorce was amicable.

The barriers to black political power were less obvious in California than in the Jim Crow South or Waters's hometown of St. Louis, but they were nonetheless formidable. Tom Bradley, a black city councilman, had run for mayor of Los Angeles once before and lost. He was making his second try in 1973 when Waters joined his campaign. The history-making race attracted national attention as Bradley became Los Angeles's first black mayor. That same year, Waters helped elect another African-American, David Cunningham, who took the seat Bradley had vacated on the Los Angeles City Council.

Cunningham made Waters his chief deputy, her first real job in politics. After she left his office and Cunningham became embroiled in ethical problems, Waters distanced herself from him. "I am the one who found the chick," he says. "But there's no such thing as a permanent friendship with Maxine Waters. You may be her friend today, but if it's not necessary, you're not her friend tomorrow." Waters defended her stance, saying, "He played it too fast and was too loose, and I don't condone that kind of thing."

The genteel Bradley ran afoul of Waters when he named financier Peter Ueberroth head of a task force to rebuild Los Angeles in the aftermath of the rioting that followed the acquittal of the white police officers tried for beating black motorist Rodney King. Waters's South Central L.A. district was at the center of the disturbance, and she objected to Bradley putting Ueberroth in charge. As the chairman of the 1984 Olympics in Los Angeles, Ueberroth had resisted an affirmative action plan that would have given black businesses a share of the commercial spinoffs of the Games. Waters also feared that Ueberroth would hold the rebuilding of the riot-torn area hostage to repeal of worker's compensation laws, long the bane of big business. "She became angry at that time and that essentially terminated our relationship," says Bradley. "She stood shoulder to shoulder with me on election night [1992] and she never spoke to me. We've seen each other from time to time, but it's still something I've not been able to understand."

Waters cannot stand passivity, and to her Bradley's quiet tenure as mayor was a missed opportunity. "He didn't do as much as he should have or could have," she said. When Bradley prepared to step down in 1993, Waters told journalist Robert Scheer that white liberals "romanticized this tall, modest, non-threatening black man because they felt comfortable and safe—until they had a rebellion—and then they thought he didn't do what he was supposed to do. He didn't keep them quiet."

What Bradley and Cunningham took as rejection by Waters, she saw as keeping her eye on the prize. Her devotion was to making widespread change. If others moved too slowly, she moved on.

After working for numerous candidates, from local school board aspirants to Hubert Humphrey's presidential campaign, she was encouraged to seek office herself by women, most of them white, who were part of the emerging women's movement. Capitalizing on her strong community base, she won her first elective office in 1976 by challenging the kind of insider arrangement that politicians love. The man who represented her district in the California State Assembly was leaving to enter the ministry. But rather than announce his plans in advance, he waited until an hour before the filing deadline to show up with his designated successor, a ploy to guarantee an uncontested race. When Waters learned what had happened, she petitioned the secretary of state to extend the filing deadline, entered the race, and won.

She recalls arriving in Sacramento "a bit naive" and with a new consciousness about language and identity forged by the women's movement. "I was a new black feminist" she says. On her first day as a member of the Assembly, she rose to introduce legislation to change "assemblyman" to "assembly member." The other legislators, caught off guard, approved the measure, forty-eight to twenty-seven. But a number of the men resented this black woman from Los Angeles telling them what to do. They complained that she was trying to "neuter" them and deny their rights as men. After a heated debate in which Waters was attacked repeatedly, the Assembly overturned her bill, forty-one to twenty-six.

Picking a fight and losing is not an auspicious way to begin a legislative career. Waters survived because she had an important ally. Willie Brown had been in the Assembly for eleven years by the time Waters arrived, and had established himself as a shrewd power broker. He stood by Waters during those awful first months, serving as her political godfather. It was Brown's way of extending a hand of friendship and making up for having supported her opponent—the handpicked candidate of her predecessor, who had denied Brown the one vote he needed to become Speaker. "The 'old boys' network was at work," she says.

Brown too had been seared by the humiliation of poverty and racism, and he understood the forces that drove Waters to challenge the Establishment. When he worked as a shoeshine boy, his white customers tossed their quarters into a spittoon for the sport of watching him fish them out. "I learned with my first breaths that being black was a definite hardship and being white a distinct advantage," he wrote in a 1995 paper defending affirmative action.

Waters admired Brown's legislative brilliance and style, and together they became a formidable team. He taught her how to play the game and, in the process, won her loyalty. "She and Willie were wonderful," said Shockley. "She gave Willie a conscience, which he could use. And he gave her true political power."

It was while attending the United Nations Women's Conference in Houston in 1977, her first year in office, that Waters discovered the power of the sisterhood and its potential as a political base. She also learned how to build coalitions in difficult circumstances, a skill that would later serve her well in the contentious California Assembly. In Houston, Waters was put in charge of bringing harmony to a diverse group of minority women who were arguing among themselves on how best to strengthen the minority women's plank in the conference platform. Waters shuttled between the Black Women's Caucus, the Hispanic Caucus, and the Native-American Caucus to hammer out a compromise. Gloria Steinem, the noted feminist author, worked with her on the language.

When it came time to unveil the plank before the larger gathering, the otherwise fearless Waters was so nervous that an Indian woman took her aside and instructed her in breathing techniques to relax. Being with other women who understood the battles she was fighting in the male-dominated political world was such an emotionally powerful experience for Waters that, for months, she would lie awake at night thinking about how to draw black women into the women's movement. Gloria Steinem had become one of her closest friends, and remains so today, but Waters knew that the women in her district would not identify with the major feminist groups, which were overwhelmingly white and seemed alien to most black women.

So in 1978 she started the Black Women's Forum in Los Angeles as her own offshoot of the feminist movement. Recognizing that she had a reputation for being abrasive, and fearing that an organization headed solely by her might be branded as extreme, Waters recruited two impeccably establishment women as co-founders. They were Ruth Washington, a respected older woman and publisher of the black-owned *Los Angeles Sentinel* newspaper, and Ethel Bradley, wife of the mayor. Mrs. Bradley felt she was not receiving proper recognition as first lady of the city, and Waters convinced her that she needed a project that would be identified as her own.

The three co-founders hoped for a respectable turnout at their first meeting. Instead, they had a clamor for more spaces. Black women found the invitation so irresistible that twice as many tickets were sold as there were seats for the first meeting. Women who arrived too late to be seated angrily demanded their money back. "It was a mess," says Water's friend Jackie DuPont-Walker. "It was truly ugly. Then Maxine got up on the table and apologized. She asked them to form a line, and she apologized to each and every one of them. She just faced the music." Waters told the women that they should take pride in their numbers because they would be a force someday.

As the Black Women's Forum grew, Waters discovered that she could rally five hundred women on short notice for almost any cause. She now had the makings of a reliable power base. Her ability to mobilize not only black women in Los Angeles, but white women in other Assembly members' districts commanded respect from her colleagues in Sacramento. She would frequently go to outlying districts to talk to women about issues that specifically affected them. During the early 1980s, she encouraged minority women and white businesswomen as well to lobby for state contracts. Unless they made their voices heard, she warned, the men would do what men always do—take care of their buddies.

Today, the Black Women's Forum is a socially conscious group of 1,500 women of all economic strata. It has task forces on issues such as teen pregnancy, health care, and criminal justice, and functions as a private social service agency as well as a social club and political force. Waters says that creating it was one of the smartest things she ever did.

All the political skills Waters had learned—in the Bradley and Cunningham campaigns, at Willie Brown's knee in Sacramento, and bringing together in Houston a diverse group of women whose only real bond was their gender—came into play when Willie Brown ran for speaker of the California Assembly in 1980. Brown had twice before run for the post and failed, losing to Leo McCarthy, the man who had made him the majority leader. Those failures made the proud Brown reluctant to put himself on the line again.

Waters moved from protégé to kingmaker, telling Brown that the race could be won. Brown needed to be convinced. The Democratic caucus was divided, with nobody commanding a majority. After scores of meetings and a great deal of dissension, a compromise candidate finally emerged, Assemblyman Frank Vicencia, a mild-mannered centrist who chaired the powerful Government Operations Committee. It was a done deal, Brown told Waters.

The words served to provoke Waters, which she now thinks was Brown's intention. Just as their faction of the caucus prepared to throw its support to Vicencia, Waters burst into the room and, according to Mike Roos, another Assembly member, declared, "There is no fucking way I'm going to support Frank." Looking straight at the stunned Vicencia, she told him that he did not have what it takes to be speaker, that he was "weak" and "indecisive." Mortified, Vicencia remained silent for a moment. Then he said, "If she thinks I cannot do it, I don't want it," and stalked out of the room. Waters did not miss a beat. "I nominate Willie," she said triumphantly.

The outburst had its shock value, which is what Waters intended. Nobody in the room doubted her willingness to back up her words. The fact that she used four-letter words added to the potency of her declaration. "Nobody else has a mouth like hers," says Oakland Mayor Elihu Harris.

Waters says she curses "not nearly" as much as the men do, "but maybe more than they've heard a woman do." Profanity is part of the fearsome manner she has cultivated over the years, and it has worked for her. Winning by intimidation is how Waters operated in the California Assembly, but she could not have done it without Willie Brown as speaker to back her up.

To win the speakership in 1980, Brown broke from tradition by going after Republican votes. Democrats did not like the promises that Brown had to make to secure those Republican votes, so Brown turned to

Waters, the most partisan Democrat in the Assembly, to sell the package to her colleagues. "If she was willing to make a deal by forming a coalition with Republicans, it was okay for everybody else," says Brown.

Waters and Brown understood one another; they confounded everyone else. Willie Brown was to remain speaker of the California Assembly until May 1995, the longest serving and most powerful speaker the state had seen. He achieved a national reputation as a brilliant, wily parliamentarian with near-psychic skills for reading and manipulating other legislators. In Maxine Waters, he found a similar spirit—unfettered by tradition, unafraid of entrenched power. Sacramento had never seen anything like them.

Under Brown, Waters became the first woman to hold the position of majority whip, the first woman on the powerful Rules Committee, the first woman on the Budget Conference Committee, and the first person without a law degree to sit on the Judiciary Committee. In 1984, she cemented what had become an unbeatable Brown-Waters team in Sacramento when she was elected chair of the Assembly's Democratic Caucus, again the first woman to hold the post.

Brown opened up opportunities for Waters that would have been unthinkable under anybody else's leadership. "A black woman would never have been chosen Democratic Caucus chair or chief whip or any of that stuff," she said. As the demands of the speakership forced Brown to move to the middle politically, he relied on Waters to carry the argument for the left, and made sure she was strategically placed to have influence.

Waters used her increasing power in the Assembly to pass legislation to aid her disadvantaged constituency. She had learned that she could not get all the votes she needed simply by arguing that her positions were correct. But she could usually get the last few votes she required through skillful use of her considerable power. Among her accomplishments were setting aside minority contracting goals for state agencies, ending strip searches for nonviolent crimes, and getting more state money for childhood education. Her legislative legacy was insured in 1986 when the Assembly finally approved a bill she had introduced six times in eight years to force divestiture of millions of dollars of state pension funds in the white, minority-ruled government of South Africa. California's action put pressure on the U.S. Congress to act, pressure that ultimately led to the collapse of the white government and the end of apartheid.

The bill passed only because Waters was relentless. Pro-business Republicans and conservative Democrats had kept it bottled up in committee. Then the day came that Waters was the swing vote on a measure to tax offshore business operations. Lawyers for major New York corporations filled the Ways and Means Committee hearing room on the day of the vote. "They were mortified when they discovered their tax liabilities would be determined by me," Waters recalls, adding that one Wall Street lawyer was overheard asking, "Who the hell is she?" For her support she demanded committee action on divestiture. With public opinion polls showing the public favoring divestiture, its passage was certain once the bill was out of committee. The one remaining hurdle was Republican Gov. George Deukmejian, whose signature was not assured. He remembers bracing for what he thought would be a confrontational meeting with Waters and other members of the leadership. Waters made her plea in a manner that struck Deukmejian as surprisingly reserved. "Maybe she thought if she used her usual approach, it might be counterproductive," Deukmejian speculated.

It is unlikely that Waters toned down to ingratiate herself with the governor; that was not her style. She had a more potent weapon than confrontation in her arsenal. Waters knew that Deukmejian was trying to get the controversial superconducting super-collider, a plum federal project, located in California. She promised to help in return for his signature on the bill calling for divestiture.

"Maxine is practical enough and flexible enough to go after the votes in whatever way the votes can be gotten," says Brown. "If it's confrontation, she'll give you confrontation. If you need an exchange, it's an exchange. If it's schmoozing, it's schmoozing. She can do it all. If you need intellectual gymnastics, she can do that. She's not one-dimensional."

Waters will on occasion stray from doctrinaire liberalism, as she did in 1981 when she refused to support efforts to unionize a local health care agency in the Watts section of her district. The union leaders threatened to run their own candidate against her in the next election if she did not back them. "Boy, Maxine got mad," Shockley recalls. "I can't even recite all the four-letter words she used to basically tell them: 'You go ahead, you run the candidate against me. I'll beat the shit out of him. I represent the people. I'm on the side of the people. No one is going to strong-arm me. No one is going to force me. I don't play politics like that.'"

It is heresy for a liberal Democrat to take on a union, but Waters resented the intrusion on two levels. She thought it was up to the health care workers, who were divided, whether or not to unionize the clinic (which they eventually did much later). And she did not like the fact that the union representatives thought they could order her around because she would need their help to get reelected.

*   *   *

Waters was now a powerhouse in California politics. Her uncompromising public persona belied her ability to strike a deal behind the scenes. It was said that "Maxine never met a back room she didn't like." Yet some who dealt with her in the back rooms considered her an uncertain ally. Her standards were high, and there was always a risk that she would take them to task in public. "I am not easily understood by traditional people," she says. "I won't do as told, so they can't trust me."

Even Brown, so close to her he is like a brother, understands the limits of Waters's allegiance. He watched her in the California Assembly deliberately kill bills in committee that he supported, and then act surprised to learn he was upset. Waters maintains she was only saving Brown from himself. As speaker, he had to make compromises, but she did not. She is so frontal, and so unapolegetic, Brown says, "She'd cut out your heart and then do your eulogy—in tears."

One politician who felt the sting of Waters's independent streak is Jesse Jackson. She ran his presidential campaign in California in 1984 and 1988, but did not even bother to call him before endorsing Bill Clinton in 1992. Jackson learned about it through news reports. "It wasn't that I considered it would create problems for Jesse—I just didn't think about it," she said. "He's a great politician, but he's got to understand that sometimes I have to do my own thing."

Waters gained national notoriety through her affiliation with Jackson. In the preliminary jockeying for the 1984 Democratic National Convention, Waters assailed "the Gary Hart yuppies" for denying Jackson an equal voice in the California delegation even though Jackson had not won half the delegates. Before she took the podium, she warned Hart's representative, John Emerson, "I'm going to blast you, but don't take it personally." Emerson, now a political aide in the Clinton White House, took Waters's remark as a sign of political maturity. "This is how the game is played," he says, "and we did business down the road."

Others who found themselves the object of Waters's wrath were not so fortunate. At a Democratic platform hearing in 1988, the Michael Dukakis forces were trying to fend off the Jesse Jackson forces, who were promoting a rebuilding plan for cities on the scale of the Marshall Plan that had rebuilt Europe, to be paid for with cuts in defense spending. Dukakis, the Democratic nominee, did not want to get into an open fight with Jackson, so the Dukakis people turned to the remnants of the Al Gore campaign to knock down the Marshall Plan idea. Roy Neel, Gore's chief of staff, was designated to deliver the counterattack.

As he testified against the idea, Neel was conscious of Waters glaring at him with such ferocity he later referred to it as "Maxine's death stare."

The amendment, supported by Jackson and sponsored by former Gary, Indiana Mayor Gary Hatcher, was soundly defeated. That night, in a show of unity, the Dukakis and Jackson people held a party at a local bar for everybody involved—except Neel. He got word that Waters had disinvited him because of his testimony that afternoon. The message, as Neel remembers it being relayed, was, "We don't want Gore's guy there."

Waters is fiercely territorial, as a number of young Jesse Jackson believers found out in 1988. California's large electoral vote always makes it a hotly contested state, but by the time its primary is held, the action is over in most other large states. Competition for jobs in the California campaign is always fierce among workers who have slogged through New Hampshire or sweltered through Mississippi.

Gerald Austin, Jackson's campaign manager, had told some of his best operatives that they had made the cut. There would be jobs for them in California. Several of them were holed up for a weekend in a Los Angeles airport hotel waiting for instructions. "We thought everything had been worked out," said one of the campaign workers. "We went to the Jackson headquarters expecting to get jobs, and instead the receptionist had plane tickets for us and said, 'You guys are going home.'" Waters, who controlled the California campaign, said the state campaign had raised enough money to make its own personnel decisions, and didn't have to make room for "the big boys" from the outside.

When Rep. Augustus Hawkins retired in 1990, after a career that spanned twenty-eight years in the California Assembly followed by twenty-eight years in the House, Waters was his obvious successor, though she could not have been more different stylistically than the reserved and mannerly Hawkins. She won with seventy-nine percent of the vote in a district that was forty-two percent black, forty-two percent Hispanic, ten percent white and six percent Asian. Blacks held a slight plurality among the voting-age population.

Along with victory came advice. People she respected told Waters that Washington was different from Sacramento. They told her to tone down her rhetoric, to watch and wait before speaking out. She listened patiently, but the notion of respecting the traditions of Capitol Hill, a place with a reputation for corruption and scandal, struck her as ridiculous. Mindful of Waters's intimidating style, House Democratic leaders were wary of dealing with her. "We fear her," said a member of the Democratic leadership.

In January 1991, two days after Waters was sworn in as a member of Congress, the Persian Gulf debate got underway, giving her an opportunity to display before a national audience the stubborn independence Californians knew so well. She was "absolutely, completely, totally opposed" to U.S. military intervention in the Gulf. The day after the invasion, Congress passed a resolution in support of the troops. Law-makers opposed to the war embraced the chance to stand behind America's young men and women—but not Waters. Although she later would go to the war zone to show her empathy for the troops, she voted against the resolution, one of only six House members to do so.

Freshman Democrats rarely were given seats on first-line committees, but Waters tried anyway. She wanted to be on the House Steering and Policy Committee, which decides committee assignments within the Democratic Caucus. She had the support of her freshmen colleagues, but Speaker Tom Foley, in an effort to consolidate the leadership's power, invoked a new rule that freshmen could not select one of their own for the committee. The Democratic elders chose Ray Thornton, who was technically not a freshman because he had served in the House once before. Thornton, who was from then-Governor Clinton's home state of Arkansas, would later vote against President Clinton's budget "even though he had made him the fucking president of Arkansas State," Waters says, her words revealing her lingering wonderment over being passed over for someone who would show such minimal loyalty.

Waters next approached Chicago Rep. Dan Rostenkowski, the iron-fisted chairman of the powerful Ways and Means Committee, to see about getting on his committee. "Rosty said, 'No way,'" Waters breezily recounts. "I didn't take it personally. There's never been a black woman on Ways and Means." If her color and gender were factors, so was the Democrats' rigid seniority system, which effectively denied newcomers major committee assignments.

Next stop was the office of Michigan Rep. John Dingell, who chaired the Energy and Commerce Committee, another plum perch rarely offered to new members. "He wondered what I was doing—the *nerve* of it," recalls Waters. Dingell later had a chance to install Waters in what had become known as "the California seat" on his committee, but went through contortions to recruit another Democrat rather than name her. "Dingell and some others were afraid of what I might do," says Waters. "Even in my delegation, some of the members representing the leadership worried about me moving too fast. And they made sure I got what everyone else was fleeing."

Waters's lobbying eventually landed her a spot on the Banking Committee, as well as on the less prestigious Veterans' Affairs Committee. "They think I'm a troublemaker, and I cannot be contained," Waters says of her party's leaders. "They don't understand my ability to disagree and then to help work things out with them."

Rather than not understanding Waters's flexibility, the leaders may have been sending her a message that she did not want to hear: that they will not reward members who challenge the old order. For all the changes that have come to the House since the post-Watergate reformers of 1974 came in, it is still a very traditional place, and its dominant culture is one of deference to the leadership. She mocks the House rules that require members of Congress to refer to each other as "the gentleman" and "the gentle lady," thus masking any anger they may feel while debating. Waters thinks these rules are "bull" and that they allow disagreements to be smoothed over, and solutions avoided. "Men in these bodies aren't accustomed to really laying it on the line," she says. Some argue that the civility, false as it is, keeps in check the kinds of passions that in the nineteenth century led to congressional arguments being settled by duels, but Waters scoffs at that. "Dishonesty is dishonesty, no matter what name you assign to it."

Everything in Congress, from parking spaces to committee chairmanships, is governed by seniority. "If you're a member without seniority, you don't really get to play unless you find a way to play," says Waters. She set out to show the leadership that, wherever they put her on the seating chart, she could draw attention to her issues.

On the Banking Committee, Chairman Henry Gonzalez, a feisty Texas populist, gave Waters free rein. "I amend every piece of legislation that comes through there," Waters boasted. In a system where most major bills are introduced by committee chairmen, the amendment process is how savvy junior members put their stamp on legislation. The Banking Committee assignment has proved beneficial for Waters and her district. Banking includes housing and community development, and gives Waters influence over the limited resources still available for cities.

G. V. "Sonny" Montgomery, a twenty-four-year member of Congress from Mississippi who chaired the Veterans' Affairs Committee, had never encountered anyone quite like Waters. She was one of three women on the committee, the only African-American and, as he was to learn, the only noncompliant member of a committee that was otherwise conservative, traditional, and white.

Waters had trouble finding the committee hearing room the first day and arrived late. At her first opportunity to speak, she dared challenge the chairman's proposal that members automatically vote against any measures that would require new spending. "By the way, Maxine, this committee starts on time," Montgomery icily reminded her when she spoke up.

Some months later, Waters wrote a letter to Montgomery demanding that he put in place a "substantial affirmative action program" for the committee, which had no black staffers even though more than a quarter of all men and women in the armed services are black. She gave Montgomery more than a month to recruit minority staffers. When he said at a committee hearing that he could not find anyone who wanted to come to Washington from his home state of Mississippi, she exploded, "God, this is chocolate city," ridiculing the notion that anybody would have difficulty finding qualified African-Americans in majority-black Washington, D.C. She asked Montgomery to stop addressing her by her first name in hearings, and told friends it sounded like he was speaking to his maid.

Others wince when Waters says things they barely dare to think, but her pressure tactics frequently produce positive results. Whether Montgomery saw the light or felt the heat, he finally added African-Americans to the committee staff. He and Waters reached an accommodation personally as well. Today, they are cordial, even friendly. After Waters was flatteringly profiled in *Ebony* magazine, Montgomery sent her a note saying he had read and enjoyed the piece.

Unlike many hearings, which play to near-empty rooms, even the most routine Veterans' Affairs Committee hearings attract numerous visitors, many of them decorated war heroes. This is not Waters's natural constituency, but she has won them over with her unwavering support for increased spending for veterans benefits, acting as a counterweight to Montgomery's fiscal conservatism. "My advocacy for veterans doesn't stop at the Budget Committee door," she says.

The way Waters has been embraced by veterans shows how self-interest can overcome almost any barrier, from political ideology to gender. Members of the committee who are veterans themselves wear their service caps to some hearings. Once, when Waters was among a handful of members advocating more spending, she declared, "I may not have a hat, but I have a heart." A grateful American Legion commander had a plaque with a service cap and the quotation made up for her.

Waters steadily made progress on her issues, but seemed to make news only when she played what has come to be known as "the race card," the injection of race, either overtly or subtly, into the debate. It is an essential element of her politics and a source of her power. In dealings with the White House and members of Congress, the normal inhibitions that hold people back, even politicians—fear of embarrassment, fear of making enemies—do not constrain Waters. She believes that people who accuse her of playing the race card do it in order to silence her, and to marginalize what she has to say.

Waters denounces the social theories advanced within the halls of

Congress by members who have little direct contact with the people they profess to want to help. She opposes tenant ownership of public housing units, for example, an idea that both the political left and right briefly advocated. "Who wants a dilapidated box in the middle of a housing project that is worth nothing, especially when you don't have the money to maintain it?" she says.

In a June 1991 debate on the House floor, she called HUD Secretary Jack Kemp's Project HOPE to advance home ownership "a silly idea" and challenged a Republican member who had risen in support of the proposal. "People do want to own their homes, but they want to live in homes like you live in and like I live in," she declared. "If they can get a job, they can be empowered. Let me tell you something, they will buy their home, and it will not be in a housing project; it will be in suburbia, or maybe next door to you." Democrats whooped and hollered.

This rhetorical victory may have scored points for her within the ranks of Democrats, who find many of Kemp's moderate and market-based proposals on social policy to be dangerously potent challenges to their standard liberal fare. But it was mainly the high initial cost of Project HOPE that sidetracked the plan.

President Bush's nomination of Clarence Thomas, a conservative black jurist, to the Supreme Court demonstrated that the race card could be played from the opposite end of the ideological spectrum. Waters watched as much as she could of the televised Senate hearings in October 1991 that examined the charges of sexual harassment brought against Thomas by Anita Hill, a black college professor who had once worked for him. "I was so fascinated that a black woman was taking on a black man in this very public arena, which you just didn't do—it's just not done," says Waters. "It was a new day for black people in terms of letting out the family secrets. I just had never seen that."

Many analysts credit Thomas's confirmation to his skillful playing of the race card, when he denounced his confirmation hearings as "a high-tech lynching." That Thomas would employ the tactic infuriated Waters. It rankled her that his blackness could serve as a shield to scare off the harshest questioning, and that his views on issues like affirmative action and abortion went virtually unchallenged.

"A person who's run away from the black community using his blackness for a defense is just nauseating," says Waters. "I hate Clarence Thomas. I hated him then and I hate him now. I believed everything Anita Hill said about him. When he intimidated the senators with his 'high-tech lynching' stuff, I thought they were stupid to be intimidated by him. It showed on television. I knew it was all over when I saw that."

*   *   *

President Bush looked unbeatable in the winter of 1991 when a long-time friend from California, lawyer Mickey Kantor, approached Waters about backing Bill Clinton for president. It was long before the New Hampshire primary, and before any of the charges about Clinton's sexual past and avoidance of the draft had surfaced in the media. Waters trusted Kantor. They had been political allies who together had founded the Los Angeles Conservation Corps for inner-city kids. Kantor had been negotiating with her for some time to persuade her to endorse Clinton, who was coming to Los Angeles for a fund-raiser. Kantor arranged for Waters to meet with Clinton at the Los Angeles airport. Clinton spelled out his vision for the country, and she got assurances that he would treat her longtime friend Jesse Jackson "with respect." Waters wanted to defeat President Bush and concluded that Clinton offered the best opportunity to do so. Kantor quotes her as echoing the very line he had pressed upon her: "We have to grow up; we can't expect purity. We have to win." She wrote her endorsement speech for the banquet that evening.

Clinton was presenting himself to the voters as a New Democrat, a fiscal conservative who emphasized personal responsibility over government largesse, so his campaign aides were surprised when Waters, a traditional liberal, was included as a regular on the campaign's morning conference calls. "We didn't know why," recalls Bruce Reed, who was issues director. "She wasn't for the same things we were for."

Waters had the title of national co-chair, and soon proved her worth to the campaign. In March 1992, when Clinton played golf at the all-white Country Club of Little Rock, raising questions about the sincerity of his commitment to black voters, Waters stuck with Clinton, thus helping to quell talk of possible defections among blacks. She remained unwavering in her support throughout the election year.

Race would soon be injected more vividly into the presidential campaign. Waters was in her congressional office in Washington when the news flash came on April 29, 1992, that the four white Los Angeles police officers who had beaten a black man, Rodney King, senseless had been found not guilty. For the next nine hours, she watched on television as rioters roamed the streets on a rampage of mindless looting, arson, and assaults. She saw flames from one of the many fires come within yards of her own house.

Videotape of black youths savagely attacking a white truck driver at the intersection of Florence and Normandie in Waters's district was shown repeatedly, infuriating white America. Waters flew home on the second day of rioting, which lasted five days. Her own office was burned out. She and aides walked the streets, trying to calm the situation. She moved through areas that few people would have ventured into, looking with horror at what had happened and anger at what she believed had caused it.

During this time, Waters made statements that seemed to suggest she was excusing the rioters. She referred to the disturbance as a rebellion, not a riot, explaining that the King verdict was the match that inflamed the long-smoldering anger of people trapped in urban blight and hopelessness. "I said it in 101 different ways that violence is not right, that I do not condone violence, that people cannot endanger their own or other's lives," she said later. But she refused to condemn the rioters the way so many white politicians were doing.

Back in Washington, she continued to push her point of view about the nature of the disturbance, even into a Republican White House. Bush and his advisers believed the rioting was the work of a criminal element that took advantage of the King verdict, rather than the outpouring of a community's grief and frustration. But Bush was in the middle of a presidential campaign, and there was enormous pressure on him to show leadership and do something to resolve the racial tension in the nation's inner cities.

Waters had just stepped out of the shower and was getting dressed for work when she heard a news report that Bush had appointed a task force on urban aid that was meeting at the White House that morning. She called her office, but nobody there knew anything about it. So she called Speaker Tom Foley and told him she had not been invited. Surely, there had been a mistake—this was *her district* they were talking about.

After listening patiently, Foley said, "That's up to the White House. I don't have anything to do with it. I don't extend the invitations."

"Well, I'm going," Waters declared. "You better tell them I'm going to be there."

Waters took a taxi from her DuPont Circle condominium to the White House, about a ten-minute ride, and showed her congressional identification card to the guards at the front gate. Waters's name was not on the list of people who had been approved to attend the meeting. Her district was the principal one affected, but she was known to be confrontational, and she was not just another member of Congress. She was an outspoken supporter of the Arkansas Democrat who was challenging Bush for the presidency and beginning to look like he might succeed.

Once again, the organizers of the meeting could fall back on tradition and say this was a meeting called for the leadership and select Cabinet members. To Waters, it was another example of how Washington has not been sensitive to the growing diversity of representation. "It is just not reasonable to discuss urban problems without the benefit of urban legislators," she says.

The soft-spoken, gentlemanly Foley, whose nonconfrontational leadership style would later be blamed for the Democrats losing the House to firebrand Newt Gingrich's Republicans, gingerly told Bush about his conversation with Waters. He said Waters had threatened to stand at the gate until he let her in. "It is better to have her here than have a big fight over this," he advised the President.

"If *you* ask me to do it, I'll do it," Bush replied stoically. "I will not do it for her—or do it under threat."

"Then I'll ask you to do it for me," Foley replied. At Bush's request, Foley went from the Oval Office to the nearby Cabinet Room, where the task force members had assembled, and told them that Maxine Waters would be joining them because he had asked the President to include her.

Around the table that morning in May 1992 were Bush, Jack Kemp, the congressional leadership, and assorted aides. They talked generally about enterprise zones and capital gains tax cuts to stimulate inner-city investment. After a respectful amount of time, Waters interjected that she had firsthand experience with the "problem" people—the aimless and angry men between the ages of seventeen and thirty—who hang out on the streets, have nothing to do, and often have never worked a day in their lives. This is the group that must be reached, Waters said.

"I went on and on and on," recalls Waters. "And then finally Bush kind of looked at Jack Kemp, and Jack Kemp, who's always got something to say, didn't have anything to say. He deferred to this mulatto black who was there representing some agency secretary. And *he* said, 'Mr. President, she's right. This country's falling apart.' The President cleared his throat and moved on to the next person."

Ten days later, Waters learned of a second meeting with the same cast. Again, she was not invited. She phoned Foley, who repeated that he did not make up the guest list. Waters told Foley that she planned to write him a letter asking that he boycott the meeting if there were no urban representatives present. On the night of May 18, an aide taped copies of the letter to Foley's office doors in the Capitol and in the Longworth House Office Building.

Dear Mr. Speaker:
    I am advised that President Bush has put together another meeting dealing with the legislative response to the urban crisis and has again excluded all members of the Congressional Black Caucus.

It is outrageous that the President would attempt to fashion solutions to inner-city problems without the advice and counsel of inner-city legislators.

I believe that you, as Speaker, should not attend a segregated meeting—a meeting where primarily white males are deciding the fate of people who, for the most part, are people of color. . . .

At 9:15 the next morning, Foley told Waters, "They're not going to let you in." Waters had one weapon left, and that was the media. She told Foley, "I'm going to tell them what I think about this. I'm going to release the letter I wrote you last night to the press."

Five minutes later, Foley called back. "They've decided it's okay," he said. In order to save face, the task force was expanded to include not only Waters, but California Republican Sen. John Seymour and Georgia Democratic Rep. John Lewis, a member of the Democratic leadership. Widely regarded as a hero for his uncompromising leadership during the civil rights demonstrations of the 1960s, Lewis has an almost mystical belief in the power of nonviolence. He raises his voice when required to but never without trying to reason calmly first. He didn't frighten anybody.

Presidents, Democratic and Republican, can usually count on the majesty of the White House to temper debate within its walls. Awe is a powerful sedative. But nothing awes Maxine Waters. No task force that included her was going to have sedate meetings. Nothing substantive came of the meeting, but Waters had succeeded in opening up the discussion to people of color.

Waters's explanations about the reasons for the riots, and her characterization of many of the looters as people who needed the basics of life, such as food and shoes, drew ridicule from Rush Limbaugh, the flamboyant conservative radio talk show host. Limbaugh mocked Waters on his program, inflaming the passions of people who had never heard of her. Trying to ruffle Waters through intimidation was no more successful for Limbaugh than for the legions of others who had tried it. Waters and Limbaugh would tangle again.

Waters could wear the attacks of a conservative radio talk show host as a badge of honor, but she could not let pass even faint praise for Bush's civil rights record. Her animosity toward Bush made headlines that summer when she called the President a racist in a public forum. The incident happened while Waters was a panelist at a July 8 conference on black voter attitudes sponsored by the Joint Center for Economic Studies. When a black conservative, representing the Republican National Committee, praised Bush for signing a civil rights bill as President, while Arkansas, under Governor Clinton, had no such protection, Waters responded emotionally.

"I believe George Bush is a racist," she declared. "I believe the Willie Horton campaign is who George Bush really is. . . . He was brought to the table kicking and screaming and literally was bludgeoned into signing a watered down civil rights bill. . . . I think that Bill Clinton is much better on the race question than George Bush—not good enough, but most whites in America are not good enough on the race question, and we all understand that. I just think that George Bush is worse than most."

Her remarks, broadcast nationally on C-SPAN, reverberated throughout the political community. Her response was not to apologize, although she did not repeat the charge when interviewers gave her the chance. Four years later, asked whether she still stands by her words, she replied, "Absolutely."

Waters knew the Bush administration would never give her community and others like it the federal help she believed they deserved. Changing Bush's mind was not an option; defeating him was. By July 1992, when Democrats convened in New York to choose a candidate, the Clinton nomination and Maxine Waters's role in obtaining it were secured. She was chosen to deliver a seconding speech for Clinton, an honor that strengthened her bond with Clinton.

In the months that followed, Democrats in Congress talked about an urban assistance bill of between $9 and $15 billion. Bush, after visiting the riot scene in Los Angeles and professing great concern, proposed only $2.5 billion over five years. The public's concern about budget deficits coupled with mixed feelings by the public over the self-inflicted damage in South Central Los Angeles forced the Democrats to scale back dramatically. They talked about what they could do that did not cost much money, and settled on enterprise zones. The idea was to encourage business investment in inner cities with tax breaks and a minimum of federal funding, and to offer some hope.

This time it was Waters's fellow Democrats who scheduled meetings to decide how to respond to the urban crisis, but once again, she was not invited. She was not a member of the leadership, or she sat on the wrong committee. Washington tradition was at work again. She showed up anyway.

"I just kept a lookout for where the meetings were," she said. "When you go in and sit down, they don't know what to do. They don't have the guts to tell you you can't be there. A lot of my ideas were adopted because they made good sense. If I followed their rules, I wouldn't be able to cover a lot of the needs of my constituents. Even though it may be considered kind of in-your-face, what do you do? Do you just go along? I would be completely impotent if I did that."

Waters gives speeches advising young people not to just knock on the door, but "knock it down." The big difference between the success of her tactics in California and the difficulties she encountered in Washington is that Tom Foley was no Willie Brown. Brown delighted in her flashiness and her defiance of authority. Foley had been in Congress for three decades, long enough that the institution's rules and rituals were embedded in his marrow. He was fair to a fault, evoking an earlier era when bipartisanship was a reality, not just a buzzword. Former House Speaker Tip O'Neill once said of Foley that he could see three sides to every issue. It was not meant as a compliment.

"I think Foley more than anybody else doesn't understand me," Waters said before Foley's defeat in the Republican landslide of 1994. "He is one of the old boys. He can sit and talk to you all day about the history of somebody's desk. He just has not dealt with people like me. So I think I really bother him from time to time. There are times we go to meetings with the Black Caucus and Foley will talk about what can't be done. I say, 'It can be done. Don't give me that.' One day, I said to him, 'Look at us. We represent all the misery in America. We represent all the poverty in America.' I am not a 'Yes suh, massuh' person. He just wished I would go away."

A miniature blue chair, a gift from an admirer, sits on a shelf in Waters's office as a playful reminder of one of her first challenges to tradition in Congress. When the Democratic Caucus met, the blue chairs were reserved for the leaders while the rank and file had brown chairs. Often, there were not enough brown chairs to accommodate everybody, but members would stand rather than sit in one of the blue chairs, which were often unused. "I just thought it was ridiculous," she said, "so I went and sat in the blue chair right next to Foley." By the time the Democrats lost power in November 1994, other members were emboldened to do what Waters had done, and the rigid seating system became a relic of the past.

Waters says she challenged the mild-mannered Foley so brazenly in front of her colleagues because she wanted to show them that they need not wait for him to confer power and status upon them. They could demand it. She would often remind Foley, "I'm elected just the same way you are."

Waters's tactics sometimes rankle even those who are her natural allies, fellow Democrats in the California delegation and the Congressional Black Caucus. But her relentlessness has paid off for her constituents, securing federal aid that they would otherwise not have gotten.

In the late summer of 1992, Waters was tipped off that $6 million of federal aid had been set aside for Rebuild LA, the task force appointed by Los Angeles Mayor Tom Bradley and headed by Peter Ueberroth. The tip came from a friendly aide who called from the room where House and Senate members were putting the finishing touches on the 1992 Housing and Community Development Act. The aide, speaking quietly to avoid being heard, said he had noticed language in the bill directing the $6 million grant to a "nonprofit public benefit corporation established by the mayor of Los Angeles and the governor of California." Wasn't that Ueberroth's group?

Indeed it was, and within minutes Waters was on the phone to the two committee chairmen responsible for directing the money. "Ueberroth can have $3 million," she said. "We want the other $3 million."

Waters wanted the money for Community Build, a grassroots organization that she had created to counter the Ueberroth group. At her insistence, the bill was rewritten to direct $3 million to the "corporation established by the Mayor of Los Angeles" and $3 million to a "nonprofit, community-based public benefit corporation which was created in response to the civil disturbances of April 29, 1992 through May 6, 1992 in Los Angeles, California," namely Community Build. She had trumped Ueberroth. Moreover, the federal aid flowing into her community would have her stamp on it.

In the fall of 1992, six months after the civil unrest in Los Angeles had unleashed a rush of publicity, promises, and enormous effort, Congress passed a modest enterprise zone bill, authorizing $500 million to pacify urban areas. Included in the bill was language authorizing job training for older youths, up to the age of thirty—the "problem" people that Waters had talked about with President Bush at the White House in the immediate aftermath of the riot. She had battled hard to win that concession, and had succeeded only after convincing Congress it was not a new program, but could be funded under an existing Labor Department program called Youth Fair Chance.

It was quite a coup for a freshman lawmaker to ram through a controversial job-training measure in a political climate where money was scarce and social programs were coming under increasing scrutiny. Perhaps if it had reached Bush's desk when the images of Los Angeles burning were still fresh, he might have signed the legislation. But racial tensions had eased somewhat by fall, and the overall package contained some tax provisions that the President did not like. Bush quietly killed the bill after he lost his bid for reelection by simply not signing it, a maneuver known as a pocket veto.

Still, this was a euphoric time. Clinton would become the first Democrat elected in a dozen years, and with Democrats firmly in control of Congress, prospects brightened for the progressive legislation that Waters sought. She won reelection in her district with eighty-three percent of the vote, and because she had endorsed Clinton early, she would have the new President's ear. She spent the months after the November election preparing an urban agenda for the 103rd Congress. It sounded more ambitious than it was. Although Waters would have loved to see a Marshall Plan for cities, she knew it was not politically viable.

So she settled on a more achievable goal, and that was to establish a job-training program that would serve the seventeen-to thirty-year-olds she was most concerned about. She had almost succeeded with George Bush in the White House; surely she could enact her 17-to-30 program with the Democrats in charge. She met with incoming Cabinet secretaries Richard Riley of Education, Donna Shalala of Health and Human Services, and Robert Reich of Labor. Her message with each was the same. "The situation is desperate. Since the rebellion last April (it was now nearly a year later), nothing has happened in my community or any community like it in America. People were led to believe that things were going to happen." The fact that Washington had failed to respond "only made conditions worse," she told them. The most encouraging words came from the President himself. Before Clinton's first official address to Congress, publicly unveiling his budget proposal, he had invited Democratic members of Congress to the White House to brief them on what he would say. Waters took that opportunity to press a copy of her urban agenda into the President's hands. The next night, after he finished delivering his speech in the House chamber, a smiling Clinton beckoned to Waters and told her he had read her urban package the night before and would start work on it right away. Waters was overjoyed. As far as she was concerned, she had the President's endorsement.

Clinton knew he owed Waters. She had not flinched even through the Sister Souljah episode, which was a calculated show of outrage designed to distance candidate Clinton from Waters's friend, the Rev. Jesse Jackson. Sister Souljah, a little-known black rap singer, had made anti-white remarks in Jackson's presence, and he had remained silent. Clinton used the opportunity to condemn racism from all quarters, but the political signal was meant to assure whites that Clinton, a New Democrat, was not beholden to his party's left wing of liberals and minorities.

Waters was not interested in a job for herself with the administration, nor was one offered. Although the incoming administration professed a desire to install a diverse Cabinet that "looks like America," Waters's

street-fighter brand of liberalism did not fit in with the Ivy League cast
that was being assembled. Waters was pleased, however, when Clinton
offered an ambassadorship to her husband, Sidney Williams. She says she
never "asked or bargained with Clinton" for Williams's assignment in the
Bahamas. "His appointment is the kind of perk a president normally
affords qualified supporters," she says. "Minorities are seldom privy to
such appointments. However, it is not a big deal." Waters had married
Williams in the summer of 1977, during her first year in elected office. A
former linebacker for the Cleveland Browns and Washington Redskins,
Williams sold Mercedes-Benzes for a dealership in Hollywood.

This was one thing Clinton could deliver. Republicans immediately
attacked Williams's nomination as a political payoff, pointing to his lack
of diplomatic experience. Aside from a brief stint as an aide to a Los
Angeles city councilman, he had never been in public life. Even some
Democrats had qualms. Connecticut Senator Chris Dodd was reluctant
at first, but a series of conversations with Williams convinced Dodd that
he was capable.

Rush Limbaugh took on Maxine Waters again. He led the charge in
belittling Williams's credentials and stirring up public opposition to his
appointment. Waters got even months later when she spotted Limbaugh
at a Super Bowl cocktail party. She was there as a member of the Los
Angeles Rams advisory committee. Introducing herself to the conservative commentator, she said, "You talk about me all the time, you ought to
know who I am. And this is my husband—you ought to know him too.
This is Sidney Williams."

Grabbing Williams's hand, Limbaugh stammered, "I know you. You
played football for the Cleveland Browns."

"And he has a master's degree from Pepperdine University," Waters
added pointedly as Limbaugh's face reddened. For once, the king of talk
show radio was at a loss for words.

"So you know what he does?" Waters recalls. "He grabs me and he
hugs me because he doesn't know what to do." She delights in telling the
story. "I had a great time making him uncomfortable, I really did. I had a
great time."

Williams's nomination had not yet been finalized when Clinton called
an evening news conference on June 3, 1993, to announce that he was
withdrawing Lani Guinier's name to head the civil rights office at the Justice Department. Black leaders were furious with Clinton for abandoning
Guinier after Republicans had labeled her a "quota queen." The Black
Caucus had initially been cool to Guinier, a black intellectual with whom
they did not connect on a political level. But when her nomination got

into trouble and Congress raised questions about some of her academic writings, the Black Caucus furiously lobbied Clinton to keep her.

The White House was grateful that Waters was "noticeably quiet" during this period, says a Clinton aide, implying that Waters did not join the chorus of criticism because she wanted to keep her husband's ambassadorship on track. Waters strongly disputes this interpretation. She says she never joins in loud protests of presidential nominations, citing her absence when other female House members marched on the Senate in protest of the treatment of Anita Hill during the confirmation hearings for Clarence Thomas. In the Guinier case, she did sign a letter to the President along with other members of the Black Caucus urging him to stand by the nomination, but did not go further with her criticism.

Other members of the Black Caucus did what politicians normally do in a situation like this. Knowing their cause was lost, they tried to turn defeat into small victories. They were merciless in assailing Clinton for "selling our sister down the river," said a White House aide, recalling the tone of the attacks. And while the harsh personal tone of the criticism failed to save Guinier, it nonetheless had the desired effect on Clinton. Members of the Black Caucus did not leave the debate empty-handed.

The White House aide explains: "If you want something from this President, look for ways that he's slighted you and make him feel guilty. There weren't two members of the Black Caucus who would have spent one iota of political capital on Lani Guinier, but they used her to pound us on other issues. There were still a lot of federal marshals and U.S. attorneys to be appointed, and they wanted their share."

Beset by a series of failed nominations and other episodes that had created a sense of amateur hour at the White House, Clinton was so weakened that the kind of deal-making the Black Caucus engaged in had become the norm. During the 1993 budget fight, the White House traded favors for votes, thus rewarding Democrats who withheld their support from the President. Legislators who backed Clinton from the start felt short-changed. Among them was California Rep. Howard Berman, who chaired a Foreign Affairs subcommittee and wanted an ambassadorship for an important political ally in his state. Berman was frustrated at seeing his colleagues' gamesmanship pay off. The White House was, in effect, teaching members of Congress to hold out for what they could get. Berman lobbied the White House at every opportunity. Finally, at a White House meeting in the fall, after much heated discussion, Clinton aide George Stephanopoulos threw up his hands and said, "The hell with it. Give it to him." Soon after, Clinton nominated Berman's choice, Californian Josiah Beeman, to be the U.S. ambassador to New Zealand.

*   *   *

Waters gave the White House an occasional break on political lapses in the black community, but she felt increasingly frustrated by the way things were going in what was supposed to be Democratic utopia. Clinton's cheery encouragement at the start of the year meant little as it turned out. She had introduced a package of four bills on February 19, 1993, which she called the Youth and Young Adult Empowerment Initiative. This was the foundation for her 17-to-30 job training program, and she had spent weeks persuading the White House to include them in the President's "stimulus package," a grab bag of programs designed to invigorate spending and job growth in urban America. When a Republican-led filibuster in the Senate forced the President to withdraw the $16 billion package on April 21, 1993, Waters sadly concluded that the Democratic Congress, even with a Democrat in the White House, did not have the muscle to pass a substantial urban aid bill, and that anything labeled "community development" could not survive in the current political climate.

But the problems of inner-city America still needed to be addressed. So liberal Democrats in the House regrouped, and with the backing of the Black Caucus, proposed a dramatically scaled-down "mini-stimulus package." It would cost only $1 billion, and it would be paid for by cuts in other programs. While there was no explicit quid pro quo, the Democratic leadership understood that they could not pass a budget without the support of the Black Caucus, so this was the political equivalent of blood money. The mini-bill provided for summer youth jobs, wastewater treatment grants, and community policing—programs that even conservative Republicans could accept. Tucked in the bill was Waters's job training amendment. With its focus on extremely poor communities, the Waters amendment was an important piece of the President's budget. It pleased Waters to discover that she had such leverage.

Because she had the full backing of the Democratic leadership, Waters was stunned when the Appropriations Committee, the only committee that has the power to authorize spending, refused to fund her amendment. "I was not the only one who had been double-crossed," she told an aide. Congressional committees are extremely turf-conscious, and the Appropriations Committee, headed by Kentucky's William Natcher, an octogenarian who had been in Congress since the early 1950s, did not like taking orders.

The next move was up to the leadership, which countered with a procedural device known as a "self-executing rule" to transfer $80 million from summer youth jobs to Waters's job training program. Any hope that Waters's amendment might slip through unnoticed and unchallenged faded with that maneuver. Self-executing rules angered Republicans since, under House rules, they were only available to the leadership of the party in power, in this case the Democrats.

"This particular self-executing rule was worse because it was rightly seen by Republicans as helping her and her pet project—so the dogs came out," legislative aide Bill Zavarello recounted.

Because it is easier to get money for existing programs than to fund new ones, Waters was once again trying to wedge her 17-to-30 proposal into the Department of Labor Youth Fair Chance program, a pilot project to train the disadvantaged begun during the Reagan administration, which had never been funded. To reach the hard-core unemployed, Waters wanted to expand the definition of youth to include men up to the age of thirty. And she wanted to provide a modest weekly stipend to the young men enrolled in the program, who might otherwise not be able to participate. The way she portrayed her goals, and the way the opposition framed them, illustrates how two sides in a debate can take the same set of facts and, without exactly lying, spin them differently.

On the House floor, Republicans mocked the $100 weekly stipend Waters said was needed for transportation, food, and grooming. "The word 'grooming,' does that mean personal grooming? Does it mean grooming of pets?" thundered Pennsylvania Republican Bob Walker, one of the Right's leading attack dog in the House.

"Grooming, as you know, means attending to one's personal needs," Waters replied. "Please do not be facetious and extend this to dog grooming. The American taxpayers do not wish us to be involved in this kind of debate. We do not have to take up this time talking about this meaning dog grooming. The gentleman knows better than that."

Walker contended that Waters's program "is including an expanded definition of welfare beyond all belief . . . to the point where we are now going to be out buying $100 cars. We may now be paying for alcoholic beverages. We are certainly paying for grooming, and she will not define what that means. . . . Does it mean clothing? Does it mean condoms?"

Indiana Republican Dan Burton, another ardent conservative, ridiculed the Youth Fair Chance program for extending the definition of teenager to include thirty-year-olds. Burton offered an amendment to strike the Waters language from the bill. But Waters had won over a handful of key conservative Democrats, and with their backing other Democrats fell into line to defeat the Burton amendment, 251–176. She even got four Republican votes.

Zavarello kept notes with the idea that he would turn them into an article for a public policy journal on the legislative process. He watched

Waters closely and wrote in her voice: "I am a target for Republicans since I aggressively and unapologetically represent low-income and minority Americans. To the right wing, I represent everything that is bad in government. The fact that the Democratic leadership was clearly going to bat for me was too much for Republicans to take."

The next hurdle was the Senate, where Waters had only a handful of natural allies from the party's liberal wing. They would not be enough, so she took her appeal to Appropriations Committee Chairman Robert Byrd, an old-time West Virginia Democrat whom she barely knew, and whose support would be essential. The "Prince of Pork," whose canny maneuvering brought federal resources to his rural home state, did not warm to Waters's program for hard-core unemployed city dwellers.

The mini-stimulus bill emerged from Byrd's Appropriations Committee without the Waters amendment contained in the House bill. The way Congress works, however, differences between House and Senate versions of a bill that has passed both chambers must be reconciled in a joint conference committee. The result was a compromise that kept the 17-to-30 job training program, but reduced funding for it from $80 million to $50 million.

President Clinton signed the bill into law on July 2, 1993, giving Waters a hard-fought prize. Still, the battle was not yet over. A staff aide noticed in a Labor Department memo describing the Youth Fair Chance program that there was no mention of the weekly stipend that is an essential part of the program. The compromise struck in the House-and-Senate conference committee had quietly eliminated the stipend.

An outraged Waters enlisted the help of Michigan Rep. David Bonior, a fellow liberal and a ranking member of the House leadership. "He's not frightened by me, worried about me, none of that," she says of Bonior, whose intensity on behalf of deeply felt causes matches her own. Bonior attached Waters's stipend language to a flood relief bill that was being rushed through Congress in the aftermath of severe floods in the Midwest. Republicans objected, saying the stipend had no place in a disaster aid bill and accusing Waters of holding up relief for flood victims.

Once again Rush Limbaugh used Maxine Waters to provoke his listeners. He railed against the stipend, calling it the "Maxine Waters Gang Assistance Program." Members of Congress were besieged with calls from outraged "dittoheads," as Limbaugh's fans like to call themselves.

But with much of the Midwest still underwater, the House could dither no longer. It passed a flood relief bill with Waters's stipend attached. A week later, on August 4, 1993, the Senate passed the same bill, but with no mention of a stipend.

Lawmakers often attach their pet projects to essential legislation, hoping their colleagues will want to pass something badly enough to accept additional measures that could not otherwise pass. Waters had succeeded in the House only after a divisive debate, and she feared she would lose in any compromise negotiated between the House and Senate. She was running out of parliamentary maneuvers. At the same time, administration officials were getting squeamish about the public relations fallout from holding up aid for flood victims because of a squabble over a job-training stipend. Waters's office received a call from the Department of Labor. "They were ready to deal," she told an aide.

Three highly placed Labor Department officials trooped over to Waters's office in the Longworth Building on Independence Avenue across from the Capitol. They told her they would implement her stipend as part of the 17-to-30 program despite not having specific instructions from Congress. "I want it in writing," Waters replied. She had been disappointed so many times in this long process that before she agreed to back off, she wanted a letter guaranteeing the commitment. When she received the letter soon after, it was signed by the general counsel of the Labor Department.

That should have concluded Maxine Waters's great job-training adventure, but in Washington, nothing is ever quite over.

When the Labor Department announced the recipients of the first round of Youth Fair Chance grants, South Central Los Angeles was not among them. Waters could not contain her rage when she told the bureaucrats administering the program that she had not gone through all that she had for others to get funded and not her own district. They explained that the grants had been awarded on the basis of evaluations made by impartial experts.

"I don't give a damn how the system works," she fumed. "You tell the Secretary that he shall never show his face over here again unless this program gets funded." As for the expertise of social scientists, Waters said, "First of all, I know that a lot of it is subjective bull. The people that they call in as the impartials don't know as much as I do."

The tally for the first-year grants for Youth Fair Chance shows that Los Angeles received $7 million, about double the average grant to other cities. Finally, Waters had won.

The battles that Waters fought in Clinton's Washington were not that different from those she had waged when Bush was in charge. She had a strong sense of déjà vu when she learned that her old nemesis, Peter Ueberroth, had been invited to the White House with former President Jimmy Carter for a meeting on how to help urban communities by cut-

ting regulatory red tape. Ueberroth was there on behalf of the task force
to rebuild Los Angeles, and Carter on behalf of his Atlanta Project to
help the poor. Waters was tipped off about the meeting by a friendly aide
in the White House and asked to attend. "After considerable discussion
about what to do, we invited her," says a then White House aide. "She
said very little. She stared at Ueberroth the whole time with this vicious
gaze on her face as if she was about to erupt."

When Ueberroth concluded his presentation about ways to leverage
private community support, it was Waters's turn.

"She chose her words carefully," says the aide, who sat in on the meeting, "but she drove home her point that Ueberroth, as an outsider,
couldn't possibly know what was best for her community, and that the
others in the room should not listen to this establishment lackey. She
didn't use that phrase directly to Ueberroth's face, but that was what she
meant." In private, Waters scolded the White House aides, "How dare
you invite a hard-core Republican who may run for office, who represents a bunch of Republican businessmen. . . ."

The difference between the way others see Waters and the way she
sees herself sometimes is dramatic. Waters maintains she was merely
there to "follow the money" and make sure that her constituents would
benefit if there was a White House initiative. She admits she does not
trust Ueberroth, but wonders, "How in God's name can some unnamed
person read my mind and determine what I was thinking?"

With her husband's nomination as ambassador to the Bahamas still in
process, Waters was heavily lobbied by Cabinet secretaries, White
House staff, and others to give Clinton her vote on the North American
Free Trade Agreement (NAFTA), the controversial pact with Mexico and
Canada that the White House touted as evidence that Clinton was a
New Democrat. Some of her Democratic colleagues who backed the
trade agreement mentioned her husband's pending nomination as rea-
son enough to back Clinton on this vote, but Waters refused.

Waters was a traditional Democrat and had long opposed the ease
with which corporations could shift plants to Third World countries and
employ cheap labor to replace American workers. She had been an early
opponent of plant closings while in the California Assembly and had
counseled Jesse Jackson to make it a big issue in his 1988 presidential
campaign. Labor unions strongly opposed NAFTA, and some of Clinton's political strategists told him that standing up against his union base
would make him look strong.

Waters objected to the notion favored by some New Democrats that if
Clinton showed independence from the party's traditional base of

women, unions, and minorities on some issues he could broaden his appeal among suburbanites who had abandoned the party.

At the same time, she felt curiously detached from the President's increasingly desperate pleas for support on health care reform, the centerpiece of his domestic agenda. Although she made many speeches and organized town meetings on health care, she did not serve on any of the committees charged with shaping health care legislation and was not a player on the issue. Waters is a single-payer advocate, that is, she favors a government-run system that would cover everybody and eliminate the need for private insurance. But she is not a zealot about it. For her, the issue is not as important as job training or welfare reform. Politicians pick their spots, and health care reform is not one of hers.

Her district, while not among the very poorest in the nation, has pockets of deep poverty that would be less affected by the failure of health care reform. People receiving welfare are provided with medical benefits, and poor children are covered by Medicaid and other federal programs. Underlying the Clintons' health care reform plan was the hope that it would lure middle-class voters, the so-called Reagan Democrats, back to the Democratic Party. Maxine Waters was part of the liberal bloc whose votes Clinton would need if health care reform ever came to a vote in the House. She was among those members of Congress who let the President know that any vote they gave him was predicated on abortion coverage being part of the final package. But because the legislation did not reach the House floor, she never had to define her stand with a vote.

Health care was nonetheless the baseline from which every other issue in Washington was interpreted. When Clinton responded to demands from the Congressional Black Caucus to alter his policy toward Haiti, it was whispered that he did so because he needed the group's votes on health care reform. Any linkage between foreign and domestic policy is always unstated, but Haiti was of prime concern to the Black Caucus. Soon after taking office, Clinton had reneged on a campaign promise to not turn back fleeing Haitian refugees as George Bush had done. The Black Caucus members were furious that the refugees received no better treatment from a man blacks had helped elect than they had from a Republican member of the establishment.

Waters protested Clinton's policy in front of the White House and was arrested on April 21, 1994, along with four other members of the Black Caucus. The incident was choreographed, with the police notified in advance and television cameras told when to show up. District of Columbia police are accustomed to handling symbolic arrests of important people in acts of civil disobedience. The police read Waters and the others a short statement ordering them to move. "And you say, 'I will not move,'" Waters said, recounting the incident. "Then they put you in the paddywagon. They're waiting for you when you come to the station, and they quickly get you out of the handcuffs and fingerprint you." Waters thought the routine paperwork took longer than was necessary, so, as she left, she informed the police, "I'm going to look into getting you guys computerized."

When a photograph of Waters being arrested appeared in a Los Angeles newspaper, a number of her constituents contacted her Washington office wanting to know why she spent her time worrying about Haiti. "Why aren't you paying attention to jobs for us?" one woman asked. Another wrote that she was "ashamed that my congresswoman ended up being a jailbird." Some young people in particular who had not lived through the early days of the civil rights movement had no concept of civil disobedience. Overall, however, her constituency approved of her challenging the President on behalf of poor black Haitian refugees. "People appreciate a fight," she said. "They really appreciate you just standing up."

Pressure on Clinton over Haiti gave the Black Caucus a high profile and enhanced the impression among white voters that the President was beholden to the minority lawmakers. A hunger strike by Randall Robinson, founder of the citizens lobbying organization TransAfrica and a highly respected black intellectual, added to the pressure on Clinton. Robinson had mobilized public opinion a decade earlier against apartheid in South Africa, which led the way to the release of Nelson Mandela. He had been one of Waters's mentors in her long fight in the California Assembly for divestiture of the state's investments in South Africa. If the President changed his policy, it would appear that he was buckling to blackmail, yet he could not cling to a policy that he had come to recognize was untenable.

"In many ways, Clinton put us on the spot with his declaration for Haiti before the election, and then turning coat," said Waters. "My God, we had to challenge that. But I was scared. I told Clinton and everybody, 'If Randall Robinson starves himself to death, it's over.'"

Clinton capitulated to Robinson's demands, as well as his own conscience, by easing restrictions on the Haitians who were trying to escape poverty and oppression in their country. A Democratic president could not continue indefinitely plucking poor black people out of the coastal waters and denying them entry to the United States. Clinton eventually sought congressional approval to intervene militarily in Haiti to restore the country's democratically elected leader, Jean-Bertrand Aristide.

As the vote neared on Capitol Hill, Lt. Gen. Raoul Cedras, head of the Haitian military, reportedly assured the ruling government that he had friends in Congress who would oppose intervention. Waters says that lawmakers who might not otherwise have supported Clinton's request backed the President to prove Cedras wrong. "The macho will do it every time," she said.

When Clinton gave the order to invade Haiti in the fall of 1994, he got scant public backing from the Black Caucus, whose members were as ambivalent about a military operation as other elected officials, especially one coming so close to the congressional election. A White House aide complained, "After jawboning Clinton to act, they weren't there when people started hitting him." Some Black Caucus members who privately favored the invasion remained silent, Waters says, in order to protect Aristide from accusations by his enemies that he was "leading us to call for an invasion."

Last-minute negotiations by a delegation led by former President Jimmy Carter assured a peaceful transition of power and halted the scheduled invasion. In planning the triumphant return of Aristide to Haiti, the White House downplayed the role of the Black Caucus. Waters figured that those preparing the invitation list for the Haiti celebration "didn't want this big black delegation drawing more attention to the argument that he had been driven to it by the Black Caucus," she said.

Once again, she found herself having to crash an official government event. She called the State Department, which said the White House was selecting the delegation. The White House said the guest list was up to the congressional leadership. The leadership said, no, the White House decides. Finally, Waters learned that the Democratic leadership had ten slots on the chartered government plane—five for the Senate and five for the House—which meant a junior member like Waters would not make the cut. "So I said fine and I told the State Department, 'I'll see you in Haiti,'" she says, laughing at her own impudence.

Advised by a State Department official not to travel alone to Haiti because she needed security, Waters retorted, "No, I don't. I'm not afraid of anybody. Who's going to do something to me?" But she would not have a place to stay, the official protested. "Oh, sure I do," Waters replied. "That's no problem. President Aristide will find someplace for me." Waters's office booked a commercial flight for her to Haiti and sent out a press release announcing she would be available for interviews. She then called the U.S. ambassador to Haiti, William Swing, who is a friend, and told him she would be arriving on American Airlines. "Come stay with us," he said. "We'll meet you at the airport."

It was not long before the State Department official called back, saying, "The ambassador has a place for you at his residence."

"I know," Waters replied. "I created it."

Waters knew where she stood on Haiti, but when a civil uprising in Rwanda pitted one tribe of blacks against another, resulting in mass slaughter, she was, in her words, "totally devastated." For perhaps the first time in her political life, Waters did not have a ready answer. "Rwanda almost took me out—it almost made me want to quit," she says. "I didn't know whether the Hutus or the Tutsis were correct. I couldn't tell anybody what I thought they should do." Waters, who is usually quick to advocate a role for the federal government, was not clear what the United States could do. Invited to the White House with other Democrats to advise Clinton, she found she was not alone. "A lot of people were like me—they didn't know from crap," she says.

Waters is moved to action by anything she perceives as unjust or unfair, especially when race or gender is involved. During congressional hearings in July 1994 on Whitewater, she assailed a Republican congressman who she felt was unfairly badgering Margaret Williams, an African-American who is Mrs. Clinton's chief of staff. The Democratic chairman had already chided the Republican, New York Rep. Peter King, when Waters jumped in and declared, "The gentleman is out of order."

King, who represents suburban Long Island, leaned over to a staffer and was heard to whisper, "This is good television." Then he lashed back at Waters: "I have the right to ask questions. You had your chance. Why don't you just sit there?"

"You are out of order," Waters repeated.

"You are *always* out of order," King shot back.

"You are out of order—shut up," Waters fumed.

After some more back-and-forth, King complained, "Mrs. Waters is butting in all the time. Nobody cares about you."

King later went on the floor of the House to comment about what had taken place in the committee. When Waters tried to respond, so many members were talking loudly that Florida Rep. Carrie Meek, the presiding Democrat, asked her to wait. Thinking she had permission to continue, Waters turned around and said, "Thank you Madam Chairwoman."

Some members pointed at her and yelled. There was some jeering and laughter. She kept talking. "The more they went at it, the more I went at it," she says.

Waters was not happy when the event made the network news, perpetuating the image of her as a troublemaker. While she believes that anger and confrontation are positive tools, and that public policy-making is advanced by airing troublesome issues, she is mindful of the danger she faces as a woman of appearing shrill. Her aides are under orders never to book her on CNN's *Crossfire,* a public affairs show that encourages rhetorical bombast by pitting extremes from the Left and Right of the ideological spectrum against each other. She has appeared on the show but says, "It is a circus, not a real debate or forum. I can't win in that format." She has since turned down many invitations to do the show.

Waters was successful in California because she knew how to operate in the back rooms. In Washington, some Democrats are wary of Waters, even those who support her goals, making it harder for her to get into the back rooms. Colleagues are afraid of being stung by her rhetoric. When committee assignments are made and task forces appointed, congressional elders evaluate a candidate's demeanor as well as credentials. "When people decide who they want on a committee, Maxine's name doesn't come forward," says a key Democrat. "She has real abilities and real concerns. She can be eloquent in discussing the problems in her district. But you have to consider it flagellation to participate in anything with her."

Characteristically, Waters refuses to be kept out by a closed door. She has worked her way into the whip's organization, the core group of Democrats given the assignment of lining up votes on important legislation. "She is surprisingly capable of doing the heavy lifts and whip calls," says a Democratic aide. "She is tough and not particularly flexible, but that's different from being unwilling to compromise."

The conventional way of getting ahead in Washington is sticking around for a long time and not making enemies. Waters gets people angry at her every day whether she needs to or not. "If you operate in the traditional ways you're never going to have a voice because the leadership is white for the most part," she says. "If you deal with just seniority and leadership, you won't have a voice. That's why I can't wait, and I can't ask."

Her challenge to entrenched leadership extended even to the Women's Caucus, which had been run for more than a decade by Democrat Patricia Schroeder, the longest serving woman member in the House, and Republican Olympia Snowe, a moderate who supports abortion rights. Keeping them in power avoided potential conflicts over successors whose views might not be so compatible, and avoided an unseemly, unsisterly contest over leadership. Waters dismissed that reasoning as "precisely what dictators say about not holding elections 'for the good of the people.'" Waters called it "cronyism" and proposed term limits for the chairs so that junior members could have a chance to serve. She says of the seniority system: "Those are the rules that men play by."

The theme of the Congress that year was no more business as usual, which Waters used to argue for the changes. Appointed by Schroeder to head up a task force on restructuring the bylaws, Waters got an attorney friend of hers to draft a new set of bylaws that called for regular elections. Schroeder and Snow resented the implication that they had selfishly stayed on as co-chairs and had grown complacent. The Women's Caucus lost much of its power after the 1994 election when Republicans won control of the Congress and abolished funding for the Women's Caucus and other legislative organizations.

Waters defends her action as simply exposing what women lawmakers had long whispered about Schroeder being "the eternal chair" of the Women's Caucus. "It's that kind of dishonesty where nobody will confront it," she said. "I don't think it was some sinister plot by Schroeder to stay in place. I think she filled a need for a lot of reasons. I think that she had the guts, she had a sense of purpose, and I think that she wanted to do it. I don't think there was anybody else like her."

Yet those feelings of respect and affection did not stop Waters from challenging Schroeder. "Sometimes I like to do that kind of stuff. I like changing the rules. That's what I like." Waters laughs heartily.

Her style means she will have to continue to force her way into the circle of decision, and that she may never be a full participant. When the leadership looks around to balance a committee with gender or geography or race, there are other women, other Californians, and other blacks who are more congenial. "It doesn't matter—and let me tell you why it doesn't matter," Waters says. "Too many people think that their power is given to them by their committee assignments. I don't believe that at all. I don't care where you sit, your power is determined by you. What you're able to accomplish and how you're able to get your issues dealt with is determined by you. To think that you are significant because somebody decides to make you significant is just so foreign to me, I mean it just doesn't fit."

Waters's ability to maneuver on the inside among Democrats has improved greatly since the 1994 election, when Speaker Tom Foley, who clashed with Waters, was defeated. She has a much better relationship with Rep. Richard Gephardt of Missouri, the current leader of the Democrats in the House. Gephardt represents St. Louis, Waters's hometown, and they have many mutual friends. She serves on the board of the Rams professional football team, which moved from Los Angeles to St. Louis.

Waters does not plan to be in Washington long enough to make the long climb by seniority to the leadership. She has a different calculation than that of most politicians, whose stature depends on the good opinion of others who are important and powerful. Waters does not think that way. She cares more what the people in the housing project think about her than what they are saying in the Speaker's suite or the White House. She derives her power from thumbing her nose at power.

She did just that in August 1994 when she joined with House Republicans to defeat a crime bill that Clinton badly needed to shore up his sagging poll numbers. The White House scrambled to put together a compromise bill that could win enough Republican support without losing liberal Democrats. Chief of staff Leon Panetta went to Capitol Hill to meet with the Black Caucus. The emerging deal eliminated the Racial Justice Act, a provision to allow additional death row pleas for minorities based on studies that show African-Americans disproportionately receive the death penalty if their victims are white.

Waters reacted with fury to Panetta's attempt to sell the deal. "She was just scathing, vile—and needlessly so to him in that meeting," recalls a White House aide who was there. "She was just pounding away on him."

That session was followed by a meeting at the White House with Clinton, where the same aide described Waters as "mean and bullying." She reminded Clinton of the role she had played in helping him get elected in 1992 and threatened to withhold her support in 1996 if he gave in to pressure from the right.

"You can't expect me to go out and get these votes for you next time," she declared angrily. Glaring at the President and his inner circle of white men, some of whom favored a New Democrat strategy of moving to the right, she said in disgust, "Throwing a bunch of black people in jail for a long time will make you all feel good."

"What would you have me do?" Clinton pleaded. "Look, I am a Democratic president confronted with Republican right-wing attitudes. If I come to Congress with a progressive prevention package, it will never pass. So in essence what I've done, I've forced them to take this prevention stuff."

Waters was unmoved by Clinton's attempt to put an optimistic spin on making concessions. She would not vote for the crime package. "My life and my career have been built on progressive politics," she said finally. "I have no credibility if I violate my own principles. In the final analysis, I'm no good to you. The constituency that you'll need when you run the next time will have no faith in me because I've turned out to be everything that they hate. I can't do it to myself, and I can't do it to them, and I'm sorry."

Observing the scene, a White House aide thought to himself that Waters's office must have a stock press release that says, in effect, "Whitey fucked us again."

Waters's own recollection of the meetings differs sharply from that of the aide who recounted the closed-door sessions. Of the reported blowup with Panetta, she says, "Leon Panetta and I are friends. . . . Many of these young staffers have no experience, no appreciation for the history of relationships and project their own insecurities rather than the feelings of their bosses." Once again, Waters purports to be stunned at the interpretation that others put on her words and demeanor. About the encounter with Clinton, she says she "never, ever" uttered the words she was quoted as saying, and that she has never spoken to Clinton in a threatening manner.

Clinton managed to cobble together enough votes to pass his compromise crime bill without Waters's vote. The White House found a way to get even. Money that Waters had requested to expand job training for low-income people was not included in the final bill because, even if it were, White House aides figured she would still vote no. "We spent the money on yes votes," said an aide.

This time her anger and her intransigence had backfired, though she was never told that directly. She is accustomed to people, particularly white people, being uncomfortable with her anger. For the most part, that has worked to her benefit, triggering guilt in others and opening doors. But in Washington, where conservative ideas were in the ascendancy, Waters's combustible personality made the hard work of compromise even harder, and threatened the fragile friendships she would need in the increasingly hostile political climate.

Waters does not think of herself as an angry person. She will tell you that she has a lot of fun in life. But when she sees injustice and unfairness, it makes her angry, and she is not going to let the white world "socialize" her into hiding that anger. She is still the little girl who stepped out in front of her mother and stood up to the bill collector. "You have to understand, this is the honest to goodness truth, I don't quite always understand why people can't be frontal and just tell people what they think," she says. "If you're African-American in America today and you're not angry, something's wrong with you."

By early October 1994, with the election looming as a common enemy, Waters was back in good graces at the White House. She and her husband were among the guests at a state dinner honoring South African President Nelson Mandela. She campaigned for a number of white lawmakers in their black neighborhoods and for black incumbents. The high recognition and flamboyant style that kept her from being included in the lawmakers' backroom deals made her a hot commodity in the black communities whose votes they needed. Privately, she felt used, complaining to aides, "They only want me when they need something."

The weekend before the November 8 election, Waters was back home in her district for some last-minute campaigning. An aide drove her in a plain sedan, stopping frequently so she could climb out and visit with the young men she saw hanging around on street corners.

"Can we talk?" she said. They all knew her, and greeted her warmly. She asked who was in school and who was working. Some youths responded proudly, and thanked her for her help. Others squirmed. "See you in church," she told one young man, whose mother she knows. "Not if I see you first," he giggled to a friend as Waters got back into the car.

Waters may be a bleeding-heart liberal on policy matters, but when it comes to dealing with people one-on-one, she is an advocate of tough love. In a pilot program on teen pregnancy that she began with government funds, she proposed that young girls see the pay stub of an average taxpayer to make them understand why working people resent teenagers having babies they cannot afford. "This is Mr. Jones's paycheck. This money is taken out every week, and part of it goes to pay for your baby," says Waters. "He hates the fact he has to pay for your baby. In fact, he hates you. He doesn't want to feed your baby. He thinks that's your responsibility, and you're getting away with something. How do you feel about that?"

Such blunt talk does not square with Waters's reputation as an uncompromising liberal, but it reflects the underlying social conservatism of African-Americans. The theme of personal responsibility resonates in the black community among older people who remember a time when families were more stable, and among young people who follow the separatist teachings of Louis Farrakhan. The reality is, however, that survival in South Central Los Angeles today is heavily contingent on government assistance.

The Maxine Waters Employment Preparation Center, a sprawling institutional-looking complex, was originally established in 1966 after the Watts riot as a job skills center. It was named after Waters in 1989, when she was at the peak of her power in the California Assembly, and now houses Waters's 17-to-30 job-training program. According to figures supplied by Waters's congressional office in Washington as of November 1995, this program for the hard-core unemployed had placed 149 young men in jobs and 32 in training programs. Hundreds more are receiving counseling, which includes a two-week "Life Skills Management Training" course to ready them for the world of work. The numbers appear promising, and Waters's insistence on designing the program to target the pervasive joblessness among young men in her district has helped make it effective. But federal dollars are its lifeblood.

At first glance driving through Waters's district, the bungalow homes with driveways and small, neat lawns do not project the kind of grinding poverty associated with a riot-torn area. But large sections that were burned out in 1992 have not been rebuilt, and the unemployment rate is among the highest in the nation.

Waters is leading the effort to restore a commercial area that is within walking distance of her own home. "If we develop this strip, it will be more than anybody has ever done to rehabilitate anything in Los Angeles," she says. She helped her neighbors in the nearby middle-class enclave of Vermont Knolls organize to resist an initial plan to convert the property into low-cost housing. Then she joined forces with Republican Mayor Richard Riordan to oppose a subsequent plan that would construct subsidized townhouses in the area. Her critics, including some local African-American leaders, say Waters is selfishly protecting the property value of her home. But she argues that no neighborhood can thrive without shops that supply basic goods.

Waters's constituents come to her for all sorts of things that have nothing to do with her duties as a member of Congress. "Sometimes I can hold a whole town hall meeting, and there's not one congressional issue," she says. "I get people who talk to me about the trash pickup. People don't know what I do, so they ask me for everything. I create out of this what I think I can do."

On election night, November 8, Waters stayed home by herself and watched television. She had been unhappy with the way things had gone in the state, from Democrat Kathleen Brown's listless race for governor to the way Dianne Feinstein stalled in opposing Proposition 187, the anti-immigration referendum. "She didn't just come out and oppose Prop 187 because it was the moral thing to do—she got jammed. She had no alternative." Feeling disconnected from her party and dispirited about the future, Waters turned off the television early and went to bed without knowing the full extent of the Democrats' losses.

She got a shock the next morning when she turned on CNN and learned the Democrats had lost control of the House and that Feinstein had barely survived a challenge from Republican millionaire Michael Huffington. Some Democrats who had been defeated she would not miss. "I almost felt detached, like I was not really a part of any of that," she recalls.

Waters's leadership style requires enemies more than allies, and she soon concluded the Democrats' loss might be a good thing. It would shake the party from its complacency. It might even force the Democrats back to the streets. "The old tools are the new tools," she said, harking back to the era of sit-ins and protest marches. Waters is not attached to the Congress as an institution the way many members are. An activist at heart, she is more at home with people who have a grievance and who are protesting than with people she describes as "those who cherish the dinner parties and the receptions and rubbing shoulders with the so-called power elite." With the Democrats in the minority, she was back in her natural political setting as the disgruntled outsider.

"You use this time to organize, organize, organize so that you can come back and try and win," she said, sounding exuberant at the prospect. "You may not control the ability to get resources to create public policy, but you sure can organize around it."

Waters dreamed of forming a winning coalition of labor unions, women, blacks, and seniors to rally against Republican extremist policies. Jesse Jackson and other liberal activists preached the same message, but most Democratic strategists were skeptical. On January 4, 1995, by staying seated while other House members rose to congratulate new House Speaker Gingrich, Waters acted in a way that symbolized the new era of civil disobedience that she envisioned for progressive Democrats.

"I wasn't in the ceremonial mood," she said. "I do think it borders on hypocritical to rejoice in his ascending to the speakership. And I think it sends a funny message to my constituents and people who watch me and who watch us. 'Why were you smiling and laughing and clapping and applauding? Were you really happy? Oh, that's those dishonest politicians again.' So I didn't feel like doing that. I didn't feel happy, I didn't feel ceremonial, and I didn't feel like sending this message that everything was all right. I didn't feel like doing any of that, so I didn't do it."

Not a single member of the Black Caucus had been defeated in November, and its strength relative to the rest of the Democratic Caucus had grown substantially. The 1994 elections shifted Black Caucus members from a minority within the majority to a minority within the minority. Yet, in an example of the sort of perverse logic that makes politics deliciously contrary, this development had the potential to make the Black Caucus more powerful than it was when Democrats had a majority in the House. With thirty-nine black representatives, thirty-seven of them Democrats, blacks constituted nineteen percent, or almost one in five, of the House Democrats.

Any effort by Democrats and moderate Republicans to organize bipartisan resistance to the sometimes extreme agenda of Speaker Newt Gingrich and his conservative following could not succeed if the black Democrats deserted their party. A coalition of moderate Republicans and Democrats without the Black Caucus would probably fail, but a coalition of the Black Caucus and conservative Republicans could thwart the rest of the Democrats and Republicans.

Waters knew that she was in a strong position to set the agenda when the White House first told her that Clinton would be visiting Los Angeles. The date that aides had selected, January 17, 1995, was the anniversary of the Northridge earthquake, which jolted the area one year earlier and caused an estimated $13 to $20 billion in damage. Waters pointed out that the country would be observing Martin Luther King, Jr.'s birthday the day before. "You can't come to L.A. and disregard that," she told Clinton's aides, "and you might as well take care of some black politics." The White House proposed that Clinton speak in a black church, a setting that he likes and that has become traditional for him. But Waters saw an opportunity for the President to showcase her 17-to-30 program and to send a message that government is doing something positive for young black men, instead of running away from government like the Republicans. Waters wanted a big, outdoor event. The White House resisted.

"What if it rains?" a White House advance man demanded.

"We'll put up a tent," she said.

"Who'll pay for it?"

"We didn't ask you for any money," Waters said.

Finally, when every objection was overcome and plans were in place, the White House wanted seventy-five seats for Democratic Party contributors. "We don't have any time to take care of the prima donnas," Waters snapped. "This is a grassroots event. We don't have any special seating." So the White House came back and asked for forty seats. "You can't have any," Waters replied. "None."

The startled advance team suggested that Clinton might not come if Waters did not make seats available. By now the event had mushroomed into a community-wide celebration with choir groups performing and children dancing and singing. She told the White House that it was fine with her if Clinton did not show up. "I'll just explain to them that the President was supposed to come, and he didn't like what we were doing, so he decided to stay away," she said, pausing to laugh as she tells the story. "So of course he came. And it was a wonderful event."

There was one more fight with the White House. The advance team

wanted to bring in four hundred AmeriCorps volunteers in their signature yellow T-shirts. Waters refused, accusing the White House of wanting to take the focus away from her hard-core unemployed and shift it to
a program that was more acceptable. AmeriCorps was Clinton's pet project to get young people involved in community service, and Republicans were threatening to eliminate its funding. "These kids that we're
working with really do believe that the President is coming to see them,
and that the focus is going to be on them," she argued. "Why would we
create that kind of jealousy between these groups?"

Waters won out, and at the conclusion of the event, one of the young
men in her program said to Clinton, "Now, Mr. President, don't abandon
us. Don't just go on over there to the right and forget about us." "I
won't," Clinton assured him.

"Now whether he does or not, I don't know," Waters said. "But he said
that to them that day, which was, I think, kind of powerful."

Clinton did move to the right after the November election, ordering a
review of federal affirmative action programs and siding with Republicans on the need for a balanced budget and slowing the growth of
Medicare. Democrats in Congress were in open rebellion over Clinton's
budget, but Waters offered only perfunctory criticism. Knowing Clinton
as she did, she knew he was acting in what he felt was his long-term
interest. As President, he had to find some common ground with the
Republican Congress. "Those are political decisions," she said. "I guess
I accept and understand."

But she drew the line at undermining affirmative action to appease
the Republicans. In a private meeting at the White House, she threatened to leave the Democratic Party if Clinton backed away from affirmative action. "You do it, I'm going, and I'm taking some people with me,"
she told Clinton's aides.

"And me too," echoed Maryland Rep. Kweisi Mfume, a past chairman
of the Black Caucus, and a highly regarded legislator who resigned his
seat later in the year to head the NAACP. "I can run as an independent in
my district," Mfume told Clinton's stunned aides. "I don't need the
Democratic Party."

To convince the White House she was serious, Waters repeated the
threat at least four times in public. She worried that because Clinton's
aides were so young, they did not have the same emotional commitment
to the civil rights movement and to affirmative action as her generation.
"No party is so important that we will belong to it if it undermines us on
this issue," she declared. "No president is so important that we will
belong to him if he undermines us on this issue."

By reaffirming his commitment to affirmative action, Clinton prevented the defection of prominent blacks, like Waters and Mfume. "I was so relieved," said Waters when Clinton announced his position in a speech on July 19, 1995. "It was like a big curtain was lifted off my back."

Gingrich had only recently become Speaker when protesters from the community-based group, the Association of Community Organizations for Reform Now (ACORN), disrupted a luncheon meeting on Capitol Hill where he was scheduled to speak. The 1960s-style tactic was roundly denounced even by many of Gingrich's opponents. But Waters applauded the action. Speaking at an ACORN gathering the next day, she held up a front-page newspaper photo of the protest and declared, "A picture is worth a thousand words." She told them that what they had done was send a message around the country that a small number of people who believe strongly can bring attention to their cause. She encouraged them to do more of this kind of action.

ACORN had already planned to disrupt a banking hearing the following day, and Waters's rousing words served as inspiration. ACORN members got in line at 1:00 A.M. to get seats at a hearing on curtailing the Community Reinvestment Act, which requires banks to lend in all communities where they take deposits. It is the one law that gives poor communities some leverage in obtaining loans. Studies show that some $35 to $40 billion has been directed into poor communities as a result. There have been efforts to undermine the law in the past, and lawmakers sympathetic to banking interests thought they had a good shot at it this time.

By waiting in line through the night, ACORN members got in ahead of banking lobbyists, who had paid couriers to hold places for them. Several influential lobbyists were denied seats and left standing outside the hearing room, which ACORN regarded as a victory. After the hearing was underway, five ACORN members, all women, stood and chanted, "Save CRA! Save CRA!" Rep. Marge Roukema, a Republican from New Jersey, tried to quiet them with the gavel and could not. After a couple of minutes, the Capitol police, stationed outside the hearing door to monitor the flow of people, entered the room and arrested the women. It was a little before noon.

Waters was not at the hearing, but was told about it on the House floor by another member. Calling an aide to find out what had happened to the protesters, Waters learned that they were in the District of Columbia jail and would not be arraigned until the following morning. That meant they would spend the night in jail. Waters did not know at the time that the five women were all over fifty years old, three of them over sixty.

Still, she was furious that they were being treated like common criminals simply for protesting at a congressional hearing.

Waters phoned the police station herself. The officer who took the call told her the women could not be released until the next day. Telling Waters that something cannot be done is the surest way to rouse her to action. She was polite, but asked to speak to his supervisor. The supervisor was not available, and neither was anybody else who could help, he said. "I want you to put down the phone and not come back until you find someone who can," Waters told him. After two minutes, a female sergeant picked up the phone. She was responsive and promised to check the status of the women.

"I will come down to the jail and you can tell me then," Waters declared. The sergeant said that would not be necessary, but Waters insisted.

"It was pouring down rain," says Bill Zavarello, the aide who accompanied Waters. "And I'm not just making this up because it's a nice story. It was pouring rain." They drove the few blocks to the station on Indiana Avenue and entered through the metal detectors. The guards tried to block Waters from going any further, but she grabbed Zavarello and the two of them headed for the elevator. They went down one floor, where the sergeant was waiting in a holding room. They worked out the details for the women's release, and Waters waited upstairs for forty-five minutes to make sure the sergeant followed through. When the five women emerged, there was lots of crying and hugging. That was when Waters learned they were all grandmothers.

The first hundred days of the Republican-controlled Congress did nothing to soften Waters's attitude toward Speaker Gingrich. Her office published a harshly negative critique that charged Gingrich with ethical transgressions related to a lucrative book deal, and said that the Republicans had "sold themselves to the wealthy special interests." When Gingrich came to the Banking Committee to ask for a special allocation in funding for Habitat for Humanity, the nonprofit group championed by former President Jimmy Carter that builds housing for the poor, he ran into the Waters buzz saw.

"You are full of rhetoric about reducing government and cutting social programs," Waters chastised the Speaker. "You really would like to get rid of HUD. But here you are at this committee with your hand out for money for a project for someone who's well-connected who comes from your state of Georgia. What does that make you?"

"Hypocrite" was the answer Waters was looking for. Instead, Gingrich reminded Waters that when the flood relief bill was going through, she had attached an unrelated provision to fund job training in South Central Los Angeles. Most members believe they are sincere about cutting back on government and managing the deficit, but scrutiny of any member's voting record will reveal instances where promoting pet projects took priority over the national interest.

Having Republicans in charge, and conservative ideas dominant, provided numerous occasions for Waters to defend her principles. When a banking subcommittee held a hearing on March 2, 1995, to look into security contracts with the Nation of Islam, which receives federal money from the Department of Housing and Urban Development to patrol public housing projects, Waters attended even though she is not a member of the subcommittee. Republican Peter King, with whom she had clashed during the Whitewater hearings, had a bill to ban federal money going to the Nation of Islam. The room was crowded, the atmosphere racially charged. Nation of Islam security guards lined the walls. Jewish groups testified against the funding on the grounds that the organization's leader, Louis Farrakhan, is anti-Semitic.

When a New York City Council member, who is Jewish, described how he went into a housing project and saw a picture of Farrakhan, which, he added, must have been put up by the security guards, Waters could no longer contain herself. She said that in any housing project in the country, you might find a picture of Malcolm X, Martin Luther King, Jr., or Farrakhan. "There are even pictures of me in some projects in my district," she added. "Just because you see a picture, you can't accuse a security guard of putting it up. I noticed the word 'nigger' scratched on one of the elevators in the Cannon Building. And I never accused Peter King of doing that." (As of February 1996, Waters reported the epithet is still there. "I see it every day.")

The comment was right up to the line of civility, if not over it, but Waters showed no contrition. She had seen too many examples of politicians using race to frighten and divide people. She was outraged when a Republican fund-raising letter featured a "Most Wanted" poster of liberal Democrats who were predominantly black, Jewish, Hispanic, and female. Only six of the twenty-eight mug shots were of white men who were not Jewish. Republicans contended that they chose the lawmakers, including Waters, based on voting patterns. But Massachusetts Rep. Barney Frank, who was also pictured, accused the GOP of including people who would "stir up their fund-raising base. . . people who think there are too many blacks, Jews, and women in Congress."

Waters and the new Republican majority could not be further apart. The GOP embraced the anti-Washington symbolism of freshman Rep.

Mark Sanford and second-term Rep. Bob Inglis, both of South Carolina, who slept in their offices and showered in the House gym. Waters saw it as a sign of privilege that a member of Congress did not have to pay rent while people are homeless and living in the streets. "I don't like that," she said. "You make a decent salary and you get to live here free because you don't want to be contaminated by Washingtonians. I think that attitude and mentality is pervasive with those new members."

Waters looked beyond the halls of Congress to leverage her power. "Being in the minority means you don't get to win legislatively," she says to describe the charged atmosphere. "Your amendments are voted down. You're constantly going to the floor and being on the losing side of whatever vote is taken. I want to tell you, it is not pleasant. It drives you to think about what else can you do to make this job meaningful and make you feel you're accomplishing something."

Waters got into politics as an organizer and a community activist, and that is who she is. If she cannot make public policy, she can bring pressure on those who do. "I believe that I can make things happen above and beyond what's supposed to happen with this kind of job," she says. The issue she settled on—bank fees—is not Bosnia, but it affects the life and pocketbook of every American, and particularly inner-city, low-income people. Her target was First Chicago Bank, which had begun charging people a three-dollar fee to use a teller.

Most legislators fill their campaign coffers with contributions from the industries they are charged with regulating, but Waters does not take political contributions from banks. The lack of a financial tie gives Waters moral high ground in her fight with the banks, but some say it also gives her less leverage because the banks have no vested interest in her. She disagrees. "The political whores can be bought any day of the week," she says. "The banks can't afford to have too many like me who can't be bought. They would lose their power and stranglehold on the Banking Committee."

A member who accepts contributions from banks would be unlikely to lead a demonstration against one. Banks do not like public embarrassment, which pleases, yet puzzles Waters. "When you're that big and you're that strong, what do you care if somebody gets in the press and talks about you, or if they organize against you?"

It turned out that First Chicago cared a lot. The bank used intermediaries to urge Waters to back off from her threat to demonstrate. It put out a public statement affirming its position, but expressing a willingness to meet with Waters. She refused. "If they don't indicate some interest in compromise, I am not interested in hearing why they have fees," she said. Ex-Panther Bobby Rush, who represents a low-income area of Chicago that the bank serves, supported Waters at first, but then changed his mind. The bank had recently opened branches in his district and put $2 million into Chicago's enterprise zone. "He just felt they were doing some things that he supported," Waters said.

The issue caught on. Jay Leno joked about it on the *Tonight* show. "Did you see that First National Bank of Chicago is charging customers $3 to talk to a teller? The good news is that for only $3.95 you can talk dirty to her." A cartoon showed a masked gunman stopped cold by a teller who, before turning over the money, demands a three-dollar fee for teller assistance. Waters introduced a bill to establish a freeze on bank fees for accounts held by average taxpayers. While the bill languished in subcommittee, she held a press conference in Chicago and led pickets in a lunch-hour demonstration in front of the bank. Soon after, the bank announced it would cut in half the amount required in savings accounts for unlimited free teller visits and halved the minimum balance for basic savings, from $500 to $250.

"In this whole process, there's *always* some room for leverage, there's *always* some opportunity, there's *always* a way to get something done that's not easily seen," said a triumphant Waters.

The experience reinforced Waters's belief that it was time to get back into the streets. The 17-to-30 jobs program that she had fought so hard to get funded was wiped out in the first wave of cuts proposed by the Republican Congress and agreed to by President Clinton. Waters had personally lobbied Clinton to keep her program. "He took notes and said he was going to take care of it," she says. Even if Clinton had wanted to reward Waters, there was little he could salvage in the post-election wreckage.

Waters reconciled herself to finding funding in the private sector. She got a half-million dollars from the music industry, telling the rap producers they had a responsibility to put money back into the community. But sustaining the kind of funding that she had gotten from Washington would be difficult, and the future of the 17-to-30 program is shaky.

Waters had gotten into politics as a result of a government-funded program. She was every bit as much a Head Start baby as the millions of three-year-olds who had profited from the program over the years. It is where she cut her teeth as a political activist. Now, at the pinnacle of her career as an elected official, she was powerless to protect Head Start from the GOP ax. The popular program faced cutbacks along with most federal spending in what the pundits proclaimed "a paradigm shift" away from reliance on government.

Waters worked up a half-dozen amendments in an effort to protect Head Start and other social programs, including the Foster Grandparents Program, originally championed by Nancy Reagan. But the Democratic leadership persuaded her not to introduce them, arguing that too many amendments would flood the process when a more targeted approach was needed to combat the GOP.

Democrats believed that in Head Start they had an issue that would capture the public's attention. Minority Leader Richard Gephardt staged an elaborate press conference, which Waters learned about through her Head Start contacts. When she sought a role, she was told she was too late, that the planning was complete. So Waters did what she always does. She showed up without an invitation. Gephardt's Boy Scout demeanor clouded over momentarily when he saw her, but near the end of the press conference, he dutifully called on Waters. Her eloquent testimonial to Head Start, and how the program had altered her life, more than justified her unexpected attendance. Everybody seemed pleased, especially Gephardt.

But when Waters negotiated with the Democratic leadership for floor time to speak about Head Start, she ran into more resistance. The Democratic strategy was in place, and Waters was not among the chosen few selected to speak. She had been relegated to a spot during what is known as "general debate," when members raise all sorts of issues and press coverage is sparse. Wisconsin Democrat David Obey, charged with orchestrating the Democratic response, is as hard-headed and self-righteous as Waters. A minor difference quickly escalated into a power struggle.

"I saw him at one point have six white males in a block just talk and talk and talk, and I was thinking, 'This is what he knows, this is what he understands, this is his world,'" says Waters. "That's all there is to it. That's the way he's always done it, you know what I'm saying. That's just the way it is. I understand it, but I don't buy it. I'm not begging him for time. I'm not just a Black Women's Forum organizer. I'm a legislator."

Waters issued an ultimatum. Either she would be permitted to speak in both slots or she would introduce her amendments. The Democratic leaders folded. So, on August 2, 1995, Waters stood on the House floor to defend Head Start against the Republican charge that it was nothing more than "a baby-sitting program."

"I know about Head Start," she said. "It changed my life."

Waters gets back to St. Louis for family reunions, organizes the brunch on Mother's Day, and responds when there are family crises. The housing project where her family last lived has been demolished, part of a federal program to level the most infamous high-rises. The community center where she danced and swam no longer exists. On her last visit to St. Louis, Waters was at a drug rehabilitation center after midnight enrolling a niece for treatment. "You can't be about everybody else's problems, and not be about your own family's problems," she says. She and her husband set aside a portion of their salaries each month to help family members. "We spend about a grand a month on our families," she says. "The way I do it, I take the ones who are most in need, try to assess what the problem is, and hope there's a beginning and an end." Laughing now, she adds, "And then I put them on my famous stipend."

By the end of the Republicans' first year in control of Congress, a record number of lawmakers had announced they would not be running for reelection. Some were Republicans, disheartened by the partisan meanness that had taken hold, but by far the larger number were Democrats. Displaced as committee chairs and powerless to stop the GOP juggernaut, they cut short their legislative careers rather than endure the humiliation of being in the minority. Even Waters was uncharacteristically silent when the Republicans ended funding for her 17-to-30 program, along with the stipend she had fought so hard to achieve. The new political order had prevailed, for now.

But unlike many of her colleagues, she had no plans to leave. "This is an inside game and an outside game," she said. If she could not get her way inside the Capitol, she would fall back on the tactics that had served her well before to rouse public indignation among the disaffected. "We've got a lot of work to do. If there's one thing Newt Gingrich has done for us, the graying of the parties has stopped. A year or two ago, people were saying, 'Aw, there's no difference between Democrats and Republicans—they're all alike.' Now there is a growing recognition that this public policy stuff, there's something to it."

CHAPTER SIX

CHIEF OF STAFF

"Where's the Middle?"

The color photograph spread over two pages in the November 28, 1994, issue of *Time* magazine shows Bob Dole and Newt Gingrich, the Republican leaders of the Senate and House, meeting for the first time since the election earlier that month that gave the Republicans control of Congress. The two met on "Dole's Beach," a sun porch just steps from Dole's Senate office, to establish important markers for the legislative season ahead. Gingrich's remarkable rise to Speaker had captured the headlines, but Dole was the senior partner, and the choice of locale reflected his venerability. The terrace, which commands a view of the Mall and its monuments, is Dole's favorite spot in the Capitol, where he retreats to reflect and bask in the sun's restorative rays. Dressed in dark business suits on a pleasantly warm day, the two leaders engaged in light banter, reflecting the cheerful mood of Republicans still celebrating their stunning victory.

Seated next to Dole and partially obscured by him in the photograph is a woman with long blond hair highlighted by the late afternoon sun. *Time* does not identify her in the caption, and few outside her family and friends would recognize Sheila Burke, which suited her just fine. Since becoming Dole's chief of staff, Burke had adhered to the admonition that staff members on Capitol Hill should be like wallpaper—seen, but not heard.

Burke's natural reticence combined with strict adherence to the staff member's code of conduct made her an anomaly in today's personality-driven politics. In her seventeen years working for Dole, her name had appeared in the papers infrequently. As an interview subject, she behaved like an unfriendly witness in a court case, volunteering little beyond bare facts, even when speaking "on background," not for attribution. She was the embodiment of the faceless staffer, the figure hovering behind the senator occasionally whispering advice on the issues of the day, or maybe just asking whether he wanted chicken noodle soup for lunch.

As Burke sat taking notes on a yellow legal pad at the first meeting of Republican heads of the two chambers of the U.S. Congress in forty years—it had been that long since the Republicans had last controlled the House of Representatives—she appeared calm, as always, but that was not how she felt. The Gingrich-led revolution presented a new dynamic. There was no staffer currently serving who could give her advice. No one in Washington had a model for dealing with a Republican House, much less one led by so restless and ambitious a personality as Gingrich.

Despite the genial mood of the photograph, there was already tension between the two men. Gingrich had decided to have the House start working on its legislative Contract With America the same day members of Congress took the oath of office. Dole had reluctantly gone along with the idea, even though the Senate Republicans had no contract of their own with the voters who had restored them to the majority. Burke later described her frame of mind as one of uncharacteristic panic. "What are we going to do for the first days? The House is going to be doing its thing, and we're going to have to find something to keep us busy." Also on Burke's shoulders was the task of interviewing and hiring staff to handle the new Majority Leader's expanded responsibilities. "Who do we want to bring back? What kinds of people do we want to take a look at?" And in the middle of this historic summit, Burke's mind drifted for just a minute to home and her three children. Her daughter Sarah's preschool Christmas party was coming up, and Burke could not remember whether she was supposed to bring the snack.

Burke, a nurse by training and a Democrat by upbringing, joined Dole's staff in 1977 as a health care specialist. She rose quickly to become Dole's representative on the Senate Finance Committee, the second woman on the prestigious committee's staff. In 1986, she was transferred from the committee staff to Dole's Senate office, and promoted to chief of staff—in charge not only of Dole's professional team, but of every facet of his legislative operation, from answering constituents' mail to negotiating with senators. On Capitol Hill, Burke is regarded as the 101st senator, a designation that some would say underestimates her actual power; yet, until recently, few people outside of the halls of Congress knew who she was.

They are an unlikely couple—Bob Dole, whose grave countenance and dark humor have made him the Darth Vader of American politics, and Sheila Burke, the fair-haired damsel worrying about baking brownies for her preschooler's party—yet everything that Dole does as Republican leader either originates with or is vetted by Burke. The arrangement had not been questioned until Dole launched his campaign for the presidency. Then prominent members of the Republican Party's right wing began to portray Burke publicly as a softhearted moderate, sympathetic to the Democrats on issues like health care, welfare, and abortion rights. They said that if Dole hoped to have their support, he would be well advised to rid himself of Burke.

Seven months after *Time*'s double-page spread on the dawning of a new Republican era, the magazine published a much different kind of story—the kind that Burke had tried hard over the years to avoid. The headline screamed, "Bring Me the Head of Sheila Burke." Conservatives quoted in the article accused Burke of inflicting her views on Dole.

Finally, a year after the barely recognizable glimpse of Burke in the *Time* photograph, her anonymity was unmasked completely by a story in *The New York Times Magazine* with a full-color, straight-on portrait of Burke staring out from the cover. Her tired eyes, tight lips, and drained countenance testify to the strain of a year in which she struggled to serve her boss while defending herself against charges that she was undermining him. Jutting out from Burke's golden locks are two red crimson horns, painted in by an artist to punctuate the cover line: "The Campaign to Demonize Sheila Burke."

Sheila Patricia Burke was born to liberal Democratic parents in San Francisco on January 10, 1951. Her father, a first-generation Irishman from Butte, Montana, met her British-born mother while he was serving overseas in the army during World War II. Joan Burke had several miscarriages before giving birth to Sheila, the couple's only child. The family eventually settled in Merced, California, a tranquil town in the San Joaquin Valley that proudly calls itself the tomato capital of the world. George Burke was an executive with the Farmers Insurance Company. His wife went to work as the dispatcher for the local ambulance company. Sheila's childhood by her own account reflected the best of the 1950s, growing up in a warm, loving nuclear family connected to a larger, caring community. Her parents were active in volunteer work, with the city park service a pet project of her father's. Burke has a photo in her office of her young son, Daniel, standing by a sign commemorating a local park in her father's honor.

Although she came of age in the turbulent 1960s, Burke never had reason to be rebellious. Her parents were her best friends until they died thirteen months apart in 1988 and 1989, and she continues to maintain the family home in Merced. Twelve years of parochial school might have primed her for an adolescent revolt. Instead, the Sisters of the Immaculate Heart, an activist order of nuns dedicated to social justice, served as powerful role models who helped set Burke on the course of fair-minded moderation that she favors today. While her contemporaries took to the streets to protest the Vietnam War, Burke studied nursing at the University of San Francisco, a Jesuit-run institution, and kept her distance from the demonstrations.

After graduation in 1973, Burke was working as a nurse in the surgical ward at Alta Bates Hospital in Berkeley when she was recruited for a job with the National Student Nurses Association in New York. She had only been practicing for a year, but she was intrigued by the prospect of a public policy position that would allow her to make a larger impact on her profession. Having never lived outside of California for any length of time as an adult, or been that far away from her parents, the move was a huge step and not altogether successful. Burke found Manhattan an inhospitable place, and was planning to return to California in 1977 when a friend told her about a job in Washington as a health policy specialist. The only hitch was that the senator who had the job opening was a Republican. Burke had always thought of herself as a Democrat, that is, when she thought about it at all. The hesitation she felt was fleeting. Having not been caught up in the student protests of the 1960s, she did not think of herself as political.

Burke's quiet intelligence and exacting efficiency quickly impressed Bob Dole, who was trying to rehabilitate his Senate career after a disastrous run for the vice presidency the year before as Gerald Ford's hatchet man. Six months after hiring Burke, he made her his staff representative on the powerful Senate Finance Committee, an appointment that violated an unwritten rule among the good ol' boys who dominated the committee that barred the hiring of women staffers. The ranking members at that time were such legendary figures as Russell Long and Herman Talmadge, southern Democrats noted for their colorful style and hard drinking. Burke never took offense at their boisterous behavior, but let them know by her stoic, pioneer woman's demeanor that she was there to stay.

When Ronald Reagan was elected president in 1980, and the Republicans gained control of the Senate, it was a new day at the Finance Committee. As the ranking Republican on the committee, Dole became chairman, and Burke became one of the most powerful staffers on Capitol Hill. Jerry Kline, the editor of a Washington newsletter, remembers first becoming aware of Burke's influence in 1982 when he happened to attend a Finance Committee "markup," a session where lawmakers put their final stamp on legislation. Assembled on the dais were a dozen or so senators, including some of the most venerable names of the day—Russell Long of Louisiana, John Heinz of Pennsylvania, and Daniel Patrick Moynihan of New York. Seated before them at the witness table was the petite figure of Burke, surrounded by stacks of papers and books, calmly fielding the most technical and often ponderously worded questions about complicated Medicare provisions in the Tax Equity and Fiscal Responsibility Act.

"I took a seat in the room, and Sheila, to my surprise, was conducting the hearing," Kline recounts. "She was walking them line by line through this very complicated legislation. And there wasn't one time where she said, 'I'll get back to you on that, senator.' I was mesmerized." Burke's command of detail was such that she could reach into the piles on her desk and retrieve the exact page with the information she needed. At the conclusion of the hearing, several senators shook her hand. As for Dole, he was "beaming like a proud papa," says Kline.

What made Burke's performance all the more remarkable was that, at the time, she was commuting regularly to Harvard's Kennedy School of Government in Boston and writing a paper on quality control in the Japanese health care system. "I said to myself, a star is born," Kline recalls.

That same hearing, however, planted the seeds of suspicion among conservatives in Dole's new right-hand woman. The Tax Equity and Fiscal Responsibility Act, which Burke skillfully helped steer through the committee, was, in fact, a maneuver to get around President Reagan's anti-tax increase policy. Under pressure from Democrats to prove the GOP was not the party of the rich, Dole had agreed to a sizable tax increase under the cover of Medicare reform, and had sold it to Reagan as a loophole-closing device. The fact that Burke helped make it happen put her in the Right's target sights.

Democratic Senate staffers call Dole "Vic Venom," but Dole is more personable than his biting, often sarcastic public demeanor suggests. He established a bond of trust with Burke when he was still a relatively junior senator from Russell, Kansas, and she came to work for him with the purest of motives as an adviser on health issues. It is the kind of relationship that politicians find almost impossible to develop later in their careers. She is his eyes and ears and second brain.

Burke changed her voting registration to Republican in the early 1980s, but she still gets along better with Democrats than with her adopted party's conservative wing. Senator Moynihan, a prickly and hard to please personality, is her biggest booster. "I don't know how the Senate would run without her," he says. When Burke's alma mater, the University of San Francisco, tried without success to recruit Moynihan as a commencement speaker, all it took was a note from Burke for him to agree. "If Sheila wants me to do it, I'll do it," he told an aide.

Burke also bonds across party lines with other female legislative assistants assigned to the Finance Committee, which is still a male-dominated preserve. As a group, they care more about broad social policy than arcane tax provisions for corporations. Burke remembers how senators' eyes would glaze over at the mention of health care reform. "You could see them scooting around on their seats, and then they'd leave to go to the bathroom and not come back," she recalls. It was the same in the Ways and Means Committee of the House, where, Burke says, "The room is packed when they're talking about butterfly straddles [a tax device], but as soon as the social welfare team comes to the table, everyone gets up and moves out the door."

When Mississippi Sen. John Stennis retired in 1989 after forty-two years on Capitol Hill, he said that the greatest change he had seen was the growth in numbers and power of women in politics, both as members and staffers. From only a token presence at the time Stennis began his career in the Senate, women held forty percent of the top staff positions by the time he retired. The "glass ceiling" of gender discrimination said to prevent women from reaching the top levels of government and industry had not been totally shattered, however. In 1995, of the 392 staffers earning more than $100,000 a year, only eighteen percent were women.

The first women to work for the federal government were hired in 1795 to weigh gold coins at the Mint in Philadelphia. They were paid fifty cents a day. Three-quarters of a century later, in 1871, Isabel Barrows, the wife of Boston congressman Samuel Barrows, became the first professional woman to work in the Capitol. Barrows was hired as a stenographer for a House committee. Her unpublished memoir, "Chopped Straw: The Remembrances of My Threescore Years," tells of the unrealized dreams of a woman who wanted more than society would allow: "Confused and tossed about, my own plans might lie like straw chopped short by the knives of the cutter. . . ."

When Barrows began at the Capitol, her superiors told her to sign only her initials on any vouchers since no woman had ever held the job of shorthand writer, and they feared she would be fired. The charade ended when she was summoned to the sergeant at arms's office to take a loyalty oath. "I can still see the surprise in the man's eyes, but I raised my right hand and swore I had never borne arms against my country and that I never would." Barrows was the official stenographer during impeachment proceedings against Secretary of War William W. Belknap for treason. "I did not even stand up once from my chair from one [in the afternoon] until one in the middle of the night," she wrote.

The first woman elected to Congress was Jeannette Rankin, a Republican from Montana, who served two terms, the first from 1917 to 1919, and the second from 1941 to 1943. She won election the first time four years before the Nineteenth Amendment to the Constitution giving women the right to vote was ratified. Montana was one of several western states that had already permitted women to vote. Rankin stood alone as the only member of Congress to vote against both World War I and World War II, perpetuating the stereotype that women's concerns were different, and perhaps not as consequential, as those of men.

With the end of the Cold War, the 1990s were an era when social issues, such as health care and welfare, once regarded as women's work, became the backbone of the political agenda. The relationships that Burke had developed with other female staffers in key positions—an informal sisterhood of professional women in the Senate—eased the way for many of the deals that were made among their bosses. "We share something," says Josie Martin, press secretary to GOP Sen. John Chafee. Reflecting on the many women on Capitol Hill whose work centers on promoting the self-interest of male politicians, Martin sighs, "All our lives revolve around one guy."

The job of any top staffer is to make the boss look good. Burke's agenda is Bob Dole. She speaks for him, advances his proposals, and negotiates on his behalf. The reason she has power is that everybody knows she is acting with Dole's authority. If he did not back her up, she would be powerless. "I've never had him undercut me in a decision," says Burke. "I've never had him come in and say, after I've agreed to do something, that we're not going to do that. That kind of support is the only way to survive up here."

Health care lobbyist Fred Graefe experienced the combined weight of Burke backed by Dole when he mistakenly thought he had won approval on a Medicare payment provision because Minnesota Sen. Dave Durenberger, then the chairman of the subcommittee that handled health financing issues, had signed off on it. When he mentioned the deal he had struck to Burke, she fixed him with her cool blue eyes and said, "Senator Dole will make that decision." Burke also made it clear that, as Dole's top aide, she was responsible for making sure the senator had all the information he needed to make the right decision.

"I thought to myself, 'Welcome to Washington 101,'" Graefe recounted. "She said it calmly, nicely. It was a week later before I figured out I got screwed. If it's a Medicare issue, if you don't have Sheila, you don't have it."

With Burke's help, Dole even managed on some health issues to outfox Reagan's budget cutters. The White House had balked at an experimental home-care program for elderly Medicare patients because of its cost, though over the long run it would save the government money. So Dole and Burke, without telling the administration, tucked a provision into the 1983 budget bill to allow the program to go forward. It was around midnight, after the bill had safely passed, when Burke got a call in her office from an irate budget official at the White House demanding to know how she could do such a thing. "We just did it," she replied. "It's over."

Although some female senators have broken the gender oneness of "the world's most exclusive club," the Senate remains predominantly a male province, so it was with some qualms that Dole made Burke his chief of staff in 1985. "He was concerned and said so, that I wouldn't be strong enough," she says. "I disabused him of that fairly quickly."

A chief of staff wears two hats: defender of the boss's political and legislative interests, and manager of his office staff and budget. That covers everything from the right to hire and fire, to the ability to act as a gatekeeper and decide who gets to see the senator. But what really sets the job apart is the ability to speak for the senator, which is why loyalty is so prized. The most powerful aides are those who are trusted by their bosses, and have earned the right to speak for them. Many senators are reluctant to give that control to anybody, and their top aides are usually called administrative assistants or AAs, because they manage the office but generally do not have the liberty to make policy or political decisions without the senator's permission.

Burke is the quintessential chief of staff. Dole trusts her to filter back information to him, to screen who he sees, and to speak for him. There is no more extraordinary bond between two people on Capitol Hill. With Dole's tacit backing, Burke gained a reputation for her willingness to confront the Republican White House. She stood up to Reagan budget director David Stockman when he favored greater Medicare cuts than she thought the system could absorb. And she spoke out at a Republican retreat in opposition to Bob Teeter, Bush's pollster, and John Sununu, the White House chief of staff, who argued that health care reform was not a matter for the federal government. Bush would later lose his bid for reelection in part because of his refusal to confront pressing domestic issues, like the need for health care reform.

Arizona Sen. John McCain, a former prisoner of war, remembers being made to feel like an errant schoolboy when, as a freshman senator in 1987, he openly lobbied for a seat on the Armed Services Committee in violation of Senate decorum. When it appeared McCain might not get the slot, he approached Burke and asked her to intercede with Dole. She heard him out, then politely said she would do what she could. But McCain, who eventually got the seat, said the manner of her response clearly conveyed that he had been out of line. McCain, who had stoically resisted his North Vietnamese captors for five and one-half years, is somewhat sheepish about how fast he capitulated to Burke. "She handled it with great skill and I never did that again," he says.

Burke's toughness is so renowned that her staff once presented her with a box of nails after a Clinton insider marveled, "The lady eats nails for lunch."

The same year that the Republicans lost control of the Senate, 1986, Burke suffered a personal tragedy. She miscarried at twenty weeks, a loss made more poignant by her portrait, in a bright red maternity dress, appearing shortly afterwards on the cover of the magazine *Nursing Economics*. As the only nurse to achieve such a prominent staff position on Capitol Hill, where most such jobs are held by lawyers, Burke is well-known and popular in the nursing community. She had to endure calls and questions for many months from well-meaning readers who did not know she had lost the baby. "She and I cried together," says former Republican Rep. Lynn Martin, a close friend.

Burke went on to have three children, a boy and two girls. She managed to give birth to two of her babies while the Senate was in recess, a fact that is cited as proof of her extraordinary efficiency. "In some ways, coming to work is the easiest thing I do in my day," she says. Balancing the demands of a growing family with her high-pressure job takes its toll, and Burke wears the dour look of the sleep-deprived. She follows a regimen familiar to working parents, a forced march that begins at dawn and does not cease until after the kids are asleep. "If you ask my husband, I'm sure he'd tell you that I'm kind of a crab face," she says.

Burke's rigorous scheduling kept the family going for the seven years that her husband, David Chew, an insurance executive, commuted to his job in Hartford, Connecticut, and was home only on the weekends. She admits that she was relieved most weekday evenings when he was not there because then she could go through her paces without the pressure of having to deal with another person. "It's a terrible thing to say, but life's less complicated when you're by yourself. I could get the kids to bed and start doing work by nine o'clock." When Chew's job situation changed and he moved back home full-time in the fall of 1994, Burke confessed that she sometimes felt nostalgic for the times when, as a single parent, she had late-evening hours alone to work, read quietly, paint her toenails, or work out on the treadmill. "Now I feel compelled to talk and do other civilized things," she says.

Burke operates on such a tightly honed schedule at home and in the office that when a staffer apologized for being "a little wound up," she replied, "That's okay. I'm the Queen of Wound." She is a minimalist communicator, using only those words necessary to convey her meaning. Her speaking style is direct, and she rarely wastes time giving examples of what she's talking about. Asking Burke for an anecdote is like asking a cow for cappuccino. The conservative columnist Kate O'Beirne says Burke's manner is intimidating—"like a nurse supervisor who is convinced you left your light on too late."

Yet Burke dutifully bakes brownies for school events and for staffers' birthdays, even if it means staying up until two in the morning. Rod DeArment, her predecessor as chief of staff, now a partner in a prestigious law firm, still gets brownies from Burke on his birthday although it has been years since he worked for Dole. Burke has a sweet tooth, and brings tins of cookies and other sweets she has baked to the office. She stashes them in cabinets and drawers and pulls them out for visitors. "Want some fat?" she says, extending a home-baked goody much the way a male chief of staff twenty years ago might have offered a guest a cigar or a drink.

Her office has the requisite power symbols: an imposing fireplace, overstuffed chairs, opulent silk swags and jabots over the windows. The rich brown conference table is strewn with papers, including a recipe for oatmeal cookies. A blender sits on the credenza, left over from a margarita party she threw for the staff months earlier. There are pictures of Burke's three tow-headed children, but no "ego wall" picturing her with presidents and politicians. A computer sits on a side table untouched. Burke writes memos in longhand and has them typed. She feels guilty about being a technophobe, and vows she will change her ways someday.

But she actually seems to like being quaintly out of touch, refusing to carry a cellular phone or a beeper. "I figure if people need me, they'll find me," she says. "I mean, short of a nuclear explosion, it can wait."

*   *   *

Burke is viewed as "the left winger" on Dole's staff, so he compensates for her by having at least one staunch conservative in a top position as a counterweight. Jim Whittinghill, a cowboy-boot-wearing, trash-talking good ol' boy, filled that role for a number of years. He says that Burke joked about how she did "the girl issues" like health care and welfare, and he did "the boy issues," like crime and gun rights. During the 1992 presidential campaign, Burke called the Bush-Quayle headquarters and scolded a mid-level aide for faxing a newsletter to Republicans around the country that mocked the idea of universal health care coverage, which she favors as a goal. After Bill Clinton was elected, conservatives worried that Burke would push Dole into a deal with Clinton on health care reform. Handing the new Democratic president such a historic achievement could prevent Republicans from reclaiming the White House for a generation.

Because Dole trusts Burke, she can sometimes get him to do things that he would not otherwise consider. In 1992, Dole was inclined to oppose a bill authorizing research on fetal tissue because that was the position of the pro-life groups, whom he supports. Burke believed that the scientific benefits of such research outweighed the argument that using fetal tissue would legitimize and even encourage abortion. Indeed, many longtime abortion opponents, including Republican Sen. Strom Thurmond, voted for the bill, as did Dole. "I convinced him it was not an abortion issue, that it had to do with the quality of life, and the quality of research," says Burke. "I felt comfortable presenting what I thought was a strong case against his natural instinct."

Anti-abortion conservatives blamed Burke for Dole's support for fetal tissue testing. Burke will never make Dole pro-choice, nor does she try, but this was a case where she had clearly influenced him. She further inflamed conservatives by making the bill a priority and taking a leadership role in soliciting the votes of other moderate Republicans to insure its passage. Connecticut Rep. Nancy Johnson recalls how Burke took her to the Democratic cloakroom, which is normally off-limits for Republicans, to lobby a senator whose vote was needed. "She's the best chief of staff I've ever witnessed," says Johnson. "If Dole won the presidency, she could run that White House in a way that rivaled [Reagan chief of staff] Jim Baker's tenure."

That is the scenario conservatives fear: If Burke were elevated to the White House, she would moderate her boss's policies in the same way that Baker, a velvet-tongued Texan, smoothed the rough edges of the Reagan Revolution. Until Dole became the front-runner for the Republican nomination, conservative grumbling about Burke was not news.

She had happily allowed herself to be insulated from the Right. Dole always had other high-level aides with the correct ideological pedigree to deal with the more conservative members. Burke liked the arrangement because it helped get the work done, so she ignored the steadily building resentment.

When Clinton put his wife in charge of health care reform, Burke became "the other woman," the one who had Dole's ear, and who was potentially the pivotal person in the debate. Her advice and counsel could move Dole toward a deal or unleash a GOP filibuster that would force the Democrats to get a super-majority of sixty votes to pass a bill. "The most powerful woman in American government, and no one knows her name," mused Moynihan's staff director, Lawrence O'Donnell, at the outset of the health care fight. "She has her hands on the controls of the veto apparatus of the Congress, and no one's ever heard of her."

Conservatives knew who Burke was, however, and their worst fears were confirmed when Moynihan, then chairman of the Senate Finance Committee, announced on NBC-TV's *Meet the Press* on Sunday, September 19, 1993, that "Sheila Burke . . . said this is an important moment [in health reform]. . . . We agree that government now has to intervene." Government intervention in health care was a conservative's nightmare, raising the specter of "socialized medicine." Hearing Burke cited on national television by a prominent Democrat as a cheerleader for health care reform convinced conservatives she would put policy above party. Behind the scenes, she had opposed their efforts to draft a set of GOP health care principles as a counterweight to Clinton's plan. "She didn't want a Republican plan that united the Republicans," says a key Republican. "She wanted a compromise. She wanted Dole to compromise with Moynihan."

Most of 1994 was a struggle for Dole's heart and mind on health care reform. He fluctuated like a human seismograph measuring sentiment for reform in his party and the country. Before it was over, he affixed his name as a co-sponsor to a half-dozen bills and ended up supporting none of them, including the alternative he himself had proposed.

Through it all, conservatives kept a wary eye on Burke. When Republican intellectual William Kristol circulated a memo in Washington in January 1994 declaring there is "no crisis" in health care, and that Republicans should not yield in their opposition, the battle between Burke and the conservatives moved into the open, at least inside the Beltway. Burke rejected Kristol's argument as semantical nonsense, using words that were sure to cause dangerously high blood pressure among her conservative critics. "The crisis is largely in people's lives," she said. "The system itself is huge and successful and makes zillions of dollars and produces massive amounts of research and extraordinary care. The crisis is that there are people who don't have it. It's a very personal crisis. It's not that the system doesn't do what it's supposed to do, it just doesn't do it for some people."

After initially endorsing Kristol's thesis, Dole backed off. Conservatives worried that he might soften and make a deal with Clinton. They blamed Burke for lessening his resolve. As it turned out, the Democrats, divided among themselves on how to finance expanded health care coverage, and fearful of a top-heavy government plan, became the principal saboteurs of significant health care reform. As Burke sat in the House chamber listening to the 1994 State of the Union address, in which Clinton vowed to veto any bill that did not guarantee universal coverage, she thought, "How stupid. Why would the President want to corner himself like that?"

Yet in the afterglow of Clinton's speech, the prospects for health care reform looked rosy. On the evening of February 22, a dozen key players, including Dole and Burke, assembled in a small dining room on the first floor of the White House for a working dinner. Clinton held forth at great length on why there could not be incremental reforms without a guarantee of universal coverage and why mandates on employers to provide coverage were essential. Mrs. Clinton said little, which Burke found surprising. As the only congressional staff member present, Burke was seated between White House aides Mack McLarty and Harold Ickes. While they had a pleasant chat, there was no substantive exchange. "The one thing I found notable was that Clinton had seconds of dessert," she says.

Burke talked briefly with Mrs. Clinton at the start of the dinner. Dole, seeing the two women together, remarked that if Hillary and Sheila could work out something, that would be fine with him. White House aides were not sure whether Dole was serious or simply wisecracking. But Mrs. Clinton, in talking with reporters after the event, said, "Senator Dole told me, 'If you and Sheila can agree, I'll vote for the plan.'"

Hillary Rodham Clinton had evolved from a Republican to a liberal Democrat. As a teenager, she had been a cheerleader for Barry Goldwater, the GOP's conservative presidential candidate in 1964. Sheila Burke had made the opposite journey, lingering near the center of the political agenda, where a potential deal might be made. The thought of these two women taking over the deal-making would tantalize people of good will in both parties, but it was never to be.

The good feelings expressed that evening disappeared almost as fast as the desserts. The First Lady and the Other Woman spoke again only occasionally and then not about anything substantive.

Public opinion had not yet begun to turn against the Clinton plan, and White House strategists thought it was too early to cut a deal. They were content to savor the warm expressions of cooperation voiced at the dinner along with the vague pledges from the Republican senators that they, too, wanted universal coverage. For her part, Burke still believed that health care reform would happen and that Republicans needed to get involved. Her thinking influenced Dole, who called Clinton after the dinner and asked, "Can't we try and work this out?" Dole instructed Burke to propose through Clinton's liaison to the Senate, Steve Ricchetti, the possibility of preliminary "framework" talks, the formula that diplomats use to break a deadlock. The White House, fearing a trap, refused.

"There was never an overt no, we don't want to talk to you," says Burke. "But it was clear that there wasn't going to be much in the way of follow-up." The White House, bowing to the Democratic congressional leaders, chose to rely on the House and Senate committees to produce a compromise bill rather than make a premature deal with the Republicans that could cost them the backing of Democratic liberals.

In the late spring of 1994, Dole scribbled a note to Moynihan during a Finance Committee hearing asking if the time was ripe for a compromise. Moynihan never responded, however much he would have liked to. He was roundly criticized in the Democratic Caucus on more than one occasion for failing to defend the Clinton plan. He could barely conceal his disdain for the complicated plan and for the President himself. Burke and O'Donnell, Moynihan's top aide on the Finance Committee, where the health care bill would be amended and brought to the floor or killed, met privately several times to explore a potential deal. Nebraska Sen. Bob Kerrey, a renegade like Moynihan, was prepared to act as a go-between. But for Moynihan to deal directly with Dole would have meant an open break from his party.

Even if Moynihan had been able to negotiate directly with Dole, the moment passed quickly. Dole became an implacable, partisan foe, and health care reform fell victim to political bickering from both sides.

The shift in Dole's attitude from conciliation to confrontation with the White House over health care can be traced to Oliver North's winning the GOP Senate nomination in Virginia in early June of 1994. Dole learned the news over the telephone from Washington as he was traveling to Sarajevo aboard a military plane on a trip that would eventually take him to Normandy for the fiftieth anniversary of the D-Day invasion. Accompanying Dole was Virginia Republican Sen. John Warner, a horse country aristocrat who strongly opposed North's candidacy. With Warner's encouragement, Dole decided to stay neutral in the race. He said on national television that North's nomination "makes it very difficult for some in the Republican Party," and announced that he would meet with Marshall Coleman, the breakaway Republican who planned to run against North as an Independent.

A firestorm within the party forced Dole to reverse himself within twenty-four hours. It was not only conservatives who were angry. Party regulars wanted to regain control of the Senate, and they thought the charismatic North was a winner. Dole called the Rev. Pat Robertson, head of the Christian Coalition, to assure him that he would not oppose North's candidacy. When Dole later campaigned with North, newspaper accounts pointed out how uncomfortable Dole appeared. But he could see the direction that his party was moving, and if he wanted to run for president, he would have to move with it.

Burke also returned from Normandy a changed person. "It sends a message about the party," she said of North's nomination. While observing the anniversary of a historic American military victory in Europe, she and Dole had lost political ground at home. The night before she left on the trip, Burke talked with health care lobbyist Michael Bromberg about the prospects for a Moynihan-Dole bill. They conspired on how Democratic Senator Kerrey might bridge the gap between the two sides. "She was still centrist," says Bromberg. Burke returned home convinced that health care reform could not be achieved in the time that remained in the congressional session. The political obstacles were too great. "Someone read her the riot act," Bromberg concluded. "She has taken a giant leap to the right."

For Republicans bent on regaining control of Congress, any talk of compromise with Clinton and the Democrats made no political sense. The pressure intensified on Republican moderates to forget health care reform and focus on November. Burke was as much a target as her boss. "Haley Barbour worked her over pretty good," says a friend. The Republican Party chairman made several trips to Capitol Hill to encourage Republicans to stand firm against a "bad" Clinton bill. For the nurse who had gone to Washington to do good, and stayed even when some outcomes were bad, this was an agonizing time. Health care was Burke's defining passion, but she had become the consummate staffer. Dole's political survival took precedence.

Not all Republicans believed that health care had to be sacrificed, however. In the end, under duress, Moynihan relinquished control of the issue to "the Mainstream Group," a bipartisan group seeking compromise, informally called "the mainstreamers." Moderate Republican Senators John Chafee, John Danforth, and David Durenberger, who led

the effort, were ostracized by conservative Republicans and derided by
The Wall Street Journal editorial page as "the three blind mice."
Together with a handful of moderate Democrats, they spent the last
weeks of the 103rd Congress in a vain effort to fashion a modest reform
bill that could win bipartisan support.

Burke was excluded from the discussions, which offended her greatly.
The mainstreamers viewed her as Dole's surrogate, and he appeared to
be impeding any progress. Public support had faded for health care
reform, and Republicans had concluded that they could block legislation
without paying a price with voters. "Are you going to get upset if I say
nice things about the Mainstream Group?" lobbyist Michael Bromberg
inquired one day of Burke. "Yes I am," she snapped. Being frozen out by
the mainstreamers, the very people she identifies most with ideologically, irrevocably altered Burke's attitude about what could be accom-
plished in the deteriorating political climate. "She was bound to get
revenge," says a friend.

The Congress ended its session with Republicans blocking legislation
on all fronts and creating gridlock for which the Democrats—the party
controlling the White House and Congress—were ultimately blamed.

Dole was on the road nonstop that fall campaigning around the country
for Republicans. Burke rarely traveled, but the tension of managing the
congressional calendar and balancing Dole's presidential aspirations
against an increasingly restive right wing had taken its toll. Her resistance weakened by near-exhaustion, she was felled by colds and the flu.
She spent a week in Washington's Georgetown University Hospital with
a rare staph infection that swelled her head and caused her skin to peel.
The infection had come on suddenly, and when Dole reached her by
phone in her hospital room, the doctors had not yet been able to diag-
nose the malady. "I can arrange for a plane," Dole said anxiously. "I'll
have you to the Mayo Clinic this afternoon." The man standing in the
way of basic health care for millions of Americans thought nothing of
ordering up a plane to insure that his aide got the very best care.

"Senator, I'm really fine," Burke replied calmly. She was hooked up to
an intravenous tube and surrounded by eight physicians. "I'm a diagnos-
tic dilemma," she said, keeping her voice even and reassuring, "but I
don't need to go to the Mayo Clinic."

Soon after, Burke's husband, David, moved back home full-time, having taken a job in the Washington area. His seven-year commute was over,
and he was now available during the week to help shoulder the burden of
raising three children. David Chew, like his wife, has made a career out of

cultivating a passion for anonymity. During the Reagan administration he was one of a handful of aides working for chief of staff Don Regan that the press dubbed "the mice." They earned the name after one of them was quoted saying, "We have no known opinions of our own."

After recovering from the infection, Burke began contingency planning in the event the Republicans won a majority in the November election. She talked to aides of former Senate Majority Leader Howard Baker about the mechanics of the transition of power. She wrote to Republican senators asking them what they would select as their top three issues for the next Congress. The answers were predictable: Welfare reform, regulatory relief, and a balanced budget topped the list. She established working groups around the key issue areas, but the planning never approached the hundred-day blitz that Gingrich was planning for the House.

Having succeeded Baker as Majority Leader in January 1985, Dole knew that power in the Senate is not concentrated in the leader the way it is in the House. Gingrich could insure Republicans' loyalty to his agenda by promising or withholding committee chairmanships. In the Senate, chairmanships had always been decided by seniority, and Dole would not tamper with that tradition.

Dole spent election night monitoring the returns on television in his office. Burke had arranged for Mexican food to be brought in, and staffers stood around eating off plastic plates, cheering and chanting, *"Tsu-na-mi! Tsu-na-mi,"* as the dimensions of the Republican tidal wave became evident. Dole's pet schnauzer, Leader, roamed underfoot. Whenever results from Kansas popped up, a staffer yelled for quiet and Dole turned his attention toward the screen. When one of the news anchors reported that Democrat Dan Glickman, chairman of the Intelligence Committee and a member of the Kansas delegation since 1977, was losing to a political unknown, Dole shook his head in amazement. "Wouldn't that be something if old Glicky lost?" he said quietly.

Burke stood in the doorway nodding agreement. Like her boss, she is of the old school in American politics, where ideology often takes a back seat to personal relationships, and a Republican can feel a twinge of sadness when a Democrat he has known for years is rudely ejected from office.

By early evening, when it was established that the Republicans had retaken the Senate, Dole asked Burke to call Democratic Majority Leader George Mitchell's office and arrange for them to get together. Mitchell's assistant proposed her boss go to Dole's office and offer congratulations. But Dole wanted to be gracious in victory, and insisted that he go to Mitchell's office instead. He found Mitchell in a buoyant mood despite the Democrats' dismal showing. "Thank God you won by a big margin,"

Mitchell exclaimed, smiling broadly and extending his hand. "If you'd only won by one seat, and I'd had to step down, I would have caught hell."

Mitchell had announced months earlier that he was leaving the Senate. The decision shocked many of his colleagues who could not believe a man in the prime of his professional life would give up such a powerful job, especially after having finally gotten a Democrat in the White House. But grinding out narrow victories for Clinton was not Mitchell's idea of fun. His Maine seat was one of eight Republican pickups that night. Mitchell was popular enough to have been reelected, but his single seat would not have made the difference.

After the election, Republican and Democratic staffers staged a musical parody of health care reform, the issue that had consumed many of their lives for the past year, as entertainment at the farewell party for Minnesota Sen. David Durenberger, one of the Republican mainstreamers. Burke was not present, but a Burke look-alike stormed onto the stage, hands on hips, to confront a staffer coiffed to look like Hillary Rodham Clinton. To the tune from the musical *Grease* "Look at Me, I'm Sandra Dee," the Hillary character launched into song.

> Look at me, I'm Hillary,
> Lousy with authority.
> Go to the Hill and they'll pass my bill,
> They must—I'm Hillary.

Unfazed, the Burke character issued a rejoinder.

> Watch it, hey, I'm Sheila Burke;
> We don't like this piece of work.
> It don't come across, 'cause the Demos have lost
> The power to Sheila Burke.

Staffers roared with delight at the body language between the two powerful women. When the staffer playing Burke referred disdainfully to Mrs. Clinton as "Ms. Number Two," those in attendance took it to mean behind Burke, not the President.

Yet Burke was out of step with much of her party. The 1994 election confirmed the rise of the radical right. Gingrich, not Dole, was the most important Republican in Washington. Dole was running for president, but his candidacy did not capture the revolutionary spirit of the newly empowered Republican Party. The intellectual center had shifted to the House Republicans, along with the energy for change.

To boost his credibility with the Right, Dole hired two defeated conservative candidates for Congress straight from the campaign trail and put them in top jobs. Burke referred to them as "the silver medalists." They were assigned to deal with the more conservative Republican members of the Senate, some of whom did not trust Burke.

The new breed of Republican senators demanded leadership that was more in tune with Gingrich's scorched-earth style. An early indication of Dole's vulnerability was the race for whip, the number-two slot for the Republicans and the party's chief vote-counter. Dole furiously lobbied members to retain his personal favorite, Wyoming Sen. Alan Simpson, a pro-choice moderate with a caustic country wit. Burke personally spoke with a number of senators to seek their votes. It was a major blow when Simpson lost by a single vote to Mississippi Sen. Trent Lott, an ally of Texas Sen. Phil Gramm, one of Dole's rivals for the 1996 Republican nomination. Lott had the allegiance of the younger and more aggressively conservative members, who were not enamored of Dole, and who viewed Burke with suspicion and even hostility. Burke downplayed speculation that she could not get along with Lott. "I assume I can work with Lott, I mean, that's my job," she protested when asked about the tension between them and their staffs.

Burke's qualms about the newly enfranchised right wing prompted her to offer to resign after the election. "If the conservatives had their choice, I wouldn't be at the top of the list," she told Dole. He dismissed her concerns about ideology, as she knew he would, so she tried a different approach. "It may not just be that you want a conservative but, you know, you've been looking at my face for seventeen years, maybe it's time for a change?" She had offered to resign before, believing that is the honorable thing for staff to do when there is a new political environment. Dole would not hear of her leaving.

There were rumors when Dole appointed Burke as Secretary of the Senate, a plum administrative job, that he was easing her out of the political line of fire. But the appointment as Secretary of the Senate was only temporary until Dole could find a permanent replacement, and Burke did not give up her place at Dole's side. Instead, she squeezed in her new duties by spending part of each day in the historic secretary's office in the Capitol. A plaque on the wall notes that Sen. John F. Kennedy occupied the office, S-208, from the time he was elected president until the inaugural. A huge cherry wood cabinet along one wall that looks like a clothes closet is, in fact, a toilet installed at the behest of Democratic Sen. Robert Byrd, who used the office when he was majority leader.

The promotion raised Burke's salary from $102,000 as chief of staff to a little over $132,000. By agreeing to fill the job temporarily after Dole's

first choice, a former Secretary of the Navy, turned it down, Burke
became the twenty-seventh person in the prestigious position. It meant
she was responsible, in addition to all her other duties, for running the
institution of the Senate, overseeing everything from the parliamentari-
ans to the operating budget. It is a fairly straightforward, apolitical job.
The hours are shorter, the pay is better, and doing the secretary's job
would mean fewer personal conflicts for Burke. But when Dole offered
it to her, she replied without hesitation that her "strong preference" was
to stay on as his chief of staff. "Fine," he said.

On Burke's last day as secretary, June 7, 1995, she returned calls, one
after another, including one from her husband. Daniel, age seven,
answered the phone. "Tell daddy I returned his call," Burke told the boy.
But this was not just another obligation fulfilled, another pink slip to
throw away. A look of consternation clouded Burke's face. "I can't,
because we're going to be in late tonight," she said patiently. A pause.
"Why? I don't know," she responded, trying to comfort her unhappy son.
"I know, sweetie . . . I know. . . ."

She hung up the phone, a mother's guilt painted on her face. "He's
pissed," she said, her normal reserve shattered by the conversation. "He
said, 'Why don't you quit that stupid job and come home?'"

Burke rationalizes the increased pressure on her private life by telling
herself it is a once-in-a-lifetime opportunity "to be this close to somebody who is running for president." She has given most of her adult life
to working for Dole, and now that he is at the pinnacle of his career she
does not want to desert him—for her sake as well as his. When Dole last
ran for president in 1988, Burke was pregnant and on the sidelines. She
delivered Daniel a month before George Bush knocked Dole from contention in New Hampshire.

In the months leading up to the 1996 primaries, Dole would need
Burke. His last run for the presidency would surely fail if he could not
simultaneously guide the Senate through one of the most dramatic periods of change in American history. He could trust Burke to run things
while he was off campaigning. Complicating Dole's dual life was the fact
that three other senators—Phil Gramm of Texas, Richard Lugar of Indiana, and Arlen Specter of Pennsylvania—were challenging him for the
Republican nomination. Only Gramm, who had money to promote his
angry populist platform, was a real contender, but the proliferation of
candidates threatened Republican unity. The conventional wisdom was
that the balky and individualistic Senate would become the black hole
for the House Republican Contract, and conservatives would blame
Dole for thwarting their revolution.

Dole had to worry about being upstaged by Gingrich and his Contract, a brilliant marketing tool for the new Republican House, and a millstone for Dole. Political analysts speculated whether the two men from different generations and perspectives could find common ground. Their first formal meeting after the election, which *Time* magazine had captured in the photograph taken on "Dole's Beach," was to send the public message that Dole and Gingrich were a team. But after the photographers and reporters were ushered out, Dole underscored his independence, says Burke, "to make sure that there was no confusion about the fact that the Contract doesn't really govern what *we* do."

The Senate would not be a rubber stamp for the House. The two bodies are different, with rhythms of their own. The House, where members are elected from districts having equal numbers of people to two-year terms every other year, is closer to the shifting passions of the people, whereas the Senate, whose members are elected statewide to staggered six-year terms, is deliberative, even dilatory. The slim majority that Republicans held in the Senate meant that Dole had to accommodate the moderates. Having first gained national attention in 1976 as a partisan slasher when he was Gerald Ford's running mate, Dole now was now telling Gingrich to cool down, take it easy. He could not get over the irony, and would often marvel, "I am now the rational voice of the Republican Party."

The rules defining and restricting debate in the House meant Gingrich could keep his party's promise to vote on all ten items in the Contract within a hundred days. In the Senate, however, a single member can delay a bill indefinitely by putting a "hold" on it, or by offering amendment after amendment to forestall a vote or even lead a filibuster that requires a super-majority of sixty votes to stop. The Senate, says Burke, is "the knights of the roundtable with no King Arthur."

Rigid seniority rules govern the way the Senate does business as well. When Gingrich put House freshmen on key committees, the freshmen class of senators appealed to Dole that its members also be allowed to short-circuit the seniority process, and sit on major committees like Finance, Appropriations, and Armed Services. Dole dutifully took the idea to his fellow Republicans, who reacted angrily. "I've been here for twelve years, and I've waited to get on the Finance Committee for twelve years, and, goddamn it, I'm not going to have you jump over me with some freshman," roared one senior Republican. "They can wait twelve years, too." The freshmen felt Dole would not push hard enough for the conservative agenda. Dole had been through enough battles to know that the really tough fights are won over time, not in a hundred days. He knew he would only be successful if he could keep the GOP majority together on the difficult votes that lay ahead.

Burke's soothing, take-charge manner reassured Dole the way a nurse would an anxious patient. "Let me sit down with everybody and figure out where we are in terms of the substance," she told him one afternoon in December 1994 when he called from out of town worried about a piece of legislation. "Then I'll give you a list of what we've got going and make sure you're comfortable with it."

Dole was in Boston where his wife, Elizabeth, had entered the hospital for an operation to clean out a blocked artery in her neck. Normally associated with high cholesterol, Mrs. Dole's condition was evidently the result of a genetic predisposition. Burke had seen to everything, from tracking down the best cardiologists and vascular surgeons to recommending that the Doles have dinner at the Union Oyster House in Boston. When the senator phoned with an update on his wife's medical condition and to report how much she had enjoyed her final meal before checking into the hospital, Burke responded in mock horror, "Oh, my God, tell her her cholesterol levels will skyrocket."

Burke was at a Senate Finance Committee retreat on the Eastern Shore of Maryland in March 1995 when she learned by reading the front page of *The New York Times* that Dole had promised the National Rifle Association that he would work to repeal the assault weapons ban passed by the previous Congress. She had been up late the night before playing billiards and relaxing with her colleagues, and was having breakfast at the time with Senator Moynihan and his top aide, Lawrence O'Donnell. "She shook her head, there was a slight grimace," says O'Donnell, adding that this minimal sign of displeasure was "a big deal" for those accustomed to reading Burke's moods. Burke is such a controlled personality that even a raised eyebrow is taken seriously by those who know her. Campaign aides had allowed Dole to make the pledge without running it by Burke, probably because they knew she would object. "I thought that was under control," she muttered at the breakfast table, which suggested this was not the first time the campaign types had kept her out of the loop.

Dole's campaign strategy in the early months required a series of shifts to the right. He called for a review of affirmative action laws with an eye to eliminating them, despite having been a friend of such programs in the past. He preached against violence and loveless sex in movies, despite not having seen the films he denounced. He returned a campaign contribution from the Log Cabin Republicans, a gay group.

And after conservative Christians said the minister in the church he attended in Washington was too liberal, he changed his place of worship. Siding with the NRA on assault weapons was just another of the rightward gestures.

Burke opposed reopening the fight over assault weapons and, even more than that, she hated being surprised. "He had stated early that he didn't think the votes were there for repeal, and that it wasn't going to be a high priority," she said. "I didn't think it made sense then to come back and say the opposite. I don't think it did him any good."

Much was made of the fact that Dole's turnaround on the ban happened while Burke was away at the Senate Finance Committee retreat. The idea that Dole's campaign strategists would not have dared to propose cozying up to the NRA in Burke's presence fed an evolving scenario that Burke was the obstacle to a more conservative Dole. "I'm not sure if it would have made any difference if I'd been there," said Burke. "Would I have argued against it? I might have. He knew that I didn't think it was a great idea."

Add to the list of things the right wing finds offensive about Burke the fact that she favors at least some gun control despite having grown up with guns. She remembers family vacations in Montana that were spent shooting tin cans and hunting. "So it's not that I am averse to hunters and legitimate sports activities. But I also find it hard to argue that assault weapons are needed by sportsmen. And I think that anything we can do to get those kinds of weapons that are used primarily against people off the streets makes perfect sense to me." The debate on whether to ban assault weapons ended abruptly with the bombing on April 19, 1995, of the federal building in Oklahoma City. The subsequent arrest of suspects with links to armed citizen militias postponed for a year any further discussion of undoing the ban on assault weapons.

A bigger test loomed for Dole to prove his ideological manhood. The House had passed the balanced budget amendment by a substantial margin, shifting the spotlight to the Senate, where the GOP fell a single vote short. Conservatives wanted Dole to punish the party's one holdout, moderate Oregon Sen. Mark Hatfield, by stripping him of his committee chairmanship. Dole, not wanting to alienate a fellow Republican whose vote he would need on other occasions, stuck by Hatfield. Dole had to find some other way quickly to demonstrate his toughness and quiet the furor over Hatfield's defection. The White House inadvertently gave Dole just the issue he needed.

When Clinton nominated Dr. Henry Foster as surgeon general, the Right demanded that Dole oppose the nomination, and, this time, Dole obliged. Foster, an African-American obstetrician, ran a successful teen pregnancy prevention program in North Carolina and had been designated one of President Bush's "Points of Light." But over his thirty-year career, he had also performed abortions. Exactly how many became an issue. When Foster offered one number at first, then a larger number later, anti-abortion Republicans assailed his credibility, although it was media savvy Foster was lacking, not honesty. "Anyone with a brain knows that an Ob/Gyn cannot survive training without confronting those issues," said Burke. "And so you would have thought they would have anticipated that kind of question and thought it through."

The White House bungling that led to Foster's defeat was unthinkable to Burke, who saw it as sloppy staff work. Administration aides failed to understand the power of the abortion issue, and that failure had compromised Clinton. "If Dole were president and this kind of thing occurred, I would have fired everybody in sight," she said. "This doesn't happen in a professional operation, it just doesn't."

Burke's hypothetical reference to managing the White House staff raised the obvious question: Does she ever think of being chief of staff to a President Dole? "No, no," she protests. Pointing out that she could be the first woman to hold the job only evokes a more violent reaction. "No, no, no, no, no. . . . I wouldn't waste three minutes thinking about it."

In disputing the proposition that she would make an ideal chief of staff, Burke reflects the selflessness of the loyal staffer. She seems to have convinced even herself that she is not the logical choice for the top staff job should Dole win the White House. "There are other people who are close to him who don't present the same problem with conservatives that I would present," she says, her tone coldly analytical. "You don't need your chief of staff to be a lightning rod."

During the late summer and early fall of 1994, Republicans battled among themselves over the size of the tax cut that Gingrich had called "the crown jewel" of the Contract. House Republicans had voted for $350 billion over seven years, a sum that Senate moderates thought profligate while government spending on popular programs like Medicare was being substantially reduced. It was up to Dole and Gingrich to reconcile the two opposing views, and to settle on a number everybody could live with. Conservatives watched Burke closely during these negotiations, and strongly objected when she suggested they first decide the funding levels for Medicare and welfare, programs targeted for cuts, or "savings," and leave the tax-cut discussion for last. Framing the debate in that fashion would help protect the social safety net. "That way she gets what she wants, and whatever is left would be the tax cut," said one of the participants.

After some heated conversation, the tax cuts were moved up on the agenda. Silence fell around the table. Neither Dole nor Gingrich wanted to go first in offering a compromise figure. Finally, Republican chairman Haley Barbour, who had been regularly attending these sessions in the name of party unity, offered a number: $242 billion, he said. Dole and Gingrich quickly settled on $245 billion, more than Burke would have liked. But she said nothing. Later, they all laughed about how it took the Republican party chairman to get them to the point where they could make progress. The $245 billion would become the party's bloody shirt, the symbol of the House freshman class's fervor. Barbour, however, had gotten himself into some trouble. Having outmaneuvered Burke, and by implication Dole, he would be excluded for a time from budget meetings.

Dole jokes that Burke's nurse's training in a psychiatric unit prepared her well for the Senate. Part of her job is psyching out the opposition, and negotiating accordingly. Burke is a crafty inside player. On every piece of legislation, she analyzes the policy and the politics, running a vote count in her head to determine what is possible. Of the famous dance team Astaire and Rogers, it was said that Ginger Rogers executed all the moves that Fred Astaire did, only backwards and wearing high heels. So it is with Dole and Burke. He leads, but only because she has mastered all the tricky steps of the legislative dance. She does everything the Majority Leader does except speak out on the Senate floor and cast a vote.

Burke's mission—to pass legislation and make government work— puts her at odds with conservative firebrands who value ideological purity above coalition-building. Burke begins almost every negotiation with the question, "Where's the middle?" That attitude waves a red flag in the face of bullish conservatives, who would rather score political points than compromise. "We can have the issue"—a way of stating the political value of being on the losing side—is a phrase that never passes Burke's lips. True partisans of the left and right would rather beat up on the opposition and "have the issue" than settle on something that will take their issue off the agenda. Dole has run three highly partisan campaigns for national office, yet Burke is able to operate in a way that is grounded more in policy than politics. "If you asked Sheila how many electoral votes there are in California, she probably couldn't tell you— and what's more, she wouldn't care," says Ron Klain, who worked opposite Burke as a top adviser to Democratic Minority Leader Tom Daschle.

How Burke handled welfare reform demonstrated her strengths and weaknesses as a legislative tactician. While Dole was off campaigning in Iowa and New Hampshire in 1995, Burke hammered out a deal on reforming welfare. But she failed to take the Right seriously enough. She assumed that mutterings of opposition from a handful of conservative senators were orchestrated by Phil Gramm to further his presidential ambition. Working with the moderates, she pulled together a welfare bill that was less severe than the one the House had passed. But the Right rebelled.

The controversy centered on provisions discouraging out-of-wedlock births. To Burke, it was a simple matter. If the Republicans remained true to their philosophy of returning power to the states, the federal government had no right to attach strings telling the states they should end welfare for unwed teenage mothers, as conservatives were demanding. She even had moral backing for her position. The National Conference of Catholic Bishops and the National Right to Life Committee opposed such anti-illegitimacy provisions, fearing they would lead to more abortions.

Burke thought the logic was so compelling that, once she explained it, critics would see it her way and the controversy would be over. The test came on the afternoon of June 21, 1995, when representatives from several conservative groups assembled in Burke's office on the second floor of the Capitol to raise their objections in person. Burke was running late, so Nelson Rockefeller, Jr., an aide to Dole who works on welfare issues and whose lineage evokes the brand of Republicanism that conservatives despise, was briefing them when Burke strode in. She settled in behind her desk and proceeded to coolly lay out the federalist argument against imposing mandates on the states, and the constraints that Dole faced on the left and the right in assembling a winning coalition.

For these activists, however, Burke's logic sounded a lot like what they heard from Republicans when Democrats controlled the Senate. The GOP was in charge now, and conservatives wanted more. Andrea Sheldon of the Traditional Values Coalition, which claims to represent 31,000 churches, spoke up first. "You know, Sheila, we represent real people. . . ."

"I was barely able to finish, and Sheila lost it," recalls Sheldon. "She just started yelling, 'Do you think I'm not a real person? I don't talk to real people?'"

Burke felt deeply insulted. "Are you trying to tell me that because I am a staff person that I don't talk to real people and have no concern about these issues? I've been a nurse, I've been in practice, I have children, I am with real people every day," she declared, the blood rushing to her cheeks and her voice rising with anger.

But what about her opposition to language in the proposed welfare reform bill calling marriage *the* foundation of society?

"I don't have a problem with marriage," Burke exclaimed, mystified at such an interpretation. She explained that it was actually an aide to Senator Packwood who had said in a staff meeting that calling marriage *the* foundation suggested that people who were not married, such as widows, widowers, and single people, were not important parts of society. "I don't think that was the message that people were trying to send," she said. And so *the* was changed to *a*, as in "Marriage is *a* foundation of society."

Burke thought the battle over a single syllable absurd on the face of it, and her exasperation showed. But conservatives saw it as a symbol of how she systematically undercuts what they care about, and as proof that she was trying to undermine the more radical reform bill that the House had drafted. The House-passed version of welfare reform took away benefits for unwed teens and had a "family cap," which ended additional benefits for children born to mothers on welfare.

"This is not about me," Burke pleaded. "There are strong differences of opinion among Republicans on these issues, and what we try to do in these staff discussions is lay out all the options for the members. I don't have a secret plan."

She explained that as a staff person, it was her job to figure out how to build a coalition between moderates and conservatives, not to satisfy one wing of the party over the other or to advance her personal views, whatever they might be. As she spoke she could see Robert Rector of the Heritage Foundation, a conservative think tank, staring at her with an expression of open disgust.

"Mr. Rector, don't give me that look," she snapped.

Conservative columnist Robert Novak would later write that Burke had "insulted" a number of organizations that represent the Christian Right. "I would challenge who was insulted by whom," Burke observed dryly.

The way Burke admonished Rector infuriated his colleagues. "That is what you say to your little four-year-old who's misbehaving," Andrea Sheldon said. Burke agrees she would have been better off keeping her mouth shut, but Rector's attitude toward her struck a nerve. Asked about it days later, she was still seething. "I was trying to explain how the staff thing worked, and he looked at me like I'd just lied through my teeth. He was very hostile, and sort of snickering. And I thought, you know, I'm not going to sit here and take this shit. I've been here too long. I mean, don't give me this crap. I'm not some eighteen-year-old staff person. I've never walked into a group where there was just this wall of animosity."

What began as an effort to close the gap between Burke and conservatives in the party ended up widening it instead. Privately Burke calls these activists "the wing-nuts." They are so paranoid, she told a friend, that they hold against her the fact that she is a nurse, "like I was a communist in my youth."

Conservatives leaked word of the contentious meeting to Novak, who they knew would be sympathetic to their cause. Five days later on June 26, 1995, under the heading "Sen. Dole's Personnel Problem," Novak portrayed Burke as the ringleader of a network of moderate staffers determined to block conservative reforms. "In an age in which the Senate's appointed mandarinate may be more influential than its elected masters, Burke is a power in the Senate," he wrote, describing how Burke "operated with stealth" in pushing out of the Senate Finance Committee a welfare reform bill that failed to address illegitimacy. When Novak called Burke before publication for her response, he volunteered that his source for the story was North Carolina Sen. Lauch Faircloth, a freshman legislator, a staunch conservative, and a backer of Dole for the Republican presidential nomination.

After the column appeared, an angry Burke called Faircloth's top staffer to point out that a Packwood aide, not she, had initially raised concern about the statement on marriage, and that she had been unfairly maligned. "And I said, 'You better get my point: A, you don't discuss these things with the press, and B, you don't take cheap shots at people.'" For months thereafter, Burke would not speak with Faircloth's staff. The conservative freshman was the only Republican to vote against welfare reform when it passed the Senate, eighty-seven to twelve, on September 19, 1995.

Dole himself had to step in to resolve the impasse with conservatives over welfare reform. The Right wanted government-imposed restraints on illegitimacy, including banning extra benefits for welfare mothers who bear additional children, but did not want to do anything that might encourage poor women to have abortions. Dealing with Dole directly, and with Burke on the sidelines, they agreed on a formula that would allow these mothers to receive government vouchers that could be redeemed for essential items like diapers and baby formula. (The entire issue became moot later in the year when President Clinton vetoed the Republican welfare reform bill.)

Burke felt betrayed by her fellow staffers, not only in Faircloth's office but throughout the conservative network in the Senate, and it had a chilling effect on the way she did her job. This was a new phenomenon where partisan staffers were not interested in splitting the difference, in finding the middle ground between John Chafee on the left and Phil Gramm on the right. This breed of GOP staffers who called themselves revolutionaries had violated the confidences among top staff that to professionals like Burke are as sacred as lawyer-client privilege. "I'm not suspicious by nature," she said, "but I find myself going into these meetings being very reluctant to engage people in honest discourse about issues unless I know everybody in the room, and know exactly who they are."

The Novak column launched the Right's attack on Burke through the media. Other opinion pieces by conservatives followed— Paul Weyrich in *The Washington Times,* and John Fund in *The Wall Street Journal*— which in turn fanned news stories in other newspapers and ultimately a ten-column piece in *Time* magazine. Conservatives wanted Burke out of the way before she could do any more damage to their agenda. The Traditional Values Coalition put out a press release that said, "If the American people like Hillary Clinton, they will love Sheila Burke."

The conservatives' real target was Dole, who needed the support of his party's right wing in the upcoming presidential primaries. Dole's ideological purity had always been suspect. Raised in a Democratic family, he had decided to run for office as a Republican mainly because Kansas was a two-to-one Republican state, and the GOP offered a more promising career path. Dole had been in Congress for thirty-four years, longer than every other Republican except South Carolina's Senator Thurmond, who was over ninety years old. A consummate insider, Dole was an unlikely standard-bearer for the new generation of Republicans who had stormed the Capitol. Although he was the front-runner for the GOP's presidential nomination in 1996, there was little enthusiasm for his candidacy among the true believers who saw Gingrich, not Dole, as the one to carry forward the mantle of Ronald Reagan's revolution. Resisting pressure from the House to go along with the Contract, Dole reminded the zealous GOPers, "I am not named Newt Dole."

If conservatives were stuck with Dole, then keeping the heat on Burke would help insure Dole's journey rightward. "I wanted to send a warning shot across the bow so that Senator Dole would realize if he didn't get more involved that conservatives might be coming after him next," said the Family Research Council's Gary Bauer. Dole evidently got the message. Shortly after Bauer was quoted in Novak's column wondering ominously "just what seat Sheila Burke would have" in a Dole White House, he received a call from Dole's office. The senator wanted Bauer's help in preparing a speech attacking Hollywood's family values.

Dole would complain privately that satisfying Bauer and his buddies was impossible, that they did not understand the nature of legislating, which inevitably involved compromise. Gingrich had sprung from that same school, Dole reminded himself. As a Republican backbencher in the House, Gingrich had called Dole "the tax collector for the welfare state" because he had supported bipartisan legislative compromises that resulted in increased taxes. What separates Dole from latter-day conservatives is that he believes the federal government can be a positive force. Dole is a legislative mechanic who works to fine tune government rather than dismantle it. After Gingrich became Speaker, he described Dole a bit more charitably as a "pre–Ronald Reagan Republican."

Not even Reagan himself could please the most ardent conservatives, and he privately called them "professional bitchers." They had preferred the conservatism of Texas Gov. John Connally and Illinois Rep. Phil Crane over Reagan in the 1980 primary, and once Reagan was in office, they found fault with virtually everything he did. A Reagan aide remembers how, with time running out on the President's second term, conservatives wanted him to take military action to aid the rebel contras in Nicaragua. Reagan had no intention of sending the marines to Managua, but as a courtesy agreed to meet with his harshest conservative critics and hear them out. When Reagan entered the Roosevelt Room for the meeting, every one of these conservatives who today hold up Reagan as their hero remained seated. It was the first time in the aide's memory that visitors had shown such disrespect to the President.

Some of the archconservatives who met with Reagan that day were at the podium for a news conference in November 1995 to announce they would actively oppose Colin Powell, the former Chairman of the Joint Chiefs of Staff, should he seek the Republican nomination for president. Powell was wildly popular with the public, and had taken centrist positions on a number of issues, including abortion and affirmative action. Conservatives dismissed him as "Bill Clinton with ribbons."

Until recently, these professional conservatives represented a minority within the Republican Party. But with the rise of the Christian Right, and the noisy assertion of the Republican freshmen, the radical Right had substantially increased its influence in Congress.

Paul Weyrich, head of the Free Congress Foundation and the acknowledged kingpin of the conservative movement, keeps a replica of the sword of Genghis Khan on the wall to the left of his desk, so that he can tell visitors, "I am to the right of Genghis Khan." Weyrich is proud that he took the first shot at Burke, "when most people didn't know who she was." In the Winter 1995 *Policy Review* quarterly published by the

Heritage Foundation, leading conservatives were asked to suggest what each of the presidential prospective candidates had to do to win more conservative support. Weyrich's advice to Dole was, "Fire Sheila Burke . . . from your Senate staff and pledge that [she] will not be hired, directly or indirectly, by a future Dole administration." After the article appeared, Weyrich saw Dole at a political function for conservatives, and Dole told him that Burke had thought better about coming after reading his comment. "You understand, she takes this stuff personally," Dole said, adding with a laugh, "I don't."

The source of the friction between Burke and conservatives is so ancient and tribal in nature that, "You'd have to go back to the days of Julius Caesar to see who drew the first blood," laughs Bert Pines, a co-founder with Weyrich of National Empowerment Television, the conservatives' cable network. She was at Dole's side throughout the 1980s when he was the principal Republican negotiator on a series of budget bills that raised taxes no fewer than thirteen times. "I was involved in every one of those bills," says Burke. Weyrich cites the 1985 crime bill and the 1988 welfare reform bill as examples where "the real issues that separate the men from the boys were taken out of the bills." In other words, he blames Burke for softening the hard-right edges of the legislation and making the bills less punitive even if such compromise was required to get legislation enacted.

The argument that Burke acted on Dole's behalf, or that such concessions were necessary to gain a majority, does not impress a purist like Weyrich. He thinks Burke is manipulating Dole to get what she wants. "Dole is about passing things—he's not about fighting good fights or changing the country in the Gingrichian sense," Weyrich says. "He's about passing things. He likes to legislate. The magic to get Bob Dole's attention is to say, 'You don't have the votes for this, but you could get them if you do such and such.'" Weyrich is correct up to a point, that Burke pushes Dole toward common ground. But what conservatives sometimes fail to take into account is that Dole, at heart, is a raging moderate passing as a conservative.

Assailing a staffer when the real target is the staffer's boss is Washington sport. Republican strategist William Kristol calls it "Groverism," in honor of the right-wing, anti-tax activist Grover Norquist, who led the charge against Reagan aides Jim Baker and Richard Darman. The tactic is often counterproductive. Attitudes harden and the besieged staffers guard the palace gates all the more against intruders. "What you have to do to get Bob Dole to do the right thing is to get over her dead body," grumbles Weyrich.

The Right resents having to go through Burke to see Dole. Weyrich pointedly refuses to return her phone calls, says Burke. When Weyrich denied that, she corrected herself. "The call back was he had no interest in talking with me. He'd wait until the leader was available." When Gary Bauer of the Family Research Council, a Christian Right lobby, learned that a meeting scheduled by Dole's office would be with Burke, not Dole, he said that he would send a staff assistant rather than attend himself. "Her reaction to that was to cancel the meeting," says Bauer. "So she can be pretty bold. I'm not a senator, but I have staff members who deal with these things for me."

On the one hand, conservatives elevate Burke as the all-powerful staffer controlling every step Dole takes. Then they turn around and denigrate her as a functionary so lowly that to meet with her is a waste of their time.

The gender issue, bubbling just beneath the surface, emerged first in Novak's column with a reference to Burke's "militant feminism." Weyrich followed with a column in *The Washington Times* summing up Burke's alleged evil influence on Dole: "She is a feminist who has mastered the art of manipulating the Senate majority leader. Men of his generation don't know how to handle aggressive women." An angry Senate Republican female aide countered, "The only thing they hate more than liberals is women. It's so sexist—the notion that this mythical woman is controlling the malleable, pathetic man. This is the raging anti-feminism of the right wing. They're little boys."

Burke was flabbergasted at being labeled a feminist. "I would never describe myself that way," she said. "I don't know what you're supposed to be if you're a feminist, but I'm good at what I do, and I would be good if I were a male or a female." She conceded that branding her a feminist just might turn her into one. "If I were a male in this job, would I be getting the same kind of grief? My sense is not. And I would never have said that a year ago. It would never have occurred to me. But this sort of talk—'She's an arrogant feminist who controls men, and men over fifty can't deal with aggressive females'—what is this bullshit? Does that mean if I were a forty-four-year-old male that they would suggest that a seventy-year-old male couldn't deal with aggressive males?" It was a defining moment for Burke, who had never before felt vulnerable professionally because she was a woman. After all, she had a string of firsts after her name. Nobody could keep her from achieving. "Maybe it comes from being an only child or from having strong parents. I've just always felt very secure about what I did."

The sustained personal attacks made Burke think seriously about leaving the Senate, though she hated the thought of giving her critics the sat-isfaction. "There's a part of me that doesn't have any interest in giving them the pleasure of watching me walk out the door. I have no reason to slink out the door," she said defiantly, then added, "There's another part of me that says, I've done this for eighteen years. I can do something else with my life. I don't need to go home every night, you know, exhausted, spend-ing eighteen hours a day. I can do something else and be happy. These jobs are stressful. I'm being blamed for having done a good job at what I do, and in terms that are really unfair. The name calling. This feminist stuff."

On July 13, 1995, a rumor swept Washington newsrooms that Burke had submitted her resignation. Burke's friend, lobbyist Michael Bromberg, said it would be a good move for her to turn in her resignation "so Dole could turn it down and send these people a signal." Indeed, a *Washington Post* editorial said that the assault on Burke had reached the point where Dole's reaction would be a measure of his character. The implication was that if Dole cut her loose, it would indicate pandering to the Right by a candidate with neither core convictions nor loyalty.

Burke denied having formally submitted her resignation, but said that if she became a liability to her boss, she would leave. The rumor of her quitting was stoked by Senator Faircloth, who was still smoldering over the way Burke had handled the welfare reform bill. Faircloth claimed that in a private conversation with Dole, the Republican leader revealed that Burke had come to him and said, "If I'm a problem, I'll leave." Fair-cloth told several leading conservatives, including Weyrich, that he responded, "Well, you better tell her to leave."

Dole deflected criticism the way he usually does, by making jokes. Asked in a Florida town meeting how he could tolerate having liberal Democrats like Burke on his staff, Dole cracked, "Half the people in this room used to be Democrats." When he returned to Washington, he told Burke she had better name identification in Florida than Lamar Alexan-der, one of his rivals for the Republican presidential nomination. Dole's view was that the attacks on Burke were really about him. "If it's not you, it's the dog," he muttered.

The stories were hard on Burke personally. Not since Roy Cohn was under fire for being the right hand of red-baiting Sen. Joseph McCarthy had a Senate staffer received such sustained press attention. Gazing at the portrait in her office of Edith Nourse Rogers, a Republican member of the House from 1925 to 1960 who wrote legislation creating the Women's Army Corps and the GI Bill of Rights, Burke groaned. "Edith, poor Edith. I'm sure she wishes she were anywhere but here. She must be looking down on this mess thinking, yuck." Propped on a nearby chair was a stuffed teddy bear sent by a school chum so that "when it gets really lonely, there'll be someone to hug."

An article in the conservative *National Review* pointedly referred to her throughout as "Mrs. Burke," despite the fact that Burke is her maiden name and that she does not use her husband's surname. "I'm glad my kids aren't old enough to read some of this stuff," she said. "Every time I pick up a paper now I just wince waiting to see what's in there." When a well-meaning colleague suggested she consider appearing on National Empowerment Television as a gesture of goodwill toward the Right, she gasped, "No, God no." The thought of mounting a public relations offensive on her own behalf was repugnant, and she kept reminding herself that the criticism was not really about her. "If I weren't working for Dole, nobody would give a damn what I did or who I spoke to or how I did my job," she said.

A groundswell of quiet support developed. Moderate staffers donned buttons to declare themselves "Raging Moderates." Several senators, including prominent conservatives like Utah's Orrin Hatch, sought out Burke to say they would defend her publicly if needed. Former budget director Richard Darman, who had felt the Right's ire during his term of public service, sent a note telling Burke to "hang in there." Retired Republican Sen. Warren Rudman sent roses along with this note:

Roses are red, violets are blue,
Novak is nuts, we love you.

After a while, the sharks moved on to other prey. Burke stayed in her job, and even gained power.

A more compelling soap opera gripped the capital in the waning days of summer 1995 as Republican Sen. Bob Packwood struggled to keep his seat despite new allegations of sexual misconduct, and the potential of public hearings that would inevitably become a circus and embarrass the entire Senate. When the Senate Ethics Committee, a bipartisan panel of six senators, voted unanimously in early September to recommend Packwood's ouster, it was up to Dole, as the Majority Leader and one of Packwood's closest friends, to orchestrate the denouement. Dole and a handful of other Republican elder statesmen, Simpson, McCain, and Hatfield, Oregon's senior senator and Packwood's former college professor, convinced Packwood to face the inevitable and resign. All that was left was setting the terms.

It was midafternoon, about three o'clock, on September 8, 1995, when Burke went to Packwood's office to pick up his letter of resignation. Packwood had called to ask her to come by because he did not trust just any aide to handle such a sensitive matter. Burke and Packwood had been close allies for almost twenty years. As pro-choice moderates, they always knew they could rely on each other. "What a jewel she is," says Packwood, who in 1985, when he first chaired the Finance Committee, had tried to hire Burke. Now here she was scanning the letter he had been forced to write, which included his wish for "a decent grace period" of some months to close out his twenty-six-year career. Burke suggested one minor change, which Packwood readily agreed to.

She was all business until it was time to say goodbye. "This place will miss you tremendously," she said, and then, her voice cracking, she added, "And *I'll* miss you tremendously." With that, she and Packwood hugged. They were both in tears.

Recounting the moment, Packwood awkwardly searches for the right words to describe his relationship with Burke. "We spent so much time alone," he says. Then, catching himself, he adds, "in the best sense of the word—not in the normal sense." The Packwood that Burke knew was a bright, talented legislator, but his other side, the side that Jay Leno ridiculed on late-night television, the pathetic gropings of more than a score of unwilling women, would forever define him, even in ordinary conversation.

Packwood's resignation from the Senate left a vacuum of leadership on the Finance Committee. Packwood had assumed the chairmanship after the Republicans gained control of the Senate in the November 1994 election, and was respected for both his knowledge and experience. Under the seniority rules, the top job fell to Delaware Sen. William Roth, a cautious septuagenarian, who few people in either political party thought was up to the task. Packwood had managed to keep the right wing at bay despite his mounting ethical problems. With Roth in charge, that task and many others would fall to Burke. "Everybody asks me who's chairman of the Finance Committee, and I say Sheila," volunteered Bromberg, voicing the view of many who do business on Capitol Hill. "She fills the power void."

Burke would soon be caught in the crossfire between moderates and conservatives, as it played out on the Finance Committee. Sen. John Chafee, a leading moderate, wanted the federal government to continue its guarantee of health coverage for poor children, pregnant women, and the disabled so that states would have to cover these groups, and could not divert the money to other programs, however worthy. When a Republican staff aide pointed out in a meeting in Dole's office that the governors opposed such a regulation, Dole retorted, "The governors are getting enough of what they want." He sided with Chafee. Staffers were told to work out the definition of "disabled" over the next several days. The Senate Finance Committee approved this limited entitlement by a resounding seventeen to three. Dole was not in the room, but Burke had his proxy and sided with the majority.

A week later, GOP staffers remained at odds over how broadly to define "disabled," a decision that could have far-reaching cost implications. A number of governors, worried that they would be saddled with a costly regulation, accused Dole of reneging on the Republicans' promise to return power to the states. So Dole sided with the governors, and blamed Burke for miscasting his proxy. He did this with a straight face. Of course, even if he had voted differently, the tally would have been sixteen to four, with the outcome unaffected.

Burke, ever the loyal staffer, said that she may have been mistaken in thinking that the disabled should be included in the mandate. The Senate parliamentarian was consulted about having an additional vote on language to cover only pregnant women and children. Roth, who had been chairman for only a month, insisted that the original language stand, which infuriated Dole. Dole had become accustomed to having his way with Packwood, whose ethics problems put him at the leader's mercy. In the end, the full Senate voted, sixty to thirty-nine, to require states to comply with federal rules for coverage of poor children, pregnant women, and the disabled under the Medicaid program—a victory for Senate moderates.

Dole's behavior was particularly perplexing because of his long history of fighting for the disabled. But he had a presidential race coming up, and he wanted to keep the loyalty of Republican governors, whose support would be key in the year ahead.

Dole looked tired much of the time, and, given the multiple pressures that he was handling, that was not surprising. "I'd be in a basket somewhere," said Burke. Simmering beneath the surface always was Dole's age. If he stumbled once physically, the age issue could defeat him. On July 22, 1995, when Dole turned seventy-two, the front page of USA Today showed the candidate on his treadmill wearing a long-sleeved blue dress shirt and striped shorts. The picture was accompanied by an exhaustive medical report, which Burke had arranged for Dole's physicians to provide the media. The image was reminiscent of Ronald Reagan pumping iron on the cover of Parade before seeking reelection in 1984. But to casual readers, not realizing that Dole wears long-sleeved shirts to cover an arm withered from a war injury, the picture did not help Dole appear particularly vigorous or more youthful.

One reason the Dole and Burke professional marriage has lasted is that they are both old-fashioned moralists. Dole's favorite television show is *Murder, She Wrote*. His taste in movies runs from *Mrs. Miniver* to *How Green Was My Valley*. After he railed against current Hollywood movies as too violent, Burke agreed with critics who questioned his credibility since he had never seen the films in question. She arranged for him to screen *Pulp Fiction* and *Natural Born Killers*. He did not make it past ten minutes on either one.

Like her boss, Burke finds much of Hollywood's output offensive to mainstream American values. She shares Dole's fondness for Hollywood classics. Her children are only allowed to see movies rated G or PG. And just as her parents turned off the television set during the Vietnam War when she came into the room while the news was on, she no longer brings home *Time* magazine since the weekly ran a photograph of the bloodied corpse of an American soldier in Somalia who had been dragged through the streets. "My kids don't need to see that stuff," she says. A P. D. James novel is about as daring as Burke's tastes go.

It is hard to say whether Burke acts like Dole because she has been with him so long, or she has been with him so long because she acts like him. He is a workaholic, and so is she. "Bob Dole has no hobbies except his treadmill," said a friend of Burke's. "He's always working, and he expects her to be there. I've seen some of his prior staff members leave bent over and shriveled up."

On Sunday, November 12, 1995, the day Burke peered out with her red horns from the cover of *The New York Times Magazine*, Dole was asked on *This Week with David Brinkley* whether she would be his chief of staff in the White House. "I think I'd probably want someone with her skill, but also with political skills—which she does not have," he replied. Dole's remark was widely interpreted as a sop to the right wing. He could have said that he was focusing on important things, like the federal budget, and had not given any thought to how he would staff the White House if elected president.

At the same time, Dole was being brutally honest. Burke is not a big-picture, political type who offers up themes and devises strategy for capturing primary states. In that way, she is a mirror reflection of her boss, a creature of the Senate who is far better at cobbling together legislative compromises than presenting a vision for the next century, or even the next four years.

No legislation would test Burke's mettle more than the marathon negotiations to reach a balanced budget agreement with the White House. They stretched through the Christmas and New Year's weekends, and shut down the government for a record twenty-one days as the two sides wrangled. Burke struggled to keep some semblance of normalcy in her life, car-pooling her children to school on the rare morning a budget meeting had not been called. In the Cabinet Room at the White House, she sat against the wall with the other staffers, saying little and counseling Dole with a raised eyebrow or a barely perceptible nod when he looked her way.

Dole had wanted to deal since Thanksgiving, and found it appalling that the House Republicans would hold the government hostage to gain leverage over the President. Sandwiched between Clinton and Gingrich for hours at a time and having to listen to them jabber away was Dole's idea of hell. He wanted to get this done and get back to campaigning. There were a couple of moments where Dole thought he could show flexibility, only to glance in Burke's direction and see her shaking her head no. He would slump back in his chair, clearly disappointed.

A White House official watching Burke noted that, contrary to her reputation, she was quite hard-line. Dole trusted her to let him know what he could get away with, and she was running the vote counts in her head as she sat there. She was concerned with procedural devices that would allow Dole to gain approval in the Senate, as opposed to how what he did looked to voters getting ready to pick a president. "You can see her mind working," said a Clinton aide, "and it's about whether she can get unanimous consent on the floor, not how many electoral votes she can get in Ohio."

The average congressional staffer is gone in two and a half years. It is a youth culture where upward mobility propels people "downtown," to the K Street corridor where they can earn bigger salaries and work shorter hours as lobbyists for corporations and trade associations. Journalist Jeffrey Birnbaum discovered that by 1990, "fully half of the aides who had worked with members of the congressional tax-writing committees [on the Tax Reform Act of 1986] had left their Capitol Hill jobs" to become lobbyists.

If Dole were not running for president, Burke would probably be gone herself. She has had job offers from companies around the world, but her friends say that she would never enter the revolving door of former staffers who cash in on their contacts by becoming lobbyists. She dreams of someday being a university president or the head of a foundation. She stays with Bob Dole out of loyalty and because she is needed, not because she thinks she might be the first woman White House chief of staff. The public attacks against her have robbed her of her precious anonymity, but she can savor the irony that the conservatives who set out to destroy her have instead watched more power flow to her.

APPENDIX

Money Matters

On October 15, 1974, barely two months after he had taken the oath of office, President Gerald Ford signed into law the Federal Election Campaign Act of 1974, which changed the rules for the getting and spending of campaign money and created the Federal Election Commission (FEC) to regulate and monitor the flow of money in national politics. "The unpleasant truth is that big money has come to play an unseemly role in our electoral process," Ford said. "This bill will help to right that wrong."

He was mistaken. The bill that was written by the Democratic-controlled Congress and reluctantly signed by Ford masqueraded as reform but served mainly to protect incumbents. It imposed spending limits too low for most challengers to overcome the advantages of incumbency and put limits on campaign contributions, making it necessary for challengers to find large numbers of backers instead of relying upon family or a few wealthy allies. The bill also paved the way for political action committees, or PACs, which allowed corporations, long prohibited from contributing to federal elections, to legally fund candidates to their liking, and to underwrite incumbents in perpetuity in exchange for access and influence.

Ford signed this last major rewriting of the federal campaign finance laws in the wake of the Watergate scandal that forced the resignation of President Nixon in August 1974. The Democrats were in a strong position to dictate the terms of the reform because Republicans, tarred by Watergate, dared not oppose anything that appeared to address the ethical behavior of elected officials. Public interest groups knew that the bill, drafted by two of the most notorious schemers in Congress, Rep. Wayne Hays of Ohio and Sen. Howard W. Cannon of Nevada, was far from perfect, but they hoped it was a step in the right direction.

Instead, it extended a long tradition in American politics whereby the democratic principle of one man, one vote is routinely undermined by the influence on elections wielded by people with large sums of money.

America's founding fathers, mostly landed aristocrats and merchants themselves, intended wealthy Americans to have influence in political affairs beyond their numbers, and to be overrepresented in Congress. In the decades leading up to the Civil War, as the costs of campaigns rose, candidates turned increasingly to wealthy interests for cash. After the war, the national economy boomed, fueled by westward expansion and manufacturing. Democracy was moving too slowly to meet the needs of fast growing populations of urban workers.

For industrialists, time was money and opportunities were slipping away as state and national legislators debated. The municipal boss system, pioneered by conservative Republicans in New York and embraced by both parties in most major cities, filled that need. At the national and state levels, this system delivered paid voters to insure election of the right legislators. Some of the money came from kickbacks on government contracts and levies on workers' salaries, and some came from wealthy industrialists.

Members of Congress could be bribed by the robber barons or threatened with defeat at the polls by the machines. Broad national policies on trusts, banking, tariffs, and trade benefited business interests greatly and directly, and hurt most individuals only indirectly and imperceptibly. Thus was begun a corrupt tradition that has never entirely died. Its zenith, at least to date, came a century later in the savings and loan scandal of the 1980s, for which the American people eventually will pay about $160 billion.

The legendary corruption of Boss William Marcy Tweed of New York's Tammany Hall was matched by corrupt establishments in Philadelphia, Boston, Baltimore, New Orleans, and, later, Chicago, Minneapolis, St. Louis, and smaller cities. These self-perpetuating political machines would take money from one or another group of industrialists or government contractors and use it to pay voters and vote organizers to elect or bribe legislators, who in turn would use their offices on behalf of the machine's benefactors.

By the turn of the century, the old French notion of *noblesse oblige* and English tradition of public service by the wealthy had been supplanted by the perception that government service was a way to make one's fortune. Idealistic aristocrats like Thomas Jefferson, who had formed the Continental Congress and the early government, often at great personal financial cost, had been supplanted by less educated moneygrubbers who had gotten their start in corrupt politics.

Bribing legislators was a common way to win a seat in the Senate, whose members were chosen by the state legislatures. Some senators bought seats for themselves, investments which paid off handsomely in bribes received in office. Others had seats bought for them by wealthy interests, men like financier Cyrus W. Field, retailer John Wanamaker, steel magnates Andrew Carnegie and Henry Clay Frick. Frick was a union-buster who once famously remarked of Theodore Roosevelt, "We bought the son of a bitch, but he didn't stay bought."

The public at the turn of the century widely understood that "interests"—wealthy self-serving financiers of elections—were generally buying off the Congress. "The Treason of the Senate," a series of *Cosmopolitan* magazine articles in 1906 by muckraker David Graham Phillips, detailed how certain senators sold out the public interest to specific private interests. Although Republicans controlled the Senate at the time, the only sense in which Democrats could have been said to be less corrupt is that they were less numerous.

In 1907, under President Theodore Roosevelt, Congress enacted a law prohibiting banks and corporations from contributing to elections, and, in 1911, a public disclosure law was passed along with spending limits for congressional elections. Many states already had begun to choose senators in popular elections. The Seventeenth Amendment, providing for direct election of all U.S. senators, was passed by Congress in 1912 and ratified a year later as a response to the tendency of the big trusts to buy state legislatures just to control the selection of senators. Neither these nor subsequent efforts in the 1920s, 1930s and 1940s were effective at curbing the harmful effects of money in politics.

Whenever elected officials propose reforming the election code, it is useful to remember that flaws generally are in the system by design, and that any changes tend to work to the advantage of some interests and the disadvantage of others. The present system has evolved from the Federal Election Campaign Act of 1971, passed in response to the growing perception in the 1960s that the Corrupt Practices Act of 1934 was being routinely violated. The advent of television had brought an ever greater need for money in campaigns, even as the old and expensive big-city machines were crumbling, and elections were once again being financed by companies and wealthy individuals.

The 1971 legislation put limits on contributions and required disclosure by presidential campaigns. It also set limits on media expenditures by congressional campaigns, but the limits were high and loophole-ridden. The law was ineffective, as was shown by the ability of Nixon's campaign committee to secretly raise and spend money to finance the Watergate burglary and other subversive activities.

Democratic liberals pushed for a new campaign finance reform bill, one that would apply to Congress as well as the president. The freshman class of Watergate babies was well-intentioned, but the personalities who shaped the bill were from the old school. Hays, the chairman of the House Administration Committee, and Cannon, who headed the Senate Rules and Administration Committee, were both masters at using the perks that help sustain incumbents in office. Hays, not coincidentally, was also chairman of the Democratic Congressional Campaign Committee.

Both men were eventually driven from office by scandal—Hays by resignation and Cannon by defeat at the polls—but not before they wrote the bill that created the present campaign finance system. The bill set up a regulatory bureaucracy that would be responsive to incumbents yet hostile and complicated for challengers, and imposed rules that would give incumbents advantages in fund-raising and protection from challengers.

Gridlock was built into the six-member FEC, which by law is comprised of three Democrats and three Republicans, who are expected to look out for the interests of their parties. To reach a majority of four, two-thirds of the six members must agree to discipline anyone for a violation, or nothing happens. Each party is effectively given a veto. On matters of no great importance to members of either party, or where the parties have common interests, a majority or even unanimity can be achieved. But action can be stymied unless all the members of one party agree with one of the other party, or two members of each party agree. Tie votes spell inaction and the status quo.

Contribution limits took power from local fat cats and gave it to national fat cats, who were more likely to make substantial contributions to many campaigns across the country. By limiting the amount that any individual can contribute, incumbents insured against challengers well-financed by a small cabal of local enemies. An incumbent could garner $1,000 gifts from Washington lobbyists and their clients nationwide, as well as from local contributors. Challengers would be far less likely to have contacts with hundreds of people wealthy enough to give the limit of $1,000 apiece to match what the incumbent could raise.

It was the beginning of dual constituency. Candidates would answer not only to their voters, but also to a national constituency of financiers, who were not eligible to vote in the elections they were underwriting because they lived elsewhere. Protecting incumbents was nonpartisan, except that Democrats controlled both chambers of Congress.

*   *   *

One of the important early decisions by the FEC legalized PACs. Corporations had in the past established "D.C. Committees," the predecessors of PACs. Such committees—really only envelopes or accounts of money, usually run by a lobbyist—collected cash from lobbyists and corporate executives to give to campaigns. With the new law, there was apprehension that someone might get prosecuted for subverting elections with money. Sun Oil Company of Pennsylvania sought an advisory opinion from the FEC, which on December 3, 1975, ruled that companies could form PACs and pay the costs of operating them, provided that the money they contribute to campaigns came from executives and shareholders of the company, and not from the corporate treasury.

Companies might not be able to vote, but they would thereafter have far more impact upon elections than had been legal since the turn of the century. The new rules allowed the operation of PACs by labor unions, trade associations, noncorporate business entities like co-ops and mutual funds, and ideological membership groups. Within five years, PACs were providing half the money in congressional elections. Roughly two-thirds of that money came from business interests. By 1984, more than four thousand PACs were registered with the FEC.

The term "political action committee" is a triple misnomer. PACs are not political; they are financial institutions, whose strength is derived from the amount of money they have, not from the number of people they represent. PACs almost never take action; they write checks as a substitute for action. PACs are usually not governed by a committee, and when they are that committee is almost always chosen by the CEO of the corporation or the head of the union or trade association, not by the employees or shareholders.

Court challenges to the new law struck down provisions limiting the amount of money a congressional candidate could raise and spend and overturned limits on how much wealthy individuals could contribute to their own campaigns. The Supreme Court upheld the $1,000 limit on the amount an individual could contribute to a campaign (really $2,000, because the law treats primary and general election campaigns as separate, yet the FEC allows them to commingle funds).

The FEC was designed to operate under almost impossible conditions. Congress can override any regulation a majority of the commission passes, and the FEC has to come to Congress every year for appropriations from the very politicians whose campaigns it is supposed to oversee.

In its early years, the FEC conducted "random audits" of congressional campaigns. This required campaigns to account for their getting and spending, much as an IRS audit requires of a citizen. Amendments to the law in 1979 did away with random audits and required that two-thirds of the commission find "reason to believe" wrongdoing has occurred before initiating an investigation.

Another feature of the 1979 legislation was to accommodate a special interest group Congress had helped create: direct mail fund-raising wizards, the most prominent of whom was conservative Republican Richard Viguerie. It was Viguerie's dream to use direct mail to create a conservative Republican congressional majority that would be independent of big business because it would be financed by millions of small contributions.

A stamp will carry a letter across the country as cheaply as across the street, so direct mail tends to lessen congressional candidates' dependency upon their local constituents and to nationalize campaign issues. Direct mail is a tool best suited for candidates with a national agenda who represent Washington to their constituents, rather than those with a local agenda who represent their constituents to Washington.

Viguerie was a power among Republicans in the 1970s because he had generated the money that put many of them in office. In many cases, he had literally financed their campaigns by bearing the initial costs of mailings for them and then reinvesting the early returns in more mailings. The catch was that members of Congress thus elected found that Viguerie owned the rights to their lists of donors, and to get reelected they would have to either find new backers or deal with Viguerie on terms more favorable to him.

Disclosure of the names and addresses of all $100-and-up contributors threatened Viguerie's assets—the mailing lists he had carefully culled by mining lists of donors to other Republicans and subscribers to right-wing publications. This was a scattershot approach, frequently getting returns lower than one percent. With contributions averaging under $20, such a low return rate did not cover the costs of mailing. To boost returns to a level of profitability, mailings would go to a mix of new names and proven donors. All the while, Vigurie was building sophisticated lists, sorted by computer to show which names responded to which kinds of pitches.

If proven donors were the cream of Viguerie's lists, proven donors of $100 or more were the *crème de la crème*. It didn't seem fair to Viguerie that his firm would go to the trouble of finding lists of potential donors, mail to them at a loss, identify the tiny fraction of them who would give to a congressional campaign, and then have to disclose the names and addresses of big donors among them in public documents that anyone could copy.

The law already made it unlawful to use FEC disclosures of contributors' names and addresses to solicit contributions. In 1979, Congress increased the threshold requiring itemized disclosure of contributions from $100 to $200, thus reducing the number of names from Viguerie's lists that would be disclosed. Congress also inserted in the law a unique provision allowing PACs or party committees or campaigns to file reports containing secret "salts," or phony names of nonexistent contributors. If anyone did mail to a list copied from an FEC report, mailings to the phony names would arrive at an address of the list manager, who would have proof that the law had been violated.

The biggest national fat cats, modern day successors to the robber barons who had corrupted the government a century earlier, chafed under the contribution limits. To appease them, Congress provided an exemption to the contribution limits for "soft money"—a means whereby unlimited amounts could be channeled to the parties, as long as the money was used for "party building" activities such as buildings, equipment and furnishings, voter registration, and get-out-the-vote efforts, as opposed to direct aid to a single campaign. This granted relief to the fat cats, who could once again buy their way into the inner circles of the parties. A steady flow of soft money allowed the parties to free up their operating budgets for helping candidates.

Like many Washington regulatory agencies, the FEC became a captive of the industry it was created to regulate. The result has been a tenfold increase since the mid-1970s in the costs of congressional elections, and a campaign financing system that divides the loyalty of members of Congress between the voters and the election financiers. The burgeoning national debt is a direct result of bidding wars whereby Congress tells each constituency what it wants to hear, then delivers. Members who vote to raise taxes risk the wrath of nationwide contributors. Members who vote to cut spending risk the wrath of the voters. So Congress tends to give both what they want—higher spending to appease the voters and lower taxes to appease the financiers.

Directly and indirectly, campaign money plays a role in the day-to-day work of the characters whose professional lives are the subject of this book. The pollster's ability to take sophisticated and frequent samples of public attitudes on vital issues depends on the extent of financing provided by the campaign. The lobbyist holds the purse strings for campaign money distributed to candidates. The elected official, whether it be a Senate chairman, the Speaker of the House, or an ordinary member, depends for political survival on the generosity of moneyed sponsors. As the gatekeeper for an elected official, the chief of staff must be cognizant of the wishes of those whose financial support helps keep the boss in office term after term.

Associations like the ones represented by lobbyists Michael Bromberg and Paul Equale direct their PAC money to those who can do them the most good, namely the winners. PACs like theirs may not have led the Republican revolution on Capitol Hill, but they surely followed it.

An examination of fifty-eight association PACs that contributed more than $50,000 to House and Senate candidates in the first ten months of 1995 shows how the pattern of heavy support for Democratic candidates in 1990, 1992, and 1994 shifted dramatically after the Republicans took control of the Senate and House in 1994. One example typical of the trend is the Wine & Spirits Wholesalers of America, which gave sixty-four percent of its PAC contributions to Democrats for the 1994 election. In the first ten months of 1995, the same association directed sixty-eight percent of its contributions to Republicans.

Fifteen corporate PACs as varied as the New York Life Insurance Company and the Pacific Gas and Electric Company that contributed more than two-thirds of their money to Democrats for the 1994 race reversed the money stream by contributing more than two-thirds to Republicans in 1995.

The following charts show how PACs administered by Bromberg's Federation of American Health Systems and Equale's Independent Insurance Agents of America shifted their money after the Republicans took over. The Ds (for Democrats) and Rs (for Republicans) at the right graphically show the shift, with each D or R representing a rounded-off ten percent chunk of the PAC's money.

FEDERATION OF AMERICAN HEALTH SYSTEMS

	TO DEMS	TO GOP	DEM%	GOP%	
1995:	$16,100	$35,200	31.38	68.62	DDD RRRRRRR
1994:	$97,000	$60,000	61.78	38.22	DDDDDD RRRR
1992:	$106,800	$73,050	59.38	40.62	DDDDDD RRRR
1990:	$118,300	$56,050	67.85	32.15	DDDDDDD RRR

INDEPENDENT INSURANCE AGENTS OF AMERICA

	TO DEMS	TO GOP	DEM%	GOP%	
1995:	$37,620	$145,388	20.56	79.44	DD RRRRRRRR
1994:	$282,745	$259,247	52.17	47.83	DDDDD RRRRR
1992:	$352,661	$237,137	59.79	40.21	DDDDDD RRRR
1990:	$395,632	$280,703	58.50	41.50	DDDDDD RRRR

Campaign money goes to individual members of Congress, but an analysis of contributions cross-referencing the many millions of dollars given to the subcommittees whose members are the greatest beneficiaries gives some clues as to how the contributing PAC hopes to benefit from its investment. Since subcommittees vary in size, the average received per member of a given subcommittee is a more accurate reflection of a particular PAC's legislative interest than the total received by all members.

In the six years ending with the election of 1994, the Independent Insurance Agents of America PAC gave money to members of the Senate and House who served on more than two hundred subcommittees. Because members each serve on several subcommittees, each contribution is counted more than once, but the important statistic is the average per member on any given subcommittee. The three subcommittees to which the IIAA's PAC contributed most heavily from 1989 through 1994 were 1) House Energy and Commerce Subcommittee on Commerce, Consumer Protection and Competitiveness, $7,492 per member; 2) Senate Appropriations Subcommittee on Commerce, Justice, State and Judiciary, $6,772 per member; and 3) Senate Small Business Subcommittee on Competitiveness, Capital Formation and Economic Opportunity, $6,419 per member.

Under the half-century-old McCarren-Ferguson Act, the insurance industry is exempt from federal antitrust laws and is therefore not regulated by the federal government. The IIAA's pattern of contributions to members of subcommittees dealing with competitiveness and consumer issues suggests a desire to keep the federal government out of the insurance business for another half-century.

Members of six subcommittees of the Senate Finance Committee are among the top ten recipients of money from Bromberg's Federation of American Health Systems PAC. The first five all are Finance Committee subcommittees: 1) Social Security and Family Policy, $7,125 per member; 2) Medicare and Long-Term Care, $5,750; 3) Energy and Agricultural Taxation, $4,166; 4) Taxation, $4,071; 5) International Trade, $3,941. The Senate Finance Committee was in the forefront of the debate over health care reform in 1994. A Ways and Means subcommittee was the leading recipient among House subcommittees, with $3,892 per member. Ways and Means was a key battleground for health care reform in the House.

Senator Daniel Patrick Moynihan has long nurtured a reputation for being above moneygrubbing, or at least blithely unconcerned about campaign dollars, yet since his first campaign for the Senate, Moynihan has never been outspent. In his first campaign in 1976, Moynihan loaned his own campaign $50,000 and ended the year with a $138,000 campaign debt. Incumbent Sen. James Buckley spent $2.1 million, almost twice as much as Moynihan, who had to spend heavily on a tough primary. Buckley's campaign chest could not overcome the anti-Republican tide in the wake of the Watergate scandal and Moynihan won with fifty-six percent.

In 1982, Moynihan won reelection by nearly two to one with sixty-five percent of the vote, the largest margin of victory by any senator in the state's history. The Republican challenger spent less than $118,000, whereas Moynihan spent twenty-three times as much, $2.7 million. Moynihan broke his own record in the 1988 election, winning with sixty-seven percent of the vote while outspending his Republican opponent, an unknown, by nine to one, with $4.8 million. This fit Moynihan's pattern of scaring off serious opposition by amassing a huge campaign chest, then clobbering his token opposition with massive spending. Moynihan's vote margin has never approached his spending margin; for every vote, he has had to spend several times as much as his opponent.

By 1994, an election year that was to prove disastrous to many Democrats, including New York Gov. Mario Cuomo, who lost to upstart challenger George Pataki, Moynihan was financially fortified against any comers. Moynihan faced a rookie Republican challenger, Bernadette Castro, heir to the convertible sofa fortune. Castro loaned her campaign more than a million dollars, but Moynihan started with almost that much cash on hand, and never stopped fund-raising. Outspending Castro by four to one, Moynihan outpolled her by twelve percent.

As chairman of the Finance Committee, Moynihan raised $1.5 million from PACs for the 1994 race, a quarter of it coming from the financial community. Health industry PACs gave him $210,000 and the energy industry, concerned about Superfund taxes and tax breaks for energy exploration, gave him another $102,000.

The reforms that Democrats passed in the 1970s to protect their incumbents now work to the advantage of Newt Gingrich and the new Republican majority in the House. With PACs shifting most of their giving to Republicans and with a huge network of $1,000 contributors ready to feed the GOP machine, the Democrats will be hard pressed to regain the majority. As the architect of the Republican revolution, Gingrich knows the value of a campaign dollar, as his own election history proves.

Gingrich lost his first two bids for Congress, in 1974 and 1976, to incumbent Democrat John Flynt, a twenty-year House veteran who showed little spark as chairman of the House ethics committee, and had ethical problems himself. Outspent in 1974, Flynt was surprised by Gingrich and held on to his seat by only a two-point margin. Flynt tripled his spending for 1976 and survived another close race.

When Flynt decided to retire rather than run again in 1978, the Democrats put up Virginia Shapard, a state senator who partly financed her own campaign. Overall, she outspent Gingrich by nearly $100,000, but much of it was spent on winning the Democratic primary, leaving her underfunded for the final days of the general election campaign against Gingrich, who won with fifty-four percent of the vote. Since then, no opponent has outspent Gingrich, or even spent half as much (see table, page 374).

As the price of a House seat skyrocketed in the 1970s and 1980s, Gingrich more than kept pace. In the 1986 race, he spent $737,000—more than was spent by 400 of the 435 House members. Gingrich rose to the fourth-ranking minority slot on the Public Works Committee in 1988, and became the ranking member on its Aviation subcommittee, where he was able to look after the interests of Atlanta's hub airport in his district. But legislation and pork were not high on Gingrich's priority list. He concentrated on his mission to make Republicans the majority party in the House. His campaign money came not from construction companies, unions, and airlines—traditional patrons of Public Works Committee members—but from small businesses across the country.

Gingrich's campaign spending has gone from under two dollars per vote in the mid-1970s to more than fifteen dollars per vote in the 1990s. Very little of his money comes from his constituents. For the 1994 race, for instance, eighty-five percent of the money Gingrich raised came from PACs or individuals who live outside his district and therefore could not vote for him. In 1992, ninety-five percent of his money came from outsiders. This reliance on outsiders' money is true in most congressional districts across the country to a lesser degree, and the voters do not seem to mind.

After winning easily in 1988, Gingrich seemed so secure in the Sixth District that the *Almanac of American Politics* concluded its 1990 assessment of him by saying he has a "safe seat." Yet, Gingrich nearly lost in 1990 to the same challenger he had beaten handily in 1988, David Worley, despite outspending Worley by nearly five to one. Worley's fundraising disadvantage was aggravated by a deal struck by the parties to withhold aid to any challenger who criticized an incumbent for voting for a pay raise for himself. True to their word, the Democrats denied

Worley any help after he attacked Gingrich for the pay raise. Worley came within 974 votes of unseating Gingrich.

Five years later, Gingrich's position as head of GOPAC, the Republican candidate development operation, helped him expand his own fund-raising base. His 1990 campaign raised money from donors in thirty-one states and the District of Columbia. In 1991–92, Gingrich found support in thirty-three states and the District of Columbia.

In redrawing congressional district lines, based on the 1990 census, the Georgia legislature gave Gingrich a constituency that is the most heavily Republican in Georgia and the most wealthy. In his first run in the new district in 1992, Gingrich had a serious primary challenge. Herman Clark, a popular Republican state legislator from the area, managed to raise $150,000, in part by loaning $21,000 to his own campaign. He came within fewer than 1,000 votes of unseating the then Republican whip. Gingrich spent a total of $1.9 million on the primary and general, and won reelection, fifty-eight to forty-two percent.

Gingrich's 1994 challenger, former Democratic Rep. Ben Jones, attacked the incumbent on ethical issues, but raised less than a third of a million dollars. Gingrich spent $1.8 million to coast to victory with a margin of almost two to one. Gingrich raised nearly a third of a million dollars in PAC money, ninety percent of which came from business interests. He also picked up money from individual donors in thirty-five states, plus the District of Columbia and Puerto Rico.

The health industry has been very good to Gingrich, a key player in scuttling the Clinton administration's proposals for health care reform. Health industry PAC money flows to candidates regardless of their positions on issues related to public health, such as abortion, AIDS, sex education, or eligibility for Medicaid. The health industry's issues concern money—medical cost-cutting, hospital cost-containment, medical malpractice liability, drug patents and licensing, and tax breaks for the wealthy and small business.

In Washington, it is not seen as ironic that Gingrich also received substantial support from the tobacco industry. Tobacco PACs contributed $23,000 to the 1994 Gingrich campaign. Executives from the cigarette industry are not prominent among Gingrich's individual contributors, but cigar manufacturers, mostly from Tampa, contributed $21,500.

Outside of business PACs, the biggest interest supporting Gingrich was pro-Israel PACs, which contributed $28,800. A generous interest group on Capitol Hill, these PACs normally favor Democrats and, because of the Senate's larger role in foreign policy, senators. But unlike many ideological PACs, the pro-Israel group is pragmatic, and probably sees Gingrich as a potential counterpoint to isolationists who would curb foreign aid, two-thirds of which goes to Israel or, in fulfillment of the Camp David accords, to Egypt in return for its making peace with Israel.

Gingrich does not do well among the CEOs of Fortune 500 companies, who tend to be establishment Republicans. He makes up for it with a nationwide donor base of hundreds of contributors associated with the health and finance industries. Most of them write checks in the maximum allowed amount, $1,000 per election.

Gingrich's support from the financial community is linked to the Republicans' advocacy of a capital gains tax cut, which would primarily benefit people who are in a position to write $1,000 checks to politicians. The tax break would provide a boon to the financial community, especially in securities and real estate. Many investors hold on to securities or property to postpone paying capital gains taxes on the profits realized at sale. With the possibility of the tax break, many are poised to sell as soon as the lower tax rate becomes effective. Brokers of real estate and securities make their money not on the rising value of their wares, but on the turnover—a commission on sales of stocks, bonds, and property.

In early fund-raising for reelection in 1996, Gingrich had the advantage of the speakership, and used it to raise $414,000 in PAC money in the first ten months of 1995. That was more than any other House member except Richard Gephardt, the would-be Speaker relegated to Minority Leader by Gingrich's success, who benefited by an outpouring of cash from labor union PACs and funds left over from a presidential campaign committee formed with the unrealized expectation that Gephardt would run in 1992.

Again, business accounted for almost all of Gingrich's PAC money and again, the financial PACs took the lead, pouring in some $95,499, or nearly a quarter of the total, and twice what any other subset of business interests gave.

By gearing his presentations for national audiences, he may not always endear himself to his north Georgia constituents. Voters sometimes punish politicians who become prominent nationally, and appear less interested in local issues. But Gingrich understands that House elections are financial enterprises, and he is one of the most enterprising members of the House. If money can win House elections—and all evidence is that it can and does—Gingrich should survive any challenge, unless it goes to how he gets his campaign money.

Maxine Waters's fourteen years in the California Assembly prepared her well for her first run for Congress in 1990. She had a network of contacts that made it easy for her to raise money. Waters raised and spent more than three-quarters of a million dollars, a higher total than ninety percent of the representatives elected that year, and higher than all but eight of the freshmen. All the other House freshmen who spent as much in 1990 had opponents who spent more than $300,000. Fund-raising by Waters's opponent did not even reach the $5,000 that triggers Federal Election Commission reporting requirements.

Waters handily won her primary with eighty-nine percent of the vote, then swept the general election with seventy-nine percent.

Nearly $200,000 of her campaign chest came from PACs, slightly more than average for House freshmen elected in 1990. She raised nearly $400,000 from individuals, most of it in $500-and-up contributions. Her financial support was mostly from the Los Angeles basin area of California, but from neighborhoods wealthier than her South Central district.

More than half of her PAC cash came from labor unions led by the Teamsters, the United Auto Workers, and the Laborers Union, each of which "maxed out," contributing the full amount allowed by law— $5,000 for the primary and $5,000 for the general election, for a total of $10,000 apiece. Business PACs provided $65,000, led by trade associations for the Realtors, who gave $6,000. Trade associations for the homebuilders, trial lawyers, and the American Medical Association contributed $5,000 each. Corporate PACs supporting Waters included tobacco giants RJR Nabisco and Philip Morris, which tend to support black members of Congress to inoculate themselves against charges that they exploit the black community, where smoking is far more prevalent than in white America.

Her business PAC supporters include many familiar names from corporate America. One might think that corporations, especially those headed by archconservatives like Bill Marriott, would not support a liberal like Waters. But money in politics often serves simply as a way for contributors to buy access. Lobbyists in Washington hand out $500 and $1,000 checks like insurance salesmen hand out business cards. Such gifts do not imply an endorsement, and certainly not a decision to become involved helping the recipient in the campaign. Rather, they are simply an acknowledgment that the candidate is likely to win, and an indication that the contributor is not going to help the opposition. It's a way of saying hello.

Waters received $23,000, a relatively small amount, from liberal ideological PACs, primarily women's groups and civil rights advocates. These groups believe strongly in Waters, but are not well-heeled.

Entertainment industry executives from Warner Brothers, MGM/UA, and Paramount made contributions of $250 to $500 apiece, and Norman Lear contributed $1,000. Hollywood stars on Waters's 1990 contribution list included screen actors Cicely Tyson, Louis Gossett, Jr., and Richard Dreyfuss at $250 apiece, and jazz great Quincy Jones, who gave $1,000.

She easily won reelection in 1992, with eighty-three percent of the vote, and in 1994, with seventy-eight percent. Her Republican opponent both times spent less than $10,000. But unlike her 1990 campaign, Waters relaxed her fund raising, and spent just $208,000 in 1992, and $177,000 in 1994.

Once in office, Waters established a "leadership PAC," a political action committee that makes it legal for a member of Congress to accept additional money from special interests and distribute it to other candidates. Contributions from the campaign committee of one member to that of another are legal, but limited to $1,000 per election. But with a leadership PAC, a member of Congress can approach anyone, whether or not they have given the limit to the member's campaign. Each willing donor, whether a PAC or individual, can give $5,000 per year to the leadership PAC. Then the leadership PAC can give up to $10,000 to any campaign, including that of its founder.

In theory, the federal contribution limit is $1,000 per contributor per election. In fact, a fat cat who wants to give more can do it via a leadership PAC, and then do it again using another leadership PAC. As a practical matter, there are no limits on the amounts that wealthy donors can legally contribute.

Some members of Congress use leadership PACs to buy support from each other in bids for spots in the congressional leadership

Waters's PAC, called People Helping People (PHP), has not attracted the usual parade of lobbyists and favor seekers. Established in 1991, its first large contribution was from actor Bill Cosby, who gave $4,000, matched by his wife, Camille Cosby. The biggest single gift was $5,000 from Georgia Frontiere, owner of the Los Angeles Rams. Another $4,000 came from Berry Gordy, the movie producer and founder of Motown Records. All told, the PAC raised $24,100 for the 1991–92 election cycle, and contributed $14,000 to federal Democratic candidates.

Waters directed PHP's biggest contribution, $5,000, to the campaign of Carol Moseley-Braun of Illinois, who was to become the first black woman to serve in the U.S. Senate. PHP gave generously to other black women running for Congress in 1992. Among them were Corrine Brown, a Florida legislator, and Cynthia McKinney of Georgia, who won in newly created majority-black districts. "When I decided to run in early 1992, I sent letters to all the women members of Congress asking for help," says McKinney. "I didn't hear back from most of them. Maxine sent a check."

In the 1993–94 election cycle, PHP raised a total of $43,800, but contributed only $11,500 to federal candidates, $5,000 of it to Louise Slaughter, a liberal representative from Rochester, New York, and a Waters ally in Congress. PHP gave gifts of $500 or $1,000 to ten other Democrats, including Democratic whip David Bonior of Michigan, whose help was key to Waters's winning passage for her 17-to-30 job training program.

Many in the Black Caucus are opposed to curbs on contributions from outside of the district and curbs on PACs. Their reasoning is that, as representatives of mostly poor people, they can't get campaign money from their constituents, and need to solicit funds from outsiders. Waters, however, would probably do all right without a lot of outside money, as she did in 1992 and 1994. Her cost per vote is among the lowest in the House. In the second most expensive media market in the country, she has learned to use people-to-people politics, instead of donor-to-consultant-to-media dollars, to win reelection easily and with huge margins.

THE COST OF A SEAT IN CONGRESS
GEORGIA'S 6TH DISTRICT, 1974–1994

YEAR	CANDIDATE	PARTY	SPENDING	NUMBER OF VOTES	MARGIN	PER VOTE
74	FLYNT, JOHN J.	(D)	$33,032	49,082	2,774	$0.67
	Gingrich, Newt	(R)	$85,505	46,308	2.91%	$1.85
	Loser's spending edge: $52,470	(159%)				
76	FLYNT, JOHN J.	(D)	$145,793	77,532	5,132	$1.88
	Gingrich, Newt	(R)	$134,517	72,400	3.42%	$1.86
	Winner's spending edge: $11,276	(8%)				
78	GINGRICH, NEWT	(R)	$219,336	47,078	7,627	$4.66
	Shapard, Virginia	(D)	$313,056	39,451	8.81%	$7.94
	Loser's spending edge: $93,720	(43%)				
80	GINGRICH, NEWT	(R)	$277,585	96,071	29,465	$2.89
	Davis, Dock Heard	(D)	$72,962	66,606	18.11%	$1.10
	Winner's spending edge: $204,623	(280%)				

YEAR	CANDIDATE	PARTY	SPENDING	NUMBER OF VOTES	MARGIN	PER VOTE
82	GINGRICH, NEWT	(R)	$365,750	62,352	11,893	$5.87
	Wood, James M. (Jim)Jr.	(D)	$154,210	50,459	10.54%	$3.06
	Winner's spending edge: $211,540 (137%)					
84	GINGRICH, NEWT	(R)	$336,065	116,655	64,594	$2.88
	Johnson, Gerald L.	(D)	$74,940	52,061	38.29%	$1.44
	Winner's spending edge: $261,125 (348%)					
86	GINGRICH, NEWT	(R)	$736,607	75,583	24,231	$9.75
	Bray, Clifton Crandle	(D)	$251,751	51,352	19.09%	$4.90
	Winner's spending edge: $484,856 (193%)					
88	GINGRICH, NEWT	(R)	$838,708	110,169	33,345	$7.61
	Worley, David J.	(D)	$358,354	76,824	17.83%	$4.66
	Winner's spending edge: $480,354 (134%)					
90	GINGRICH, NEWT	(R)	$1,559,052	78,768	974	$19.79
	Worley, David James	(D)	$342,296	77,794	0.62%	$4.40
	Winner's spending edge: $1,216,756 (355%)					
92	GINGRICH, NEWT	(R)	$1,962,810	158,761	42,565	$12.36
	Center, Tony	(D)	$411,794	116,196	15.48%	$3.54
	Winner's spending edge: $1,551,016 (477%)					
94	GINGRICH, NEWT	(R)	$1,817,792	119,432	52,732	$15.22
	Jones, Ben Lewis	(D)	$321,774	66,700	28.33%	$4.82
	Winner's spending edge: $1,496,018 (465%)					

Source: Sunshine Press Services computer analysis of Federal Election Commission data obtained through the federal Freedom of Information Act.

NOTES

For each chapter, we have listed our sources in the order that the information they provided us appears. We also spoke to a number of people who agreed to be interviewed only if we did not identify them by name. We have reconstructed dialogue in a number of instances based on the recollections of those involved. Where we had only one primary source, we sought confirmation from others. Where there was disagreement over what took place, we say so. Our heartfelt thanks to those who took the time and risk to cooperate in this project.

1. THE POLLSTERS

Sources: Stanley B. Greenberg, Paul Kirk, Frank Greer, Jill Buckley, Dick Wirthlin, Samuel Popkin, Paul Curcio, Doug Bailey, Frank Luntz, Rep. Bob Livingston, Rep. Chris Shays, Tony Blankley, Jennifer Laszlo, Phyllis Luntz, Sen. Daniel Patrick Moynihan, Bill McInturff.

29   Stanley Greenberg, "From Crisis to Working Majority," *American Prospect*, September 1991.
35   "to allow a continuing conversation": Memo by Stanley Greenberg, "The Clinton Polling/Research Program," November 23, 1992.
35   "a first draft of political tasks": Memo by Stanley Greenberg, "Post Election Survey," November 4–8, 1992.
36   "Voters are deeply worried": Memo by Stanley Greenberg, "The Clinton Presidency: Political Goals," November 18, 1992.
40   "growing majorities": Memo by Stanley Greenberg, "Health Care Positioning," February 2, 1993.
41   "We have let slip away": Memo by Stanley Greenberg, "Post-Inaugural: New Kind-of-Democrat?" February 5, 1993.
42   "It sounds too good": Focus group, Paramus, New Jersey, April 27, 1993.
48   Richard L. Berke, "Pollster Advises Democrats: Don't Be Too Close to Clinton," *The New York Times*, August 5, 1994, p. A-1.
54   *Harper's Index*, June 1994. James M. Perry, *The Wall Street Journal* (Washington)/Coldwater Corporation (Ann Arbor, Michigan)/U.S. Federal Election Commission.
56   Stanley B. Greenberg, *Middle Class Dreams: The Politics and Power of the New American Majority* (New York: Times Books, 1995).
57   Ann Devroy, "Clinton Aide Urges Shift on Affirmative Action," *The Washington Post*, March 9, 1995, p. A-4.

60   Sam Roberts, "Private Opinions on Public Opinion: Question Is, What Is the Question?" *The New York Times*, August 21, 1994.

60   "He would say": American Enterprise Institute forum with presidential pollsters, Washington, D.C., December 8, 1993.

62   "Whatever the realities": 1980 "Black Book" campaign document for Ronald Reagan.

73   "Americans think politicians": Frank Luntz, "Looking for Waterloo: A Strategy for the Republican House Leadership," January 1994.

73   Chuck Raasch, "Pollster Tells GOP It's Out of Touch," *USA Today*, February 17, 1994, p. 4-A.

73   "academic quality and overall reputation": Samuel M. Hughes, "What Students Are Thinking—And Doing," *The Pennsylvania Gazette*, December 1993, p. 20.

78   *TV Guide*, October 22, 1994, Vol. 42, No. 43, Issue #2169.

78   Ralph A. Hallow, "GOP Unveils Down-the-Stretch Ad Blitz," *The Washington Times*, October 28, 1994.

79   "the enemy of normal Americans": Ann Devroy and Charles R. Babcock, "Gingrich Foresees Corruption Probe by a GOP House," *The Washington Post*, October 14, 1994, p. A-1.

80   *Face the Nation*, CBS News, October 23, 1994.

81   *Inside Politics*, CNN, December 29, 1994.

87   "Periscope," *Newsweek*, February 27, 1995, p. 4.

87   "gray walls and low ceilings": Katharine Q. Seelye, "Democrats in Congress Seem Stuck in Denial Stage of Grief," *The New York Times*, February 23, 1995, p. A-1.

2. THE LOBBYISTS

Sources: Michael Bromberg, Louise Caire Clark, Dan Rostenkowski, Ira Magaziner, Bill McInturff.

90   "We've got a bombshell here": Interview with Michael Bromberg, corroborated by Charles Kahn.

91   "This could harm you if it became public": Interview with Michael Bromberg, corroborated by David Gergen.

97   "If you want to discuss health care": Sandra G. Boodman, "On the Pulse," *The Washington Post*, Health Magazine, February 22, 1994.

98   "It's better to be a chess player": Sandra G. Boodman, "Health Care's Heavy Hitter," *The Washington Post*, February 6, 1994, p. H-1.

108 "over my cold, dead, political body": Dan Balz, "For Gramm, Hardship Fostered Determination," *The Washington Post*, February 19, 1995, p. A-1.

109 "the best deal in town": May 4, 1994, press conference in which Nebraska Sen. Bob Kerrey and Oklahoma Sen. David Boren endorsed the Chafee plan.

110 "Three Blind Mice," Review and Outlook, editorial, *The Wall Street Journal*, June 27, 1994, p. A-12.

112 The word "lobby" dates back: William Safire, *Safire's Political Dictionary* (New York: Random House, 1978), p. 383.

112 "lobby-agents": Douglass Cater, *Power in Washington: A Critical Look at Today's Struggle to Govern in the Nation's Capital* (New York: Random House, 1964), p. 206.

112 "crawling serpentine men": Margaret Susan Thompson, *The "Spider Web": Con-*

gress and Lobbying in the Age of Grant (Ithaca and London: Cornell University Press, 1985), p. 54.

112 "The host of contractors": Karl Schriftgiesser, *The Lobbyists* (Boston: Little, Brown, 1951), pp. 5–7.

112 Third House of Congress: William Safire, *Safire's Political Dictionary,* p. 383.

112 "The consumer is the only man": Campaign speech by John F. Kennedy, Wittenberg College, Springfield, Ohio, 1960; *The Macmillan Dictionary of Political Quotations* (New York: Macmillan, 1993).

114 "the seventeenth person to do so": John F. Persinos, "Words of Wisdom 1994: Useful Political Insights from Top Pros," *Campaigns & Elections,* July 1994, p. 34.

117 "it's going to be the two coldest years in Washington": Dan Balz, "GOP Plays Hardball with PACs," *The Washington Post,* October 13, 1994, p. A-1.

121 "I'm assuming anyone as obviously brilliant": Greg Steinmetz, "Clinton Health-Plan Casualty: The Health Insurance Agent," *The Wall Street Journal,* November 17, 1994.

121 "Top officials on the President's health care task force": *Newsmaker Saturday,* CNN, September 18, 1993.

123 *PrimeTime Live,* ABC News, January 20, 1994.

130 Paul Starobin, "Wired," *National Journal,* March 4, 1995, pp. 535–39.

132 "The O'Leary Report's 1993–94 PAC List of Shame: The PACs That Shunned Newt and the GOP's Contract With America," *The O'Leary Report,* July 1995.

135 Jonathan D. Glater, "Rubin Urges Changes in U.S. Banking Laws: Treasury Chief Would End Curbs on Competition," *The Washington Post,* February 28, 1995, p. C-1.

135 Jeffrey Taylor, "Plans Compete for Relaxing Banking Laws," *The Wall Street Journal,* February 28, 1995, p. A-2.

135 Keith Bradsher, "Rubin's Plan for Banking Spurs Fight," *The New York Times,* February 28, 1995, p. D-1.

3. THE CHAIRMAN

Sources: Lawrence O'Donnell, Jr., Ira Magaziner, Sen. John Breaux, William J. Baumol, Liz Moynihan, William Kristol, Sen. Daniel Patrick Moynihan, John Carpenter, Donna Kass, James Q. Wilson, Stephen Hess, Al Shanker, Bob Packwood, Tom Harkin, Midge Costanza, Michael McCurry.

141 "I never know what he's going to do": Robert Mann, *Legacy to Power: Senator Russell Long of Louisiana* (New York: Paragon House, 1992), p. 360.

143 "roll right over him if we have to": Michael Kramer, "Still Waiting for Bill's Call," *Time,* February 1, 1993, p. 37.

143 "fantasy, but accurate fantasy": *Meet the Press,* NBC News, September 19, 1993.

149 "Everybody on welfare is in crisis": *Meet the Press,* NBC News, January 23, 1994.

149 "boob bait for bubbas": *Meet the Press,* NBC News, January 9, 1994.

150 "Republican senators do not operate on their own": Ira Magaziner, "The Ultimate Congressional End Game—Or Is There Life After Dole?" January 1994.

157 "over my cold, dead, political body": Dan Balz, "For Gramm, Hardship Fostered Determination," *The Washington Post,* February 19, 1995, p. A-1.

159 Meeting with Senator Moynihan, John Carpenter, Donna Kass and others, May 10, 1993.

163 Daniel Patrick Moynihan, "The Negro Family: The Case for National Action,"
     Office of Policy Planning and Research, United States Department of Labor,
     March 1965.

163 "Moynihan's Scissors": William Raspberry, "Moynihan's Scissors," *The Washing-
     ton Post,* February 10, 1995, p. A-23.

164 Rowland Evans and Robert Novak, "Inside Report: The Moynihan Report," *The
     Washington Post,* August 18, 1965.

165 Daniel Patrick Moynihan, "The President and The Negro: The Moment Lost,"
     Commentary, Vol. 43, No. 2, February 1967, pp. 31–45.

166 "Moynihan in to see me": Haldeman, H. R., *The Haldeman Diaries: Inside the
     Nixon White House* (New York: G. P. Putnam's Sons, 1994), p. 144.

168 Daniel Patrick Moynihan, "Qui Bono—In Whose Interest?" *Public Interest,* Fall 1972.

169 "briefly been a member of the Ku Klux Klan": Michael Barone and Grant Ujifusa
     with Richard E. Cohen, *The Almanac of American Politics 1996* (Washington, D.C.:
     National Journal Inc., 1995), p. 1428.

170 Lawrence F. O'Donnell, Jr., *Deadly Force: The True Story of How a Badge Can
     Become a License to Kill* (New York: William Morrow, 1983).

172 "Eggs McBentsen": Thomas B. Edsall, "Breakfast with the Senate Finance Chair-
     man for $10,000," *The Washington Post,* February 3, 1987, p. A-1.

172 "doozy": Thomas B. Edsall, "Bentsen Decides to Disband His $10,000 Breakfast
     Club," *The Washington Post,* February 7, 1987, p. A-1.

172 "where he will oversee": Clifford Krauss, "Moynihan Holding Well-Timed Party,"
     The New York Times, June 11, 1993, p. A-20.

173 Adam Clymer, "Moynihan Asks Big Tax Increase on Ammunition," *The New York
     Times,* November 4, 1993, p. A-1.

178 Robert D. Putnam with Robert Leonardi and Raffaella Y. Nanetti, *Making Democ-
     racy Work: Civic Traditions in Modern Italy* (Princeton, N.J.: Princeton University
     Press, 1993).

184 "class warfare": "Lawmakers' Pay Raised, Fees Curbed," *Congressional Quarterly
     Almanac, 101st Congress, 2nd Session, 1990* (Washington, D.C.: Congressional
     Quarterly, 1990), pp. 73–74.

185 "writes more books than some political people read": George F. Will, "The Pres-
     ence of Malice," *Newsweek,* December 7, 1987, p. 106.

187 Todd S. Purdum, "Democrats Pick New York Slate of Incumbents," *The New York
     Times,* June 2, 1994, p. A-1.

189 "Find out what Moynihan drinks": George F. Will, "The Presence of Malice,"
     p. 106.

189 Garry Trudeau, *Doonesbury,* Universal Press Syndicate, 1978.

191 "discussion on policy toward the People's Republic of China": Frank Lynn, "Two
     Senators: More Than a Contrast in Styles," *The New York Times,* September 13,
     1983, p. B-1.

197 "Periscope," *Newsweek,* April 24, 1995, p. 4.

197 "You start by being born a Norwegian": Mary McGrory, "No Legitimate Solution
     in Sight," *The Washington Post,* March 16, 1995, p. A-2.

198 "It is beyond belief": "What Kind of Reform? Mr. Moynihan on Welfare," editorial,
     The Washington Post, May 21, 1995, p. C-6.

199 "Children will be sleeping on grates": Barbara Vobejda and Judith Havemann,
     "Dole Concedes Some Major Points to Gain Support for Welfare Bill," *The Wash-
     ington Post,* September 9, 1995, p. A-8.

200   Alison Mitchell, "President Voices Optimism on Hopes for Welfare Bill," *The New York Times*, September 17, 1995, p. A-1.

200   Gerald F. Seib and Michael K. Frisby, "As Welfare-Reform Bill Moves to the Middle, Concerns Arise Whether the Center Can Hold," *The Wall Street Journal*, September 19, 1995, p. A-24.

4. THE SPEAKER

Sources: Christina and Robert Jeffrey, Newt Gingrich, Kip Carter, Reg Murphy, Mel Steely, Floyd Hoskins, Lee Howell, Frank Gregorsky, Ray Abernathy, Rep. Ed Derwinski, Paul Weyrich, Bert Pines, Fritz Rench, Rep. Lynn Martin, Marianne Gingrich, Rep. Nancy Johnson, Rep. Bob Michel, Vin Weber, Rep. Steve Gunderson, John Sununu, Tony Blankley, Frank Luntz, Bill McInturff, Rep. Fred Grandy, Tony Coelho, Bob Strauss, William Kristol, Ben Jones, Rep. John Kasich.

203   "The program gives no evidence": Kevin Merida and Serge Kovaleski, "Fired House Historian Says She Is Victim of 'Outrageous' Charges," *The Washington Post*, January 11, 1995, p. A-6.

205   "You could always swear": Robert A. Caro, *The Years of Lyndon Johnson: The Path to Power* (New York: Alfred A. Knopf, 1982), p. 312.

211   "We were starving for intellectual discussion": Conversation with Myron Arons.

218   David Halberstam, *The Powers That Be* (New York: Alfred A. Knopf, 1979).

223   "Republicans should rethink": Meeting of the Congressional Task Force, June 14, 1979.

224   "Junior House Republicans concocted": David Broder, "Capitol Steps Theatrical," *The Washington Post*, September 10, 1980, p. A-19.

225   "Several GOP congressmen": Steve Neal, "Reagan, GOP Congressmen Vow to Keep Five Major Campaign Promises," *Chicago Tribune*, September 16, 1980, p. 7.

229   "It is the lowest thing": *Congressional Record*, Proceedings and Debates of the 98th Congress, Second Session (Washington, D.C.: U.S. Government Printing Office, May 15, 1984), Vol. 130, Part 9, p. 12,201.

231   "I have an enormous personal ambition": Lois Romano, "Newt Gingrich, Maverick on the Hill," *The Washington Post*, January 3, 1985, p. D-1.

231   "doesn't gear up every morning to be a Viking": Myra MacPherson, "Newt Gingrich, Point Man in a House Divided," *The Washington Post*, June 12, 1989, p. C-1.

241   Frans de Waal, *Chimpanzee Politics* (Baltimore: The Johns Hopkins University Press, 1989).

241   "political animal": Aristotle, "Politics," *The Basic Works of Aristotle*, Richard McKeon, ed. (New York: Random House, 1941), Book I, Ch. 2, p. 1,129.

241   "Whole passages of Machiavelli": Albert Somit, "Review of Chimpanzee Politics," *Politics and the Life Sciences*, August 1984, Vol. 2, pp. 211–13.

251   "In politics, you've got a product": Interview with Barry Jackson.

254   "marching orders": David S. Broder and Dana Priest, "Health Bill Funding Snarls House Panel," *The Washington Post*, June 16, 1994, p. A-1.

257   "For anybody who's not on board now": Dan Balz, "GOP Plays Hardball with PACs," *The Washington Post*, October 13, 1994, p. A-1.

257   "the enemy of normal Americans": Ann Devroy and Charles R. Babcock, "Gingrich Foresees Corruption Probe by a GOP House," *The Washington Post*, October 14, 1994, p. A-1.

257 "He's done Lord Acton one better": Interview with David Dreyer.

259 *Inside Politics*, CNN, September 27, 1994.

262 "vividly reminds every American how sick the society is": Howard Kurtz, "Scourge of the GOP Whip: Gingrich Dukes It Out with the 'Elite Media,'" *The Washington Post*, November 16, 1994, p. B-1.

264 "Newt Gingrich didn't elect me to anything": Lloyd Grove, "Newt Who?," *The Washington Post*, December 8, 1995, p. F-1.

5. MEMBER OF CONGRESS

Sources: Rep. Maxine Waters, Brenda Shockley, Jackie Dupont-Walker, State Sen. Teresa Hughes, Stan Di Orio, State Sen. Jim Costa, Alice Huffman, Elihu Harris, David Cunningham, Tom Bradley, Gloria Steinem, Mike Roos, Willie Brown, Gerald Austin, Frank Watkins, Bill Zavarello, Patrick Lacefield.

273 "She told us the social worker": Interview with Jackie Dupont-Walker.

273 "I am the one who found the chick": Interview with David Cunningham.

274 "She became angry": Interview with Tom Bradley.

274 "romanticized this tall, modest, non-threatening black man": Robert Scheer, "Veteran Legislator Makes People Angry—But She's Never Ignored," *Los Angeles Times*, May 16, 1993, p. M-3.

275 "I learned with my first breaths": Jenifer Warren, "Brown Presses His Case for Affirmative Action," *Los Angeles Times*, April 11, 1995, Metro Desk, p. A-3.

277 "Nobody else has a mouth like hers": Interview with Elihu Harris.

279 "Maybe she thought if she used her usual approach": Conversation with George Deukmejian.

280 "This is how the game is played": Interview with John Emerson.

280 "Maxine's death stare": Interview with Roy Neel.

284 Richette Haywood, "A Black Woman's Place Is in the House of Representatives," *Ebony*, January 1991, p. 105.

285 "People do want to own their homes": *Congressional Record*, Proceedings and Debates of the 102nd Congress, First Session (Washington, D.C.: U.S. Government Printing Office, June 6, 1991), Vol. 137, No. 86, H4109.

286 "We didn't know why": Interview with Bruce Reed.

297 "The word 'grooming,' does that mean personal grooming?": *Congressional Record*, Proceedings of the 103rd Congress, First Session (Washington, D.C.: U.S. Government Printing Office, May 26, 1993), Vol. 139, No. 76, Part 2, H 2893.

304 "I have the right to ask questions": Testimony before the Banking, Housing and Urban Affairs Committee hearing on Whitewater, July 28, 1994, plus interviews with Bill Zavarello and other aides who were present.

315 "sold themselves to the wealthy special interests": Maxine Waters, "The *Real* Story of Newt Gingrich's First Hundred Days," press release, April 6, 1995.

316 "stir up their fund-raising base": Kenneth J. Cooper, "'Wanted' by GOP: Selected Liberals," *The Washington Post*, July 11, 1995, p. A-7.

318 "Did you see": William M. Isaac, "First Chicago Got a Bum Rap on $3 Teller Fee," *The American Banker*, June 15, 1995, p. 5.

6. CHIEF OF STAFF

Sources: Sheila Burke, Josie Martin, Fred Graefe, Sen. John McCain, Rep. Lynn Martin, Jim Whittinghill, Rep. Nancy Johnson, Lawrence O'Donnell, Jr., Michael Bromberg, Ron Klain, Andrea Sheldon, Paul Weyrich, Bert Pines, Gary Bauer, Bob Packwood.

323 Karen Tumulty, "Bring Me the Head of Sheila Burke," *Time*, July 24, 1995, p. 30.

323 Jason DeParle, "The Campaign to Demonize Sheila Burke," *The New York Times Magazine*, November 12, 1995, p. 32.

325 "I took a seat in the room": Interview with Jerry Kline.

326 "In 1995, of the 392 staffers": Michael M. Lazarow and Amy Keller, "A Tough Year for the Six-Figure Club," *Roll Call*, September 11, 1995, p. B-45.

326 "Confused and tossed about": Isabel Chapin Barrows, "Chopped Straw: The Remembrances of My Threescore Years," Washington, D.C., 1908.

329 "The lady eats nails for lunch": Gloria Borger, "Health Reform's Other Woman," *U.S. News & World Report*, March 28, 1994, p. 38.

333 "Senator Dole told me, 'If you and Sheila can agree, I'll vote for the plan.'" Hillary Rodham Clinton at a working White House dinner on health reform, February 22, 1994.

335 "makes it very difficult for some in the Republican Party": Helen Dewar, "In Fractious GOP, Dole Learns Tough Guys Don't Take Sides," *The Washington Post*, June 9, 1994, p. A-1.

336 "Three Blind Mice," Review and Outlook, editorial, *The Wall Street Journal*, June 27, 1994, p. A-12.

339 "Dole's first choice, a former Secretary of the Navy": Mary Jacoby, "Aftershocks," *Roll Call*, February 27, 1995.

342 Jerry Gray, "Dole, In a Second Nod to Right, Pledges to Fight Gun Ban," *The New York Times*, March 18, 1995, p. A-1.

349 Paul Weyrich, "Who Will Run the Dole Administration?," *The Washington Times*, July 11, 1995, p. A-19.

349 John H. Fund, "Bob Dole's Dealmaker," *The Wall Street Journal*, July 7, 1995, p. A-10.

349 Karen Tumulty, "Bring Me the Head of Sheila Burke," p. 30.

349 "If the American people like Hillary Clinton": Traditional Values Coalition, "Does Dole Really Support Welfare Reform?" press release, June 21, 1995.

349 "just what seat Sheila Burke would have": Robert D. Novak, "Senator Dole's Personnel Problem," *The Washington Post*, June 26, 1995, p. A-21.

351 "Fire Sheila Burke": "Advice to the Lovelorn: How Presidential Candidates Can Woo Conservatives," A Symposium, *Policy Review*, Winter 1995, No. 71, p. 37.

352 "She is a feminist": Paul Weyrich, "Who Will Run the Dole Administration?," p. A-19.

353 "The Travails of Ms. Burke," editorial, *The Washington Post*, July 23, 1995, p. C-8.

354 "Mrs. Burke": Rich Lowry, "The 101st Senator," *National Review*, July 31, 1995, p. 19.

358 Jeffrey H. Birnbaum, *The Lobbyists: How Influence Peddlers Get Their Way in Washington* (New York: Times Books, 1992), p. 127.

APPENDIX: MONEY MATTERS

359 "The unpleasant truth": *Weekly Compilation of Presidential Documents*, week of October 13–19, 1974.

360 "The municipal Boss system": Thomas C. Reeves, *Gentleman Boss: The Life of Chester Alan Arthur* (New York: Alfred A. Knopf, 1975), pp. 45–47.

360 "will pay about $160 billion": Brooks Jackson, *Honest Graft*, revised edition (Washington, D.C.: Farragut Publishing Co., 1990).

361 "We bought the son of a bitch": Peter Collier and David Horowitz, *The Rockefellers: An American Dynasty* (New York: Holt, Reinhart & Winston, 1976), p. 57.

INDEX